D0117033

the
GOLDEN
GAME

Kevin Nelson

Foreword by
Hank Greenwald

the
GOLDEN
GAME

The Story of California Baseball

California Historical Society Press, San Francisco, California
Heyday Books, Berkeley, California

California Historical Society Press gratefully acknowledges major support for this project from the Louise M. Davies Foundation and the Richard and Rhoda Goldman Fund.

California Historical Society Press is a collaboration between the California Historical Society and Heyday Books. California Historical Society Press is supported by grants from The William Randolph Hearst Foundation and The Mericos Foundation.

The Publishers dedicate this book to the memory of Donald Crawford, Jr., whose dedication to the California Historical Society and the California baseball project was unwavering.

© 2004 by Kevin Nelson
Foreword © 2004 by Hank Greenwald

All rights reserved. No portion of this work may be reproduced or transmitted in any form or by any means, electronic or mechanical, including photocopying and recording, or by any information storage or retrieval system, without permission in writing from Heyday Books.

Library of Congress Cataloging-in-Publication Data

Nelson, Kevin, 1953–
The golden game : the story of California baseball / Kevin Nelson ;
foreword by Hank Greenwald.
    p. cm.
Includes bibliographical references and index.
ISBN 1-890771-80-5 (pbk. : alk. paper)
1. Baseball—California—History. I. Title.
GV863.C2N43 2004
796.357'09794—dc22
2004000442

Cover Art: Background: Rod Dedeaux, 1935 (Courtesy University of Southern California, on behalf of the USC Special Libraries and Archival Collections); L to R: Ted Williams, circa 1941 (San Diego Hall of Champions); Oakland vs. Chicago ticket, 1947 (Doug McWilliams Collection); Joe DiMaggio and Marilyn Monroe (Security Pacific Collection/Los Angeles Public Library); Jackie Robinson with teammates on the Pasadena Junior College Bulldogs, 1939 (Security Pacific Collection/Los Angeles Public Library); Tommy Lasorda celebrates the Dodgers' 1981 world championship (Security Pacific Collection/Los Angeles Public Library); Babe Ruth with Hollywood starlets, 1927 (Security Pacific Collection/Los Angeles Public Library).

Cover and Interior Design: Jack Myers, Tracy Dean, Tania Kac
Printing and Binding: Phoenix Color, Hagerstown, MD

Orders, inquiries, and correspondence should be addressed to:
        Heyday Books
        P.O. Box 9145, Berkeley, CA 94709
        (510) 549-3564, Fax (510) 549-1889
        www.heydaybooks.com

Printed in the United States of America

10 9 8 7 6 5 4 3 2 1

For Hank and Gabriel Nelson,
two young California ballplayers on the rise

CONTENTS

Foreword

Hank Greenwald

Like the precious metal that drew thousands to the Golden State over one hundred and fifty years ago, there are nuggets galore to be found in the mining of California's rich baseball heritage. Fortunately, Kevin Nelson has successfully dug them up for us in *The Golden Game: The Story of California Baseball*.

The westward migration did not stop with the Gold Rush; the flow of those seeking a better life, and certainly a better climate, continues daily, enriching both California and those she welcomes. And, as was the case a hundred and fifty years ago, people continue to bring their baseball interest with them. But there is no residency requirement mandating that those who relocate will adopt local teams. Therefore, it is a common sight at ballparks in San Diego, Anaheim, Los Angeles, San Francisco, and Oakland to witness fans cheering for teams like the Cubs, Yankees, Red Sox, and many others. Affection for the old hometown team is a transportable commodity, as is the love of the game itself. There are no geographic restrictions.

Much has been written about the imprint of baseball upon American life. Unlike sports whose presence seems to die at the end of the season, baseball knows no such boundaries. It remains with us through the long winter months, manifesting itself in the rehashing of playoffs and World Series outcomes. With the ushering in of a new year, the anticipation grows daily as we await the news heralding the rebirth of a new season: "Spring training opens tomorrow." Only the true baseball fan knows the exhilaration that accompanies those words.

In another of his books, *Baseball's Greatest Quotes*, Kevin Nelson includes the following passage from novelist James T. Farrell:

> Baseball *is* America's game. Since around the middle of the nineteenth century we've been playing it and watching it. Kids, poets, presidents, thieves, senators, generals, shop clerks, steelworkers, movie stars, teamsters, farmers, writers, all have been drawn to the game and have been moved by it. Baseball is our language, our history, our blood. Without it, the world would be far different for many of us.

As Nelson points out, even the vast Pacific Ocean was not capable of confining baseball's popularity to the continental United States. When New Yorker Alexander Cartwright, an early visitor to California, found that his dream of finding gold had faded, he continued west to Hawaii, where he began spreading the baseball gospel. Evidence of this was clear to me in 1965 when I was broadcasting the games of the Pacific Coast League's Hawaii Islanders. One of the first things I noticed at the old Honolulu Stadium on King Street was a plaque commemorating Cartwright's days in the islands and recognizing him as modern baseball's creator. (In fact, if the stadium's condition was any indication, it must have been the venue for Cartwright's first game there.)

It seems reasonable that a state large enough in size, population, and economy to be a nation of its own might export baseball along with many of its more conventional products. In reading *The Golden Game,* you'll discover how baseball in California helped to sow the seeds of fanatical interest so evident in the Land of the Rising Sun, for example. In this regard the role of San Francisco's own Lefty O'Doul is fully explored. It was O'Doul who, both before and after World War II, helped popularize the game in Japan by organizing tours of major league ballplayers. Perhaps only he could have arranged for the likes of Babe Ruth, Lou Gehrig, and many others to make the long journey. As Nelson points out, Lefty wasn't simply involved in running a tour, but in fostering a friendship with the Japanese people. He worked with young players, imparting wisdom and nurturing skills in a way that only one of his ability and personality could accomplish. O'Doul became known as "the Father of Baseball in Japan" by suggesting a means by which players could work for industry, which in turn formed the basis for professional baseball in that country.

It would be wrong to suggest that the export of baseball to Japan was a one-way street. Second-generation Japanese in California, the Nisei, formed a league of their own in the 1930s and played in such Central California towns as Fresno and Watsonville, led by Kenso Nushida, Kenichi Zenimura, and other fine players. In 1965 it was Masanori Murakami who became the first native Japanese to play in the major leagues when he joined the San Francisco Giants. Today it's commonplace for a big league club in America to have a Japanese player on its roster. From Latin America, Korea, and Australia as well, we see more and more players reaching the major leagues.

A generation of Americans has emerged believing the history of sports began with ESPN. While ESPN might have you believe the same thing, the fact remains that the history of sports has a far greater frame of reference. In a similar vein, it might be said there are many who believe the history of baseball in California began with the arrival of the San Francisco Giants and Los Angeles Dodgers in 1958. Those who subscribe to such a theory do themselves a great disservice. Baseball flourished long before their arrival and is still played today at varying levels below major league. While the glory days of the Pacific Coast League ended with the arrival of the New York and Brooklyn clubs, the league is still represented by teams in Fresno and Sacramento. The California League continues its operation with such entries as San Jose, Modesto, San Bernardino, Rancho Cucamonga, High Desert, Bakersfield, Visalia, Stockton, Lake Elsinore, and Lancaster. The health of these franchises is reflected in the appearance of many upgraded playing facilities and, in the case of Fresno and Sacramento, brand-new ballparks in the first two years of the twenty-first century.

California high schools and colleges continue their tradition of offering first-rate baseball programs. Journeying through these pages, the reader discovers that schools in the Golden State produced the likes of Ted Williams, Joe DiMaggio, Jackie Robinson, Willie Stargell, Joe Morgan, Harry Heilmann, Frank Robinson, and countless others who not only went on to the major leagues but to the Baseball Hall of Fame as well. But to acknowledge only the players fails to do justice to the dedicated coaches and educators whose instruction and guidance helped make fame and fortune possible. Nelson recognizes the contributions of these lesser-known individuals as well.

The California sun has made it possible to feed much of the United States and the world. It has also helped feed baseball's need for heroes. In speaking of his alma mater, West Point, General Douglas MacArthur said, "Upon the fields of friendly strife are sown the seeds that upon other fields, on other days, will bear the fruits of victory." In a manner less military in nature, the seeds sown upon California's playing fields have borne the ballplayers who've helped produce many a pennant and World Series championship.

Another level of baseball, not often discussed, involves the inland desert area of southern California, which is home to various Indian tribes. In this book you'll read of the emergence of California Indian ballplayers, including Chief Meyers, a Cahuilla who became a catcher for John McGraw's famous New York Giants. Baseball was adopted as a form of recreation not only by the Cahuillas of Riverside County, but by other tribes throughout the state.

No other sport in America has become as much a part of our culture, especially our literary landscape. The language of baseball has embedded itself into everyday usage, becoming so commonplace in American speech that we fail to give a thought to its origin. Novels, histories, anthologies, the stage (musical and dramatic), movies, and biographies have all heralded the accomplishments and failures of those who have been a part of the game. Not included in the previously mentioned vehicles of expression is another art form, one that was most likely the first to relate baseball to the highs and lows of everyday life. While schoolchildren study the likes of Whitman, Cummings, Frost, and Poe, perhaps a greater life lesson can be learned from a man named Ernest Thayer, whose "Casey at the Bat" appeared in the pages of the *San Francisco Examiner* in 1888. Renditions of "Casey" have been performed for well over a hundred years by personalities ranging from De Wolf Hopper over a century ago to the colorful Mets' and Phillies' reliever Tug McGraw in more modern times. To this day, it remains one of our most popular poetic ballads. Though Thayer claimed no intent to link the setting of his work to the city of Stockton, the similarities, as Kevin Nelson points out, are too strong to ignore. In fact, in the late 1990s the California League's Stockton ballclub even changed its name to the Mudville Nine.

California's contribution to baseball also takes an electronic form. No means of disseminating game accounts reaches the public faster than radio or television. Both locally and nationally, baseball broadcasts and telecasts are followed avidly. The Golden State can claim, either by birth or by absorption, some of the great voices of the game. Although Vin Scully cut his teeth describing the exploits of the Brooklyn Dodgers, his nearly half a century in Los Angeles is more than enough for California to claim him as her own. Al Michaels, a Hamilton High product of Los Angeles, made an early name for himself broadcasting baseball in Cincinnati and San Francisco before moving on to ABC. Another legend, Jon Miller, a native Californian who grew up in Hayward, broadcast with several major league teams. He's also known as the voice of ESPN's *Sunday Night Baseball*. Former Yankee infielder Jerry Coleman, out of Lowell High in San Francisco, has been describing San Diego Padre baseball for more than three decades. These names represent but a few of the Californians whose voices have spread the baseball gospel and helped produce new generations of fans; countless followers of the game have testified to their interest having been stimulated by the voices announcing their hometown teams.

While it's easy to recognize radio and television as a positive force for baseball, there were great concerns in the early days of those media. While some major league clubs embraced the idea of radio in the 1930s, the Yankees, Giants, and Dodgers felt otherwise. The three New York teams actually entered into an agreement to keep their games off the air for fear of the impact on attendance. Not until Larry McPhail brought Red Barber from Cincinnati to Brooklyn did the embargo finally end. Years later it was felt that television would have a similar impact. Minor league operators were even more concerned about it. They had reason: several of the minor leagues folded, forcing a reorganization and eliminating such classifications as B, C, and D.

In recent years the minors have had a rebirth, in terms of both interest and franchise value. Minor league teams even televise some of their games. Independent leagues have sprung up in various places around the country. These are entities comprised of teams not affiliated with major league clubs, but which play a brand of ball comparable to the lower minor leagues. For several years the Western League (an independent) operated a franchise in Rohnert Park, California, called the Sonoma Crushers, whose logo showed the team's initials in a wine-purple color suspended over a wine-blue foot.

In Rodgers and Hammerstein's musical *South Pacific,* there's a character named Bloody Mary. From her island of Bali Hai she sings a song called "Happy Talk" that includes the passage, "You gotta have a dream, if you don't have a dream, how you gonna have your dreams come true?" One could certainly make the argument that all great things have happened because someone had a dream and acted upon it. For centuries, people have dreamed in terms of exploration, science, medicine, music, literature, and so much more. While there have been wonderful accomplishments in various fields, the dreams continue. The cure for cancer will be found. Birth defects will be a thing of the past. Dreams drive people and lead them to goals once believed unreachable. In my youth the popular response to seemingly outlandish dreams was "Yeah, and someday there'll be a man on the moon." Well, guess what?

Alexander Cartwright had dreams. While the dream of finding gold apparently eluded him, a byproduct of that dream was the introduction to the Golden State of what came to be called "baseball." Another was his ultimate recognition as "the Father of Modern Baseball." From those pioneering days into the twenty-first century, the dream of a better life in California continues. Alexander Cartwright could not have imagined that, long after he was gone, youngsters would dream of playing the game he helped to create, or that the riches he failed to uncover in California would be realized by those who have struck gold playing his golden game.

Introduction

The story of California baseball begins in New York in the years before the Gold Rush. Base Ball—it was two words then—was just getting started, and men from Manhattan Island and Brooklyn were among the earliest to play it. When gold was discovered in the Sierra Nevada foothills and the dream of instant riches swept across America, some of these New Yorkers came to California and brought the game with them. Then, more than a century later, New Yorkers again had a hand in bringing baseball to California. In this case it was major league baseball. Two of New York's major league teams, the Brooklyn Dodgers and the New York Giants, transferred to California, and the state's first big league clubs, the Los Angeles Dodgers and the San Francisco Giants, began play in April 1958.

The Gold Rush begins the story of baseball in California, but the arrival of the Dodgers and Giants certainly does not end it. The Anaheim (originally Los Angeles) Angels, Oakland Athletics, and San Diego Padres all set up shop in the decade that followed, adding still more layers to an already rich story.

For decades California has produced more major league ballplayers than any other state. As impressive as this may be, it is not the central story of California baseball. The central story is the astonishing mix of people—people from all over the United States and all over the planet—who were and are involved in it.

The man who broke organized baseball's color barrier was Jackie Robinson, who grew up in Pasadena, California. Born in Georgia, the man selected by *Time* magazine as one of the one hundred most influential people of the twentieth century came west with his family when he was only a baby. They lived on Pepper Street near Brookside Park and the Rose Bowl, and Robinson attended Pasadena public schools, Pasadena Junior College, and the University of California at Los Angeles. Brooklyn Dodgers executive Branch Rickey chose Robinson to carry the burden and honor of being the first black to play modern major league baseball largely for two reasons: he was educated and he had played all his life on integrated sports teams.

The Dodgers' welcoming parade, Los Angeles, 1958. Security Pacific Collection/Los Angeles Public Library

The media sometimes portray Robinson as a "child of the South" because that was where he was born, but his childhood and early manhood more accurately belong to California. His often painful years there, where he encountered harsh unfairness solely because of the color of his skin, are an essential part of this state's, indeed this nation's, baseball story.

The last man to hit .400 or above in a regular season was Ted Williams, who is regarded today as one of the two or three best hitters ever. He was born and raised in San Diego. His father was an Army veteran and his mother, who was of Hispanic descent, was a deeply devoted religious crusader. Unhappy in their marriage, Ted's parents frequently left him and his younger brother alone in their house to fend for themselves, and Ted found refuge in baseball, developing a lightning-quick batting stroke that took him from the playgrounds of San Diego to fame and glory with the Boston Red Sox.

The man with whom Williams is frequently paired in baseball history, Joe DiMaggio, was born in the East Bay town of Martinez but grew up across the bay in San Francisco. With his brothers Vince and Dominic—both future major leaguers themselves—Joe learned the game by playing pickup ball at North Beach Playground in the city's Italian district. But their immigrant father, Giuseppe, a fisherman on San Francisco Bay, disapproved of his sons playing baseball because young men needed to work, not waste their time with childish games. Only after Joe achieved fame (and an excellent salary) on San Francisco's Pacific Coast League team did Giuseppe open himself up to the pleasures of baseball. Joe, of course, went on to greater glory in New York with the Yankees: in 1941, with America on the eve of world war, he galvanized fans across the country by hitting safely in fifty-six consecutive games, thereby establishing one of the game's most enduring records.

DiMaggio, Williams, and Robinson were the three best players of their generation and three of the best of all time. All overcame challenges to achieve what they did, all are in the Baseball Hall of Fame, and all grew up, at basically the same time, in California.

California and Californian ballplayers have frequently played lead roles in the national baseball drama, although because the major leagues arrived only in the 1950s, the state's impact on the game is not widely understood or recognized, by people in both the East and the West. The national game helped shape the California game, and the California game influenced the national one, dating back to the nineteenth century.

In the 1880s San Francisco was California's largest city, the railroad hub of the Far West and the heart of organized baseball activity in the state. Baseball was so popular that an aggressive young newspaper editor, William Randolph Hearst, decided to feature it regularly on the front page of the *Daily Examiner* in order to boost the paper's circulation. With this same goal in mind he also hired a shy, bookish friend from Harvard, Ernest Thayer, to write a satirical column for the paper. Writing under a pen name, in June 1888 Thayer published in the *Examiner* the most famous baseball poem and arguably one of the most popular American poems ever, "Casey at the Bat."

Since its publication, "Casey at the Bat" has become a fixture of popular culture, endlessly reprinted in newspapers, magazines, and books. It has spawned untold numbers of parodies, in print and song; there have been cartoons, television programs, movies, and even a full-length opera based on it, with many more novels and movies borrowing from its funny-sad theme of a mighty slugger who, rather than hit a home run to win the game as people are led to expect, breaks the hearts of Mudville's fans by striking out. Though some have claimed that Stockton, in California's San Joaquin Valley, served as the inspiration for Mudville, Thayer repeatedly denied there was any real-life basis for Mudville or, for that matter, Casey. They were purely works of the imagination.

Another colorful character named Casey, this one not imaginary, is best known as the manager of the world champion New York Yankees in the fifties and the somewhat less successful New York Mets in the sixties. One of the many significant baseball figures associated in the public mind with the East but who have long and deep ties with California, Casey Stengel lived for more than half a century in Glendale, near Los Angeles. In the late 1940s, considered a clown and a loser by many in baseball, he took a job as manager of the Oakland Oaks of the Pacific Coast League, and his success there helped revive his reputation and led to his being hired by the Yankees. It was also in Oakland where Stengel met Billy Martin, a feisty Berkeley-born and -raised teenager who would go on to become one of the most controversial and embattled managers in big league history. But Casey and Billy were like father and son, forming an enduring bond. Wherever Martin managed, including in his Coliseum office with the Oakland Athletics, a photograph of his former mentor hung on the wall.

★   ★   ★   ★   ★

One of the most fascinating aspects of California baseball is how the history of the game in the state is interwoven with the history of the state itself. In the 1850s reaching California from the East required hard overland travel or an ocean voyage of several months. Baseball reflected this geographic isolation. It was essentially a provincial affair headquartered in northern California, which, at the time, had a far bigger population than the south of the state.

The building of the transcontinental railroad in 1869 changed all this, opening up the state to East-West traffic and increasing exchanges of all kinds, including those related to baseball. The sport's first professionals, a glamorous all-star dream team known as the Cincinnati Red Stockings, arrived in California in the early months of the railroad's operation, wowing the locals with their diamond prowess and style. They would only be the first of countless outsiders who would vitalize the California game over the years. The railroads, coupled with the steady wave of immigrants into the state, ensured that baseball on the Coast would not merely be a homegrown affair. Easterners, Midwesterners, Southerners, and people from around the world would transform California baseball, just as newcomers in industry, agriculture, science, government, art, and other areas of endeavor would shape the larger history of the state itself.

In 1903 a group of baseball men in California and the Northwest formed the Pacific Coast League, the backbone of organized baseball in the state until the Dodgers and Giants arrived. The Coast League was a minor league but not in the sense we understand the term today: a group of farm teams vastly inferior to the major leagues. For most of its early history the Coast League was a proudly independent league with clubs in San Diego, Los Angeles, Hollywood, San Francisco, Oakland, Sacramento, and in other western states. It had charmingly idiosyncratic parks, a unique cast of characters on the field, and fans who cared as deeply about their teams as today's fans do about their favorite major league clubs. Though Coast League pitching was not up to major league quality, many other aspects of its play were, and some of the most storied names in baseball history—DiMaggio and Williams, to name but two—made their professional debuts in Coast League uniforms.

The same year of the Coast League's founding, another event occurred that influenced baseball in the state: the formation, in San Francisco, of the first Issei baseball club in mainland America. Today California has the largest population of Japanese Americans of any state in the country, and the first generation of Japanese immigrants—known as Issei—began arriving in the late 1800s and early 1900s. Soon they became part of the state's baseball mix, competing with and against whites who, like them, were the children of immigrants or immigrants themselves.

But in many towns around California the Japanese were not permitted to play in ballparks used by whites. In response they built their own parks in their own neighborhoods. On Sundays everybody came together for what they called "Baseball Crazy Day," in which even the most reserved members of the community laughed and yelled and placed wagers on the action on the field. Baseball was one of the ways the Japanese connected with mainstream society. With the advent of World War II, however, some 120,000 Japanese and Japanese Americans in this country, mostly from California, were rounded up and held against their will in internment camps in the state and around the West. While in these camps, the internees built ballfields, organized teams and leagues, and played baseball almost every day. Their story is part of California baseball, too.

Many different kinds of people, coming together on a ballfield, have made the California game what it is today. The Cahuilla Indians of Riverside County and other tribes of the inland desert of southern California have played baseball for generations. The best and most famous Cahuilla player was Chief Meyers, whose mother was a Cahuilla and whose father was of German descent. After playing school and reservation ball in and around Riverside, Meyers, like so many Californians before and after him, traveled east to join the major leagues, becoming a catcher for the New York Giants under manager John McGraw.

During one season of winter baseball in southern California, Meyers played on the semipro San Diego Pickwicks with Walter Johnson, the second-winningest

San Fernando Valley Aces and their wives and girlfriends, 1930s. Courtesy of Pete Mitsui.
From Through a Diamond: 100 Years of Japanese American Baseball, *by Kerry Yo Nakagawa.*
NBRP (Nisei Baseball Research Project)

pitcher in baseball history and one of a phalanx of Hall of Famers with California ties. (California's high schools alone have produced more than thirty Hall of Famers.) Conventional stories about Johnson's boyhood emphasize his Kansas farm roots, but he spent his teen years in the oil fields of southern California. It was in places like Olinda, Fullerton, and Anaheim where he first developed into a pitcher and his fastball started jumping past batters. While working in the oil fields he drove a team of horses, stopping between errands to practice his pitching by throwing rocks at tin cans.

Johnson and Meyers were both part of the southern California baseball scene, a scene that, like the one up north, attracted people from all over. McGraw of the Giants frequently came to Los Angeles in the off-season to play the ponies at the winter horse-racing circuit, and Chicago Cubs manager Frank Chance, McGraw's hardheaded, never-back-down rival (both are members of the Hall of Fame), also retreated to southern California in the off-season, running an orange ranch in Glendora known as Cub Ranch. Though McGraw, who did not come from California, and Chance, who did (Fresno, born and raised) made their living back East, when they came west for the

San Francisco Seals, 1914. California Historical Society, FN-40034

winter they were both part of the informal warm-weather fraternity of southern California baseball.

The movies were another part of this scene, one more reason why baseball in California was not quite like baseball anywhere else. Even if there were no major league teams in the state in those days, there were plenty of major leaguers around in the off-season, and virtually all of the game's greats went to Hollywood at one time or another. Babe Ruth regularly visited Hollywood to appear in movies and traveled around the state playing exhibitions in front of awestruck crowds who had only read about him in the papers or seen pictures of him in newsreels at the theater. Ty Cobb, second perhaps only to Ruth as the greatest of his time, starred in one of the earliest silent movies made in Hollywood with a baseball theme, and after ending his major league career, the wealthy Georgian retired to California, spending the tormented final years of his life at his estate in Atherton and mountain chalet at Lake Tahoe.

San Francisco baseball team in front of the Bay Bridge under construction, circa 1935.
California Historical Society, FN-40045

Yet another famous personality came to California in the 1930s because of baseball, although he wasn't a player. He was an Iowa sportscaster covering the Chicago Cubs at their spring training site on Catalina Island off the coast of Los Angeles. While on assignment with the Cubs one spring, he took a screen test for the movies that turned out so well it ended his broadcasting career and started a successful new one in Hollywood. After making more than fifty motion pictures he branched into politics, later serving as governor of California and president of the United States. He was Ronald Reagan.

★   ★   ★   ★   ★

There are many reasons why California is such fertile ground for baseball. Its population—the largest of any state—is an obvious reason because there are more players to draw from, but the numbers alone do not tell the whole story. The generally mild climate, allowing the game to be played in many areas of the state year-round, is surely important. Yet another factor is the state's geography. Isolated from the rest of the country for much of its early history, California developed at its own pace, in its own inimitable fashion. With so many new-comers constantly arriving from somewhere else, what your father did, or your father's father, was not quite so important to people. This may have contributed to a more casual, less rigid social structure and a somewhat more tolerant racial atmosphere than in other parts of the country, although the state has certainly shown that it is not immune to the extremes of prejudice and intolerance.

In the whole history of California, those living in the state who were born outside it have always outnumbered those living in the state who were born in it. This is as true today as it was in 1850. People take a gamble when they leave their home to come to a new land in a faraway place. Sometimes this gamble works out, sometimes not. But the journey begins first with a decision to take a risk.

And so, this is how this story begins, with a young man from the East who risks everything to come West.

The Seed
Is Planted

SATURDAY, MARCH 22 — 2:15 P.M.
SUNDAY, MARCH 23 — 2:15 P.M.
— 1947 —

ABLISHED PRICE - $3.33   Total $4.00
ERAL TAX - .67

HIS PORTION OF TICKET NOT GOOD FOR ADMITTANCE
DETACH SEPERATE COUPONS FOR INDIVIDUAL GAMES

In the fall of 1845 a group of New York men formed the first organized base-ball club. They called it the Knickerbockers, and the following spring they played a game in a meadow across the Hudson River in Hoboken, New Jersey. Elysium was for the ancient Greeks a blessed state, the heavenly paradise where souls went after death. This meadow in Hoboken, this green space where the Knickerbockers played their first game of baseball, was called Elysian Fields.

The founder of the Knickerbockers was Alexander Joy Cartwright Jr.—"Alick" for short. Born on Lombardy Street in New York City, Alick was the son of a retired ship captain. Over six feet tall, a big man for his time, he had brown eyes, a thick crop of wavy hair, and a beard, which was practically stan-dard dress for men of the era. In his mid-twenties, he lived in Manhattan with his wife and children, working as a teller at Union Bank while also serving as a volunteer firefighter. Several of his teammates on the Knickerbockers were also firefighters.

When Cartwright and his friends began their sporting experiments, there was already a game popular in New York and Boston called "town ball," a bat and ball game played on a square field. The rules changed according to where the game was played and were often made up on the spot by the players themselves. The number of men in the field varied and so did the number of bases—three, four, or five, depending on the rule makers of the moment. The team on the field got a runner out by trying to hit him with the ball or by catching a pop fly.

What the Knickerbockers did was take the raw materials of town ball and craft them into a new shape. They devised the first set of baseball rules, the original seedbed for all the refinements that have come since. They changed the square into a diamond. Before the Knickerbockers there was no concept of fair territory versus foul; that was their idea. In a simple yet daring burst of inspi-ration, they decided that the players on the field had to throw to a base to get a runner out, rather than hit him with a ball. This last rule made for close plays at the bases and created the need for an arbiter, or umpire, to resolve any dis-putes that arose.

At the National Baseball Hall of Fame in Cooperstown, New York, the plaque that honors Cartwright describes him as "the father" of modern base-ball. Contemporary baseball historians have challenged this claim, saying that the game evolved over time and that many men, not just one, originated it, but no one disputes that Alexander Cartwright was one of the architects of early baseball, a witness to its creation. He played in that first Knickerbocker game in Hoboken and remained with the club until a force stronger than any game pulled him away from New York City, causing him to leave behind his wife and children and all that was settled and known.

★   ★   ★   ★   ★

In January 1848 one of the most famous accidents in American history occurred. James , a carpenter, found gold on the banks of the American River in the foothills of the Sierra Nevada. This discovery set off a mass global migration unlike any before or since. People poured into California territory from all over, lured by stories that gold could be had as easily as plucking an apple off a tree, stories that, incredibly, sometimes turned out to be true. In the first year, when the plucking was best, gold seekers came from Mexico, Latin America, the Oregon territory, the sun-kissed islands of Hawaii. Indians and local Californios feverishly worked the diggings too. Easterners tended to view the news from California with skepticism until President James Polk, in December 1948, made the headline-grabbing announcement that yes, the claims appeared to be real. It was like firing a pistol to start a race. Now it seemed every young man with a bounce in his step and a wink in his eye was heading west to make his fortune.

The entire nation was swept up in the excitement. The New York *Herald* wrote: "All classes of our citizens seem to be under the influence of this extraordinary mania." The *Express* agreed: "We have seen in our day manias, fevers, and excitements of sorts, [but] this last gold news has unsettled the minds of even the most cautious and careful among us." The papers contained sensational stories and accounts from California, as well as the advertisements of companies eager to sell supplies to gold seekers before they left. Being a Manhattanite working in the Wall Street district, Alick Cartwright heard the wild stories and read the newspapers with avid interest, for he was among those who had caught the bug.

Other New York men had caught it too, including his brother Alfred. Though not a ballplayer like Alick, Alfred had umpired a Knickerbocker game. Now the brothers Cartwright, who had once run a Wall Street bookshop together, were each about to have the adventure of a lifetime, the stuff of storybooks.

Alfred left for California first, setting sail on a clipper ship out of Newport Harbor in January 1849. Alick chose the land route, departing two months later from Newark, saying goodbye to Rebecca, his wife of six years, and their four children, including the youngest, little Alick, who was still only a baby. All around the States, men were diving off the edge of the known world into the unknown. They left families, friends, loved ones—perhaps never to see them again.

From his papers, correspondence by his family, and research by biographer Harold Peterson, we know Cartwright traveled on trains and wood-burning side- and stern-wheel steamboats from New York City to Independence, Missouri, on the edge of the western frontier. Dreaming private dreams of riches, the gold seekers banded together for the hard journey ahead, forming temporary, mutually held companies that bought wagons, animals, and the million and one things they needed to survive. Cartwright bought into one of these companies and joined a party of more than thirty wagons and one hundred men. Nearly all of the early Gold Rush emigrants were men, and young men at that. When his wagon, pulled by mules, set off down the trail, Cartwright was twenty-nine years old.

The wagon trains of the forty-niners may appear to be far afield from the world of baseball, but this is not the case. Wooden wagons actually became part of the game—pieces of them anyhow. Until the coming of the railroads, goods being shipped from the East Coast to the West mainly came by sea and carried a high price tag. If people wanted to play "base ball"—it was two words in those days—and needed a bat, they had to make it out of materials that were available locally. "Wagon tongue" bats, made of ash and hickory, derived their name from the old-fashioned bats cut from the tongues and axletrees of farm wagons. Of course, many early bats had equally humble origins. The hitting stick used by a boy to sock a clutch single and win a game for his team may have come from his mother's washroom; she had used it to stir a tub of laundry.

Hundreds of wagon trains embarked on journeys down the California–Oregon Trail during this raucous moment in American history when the country's borders were being pushed outward. But on this particular wagon train, tucked into the bag of one of its passengers, was a ball.

Cartwright had brought with him from New York a ball with a core of yarn or rags and a catgut cover. Certainly it more resembled an antique town

Gold Rush pioneers playing cricket on the way west. "Sunday on the Plains," drawing by Chappel from daguerreotype by J. Wesley Jones, circa 1853. California Historical Society, FN-00892

ball than any regulation hardball in use today in that it was soft, perhaps a little squishy. Nor did it go far when you hit it.

From time to time on his way west the founder of the Knickerbockers apparently tossed the ball around with his fellow travelers. Participants may have included Indians and frontiersmen. "It was comical to see mountain men and Indians playing the game," Cartwright later told friends.

As the journey progressed and the trail became too tough for idle play, however, there were undoubtedly fewer and fewer chances to play with this ball, and much less inclination to do so. Not long after leaving behind the white settlements, the travelers entered Indian territory. The New Yorker carried a double-barreled rifle for protection but, mirroring the experiences of many other emigrants, his wagon party passed freely through these lands. A far greater danger was cholera, which killed hundreds of gold seekers before they breathed one breath of California air. Indians caught the disease too and it made them, like so many others, go crazy with pain before they died.

The long, hard road across the desert and the mountains ended in August, five months after it began on the other side of the continent on the shores of a different ocean. Cartwright walked virtually the whole way. After crossing the Sierra Nevada, his party came to a valley, probably what is now Grass Valley, before turning south to Sacramento City.

A bustling inland river city, poised on the doorstep of gold country, Sacramento City was the main staging area and supply center for the Northern Mines. As such, it surged with the energy of men in pursuit of instant fortune. Everything and everybody seemed to be in motion, with most of the citizens on their way up to the diggings or just getting back from them. The mining sites were called diggings because that was what you did when you got there: dig. You used a pick or shovel or anything you could get your hands on to unearth those gold flakes buried in the hillsides and streambeds.

Downriver from Sacramento on a peninsula at the mouth of a bay, on the far western edge of land, was the headquarters city of the Gold Rush. San Francisco was like Sacramento only more so: everybody moving in quick time, spinning fabulous schemes of how they were going to make a bundle, and fast. Once-proud square-masted clipper ships, having weathered the eighteen-thousand-mile voyage from the East Coast around South America up to California, sat rotting in port, abandoned by captain and crew who had run off to the diggings. Along the waterfront men lived in makeshift wooden huts or canvas tents that provided scant protection from the chill ocean winds and layers of fog blowing in across the sandy hills. *Everything* was makeshift in a way, with no thought for tomorrow except How much is in it for me? Drunken rascals of every description—"cholos," to use the Spanish word—crowded into the smoky saloons and spilled onto the streets, looking for their next hustle. There were few women and fewer children. Some of the women were working girls who never lacked for customers willing to pay with nuggets of real gold.

Into this wild, testosterone-charged place came the bearded young patriarch of baseball, beaten down by how hard it had been to get there. Cartwright's wagon train had collapsed late in the journey. Mules had quit or died, their converted farm wagons had broken down on the rocky, rutted trails, and they had lost "most of their truck," as his brother Alfred put it in a letter to Alick's wife. Alfred explained that Alick and his wagon party had arrived in San Francisco only with "what they had upon their backs, a cup and a spoon apiece." In the land of El Dorado, where legend said you could scoop up handfuls of gold like sand at the beach, he owned almost nothing except dented dreams and that catgut-covered ball. On top of it all, a bad case of dysentery raced through his weakened body.

Alfred Cartwright, who had left the East Coast nearly two months before his brother yet reached San Francisco at about the same time, had a harrowing story of his own to tell when the two met on the waterfront amidst the empty, rotting ships and makeshift huts. Alfred had set sail on the *Pacific*. Its route was down the eastern coast of the Americas, around Cape Horn, and on up to California. (In baseball, when infielders whip the ball from first base to second to third during practice or after a batter makes an out, this is called throwing it "around the horn." The term likely stems from this ancient, storied sailing route.) But problems arose almost as soon as they put land behind them. The ship's tyrannical captain refused to give the passengers food or medical treatment. One of the other passengers on board was Mark Hopkins, a New York shopkeeper who would later play a monumental role in the shaping of the American West, becoming a founder of the company that built the transcontinental railroad linking California with the rest of the country. Slowly starving to death, Hopkins, Alfred Cartwright, and the other passengers plotted mutiny until they managed to get a Rio de Janeiro physician to examine Captain Tibbets, who was declared insane and relieved of his command. The voyage proceeded less eventfully from there.

What the Cartwrights realized—indeed what men all over gold country were realizing—was that they were too late. Other men had gotten there before them and beaten them to the spot. The days of easy pluckings, if they had ever existed, were over. Jacob Stillman, a New York physician who was also on the embattled *Pacific*, related in his diary the word they were hearing on the street: "Many who went to the mines returned unsuccessful and report that the exertion in getting gold is too great." For some men it was no longer worth the effort. "Some are leaving for the Sandwich Islands and beyond," wrote Stillman.

One of the men leaving was Alexander Cartwright, who booked passage on a Peruvian ship for the Sandwich Islands—Hawaii. A friend from New York who had lived there told him, no kidding, the islands were truly paradise. So after less than a week in San Francisco, Alick set off on the next leg of his epic journey, sailing through the Golden Gate and leaving behind the mystery that is at the heart of this story.

Contemporary accounts often refer to Cartwright as the "Johnny Appleseed" of the game, planting baseball seeds across the Western frontier. His Hall of Fame plaque records how he carried a ball (gone now, apparently tossed aside and lost) to the Pacific Coast and onto Hawaii, where Rebecca and the children later joined him and he lived the rest of his life. But given his condition when he arrived in gold country, how long he stayed, and the atmosphere he encountered when he got there, Cartwright almost certainly did not plant any seeds in California.

But if baseball's Johnny Appleseed did not bring the game to California, who did? Although Alick may have been disillusioned by his prospects in this new land, thousands of other outsiders continued to pour in from all over. Men from such early baseball hot spots as Manhattan and Brooklyn ranged all over the boom country map, testing their luck in the now-forgotten mining towns of the era. Most of these men sooner or later ventured through Sacramento City or San Francisco or both. One New York Knickerbocker, Frank Turk, served as an alcalde—an attorney, judge, sheriff, and mayor rolled into one—in frontier San Francisco.

By 1850, California the territory had become California the state. Even as the early euphoria of the Gold Rush faded, more people—and more New Yorkers—kept coming west. Two years later, on January 14, 1852, the *Daily Alta California* carried an intriguing item. It described how, on a street in San Francisco, "full grown persons [were] engaged very industriously in the game known as town ball." The newspaper did not provide the names or any details regarding the identity of these full-grown persons. But the seed had been planted. The game had arrived. Guys were playing ball, winter ball, in California.

Stagecoach
Baseball

THE " PACIFICS," 1866

S. H. WADE
SECOND BASE

W. SHEPARD
THIRD BASE

W. F. HALE, JR.
PITCHER

ECK

J. KERRIGAN

J. W. HARRISON

SATURDAY, MARCH 22 — 2:15 P.M.
SUNDAY, MARCH 23 — 2:15 P.M.
— 1947 —

ABLISHED PRICE - $3.33   Total $4.00
ERAL TAX - - - .67

HIS PORTION OF TICKET NOT GOOD FOR ADMITTANCE

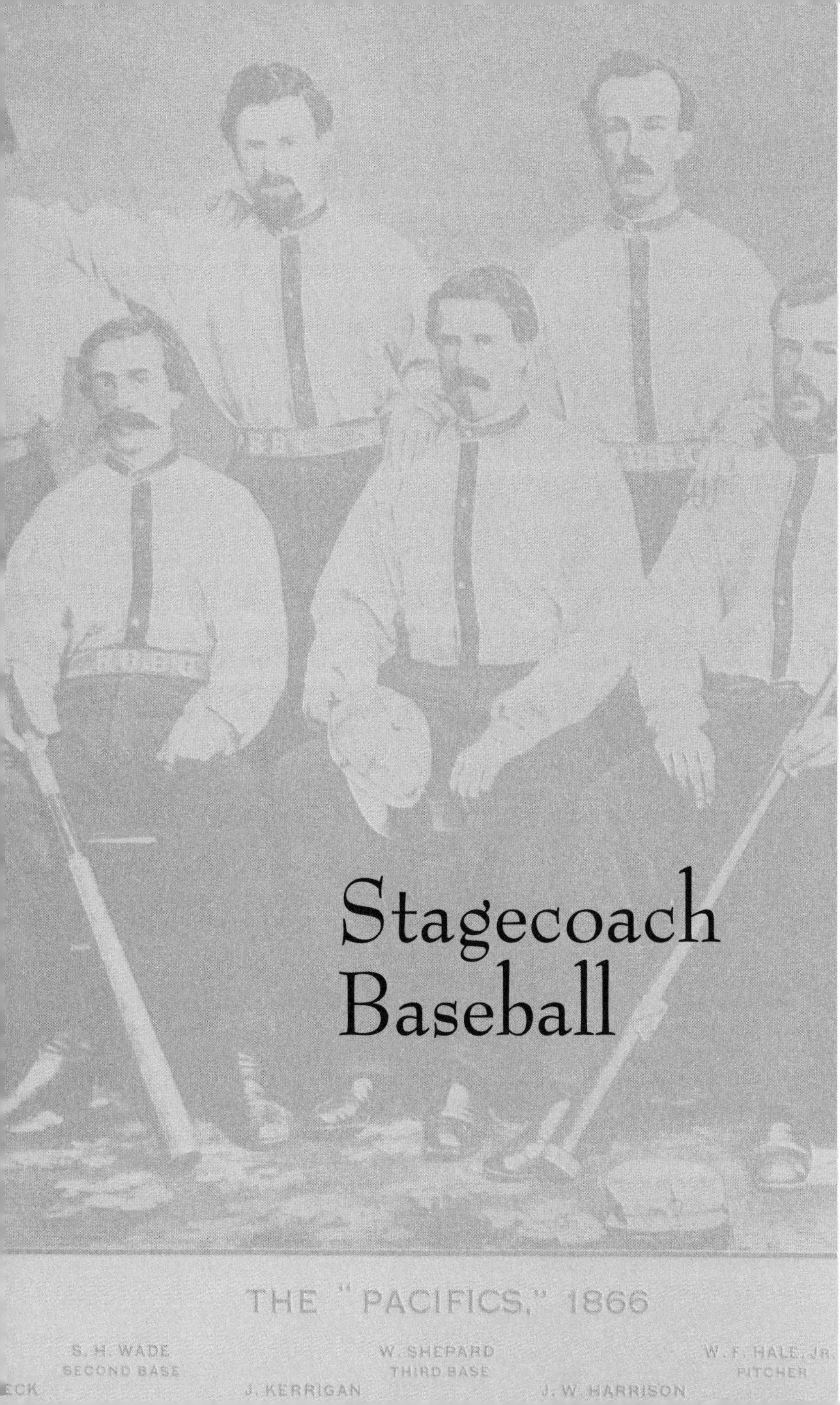

Perched on the western edge of the continent, walled off by mountains and desert on the one side and ocean on the other, accessible only by ship or hard travel overland, California was a distant planet far removed from the orbit of New York and other Eastern cities. Nevertheless, residents of America's newest state found they had at least one thing in common with their brethren across the country: a fascination with baseball. Interest in what would later be dubbed "the national pastime" surged in the 1850s, particularly in the metropolitan centers of the East Coast. Meanwhile, Easterners continued to come west to seek their fortune, and the Gold Rush cities of San Francisco and Sacramento became early hotbeds of baseball activity in the state.

Sacramento can lay claim to the first active ballclub in the state: the Sacramento Base Ball Club, established in the closing months of 1859. This development caused feathers to be ruffled all over San Francisco, where a local newspaper wondered how Sacramento could have beaten California's largest city to the punch. Within days the San Francisco Base Ball Club was born, and almost immediately, and for the next decade, it was the most successful team in the state.

As baseball historian David Nemec points out, the nineteenth-century game contains many hard-to-unravel mysteries. Records about individuals and the games they played are sketchy and draped in shadow. What has survived are fragments. Such is the case with John M. Fisher, one of the founders of the San Francisco club. Not much is known about him except that he grew up in New York, where he played for the Empires, one of the early teams that sprung up in the aftermath of the Knickerbockers. He came to California and settled in San Francisco, bringing his baseball knowledge with him. Fisher, a shortstop, recruited other East Coast transplants to be his teammates.

The first organized baseball game in California took place on George Washington's birthday, February 22, 1860, between Fisher's San Francisco Base Ball Club and a rival club, the Red Rovers. The game occurred at a long-gone spot in San Francisco called Centre's Bridge. Centre's Bridge, probably in what is now the South of Market area, was California's version of Elysian Fields, but it achieved this honor only by hours. That same day, the Sacramento Base Ball Club squared off against the Unions in an afternoon contest in the capital city—the second organized game in the state's diamond history.

In the game at Centre's Bridge, a nasty squabble broke out after the Red Rovers charged the opposing pitcher with cheating. When the San Franciscos felt their teammate was being unjustly maligned and stood by him, the Red Rovers walked off the field in protest although the game was tied, 33 to 33. They lost on a forfeit, which so ticked them off they refused to pay for the post-game dinner, as the losers traditionally did. The victorious San Francisco club celebrated at a saloon.

At this time, and for years to come, the pitchers tossed the ball underhand. If a batter did not like what he saw, he could ask for a better pitch more suitable to him. This may have been what caused the row: the San Francisco pitcher accused of cheating would not put the ball where the Red Rover batsmen wanted it.

The ball used in this game was almost certainly livelier than the rag ball carried west by Alexander Cartwright ten years earlier. Perhaps too lively. The core likely contained strips of wound rubber, making it hard for fielders to follow the bouncing ball on a field pocked with holes and rocks. There was no fence at Centre's Bridge or any other ballfield in California, but the goal of a hitter was not to hit a home run. Rather, it was to scratch out a single, keep the ball in play, and advance the men on base in order to score runs.

Fielding gloves were also unheard of; players caught with their bare hands. It would have been considered unmanly and unsportsmanlike to wear protection on your hand.

In September, two thousand people attended the first state baseball tournament, held in Sacramento as part of an agricultural fair. Some San Franciscans may have traveled via stagecoach to see their ballclub, now known as the Eagles, face rival Sacramento. Accounts of this best-of-three championship series vary. The visitors, led by John Fisher, either took two straight or won the first game easily and were leading the second by a wide margin when daylight ran out and play was halted. In any case, the Eagles claimed the $350 winner's prize and a silver championship trophy, confirming their pre-tourney reputation as the best team west of the Mississippi.

In April 1861, little more than a year after that first California series, Confederate forces bombarded Fort Sumter, starting the Civil War. Pony Express riders brought the first news of it to California. This horrible nation-splitting conflict brought together huge assemblies of young men in the scarred battlegrounds of Virginia and other eastern states. In periods of forced idleness between battles or after marches, the soldiers made the hours pass by playing ball in camp. Boys and men from around the country learned how to play baseball during the war, and in this way knowledge of the game spread. When the nation, as one nation, returned to blessed normalcy after years of bloodshed, baseball experienced a boost in activity. The lucky ones, the ones who had made it out alive, came home and showed off this new game to their family and friends. Hundreds of new baseball teams, arrayed in their colorful uniforms, suddenly bloomed like wildflowers across the States.

In 1866, the year after the war drew to its mournful close, about a half-dozen California baseball clubs sent representatives to the first Pacific Base Ball Convention in San Francisco. This was primarily a San Francisco affair; only one team, the Live Oaks from Oakland, came from outside the city. This gathering of baseball tribes sought to standardize rules and organize a local championship. The powerhouse Eagles sent John Fisher as their representative. Likely appearing for the Pacifics, a rising power, were the Shepard brothers, William and James. Like Fisher, they were New York transplants. They had played with the Knickerbockers and possessed real ballyard skills, the mustachioed William at third base, and James, sporting a dark goatee, holding down first. In this and coming years their club would challenge the Eagles for northern California baseball supremacy.

THE "PACIFICS," 1866

J. SHEPARD		S. H. WADE		W. SHEPARD		W. F. HALE, JR.		J. H. WETMORE
FIRST BASE		SECOND BASE		THIRD BASE		PITCHER		RIGHT FIELD
	H. T. WHITBECK		J. KERRIGAN		J. W. HARRISON		T. CAMPBELL, JR.	
	CENTER FIELD		SHORT STOP		CATCHER		LEFT FIELD	

San Francisco Pacifics, 1866. James Shepard is seated far left, William Shepard is seated center.
California Historical Society, FN-40036

The second Pacific Base Ball Convention, held the following year, showed how baseball was expanding geographically around the state. It was again hosted by San Francisco, but this time players from twenty-five clubs from as far away as San Jose attended the meeting. One account claims that one hundred clubs from around California sent emissaries, although considering the difficulty in getting around the state in those days, this is probably an exaggeration.

San Francisco ballplayers during this era liked to practice and play games in what is now the Civic Center area. Once hilly and rolling, it was used as a cemetery during the Gold Rush until the city flattened the land and removed the gravestones. Baseballers quickly gravitated to this empty sandy lot, running down fly balls and fielding grounders over the bones of the pioneers. The area became so identified with the game that city residents began referring to ballplayers as "sandlotters," guys who played "sandlot ball." The term grew into widespread use and has since become an indelible part of the language of the game.

A different sort of baseball hangout opened in San Francisco in 1868: a new gem of a park in the Mission District, at that time the Irish section of the city.

Owned and built by the Hatton brothers, both Australian immigrants, they called their new showplace the Recreation Grounds and proudly proclaimed it to be the first ballfield in the state with a fence around it. The fence was made of wooden planks, same as the sidewalks of the city, and had a dirt infield and grass, real grass, in the outfield. Young sandlotters had never seen anything like it.

The park opened on Thanksgiving Day and featured a match between the Eagles and the Wide Awakes of Oakland. ("Wide Awakes" was a popular team name of the time, describing men who got up early to play before they reported to their day jobs.) Three thousand fans saw the Eagles beat the Wide Awakes in an early installment of what would develop into a 150-year-old baseball rivalry between Oakland and its larger, more glamorous neighbor.

Much is not known and cannot be known about that first game at the Recreation Grounds. A careful description of its first-in-the-West fence does not exist. Did the fence have holes in it or cracks of light between the planks wide enough for children on the other side to peer through to the field? If so, pioneers of another sort may have been on hand: charter members of California's first knothole gang.

Recreation Park, San Francisco, 1896. California Historical Society, FN-40035

Opening Day at the Rec Grounds was a big success, but any smart business-man could see that eventually the novelty would wear off. In order to keep people coming to the park and paying for the privilege, the Hatton Brothers needed to bring in attractions such as the circus and other crowd-pleasing spectacles. For the moment all the attractions were local. But the time was rapidly approaching when people in the West would be able to travel easily and relatively quickly to the East, and Easterners would be able to go West, opening up San Francisco and California to national personalities and attractions. All over the country Americans from all walks of life were watching with a mixture of national pride and self-interest the railroad-building race roaring to a climax in the plains of Utah.

"The grandest and noblest enterprise of our age," as famed New York editor Horace Greeley put it, was a team effort. Two teams of workers—the Central Pacific team and the Union Pacific team—competed against one another in a railroad-building race to connect California with the rest of the nation. The Union Pacific Railroad laid track starting in Nebraska, moving westward across the prairie. Its rival was the Central Pacific, founded and managed by four powerful Sacramento businessmen, Charles Crocker, Collis P. Huntington, Leland Stanford, and Mark Hopkins. The Central Pacific began its tough task in Sacramento, advancing eastward across the barrier of the Sierra Nevada, buried half the year in deep snow. Thousands of Chinese immigrants, working harder than any athlete ever has, did the hard labor for the enterprise, all of it by hand. Many lost their lives in the dangerous and unrelenting work. The foremen for the work gangs were mainly Irish immigrants. They followed the path laid down by engineers whose surveying was so spot-on that cars traveling on Interstate 80 today pass along the original route.

After six years of monumental work the Central Pacific linked up with the hard-charging Union Pacific, and on May 10, 1869, East and West were formally joined in a ceremony at Promontory, Utah. They attached a telegraph wire to the last spike on the line and another wire to a sledgehammer. When the hammer hit the spike, the connection sent a telegraph message simultaneously to operators standing by around the country. A nation rent by war at the start of the decade was being fused into one at the end. Button-bursting parades and celebrations broke out everywhere.

The effect of the railroad was profound and immediate, and waves of change spilled over into every sphere of society. Before the railroad it took months and a small fortune to go between the coasts. Now it took a week or two and much less money. The spike that connected the final railroad tie had driven a hole into the wall that separated far-off California from the rest of the nation. Through this opening would come exchanges of people, ideas, energy, trade, materials, tools, language, culture, and know-how. These exchanges would lead to more exchanges, and greater openings, that no one could anticipate or predict. The world had suddenly gotten a lot smaller.

During that heady spring and summer of 1869, something new was afoot in the world of baseball too. Baseball at its inception was a game practiced by amateurs—men who played solely for the love of it, for its healthful benefits, for the joy of sport. Over time, though, this became more the ideal than the reality. As teams became more competitive with one another, the market for top players heated up. Clubs attracted talented players by giving them do-nothing jobs for which they were paid. But their real job was to play ball. Sometimes the clubs simply paid players on the sly, not bothering with the cover of a job. All of this changed with the arrival of the hired guns of the Cincinnati Red Stockings, who blew the cover off baseball's sham practices.

The Red Stockings were baseball's first dream team, an all-star collection of diamond talent. What's more, they were professionals. They were paid to play the game, openly so, and the way they pounded amateur teams only added to their mystique. Touring around the East and Midwest, they had taken on all comers and beaten them with a sharp stick. They had won all their games, virtually all by lopsided scores, and thousands of fans in Cincinnati and around the country had flocked to see the beatings.

That summer the Red Stockings were baseball's top gate attraction. During their triumphant tour, W. S. Hatton of San Francisco made them an offer to come to California, and they accepted. The Recreation Grounds owner had landed a real plum. The Red Stockings were sure to bring out the crowds in baseball-crazy Frisco. What people may not have known was that stagecoach baseball in California was coming to an end and that a new era in keeping with the steam engine—faster, more explosive, and fueled by money—was about to begin.

Enter the Professionals

SATURDAY, MARCH 22 — 2:15 P.M.
SUNDAY, MARCH 23 — 2:15 P.M.
— 1947 —
ABLISHED PRICE - $3.33
ERAL TAX - .67   Total $4.00

IS PORTION OF TICKET NOT GOOD FOR ADMITTANCE

The most glamorous baseball team in existence rode first class in a Central Pacific Silver Palace car across the vast open spaces of the American West. In Nevada, before crossing into California, Central Pacific workers attached a second locomotive to the train, which needed extra power to make it to the top of the mountains rising above them like the walls of a fortified castle. On this train were the best baseball players of their time. They included player-manager Harry Wright, the man who assembled the Red Stockings with the financial backing of the city of Cincinnati, and his brother George, a razzle-dazzle shortstop (both are in the Hall of Fame). The youngest and lowest-paid player on the squad was nineteen-year-old Cal McVey, a slash-hitting, play-any-position phenom from Indianapolis.

Harry Wright, with Boston. National Baseball Hall of Fame Library, Cooperstown, N.Y.

This was not a simple train trip for these players; it had the look and feel of an adventure. For them Chicago was "the West"; California was, well, it was way, way out there, an island attached to land. The railroad had only been in operation five months, and while it had instantly made passage to and from California simpler and faster than ever before, it was hardly what anyone would describe as easy travel. The trains ran up to sixty miles per hour, jarring the bones of their passengers every foot of the way. The scenery streaming by the window was at times gorgeous, other times boring as unsweetened mush. But these lands were not at peace. Sioux warriors and other Indian tribes defending their homelands against white settlers offered armed and bloody resistance to the United States Cavalry. Once you made it to the coast, assuming you did, who knew what to expect? The land on the other side of the Sierra was a world unto itself, as exotic in its way as India and the spice lands of the Far East.

After crossing the seven-thousand-foot summit and coasting down the western slopes of the Sierra, the ballplayers reached Sacramento, then the end of the railroad line. After a night in "the Queen City of the Plain," as the guide-books called it, they rode the *Capital* steamer down the river to a hero's welcome in San Francisco. It was late September 1869, and a welcoming committee greeted them at the Embarcadero, taking them by horse-drawn carriage to the Cosmopolitan Hotel, one of the city's finest. Later the Stockings paid a visit to the pride and joy of the Hatton Brothers, the Recreation Grounds, where they would be playing the next day. In the evening the out-of-towners put in a head-turning, whisper-causing appearance at the opera house.

They were the talk of the city, page one news. On Saturday, the opening day of their big series, stores, banks, and public offices declared a half-day holiday. Grown men shuttered their shops and gazed with a boy's wide-eyed wonder upon the storied visitors from the East, the grandest (and richest!) ballplayers in the world. No one in the West had seen players with such style and polish. They wore flannel knickers with brightly colored crimson socks—hence, their name. Their plumage rivaled that of peacocks, and a few of the players strutted like them too, aware of the thousands of pairs of eyes keenly following their every casual gesture. Some of the watch-ful eyes belonged to women. No one could overlook the impressive physicality of these men—these fit, athletic, hard-bodied men. One reporter for the morning *Chronicle* noted the "well-formed calves" of the players bulging underneath their red-hot legwear.

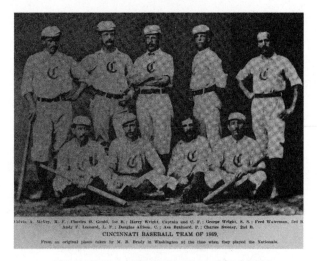

Cincinnati Red Stockings, 1869. Standing, from left: Cal McVey, Charles Gould, Harry Wright, George Wright, Fred Waterman. Sitting from left: Andy Leonard, Doub Allison, Asa Brainard, Charles Sweasy. Doug McWilliams Collection

Among his many bright baseball ideas, ideas that have long been consolidated into the customs and traditions of the sport, Harry Wright is said to have introduced the pre-game rituals of batting practice and hit-ting fly balls to outfielders to help them warm up. It is not known whether the Stockings took bat-ting practice or shagged fly balls that day, but we do know fans began arriving at the Rec Grounds a full three hours before the scheduled first pitch, and the Wrights, Cal McVey, and the other stars may have treated them to an early show.

The ball joint at Twenty-fifth and Folsom was jumping, the place to see and be seen. Two thousand people throbbing with energy and excitement turned out. But for all the build-up leading up to them, the games were a let-down, an awful mismatch. First the Stockings played the Eagles, winners of a recent championship tournament in San Francisco, and scored twelve runs in the first inning of a 35 to 4 win. The next days only got worse for the home-town boys. After pummeling the Eagles a second time, the Stockings took on the Pacifics, led by the talented Shepard brothers. It hardly mattered; they received a thumping too. Then came the Atlantics, more lambs to the slaugh-ter. After five innings the Red Stockings led 76 to 5. It was reasoned that the

Atlantics were probably not going to catch them, and the game was brought to a merciful halt.

The night before they left San Francisco the Red Stockings attended a banquet in their honor at Pacific Hall on Bush Street. Post-game banquets in those days were quite common. Civic dignitaries and prominent base-ballists—an early term for ballplayers—were present. Harry Wright, a onetime New York Knickerbocker renowned for his sportsmanship and muttonchop whiskers, toasted the generosity and hospitality of the hosts, who responded with their own gracious remarks. One San Franciscan, raising his glass, said about the Red Stockings, "May they never meet the wash in which they will be bleached." The next day, the visitors from the East returned to Sacramento for a farewell appearance, after which they climbed back aboard the Central Pacific for the long, clattering train ride home.

After leaving California the Red Stockings kept playing and winning, never letting the ideals of sportsmanship and fair play get in the way of a good thrashing of their opponents. Their eighty-one-game winning streak, the longest in professional baseball history, came to an end the following year when a team from Brooklyn nipped them 8 to 7 in an extra-inning thriller. The club disbanded after that season and the players all went their separate ways. But the skill and professionalism of the Red Stockings forced changes in baseball everywhere.

The initial reaction in California bordered on depression. Some had previously thought their brand of ball measured up to the Easterners'. Clearly, the lopsided nature of the games deprived them of this illusion. They recognized, as did people across America, that if you wanted to field a top-level baseball team, you needed to pay your players on the square. And this required money, lots of it.

One group of baseball fans, the gamblers, viewed these unfolding events with keen interest. Gambling was the mother's milk of baseball, California included. California *especially*, settled as it was by people who had come there, in essence, on a gamble, often at great personal risk to themselves and their families. With the railroad, many of the physical risks associated with travel to and from the West had largely fallen away, at least for those in the continental United States, but to leave your home to make a new life in a distant place you've never been—that takes guts, whatever era you live in. Compared to that, compared to the big gambles of life, betting on a ballgame was not much of a risk. Anybody could do it, and lots of people did and got a kick out of it.

When the Red Stockings blew through San Francisco, spectators formed gambling pools and made side bets in the crowded grandstands of the Recreation Grounds. This practice was commonplace for games in the city and around the state. City gamblers supposedly fired pistols into the air to startle outfielders who were about to catch a fly ball or field a grounder, hoping to cause a bobble to change the outcome of the play and possibly the game.

Gamblers—successful ones, anyhow—are smart people, and they realized early on that there were better ways to reach ballplayers than by shooting bullets into the air. Money buys influence; it is the greatest persuader of all. Gamblers knew this and they paid players to throw games. Batters on the take struck out with the bases loaded or swung and missed at bad pitches. Those in the field misjudged fly balls or booted grounders, and pitchers served up easy offerings that surprised but grateful hitters laced into the outfield gaps. With baseball's popularity surging in California, the influence of gambling and gamblers on the national pastime would only grow stronger.

During this same period, a small but noteworthy event took place in the south of the state, down Mexico way. A new ballfield was built in the coastal community of San Diego. The field, possibly the city's first, was the property of L. L. Lockling, a surveyor who received the land in payment for some mapping work he did for the previous owner. Located between Sixth and Seventh Streets, it served as home park for the Young Americans, Golden Eagles, and other clubs.

At the groundbreaking, about fifty people, all men and boys, came together to record the moment for posterity and pose for a photograph. Some men wore long-sleeve white shirts and vests, the more formal ones kept their coats on. All the men, four of whom leaned jauntily on bats, wore hats. Clumps of boys squeezed in line next to the men to get their faces in the picture. They wore caps too.

San Diego in the 1870s was a small, sleepy border town isolated from the rest of the nation. No railroads connected it to either Los Angeles or the northern part of the state. But railroad or no, they had built a place to play ball. This

The newly constructed baseball field, San Diego, early 1870s.
San Diego Historical Society Photograph Collection, www.sandiegohistory.org

was occurring not only in San Diego, but all around the state, in small towns and out-of-the-way places too small to be called towns. People cleared off a flat piece of dirt and set up a diamond. Families and friends split into teams and played until they got tired, which, for some youngsters, was never. They did this without fanfare, without the local newspapers paying any attention at all. It was just something boys and men did, and, if they let them into the game, girls too.

Baseball proceeds unofficially. You do not need to belong to an organized team or league to play. You do not need a uniform or cap or shoes. A stick can substitute for a bat, a rock or wad of paper can act as the ball. You do not need gloves; in a pinch your bare hands will do. All a person really needs is a little imagination and a sense of play.

Organized professional baseball, however, is a different animal. Obviously, a professional club needs money—the more the better. It also needs people, a fan base to support the team—again, the more the better. Both these ingredients depend on the basic necessity of transportation. For people to live in a city in the first place, they need a way to get there. This was why organized baseball first flourished in northern California, particularly San Francisco. When the railroad brought people and money in droves, organized baseball followed shortly behind.

Women's ball team, with women spectators in the stands, 1890s.
California Historical Society, FN-40044

Cal McVey. National Baseball Hall of Fame
Library, Cooperstown, N.Y.

The railroad and the waves of immigration from overseas also guaranteed that baseball in California would not simply be a local, homegrown affair. Easterners, Midwesterners, Southerners, and people from Europe and other continents would be part of the story. These so-called outsiders poured into the state and made it their own, transforming California baseball just as onetime outsiders in other areas of endeavor shaped the larger history of the state itself.

The development of organized baseball leagues in California roughly coincides with the founding of the National League, which began play in 1876. Although separate in many ways from what was going on in the East, California remained part of the larger growth of the game nationally. The state's first organized baseball league was the Pacific Base Ball League, which played its inaugural season in 1878. All four of its teams called San Francisco home. They played their regular season schedule at the Recreation Grounds, though the championship game took place across the bay at an Oakland racetrack. Five thousand fans paid twenty-five cents apiece to see the Athletics nip the Californias, 9 to 7, in a hotly contested game played under protest. The losers claimed the umpire missed a call that cost them the game and the title.

The next year the California League started up as a rival to the Pacific. Three of its teams came from San Francisco but one hailed from Oakland, where the league played all its games at a park on Center Street. In September the San Francisco Knickerbockers, champions of the Pacific, battled the Californias, winners of the junior circuit, who had jumped over to the new league. The Knickerbockers won, 6 to 5, to claim the unified state title.

Then, in another example of how outside influences were changing baseball in the state, the Cincinnati Red Stockings reappeared in San Francisco after an absence of ten years. After finishing their season in the East they had set off on an exhibition tour of the West, not unlike the one they had taken when the transcontinental railroad first opened up. But much had changed in the interim. Though still in an orbit of its own, California had become a popular wintering ground for Eastern major leaguers who came out to relax, indulge in whatever pleasures struck their fancy, and pick up some extra money in the off-season playing in exhibitions. These Red Stockings were only one of many big league teams that would pass through the state in the years to come.

The team's roster had changed as well. This version of the Red Stockings was nothing like the freight train that had flattened everything in its path in 1869. The Wright brothers and just about everybody else from that famous lineup were long gone. But there was one familiar face, a star on the original club who had seen California as a boy and was now coming back as a man: Cal McVey.

Approaching his thirtieth birthday, McVey was no longer a wide-eyed teenager. After the original Red Stockings disbanded he had continued playing professional baseball, starring on championship teams in Boston before signing up with Chicago in 1876, the inaugural year of the National League. His pitching and hitting helped lead the Chicago White Stockings to the first pennant in National League history. At the time of this, his second trip to

California, McVey had returned to his professional roots as player-manager of the Red Stockings, which had reformed as a National League club.

No one knows what was going through his mind. Did he like what he saw on his first trip and vow to come back if he ever got the chance? Had he been planning to return for some time? Or did he make a spur-of-the-moment decision that this was the place for him after all? All we can say for certain was that at the end of their second tour, the Red Stockings returned to Cincinnati with one less passenger. This time Cal McVey was staying, and California was his new home.

Details about him following this life-changing decision remain sketchy. At different times he lived in San Francisco, Oakland, and other California cities. Though his major league career was over, he remained active in Bay Area baseball circles, forming the semipro Bay Cities club in Oakland. One account says Bay Cities was skilled enough to beat a visiting team of Eastern major leaguers; another has the club playing only a short time before folding. McVey also played for a time in local California League games, his name last appearing on a professional baseball roster in 1886.

McVey's most valuable role in California baseball, however, may have been as mentor and advisor to local players, encouraging them to test their skills

Providence Grays, National League, 1882. Catcher Sandy Nava is sitting on the floor, center. Third-baseman Jerry Denny is standing above him. Manager Harry Wright is in street clothes, and his brother George is seated to his right. National Baseball Hall of Fame Library, Cooperstown, N.Y.

against the best of the East. He was not the only person who did this, but he was one of the most prominent. And as a retired major leaguer, a man who had played with the best in the game, his words carried weight.

Andrew Piercy, a native of San Jose, debuted with McVey's former club, the Chicago White Stockings, in 1881. Although his stay in the National League did not last long (he played only two games before returning to his home state), he was the first native Californian to play in the major leagues.

The year after Piercy's appearance, Sandy Nava, a catcher from San Francisco, broke in with Providence, then a National League city and part of the major leagues. Nava's father was English and his mother was Mexican, which made him one of the earliest ballplayers of Hispanic descent to play in the majors. Nava saw limited duty in his five years in the East.

Bare-handed third baseman Jerry Denny made a much greater impact on the game. His parents migrated from New York to the Bay Area when he was a boy. Both died when he was still young, and he grew up in an orphanage. He played for St. Mary's College (then in San Francisco) and in the California League before graduating to the big time. He made his debut with Providence around the same time as Andrew Piercy but lasted considerably longer—thirteen seasons in all. Playing with his bare hands, he was considered one of the best fielding third baseman of his day, ranging to his left and right with equal ease and gobbling up everything hit in his vicinity. In 1884 he began one era—hitting the first home run in what was the equivalent of World Series competition—and then, ten years later, ended another, retiring as perhaps the last major leaguer not to use a fielder's glove.

Jerry Denny, 1887. National Baseball Hall of Fame Library, Cooperstown, N.Y.

Piercy, Nava, and Denny were among the first California-bred ballplayers to play major league baseball, but they would certainly not be the last. The baseball express that had brought Cal McVey and other stars to the West was no longer running in one direction. Players from the land beyond the mountains were turning their sights on the distant cities of the East.

How Casey
Advanced
to the Bat

st Lawrence Thayer   Illustrated by

SATURDAY, MARCH 22 — 2:15 P.M.
SUNDAY, MARCH 23 — 2:15 P.M.
— 1947 —

ABLISHED PRICE $3.33   Total $4.00
ERAL TAX —   .67

HIS PORTION OF TICKET NOT GOOD FOR ADMITTANCE
DETACH SEPERATE COUPONS FOR INDIVIDUAL GAMES

One fine day in the fall of 1886 a twenty-three-year-old Massachusetts man arrived in San Francisco with bright hopes. While touring Europe he had received a telegram inviting him to write for the *Daily Examiner,* one of the newspapers in town. Born in Worcester, near Boston, he was the son of a well-to-do textile manufacturer. Not ready to follow his father's path just yet, and wishing to explore more of what the world had to offer, he agreed to come to California, a place he had never been before. His name was Ernest Lawrence Thayer—"Phinney" to his friends at Harvard College, where he had graduated.

It was William Randolph Hearst, a friend of Phinney's from Harvard, who had extended the offer, cabling him overseas. W. R.'s father, George Hearst, a self-made millionaire who had come west during the latter years of the Gold Rush, owned the *Examiner.* In November he had become a United States Senator from California, and plans were afoot to remove George's name from the paper's masthead and replace it with his son's, as soon as Hearst senior was officially sworn in the following spring. But W. R.—that was how friends and colleagues referred to him—was a bright, ambitious young man with no time to waste. Only twenty-three himself, he was already making decisions about the paper, one of which involved bringing in fresh voices and humor. That was why Phinney got the call.

W. R. and his newest employee shared many interests, including baseball. Although not a player himself, Hearst had made financial donations to Harvard baseball and in his sophomore year hosted a dinner for the team. The next year he became vice president of the Intercollegiate Base-Ball Association, an election win he credited to putting on lots of drunken parties for his classmates.

Among his other activities, Will was business manager of the *Harvard Lampoon,* the school's humor magazine. There he met Phinney, the *Lampoon's* editor and star writer. With crisply parted hair, a slender clean-shaven face, and almost delicate features, Thayer was something of a loner, quiet and reserved. His interests tended more toward philosophy and literature than the hurly-burly world of commerce. But he had a lively wit and quirky comic sensibility that came out in his humor pieces for the *Lampoon.* "Thayer, although very young, is already noted for his letters, some of which have appeared in the New York Times," wrote an admiring Will Hearst to his mother. Phinney loved baseball too. He frequently attended Harvard games and his best friend was captain of the team.

Upon his arrival in San Francisco, Thayer stayed at first in the Hearst family home on Taylor Street. Later, when he got his feet under him, he found a place of his own near Union Square. Phoebe Hearst, Will's mother, a former Missouri schoolteacher who had grown into one of the city's cultural and educational leaders, took a liking to him, treating him kindly and encouraging him in his writing. This was not unusual; Phoebe enjoyed young people and did what she could to help their talents blossom. The bookish Thayer, who spoke with a soft Massachusetts accent, felt awkward around society people and not entirely comfortable in the city in general. But the Hearsts tried to make him feel welcome, inviting him over to the house for Thanksgiving dinner.

Thayer wrote about baseball and other subjects for the *Examiner* with the same deft touch he had shown at the *Lampoon*. His reporting was unsigned, characteristic of the time. But he was not happy at the paper. In a letter to his parents that winter, he explained the reasons for his discomfort:

> I see nobody at all outside my professional colleagues & I think that journalists are very much like cattle in that respect. They move in herds. As a rule they are very amusing fellows, for they have all had varied experiences & they are brighter & more intelligent than the average of men. Sometimes, however, I get very tired of their society, for with all their good points they certainly lack steadiness and respectability. They are wild, happy go lucky fellows, tied to nothing and nobody.

When not in the office Thayer could be found, at least some of the time, at the ballpark. That spring San Francisco inaugurated a new park, the Haight Street Grounds, on the eastern edge of Golden Gate Park. Fans reached it by trolley. As the home for California League games, it quickly became a popular in-crowd spot. Charles Crocker, the bear of a man who supervised the building of the transcontinental railroad and was one of the state's wealthiest and most powerful individuals, had a private box there. The swells of the Bohemian Club also reserved a box for their members only. On Opening Day ten thousand people saw the Haverlys beat the Pioneers, 5 to 4, in a preview of the season to come. The men from the Haverlys, sponsored by a city theater, were four-time defending champions, but the talent-packed Pioneers promised to challenge them for the flag.

Haight Street Grounds, San Francisco, 1887. California Historical Society, FN-40029

The size of this event and the excitement it generated did not escape notice in the newsroom of the *Examiner.* W. R. was pushing hard to boost the paper's circulation and one of the ways he determined to do it was to beef up its sports coverage. Box scores began appearing on page one. Articles on baseball, boxing, and horse racing popped up on the front page as well. Along with the high-profile sports coverage, Hearst doubled the headline size on the front page, added more illustrations, and signed high-priced editorial talent such as the satirist Ambrose Bierce. The paper also splashed more crime stories across its pages and published spicy drawings of scantily clad young females.

Besides Ernest Thayer, Hearst had brought in a few other Harvard classmates to help him turn the *Examiner* around. These Cambridge Yard refugees usually dined together in the evenings after work. "We spend about two hours at table trying to get each other to praise our individual work," joked Thayer in a letter home. Three or four times a week W. R. joined the party. As Thayer said, "We tell him how to run a newspaper. He should have a great many excellent ideas on this subject by this time."

Despite these apparent good feelings there was friction below the surface. With new talent being imported from around the country, Thayer felt himself being steadily pushed out of the *Examiner.* His contributions to the paper were reduced and his pay was cut ten dollars to twenty five dollars per week. Nor was his friend quite as solicitous as he once was, now that he had officially become publisher. "Hearst is no longer a boy," wrote Thayer, "but a man with a scrupulous regard for his own interests." Some of the older hands in the newsroom had been let go, and he worried about being fired. While not falling into despair, Thayer had, in his short stay at the *Examiner,* decided one thing absolutely. As he wrote to his parents in the spring of that year:

> My mind is made up on one point. If I cannot hold my own in
> my present position, I will give up the Examiner entirely. I will
> not go back to reporting under any circumstances. The life of a
> reporter on a Frisco paper is one of a man accursed of God.

But Thayer did not get fired as he feared, and San Francisco was not yet finished with him. Still ahead were more games to see, more writing and exploration, and one of the grandest, most surprising achievements in all of baseball history.

★ ★ ★ ★ ★

As hoped, the 1887 California League pennant race was turning into a real dilly. The Pioneers and the Haverlys were battling neck and neck. But the Sacramento Altas, who were breaking in a new ballpark of their own, Snowflake Park, were making noises like they were going to take a run at the crown. The fourth team in the four-team circuit was sponsored by Greenhood and Moran, a tailor and clothing shop in Oakland. Like the Altas, the G&M's had joined the league the previous season. Its pennant chances were hurt badly

Sacramento Altas, 1886. California Historical Society, FN-40037

when its twenty-year-old left-handed pitching and hitting sensation, George Van Haltren, signed a major league contract, agreeing to the deal with his father's blessing, at a saloon. By June his talents were on display back East in the National League, and as a result the Oaklanders were struggling.

With two teams from San Francisco and two from outside the city, the California League had become, truly, a California league—or at least a northern California one. Its former rival, the Pacific Base Ball League, had come and gone. A new competitive league had appeared on the scene earlier in the season, boasting four teams of its own and big plans, only to get shellacked in ticket sales and die after only a couple of months. The California League reigned as the state's leading professional baseball organization.

Still, it had its problems. For instance, many people opposed playing baseball on Sunday because it was the Lord's Day and was not to be spent indulging in frivolous activities. In some jurisdictions, Sunday baseball was against the law. But both players and fans worked during the week, so the only free days they had for baseball were Saturday and Sunday. For practical and economic reasons, then, the California League adopted Sunday play—a policy that caused teenager

Fred Lange and some other younger players to be less than forthcoming with their parents. Lange, a catcher with the G&M's who grew up to write a history of early California baseball, used the name of "Dolan" so his parents wouldn't catch him playing on the Sabbath. His folks eventually found out but let him stay in the club anyhow.

Lange's parents worried about him because baseball players were to polite society what California was to the rest of the nation: on the rough edges. They drank and smoked and used bad language. They gambled and it was well known some of them cheated and threw games—"hippodroming," as the practice was called then. Ballplayers ran with fast women, went through money like they had a private pass to the U.S. Treasury, and consorted with dubious characters who, like them, felt more at home in a poolroom than a schoolroom.

"Going to the Game," 1890s. Illustration by Ralph Yardley. The Haggin Museum, Stockton, CA

While decent families were tucked away in bed, ballplayers were out carousing till the wee hours of the night. Many a California Leaguer played on Sunday with a major hangover from the night before, and some of them—real "lushers," to use the vernacular of the time—took the field drunk.

But the antics of players were only one part of a larger problem—the loss of public confidence in organized baseball. Gambling and booze were poisoning the game. Both players and fans raged at umpires and acted like jerks. Another issue was the practice known as "revolving," in which players ignored signed contracts and jumped to whatever team offered them the best deal at that moment.

When San Francisco attorney John Mone became league president in the early eighties, his charge was to clean house—assert control over rowdy players and fans, kick out the gamblers, and make it safe for non-drinking, non-gambling, non-swearing customers to come to the ballpark. While Mone was no miracle worker, he did achieve progress in these areas. In 1886 the sale of liquor was banned at all California League ballparks. And in May of the following year the league initiated its first Ladies Day promotion. In the eyes of Mone and league owners, women improved the atmosphere at games, exerting a civilizing influence on the rough male-dominated surroundings. Seated together in the special ladies pavilion reserved for them at the Haight Street Grounds, women often came dressed in the colors of their favorite team. Hardcore male fans may have grumbled, but league officials smiled at the swatches of pink and blue and white brightening the stands like spring flowers.

★   ★   ★   ★   ★

The race for the title came down to nearly the last day of the 1887 season. George Van Haltren, the brilliant young Oakland star, had returned to the G&M club after his major league season had concluded. Van Haltren would do something similar for the next sixteen seasons—excel in the East (his career batting average was .316) and then come home in the winter to play and coach, including in the Pacific Coast League. But this year his presence in the final days was not enough to put the G&M's over the top. They dropped out of contention, as did the Altas of Sacramento, leaving the Pioneers and the Haverlys to duke it out for the championship in the next-to-last game of the season.

The deciding tilt took place in October in front of a full house at the Haight Street Grounds, which had been expanded during the season to accommodate the swelling numbers of fans who wanted to see games there. It now held twenty thousand people, double the attendance of Opening Day. Eddie Lorrigan, a former St. Mary's College man, took the hill for the upstart Pioneers, while Haverlys manager Henry Harris gave the ball to his main man, Pete Meegan. In the middle part of the decade, California League pitchers had abandoned underhand throwing and adopted an overhand motion, part of a national trend toward throwing the ball harder and more like the way it is done today. This, along with the development of a wicked new type of pitch, the curveball, had reduced the number of runs scored in games. In the end, Lorrigan and the Pioneers bested the defending champions, 6 to 4, and claimed the pennant.

George Van Haltren, late in his career.
Courtesy of the Oakland Museum
of California

Ernest Thayer may have attended this game. He certainly was in the city during this time—watching baseball, soaking up the atmosphere, and commenting on the personalities as he filed his once-a-week satirical pieces on life on the Pacific Slope. What influence, if any, did all of this have on what was to come? More important, perhaps, than any of the baseball Thayer witnessed was the fact that he had a publishing home, where he could write what was on his mind and see what he wrote in the paper the next day or soon after. During this fall, as the Haverlys and Pioneers were streaking to the wire, he began experimenting in print with the comic ballad, a new literary form for him. Despite being bothered by poor eyesight, he had been reading W. S. Gilbert's *Bab Ballads*. Thus inspired, he published a half-dozen or so similar ballads in the *Examiner*. "The Strange Story of a Highly Educated Young Lady" tells the tale, in comic verse, of a woman being courted by two men. "The Shocking Tale of an Extremely Accomplished Villain" covers a murder:

> The time is twelve o'clock about, the scene a narrow street;
> A cry of murder rouses a policeman on his beat;
> He rushes to the rescue and discovers with a start
> Mr. Jonathan Depew with two daggers in his heart.

A sea ballad by Thayer, subtitled "The Thrilling Account of an Incident in American Navy Life," appeared in the paper in early December. There is disagreement over what occurred next. One authority on Thayer says he became ill and left San Francisco for Worcester shortly after the ballad's publication; two others say he continued writing unsigned editorials for the *Examiner* until late February of the next year, amid the stirrings of a new baseball season. What is certain is that he did eventually give up the life of a San Francisco journalist and go back to Massachusetts. There, in Worcester, in the spring of 1888, he sat down to write a ballad about baseball. The opening line of his poem reads,

> The outlook wasn't brilliant for the Mudville Nine that day…

He continued writing. When he finished he folded the piece up and sent it off to the *Examiner,* which paid him five dollars for it. Thayer never asked for, nor received, another penny for his creation. It was the last piece he wrote for the *Examiner* and virtually the last piece of professional writing he ever did.

On June 3 the San Francisco *Examiner* published "Casey at the Bat," subtitled "A Ballad of the Republic, Sung in the Year 1888." Thayer's previous ballads had all received prominent treatment at the top of a page with an accompanying illustration, but "Casey at the Bat" appeared at the bottom of page four next to an Ambrose Bierce piece. The headline was tiny, and no drawing attracted readers' eyes to it. As was the case with his other ballads for the paper, Thayer did not use his real name. The poem's author was listed only as "Phin"—a reference to his Harvard nickname.

What came next was a happy accident—actually, a string of them. A novelist named Archibald Clavering Gunter, the author of the best-selling *Mr. Barnes of New York* and thirty-nine other now-forgotten books, happened to see the poem and clip it from the paper. Later that summer, while in New York, he sent a copy over to his friend De Wolf Hopper, who was starring in a comic opera at the Wallack Theater in Manhattan. Gunter suggested Hopper perform the poem the next evening, when several ballplayers from the New York Giants and Chicago White Stockings were planning to attend.

Initially unimpressed by what he read, Hopper did not want to deliver the poem. A longtime veteran of the theater, he was a commanding figure on stage, as big as an athlete and with a voice that could shake a chandelier. But on the day of the scheduled appearance by the ballplayers, Hopper reread the poem and decided to do it after all. Always a quick study, he committed the lines to memory and prepared for his performance.

As previously announced, members of the Giants and White Stockings appeared that evening at the Wallack Theater, settling into their box seats. The presence of the players had caused a stir in the audience before the curtain went up but soon they, like everyone else, fell under the spell of De Wolf Hopper's powerful recitation. When he uttered that epic last line—"But there is no joy in Mudville—mighty Casey has struck out"—silence followed. The ending was so shocking it caught the audience by surprise. Then, almost in unison, the ballplayers and the others in the theater jumped to their feet, clapping and cheering for the man who had delivered the words. A legend, as they like to say in show business, was born.

Historian Jules Tygiel has said that "Casey at the Bat" represents the "first major expansion of baseball into popular culture," when the game reached beyond the playing field into society at large. This expansion occurred almost immediately. Hopper's performance received a rave review from the *New York Times*, and in the weeks and months that followed, newspapers around the country printed the poem in their editions. Hopper became a man in demand. Everyone wanted to hear him speak those words about Mudville, not just theater lovers and the cultural elite but also shopkeepers, bartenders, steamfitters, woodworkers, grocers, waitresses. But as the fame of "Casey at the Bat" spread, several mysteries swirled

"Casey at the Bat" liquor bottle. Doug McWilliams Collection

"Casey at the Bat" children's book, 1989.

"Casey at the Bat" Centennial Issue,
Sports Illustrated, 1988.

around the poem. One of the biggest centered on the identity of the author. Who was "Phin"? Only a handful of people in all of America knew the answer, and the author himself did not step forward to solve the mystery.

Remaining tucked away in his Worcester, Massachusetts, home, in the years to come Ernest operated one of his father's textile mills and led an introspective life in keeping with his quiet, philosophical bent. He stayed true to his vow not to practice journalism anymore, at times regarding the hubbub surrounding his poem as a nuisance. He never authorized a reprint of it and only seldom gave readings, occasionally passing along copies to his friends for their amusement. People across the United States could recite snippets of "Casey" by heart, but mentioning the author's name to them would have drawn only a blank stare.

Into this void stepped various imposters claiming to have written the piece. These false claims disgusted Thayer and, after he was accused of stealing his own poem, forced him to take his case to the public. "I think that if the matter were of any importance the easiest way to establish the authorship would be to let the different claimants furnish a copy which might be compared with the poem as it was first printed in the Examiner," he wrote in a letter to a sports editor. Reporters did exactly that and found that Thayer was truly the author and the *Examiner* the original publisher.

Even so, literary fakes kept making specious claims of authorship, just as other controversies attached themselves to the poem. Who was Casey? Was he modeled on a real player? Many say he resembles Mike "King" Kelly, a famous player of the time, and one early newspaper reprint substituted his name in place of Casey's. Another alleged inspiration was John Patrick "Patsy" Cahill, a hard-drinking San Francisco–born California Leaguer of the 1880s. Upon his death in Pleasanton, the *Oakland Tribune*'s obituary claimed that he served as the true model for Casey's character. Other local heroes made similar claims around the country.

Another controversy focused on Mudville, the setting for the poem. Does this fictional place have a basis in fact? Many cities in the United States have claimed the title. Indeed almost any nineteenth-century town with dirt streets might, after a good rain, turn into a mudville. Stockton, California, was known as "Mudville" at the time Thayer was living and writing in San Francisco. Stern-wheeled steamboats traveled back and forth between the two cities every day. In 1887 Stockton fielded a scrappy club that played its home games at the Banner Island Grounds along the Stockton Channel, the main shipping channel for the inland river city. Two members of that club were Billy Cooney and Dan Flynn, whose last names are the same last names of two characters in the poem. "Casey at the Bat" also refers to cheers rumbling through "the valley" and knocking up "the mountain." Could these landmarks be the San Joaquin Valley, the home of Stockton, and Mount Diablo, which is visible from the town?

"I am sorry to say there is no story connected with the writing of those stanzas," Thayer wrote in another letter to a newspaper, trying unsuccessfully to end the speculation about Mudville and Casey. "The verses themselves own their existence to my enthusiasm for college baseball, not as a player but as a fan, and to my association while in college with Will Hearst, who engaged me to come to the Examiner in San Francisco after I graduated.... The poem has no basis in fact."

Nearing fifty, having had his fill of the textile business and New England winters, Thayer retired to Santa Barbara, where the shy bachelor met his Rosalind—Rosalind Buel Hammett, a widow. After being married in San Diego they made a home together in a cozy Montecito bungalow on the shores of the blue, blue Pacific.

Thayer lived in the area nearly thirty years until his death on the eve of World War II. Though mellowing some, he still expressed unhappiness with all the unsought attention his poem had brought him. He said once that his youthful writing for the *Examiner* was mostly "nonsense" and that "Casey at the Bat" was "neither better nor worse than much of the other stuff." He added, "It would be hard to say, all things considered, if it has given me more pleasure than annoyance."

But others could feel the pleasure of his creation even if he could not. At the fiftieth anniversary of his Harvard graduating class, his classmates posted a banner that said, "An '85 Man Wrote 'Casey'!" This was said to have given him some satisfaction. When he died, at seventy-seven, the *Santa Barbara News-Press* noted that Thayer's friends had encouraged him to write more but he had always resisted, claiming he had nothing to say. "Now I have something to say," he said at the end of his life, "and I am too weak to say it."

The other major player in the "Casey" saga, De Wolf Hopper, also has a California footnote to his story. In 1916, the Triangle Film Corporation of Hollywood decided to make the first movie adaptation of "Casey at the Bat," and they naturally called on the man who had recited it thousands of times across the country to play the title role. Trouble was, Hopper was then in his fifties, a little too old perhaps to play an athletic young baseball hero. Also working against him was the fact that this was a silent movie and his greatest acting attribute was his voice.

The movie received terrible reviews and flopped at the box office, wrecking Hopper's dreams of a movie career and sending him back to the New York stage. But his association with Hollywood did not end there. His fifth wife, Hedda Hopper, became a famous and powerful show business gossip columnist. Their son, William De Wolf Hopper Jr., played the Paul Drake character in the *Perry Mason* television detective series.

Train Ride
South

SATURDAY, MARCH 22 — 2:15 P.M.
SUNDAY, MARCH 23 — 2:15 P.M.
— 1947 —

ABLISHED PRICE $3.33   Total $4.00
ERAL TAX   .67

THIS PORTION OF TICKET NOT GOOD FOR ADMITTANCE
DETACH SEPERATE COUPONS FOR INDIVIDUAL GAMES

Days after the close of the 1888 major league season in the East, baseball's first round-the-world tour set off from Chicago. The players on the tour consisted of a handpicked collection of talent from the Chicago White Stockings and other National League clubs. A traveling band of star players, in many ways they resembled the original Cincinnati Red Stockings of twenty years before, only with a more ambitious road trip ahead of them. After touring parts of the United States they planned to cross the Pacific to Australia, staging exhibitions for people who had never seen baseball before.

This band of baseball globetrotters arrived in San Francisco in the first days of November. Twenty players were in the group—ten from the White Stockings and ten from around the league. This latter group was called the "All-Americas." In the opener, the All-Americas whipped the White Stockings in front of fifteen thousand fans at the Haight Street Grounds. After that a few California League teams got into the act. Both the Pioneers and Greenhood and Moran soundly thumped the All-Americas in a display of local baseball muscle. These games, crowed the *San Francisco Chronicle,* showed that "we have players here who are not many paces behind their celebrated brethren of the East in point of ability."

After their games in San Francisco the Easterners packed their bags for Stockton, home to the winners of that year's California League pennant. They played to a tie with the men from Stockton before darkness shut down the game at the Banner Island Grounds.

When the original Cincinnati Red Stockings came to California they stopped in Sacramento and San Francisco before heading back East. But these major leaguers took a different tack. Instead of visiting only the northern part of the state, they turned south to the suddenly no-longer-sleepy town of Los Angeles.

Having been left out of the Gold Rush, this was the first time the southern part of the state had experienced a substantial economic boom. Outsiders poured into the area, lured by cheap land and cheaper railroad fares.

Formerly the Central Pacific, the Southern Pacific Railroad was battling its chief rival, the Santa Fe, for power and passengers. Three years earlier the Santa Fe had done what Los Angeles civic leaders had been dreaming of for decades: provide a direct railroad link with the eastern United States. The Santa Fe roughly followed the old Butterfield stagecoach route from Missouri across the Southwest to Los Angeles and then down the coast to San Diego. This put it at odds with the Southern Pacific, which had controlled East-West traffic and rail service within the state. The two companies started trading price cuts like heavyweight boxers exchanging punches, making the trip to the coast a bargain. Passengers could get there from halfway across the country for a measly twelve bucks.

Those crossing into Los Angeles and surrounding communities came mainly from the Midwest. Attracted by land prices set low enough to encourage settlement, they brought their families, built homes and churches, and started businesses. Some of these white newcomers married Mexicans who already lived in the area, forming new families.

These settlers were different than the ones who stormed California during the Gold Rush. They arrived not with expectations of a quick score; rather, they were digging in for the long haul, sinking roots into the sunbaked earth. They liked that there was lots and lots of level land. Orange groves carpeted the valleys, and orchards bloomed seemingly everywhere you turned. Sure, the place was being buried in hype; the railroads advertised its virtues around the country, and the city and the *Los Angeles Times* did plenty of cheerleading too. But people could see this was no magician's trick—there was something vital going on, something real. Besides, it was a place that was good for your bones, warm all year round. Sure beat the snow and sleet and those cold Midwestern winters.

New towns were springing up like umbrellas in a summer shower: Santa Monica and Long Beach along the coast, Pasadena and Burbank in the inland valleys. New schools and cultural institutions were being formed, and the ones that already existed were flourishing. With transportation established in the

Mexican-Anglo ball team, Los Angeles, circa 1870s.
The Huntington Library, San Marino, California, photPF 08187

region, people and money followed, and here came a big-time major league baseball tour—traveling on the Southern Pacific line in two Pullman cars, a dining car and a sleeping car—to see what all the fuss was about.

The leader of the tour was Chicago White Stockings president Albert Goodwill Spalding, who conceived, organized, and paid for it. He also chose the players who were on it, making his selections based on their skills as well as their character. "It was absolutely essential," he later wrote, "that all who did go [on the tour] should be men of clean habits and attractive personality, men who would reflect credit upon the country and the game." Spalding loved his country and he loved baseball, and he wanted his global barnstormers to be ambassadors for both.

Everywhere you dig in the ruins of old-time baseball, you find the remnants of Spalding's footprints. Born in 1850 and growing up in tiny Rockford, Illinois, he said he first learned about baseball from a Union soldier returning home from the ravages of the Civil War. Shy as a teenager, so shy he could not bring himself to ask other boys if he could play in their pickup games, his personality grew bolder once he stepped onto a diamond. His pitching helped turn the small-town homegrown club of Forest City into a national dynamo

Los Angeles ballplayers on the way to a game, circa 1880s.
The Huntington Library, San Marino, California, photCL 58(342)

that could stand toe to toe with the big city boys and lick 'em in a fair fight. Though beaten by the original Red Stockings in their streak year of 1869, Forest City came back the next season and handled them by a score of 12 to 5. That same year, Spalding signed a $2,500 contract, $500 of which was paid up front in cash, to play professional baseball.

Blessed with a "cannon shot" throwing arm, as one observer described it, the twenty-year-old quickly found stardom. He pitched for Boston and mowed down National Association hitters like they were little kids batting on the Rockford Commons. One of his teammates was another talented young Midwesterner, Cal McVey. After a string of championships in Boston, Spalding jumped to the National League in its inaugural year of 1876 and became player-manager of the Chicago White Stockings, one of the league's eight original clubs (now known by a more familiar name, the Cubs.) But the man from Rockford was more than just a hired hand: he contributed ideas and leadership that helped the fledgling league take wing.

In February 1976 the *Chicago Tribune* reported that Spalding had opened "a large emporium in Chicago where he will sell all kinds of baseball goods." From such humble beginnings are empires built. A. G. Spalding & Bros. entered into an exclusive contract with the National League, agreeing to pay one dollar to the league for every Spalding ball it used so long as it used only Spalding balls. The public rushed to buy equipment endorsed by the professionals, and the Spalding brand became gold. His company, which still exists today, made balls, bats, gear, and uniforms for the major leagues, the California League, and later the Pacific Coast League, dominating the baseball manufacturing business well into the early years of the twentieth century.

After two seasons in the National League, Spalding had retired from active play, but in his early thirties he returned to baseball to become president of the White Stockings, splitting time between the executive suite and his expanding business interests. It was around then that he conceived the idea for a global baseball tour. If people around the world discovered the joys of baseball, learned about it and began to play it, they would need gear. For Spalding the tour functioned as a kind of extended sales trip, part of a long-term business development strategy.

With so many former Midwesterners living in the area, Los Angeles baseball fans knew who Albert Spalding was. But another member of the tour, Cap Anson, player-manager of the White Stockings, commanded even greater attention. The thousands of fans who came out for the exhibitions wanted to see him most of all, for he was the most famous baseball player in America the greatest star of his time.

Adrian Constantine Anson was a Midwesterner too, born in Iowa. His nickname of "Cap" was shortened from Captain, a tribute to his talents in leading men. Over six feet tall and sturdy as a barn, he played first base with steadfast durability. But it was his hitting that brought him fame. Sandlot players around the country who wanted to be like Cap used Anson-label bats. Earlier in August he had been one of the ballplayers who witnessed the premiere of

"Casey at the Bat" at the Wallack Theater in New York. His stature among players and fans, along with his proven ability to sell tickets, had earned him a
prominent berth on the tour.

Despite his gifts as a player and manager, time has not been kind to Anson.
Modern biographers cannot fail to note an ugly piece of business he engaged
in the season before the world tour. In July 1887, Anson's White Stockings were
poised to play an exhibition against Newark of the International League. Slated
to pitch for Newark was George Stovey. But Anson held his team off the field
and refused to play because Stovey was "a no-account nigger."

Los Angeles ball team, 1880s. The Huntington Library, San Marino, California, photCL Pierce 10,093

Anson used epithets of this type in his autobiography published years later. He hated blacks and virulently opposed their participation in what he felt was the white man's domain. This incident, imbued with power by his commanding prestige and personality, contributed to the spread of what was known as "the unwritten rule." The unwritten rule, which drummed Stovey and a few other blacks from this period out of organized baseball, was brutally simple: no blacks, no Hispanics with dark skin and Negroid features. They need not apply for jobs in the minor or major leagues. Anson's refusal to play against a black man encouraged others around the country to do the same.

But Anson was not alone; the unwritten rule would have had no force if he were its sole advocate. Nor were the epithets he used uncommon; they were part of the vocabulary of players, managers, owners, league officials, sportswriters, and the people in the grandstands, both men and women. Uniformly, the color of their skin was white.

In his book *America's National Game,* published years later, Albert Spalding carefully noted the names of each member of his global tour. Two of the ballplayers—Anson and John Montgomery Ward, a shortstop with the New York Giants—are now enshrined in the Baseball Hall of Fame. Another of the players, John Tener, went on to become governor of Pennsylvania after leaving the game. George Wright, the onetime Cincinnati Red Stockings star, served as umpire on the tour. He and Spalding are in the Hall too.

Other lesser-known individuals joined the tour to see the sights and assist where they could. Spalding's mother, Mrs. Harriet I. Spalding, was aboard. So were Cap Anson's wife and two other wives. Three reporters from the Chicago and New York papers covered the trip.

But in his book Spalding neglects to mention one person who was also part of the tour: Clarence Duval. Duval was not welcome to dine at the same tables with the others or share a sleeping car with them. Nor could he use the same bathrooms they did. The reason for this was the color of his skin. He was black.

Anson had opposed bringing him on the tour, but Spalding overruled him. According to Spalding biographer Arthur Bartlett, Duval was a song and dance man in vaudeville who had served as a "mascot" for the White Stockings in Chicago, earning the loyalty of the team president. Duval's job on the tour was to entertain the fans before the game. When the players made their entrance onto the field he marched ahead of them, wearing a checkered suit with patent leather shoes and a cane or a navy blue suit with brass buttons.

Once they arrived in Los Angeles, the travelers likely held their exhibition at the Sixth Street Base Ball Park. Built on the site of a former hay market between Flower and Hope Streets, it was the first ballpark in the city with a fence around it, though its most popular use was as a bicycle racing track.

After their games in southern California, the tour returned to San Francisco, where a gala bon voyage dinner was held at the Baldwin Hotel. The dinner menus were printed and designed to resemble baseballs, and diners chose from such dishes as "Oysters on the Home Run," "Petit Paté a la Spalding," and "Frisco Turkey a la Foul." The next day the group boarded the steamship *Alameda* and chugged out through the Golden Gate, ending the California leg of its trip.

The travelers headed to Hawaii, mirroring the journey taken decades earlier by Alexander Cartwright, the aging New York Knickerbocker founder who had lived on the islands for nearly thirty years and likely met Spalding when he was there. The tour stayed in Honolulu long enough to be the invited guests at a feast hosted by the royal family. When Duval performed, the king tossed him a ten-dollar gold coin in appreciation.

The steamer took two weeks to reach New Zealand and Australia. Originally the group planned to head back across the Pacific at this point, but instead decided to push onto Egypt. They played ball in the shadows of the pyramids. From there they went to Italy, France, and Great Britain, drawing curious and often baffled onlookers wherever they went, before returning to the States.

★   ★   ★   ★   ★

In the decade that followed the world tour, Albert Goodwill Spalding experienced a series of changes in his life that made him not just a visitor to California but a year-round resident. After relinquishing partial control of the White Stockings and stepping away from baseball management to pursue other endeavors, he took another move toward retirement by giving up day-to-day management of A. G. Spalding & Bros., then the largest sporting goods company in the world. Then came possibly the biggest change of all: marriage, for a second time. A widower, he exchanged vows with a woman named Elizabeth Mayer.

"She is really very handsome," a journalist wrote of Mayer, "and she does what the 'Advice to Wives' departments in women's magazines always urge young wives to do: she takes an interest in her husband's soul enthusiasms." Perhaps, but it was Mayer's soul-enthusiasm that led to yet anther change in her new husband's life. Mayer belonged to a small religious sect known as the Theosophical Society, which believed the key to wisdom lay in the study of God's nature. The Theosophists had established a spiritual community in Point Loma, California, and the newlyweds moved there on the eve of the new century. Lomaland, as this community was called, consisted of places of worship, an open-air theater, and cottages for the five hundred or so people who lived there. The Spaldings built their own home and, befitting a man of Albert's station, it was no cottage. Their residence, one of the grandest buildings in all of Lomaland, possessed sweeping vistas of San Diego Bay. (It is now part of Point Loma Nazarene University.)

At this stage in his life Spalding was one of the wealthiest men in the country, with an estimated income of $85,000 a year. He was one of the game's elder statesmen, as famous as he was powerful. And his commanding personality only added to his reputation. A photograph of him in his mid-fifties shows him in a banker's suit and tie. His hair is gray, his chin square and firmly set, and he wears a tough, no-nonsense expression for the camera. Those who opposed his will knew this was no bluff.

It is not clear if Albert ever became a practicing Theosophist or not; he told one interviewer he followed it mainly to please his wife. In any case he and Elizabeth settled into their new life far away from the baseball power centers of Chicago and New York. Spalding's purpose in coming west, he said, was "to seek a change and rest from the active duties of life," but in many ways he remained active as ever. Visitors from around the States came calling on Lomaland's most famous resident. He owned a stable and rode horses even as he became fascinated with another form of transportation, the automobile. Expensive and rare, automobiles in the early 1900s were regarded mainly as the playthings of the wealthy, less reliable than a horse and certainly never to replace trains as the primary method of moving people and goods. Nevertheless Spalding's enthusiasm grew. He joined a San Diego commission that oversaw new road building in the county, and he personally paid for the construction of many of them.

Spalding's interest and involvement in local civic affairs—he also played an influential role in the passage of a bond measure for new highways—made him a popular figure in San Diego County, so much so that a group of citizens asked him to be California's Republican Party candidate for the United States Senate. In those days senators did not gain office by a direct vote of the people; the state legislature appointed them. But beginning with this election, a non-binding advisory vote would be held to guide the legislature in making its choice. The voters would vote after a thirty-day campaign, after which the legislature would name the state's next senator. With the legislature controlled by Republicans, it was a given that a Republican would be named to the office. Spalding did not agree to be a candidate until the last day, filing his nomination papers one half hour before the deadline.

His opponent in the contest was John P. Works, a Los Angeles attorney and former judge who was a member of the Progressive wing of the Republican Party. Works and his supporters criticized the political newcomer as a captive of California's powerful railroad interests and as a man who knew only baseball and nothing else. Spalding denied the railroad accusations but proudly boasted of his ties to the game, saying that politics would do well to copy baseball's reliance on fair play. "Politics can be played just as squarely as baseball," he said. "Let the game be played in a manly, straightforward manner, and I will gratefully accept the umpire's decision." At another point he added: "The introduction of a little of the integrity of baseball into politics would not hurt politics."

The connection between baseball and politics entered into a newspaper interview Spalding gave a few days before the November advisory vote. Edward Marshall, a correspondent with the *New York Times,* asked if his ties to baseball had helped or hurt his candidacy. "How do I know yet?" replied Spalding, saying confidently, "Give me the baseball votes of California and my opponents may have the rest."

Also present in the room were his wife, Elizabeth, and cartoonist Homer Davenport, who was drawing a sketch when this comment was made. "The political game is easy when you stack it up against Base Ball," Davenport said, not looking up from his sketchpad. "You're talking to a Senator-to-be all right."

Mrs. Spalding, the reporter noted, "flushed with pleasure" at this remark.

But the political game turned out to be tougher and more conniving than they thought. Spalding did indeed win the approval of the majority of Republican voters in seventy-four districts around California, compared to thirty for Works. But since the Progressive Republicans had gained control of the state legislature, they ignored the advisory vote and appointed Works to be senator.

In 1911, the year after his thwarted Senate candidacy, Spalding published *America's National Game* with Davenport's illustrations. This landmark book, which is part autobiography, was written while Spalding lived in Point Loma. In it he tells the story of baseball in the late nineteenth century, describing many of the game's early pioneers and events, including the volatile, fiercely contested area of player-manager relations, which was as divisive in Spalding's time as it is today. Being a man of management and of forceful views, his opinions naturally color his observations, but the work remains an important record of baseball in its formative years. Spalding died four years after *America's National Game* was published; his grave is in Point Loma.

From Robinson to
Lange to Chance

CHAPTER

6

SATURDAY, MARCH 22 — 2:15 P.M.
SUNDAY, MARCH 23 — 2:15 P.M.
— 1947 —

ABLISHED PRICE - $3.33   Total $4.00
GERAL TAX -   .67

THIS PORTION OF TICKET NOT GOOD FOR ADMITTANCE
DETACH SEPERATE COUPONS FOR INDIVIDUAL GAMES

They called him a shameless baseball promoter. They said he made up stories to get his name and his team's name in the press. He was the fast-talking ringmaster of Oakland baseball, Colonel Tom Robinson. A charming rogue perhaps, but also a winner who steered Oakland to its first California League pennant, the owner-manager was so popular in the East Bay city he could have run for mayor and won except it would have represented a step down from his current position. His club celebrated its 1889 title by unveiling a huge red, white, and blue championship banner at a ceremony. In his early thirties, Colonel Tom was proud as a new papa.

The man at the helm was so identified with his club that its nickname was the Colonels. If there was any doubt it was his baby, all you had to do was see the team photograph: wearing a suit and bowler hat, with a rakish mustache that curls slightly upward at its ends, the Colonel sits in the center surrounded by his players, who were also his employees. There is no question who was the star of the team, and it was not the fellows in the uniforms.

But in a matter of two short years, Colonel Tom's star—and his team's—had dimmed considerably. Things got so bad at one point that Colonel Tom

Oakland Colonels with manager Tom Robinson in center, 1891. Doug McWilliams Collection

and his players burned the championship banner in order to rid the Colonels of the jinx that was making them lose so many games. In those days a team normally carried ten or eleven men on its roster, and in a desperate effort to shake things up, Colonel Tom shuffled forty players in and out of Oakland over the 1891 season. But nothing worked. The Colonels finished dead last—fourth in a four-team race behind Sacramento, San Francisco, and first-place San Jose.

As the 1892 season approached, the prospects for the Colonels appeared equally grim. The team to beat was the defending champion of San Jose, which was known as "the Garden City" for its acres of fruit orchards and lovingly tended gardens. The city had joined the California League only the year before, cruising to the title on the strength of two rubber-armed pitchers, George Harper and Nick Lookabaugh. Standing on a mound that was only fifty feet away from home plate, either Harper or Lookabaugh had pitched every inning of every game during the 147-game season. And both were back, rested and ready for the new campaign.

Teams were always coming and going in the California League, its composition often changing from one year to the next. San Jose had replaced Stockton, which itself had taken the place of the Altas of Sacramento a few years earlier. Another club from Sacramento then entered the league the next season. But amidst these ever-shifting franchises a permanent change was taking place in the way baseball operated. The Oakland clothing store Greenhood and Moran no longer sponsored a club; neither did Haverly's, the San Francisco theater. California League teams now included their home cities as part of their names. The owners believed this lent prestige to their teams, boosted their appeal among the local populace, and encouraged regional rivalries. Fans now identified with their home team because the name of their city was scrawled in bold letters across the front of each player's jersey. (Another way fans identified with players was through trading cards. During this era S. F. Hess and Co. produced the first California baseball cards. Buy a pack of Creole cigarettes and inside was a card featuring a colorful illustration of a California League player.)

The latest city to enter the league's revolving door was Los Angeles; this year, 1892, marked its entry into organized professional baseball. The real-estate boom of the previous decade was sputtering out, but this was California, the land of boom and bust. If there was a bust, just you wait—another boom was right around the corner. (Later that year oil was discovered near West Second Street and Glendale Boulevard, indeed triggering another boomlet in the area.) Through all the ups and downs, Los Angeles was growing faster than any city in the state. Trains ran regularly between the city and the Bay Area, the home base for the other three teams. Although league officials worried about the extra transportation costs and whether Los Angeles had enough people to support a team—worries that extended to every city in the league save for San Francisco—they felt it was a risk worth taking. The owner of the new franchise was G. A. Vanderbeck, and the team played its home games at Athletic Park on Seventh Street. Opening Day took place in late March, drawing more than three thousand spectators.

Los Angeles Consolidated Railway's semipro team, 1891.
The Huntington Library, San Marino, California, photCL 58(332)

The pennant chase rapidly became a two-team race between San Jose and Los Angeles. Vanderbeck had opened his wallet for a bunch of new talent, and his club shot to the top of the standings. But the defending champs rose to the challenge. Although they did not pitch all the innings as they had the previous season, Harper and Lookabaugh pitched enough of them to help the boys from Garden City keep pace with the newcomers from the south.

By summer, though, the early enthusiasm had faded. Attendance was down, way down, around the league, prompting officials to split the season in half and declare San Jose the winner of the first part. Los Angeles took second, San Francisco third, with the Oakland Colonels bottom-feeders once more.

Part two of the California League season then kicked off in late July but, to the despair of Tom Robinson, the Colonels played as badly as they did in part one, winning only twelve games against twenty-five losses. This sent him into a wheeling and dealing frenzy. Out went the old players and in came the new in a late-season bid to get his team back into the race. Lucky for the Colonels, one of his acquisitions was a big, speedy outfielder from San Francisco named Bill Lange.

No doubt about it, this kid could play. He could flat-out play. You didn't have to be a genius to see what Tom Robinson saw in him. His size, for one. In the full extent of his manhood Bill Lange stood a whisker under six feet, two inches tall and tipped the scales at a rock-hard two hundred pounds. That's why they called him "Big Bill." But he was no lunk; dude could fly. Big Bill roamed center field like it was his own private preserve, charging hard and grabbing out of the air any balls that trespassed into his territory. Not only was he a gifted fielder, he knew how to handle a bat too. No pitchers liked to see him come to the plate. Sure, they were the ones with the ball, so that gave them the advantage, but when Big Bill waggled that club in his hands, the odds seemed to tilt back in his favor.

The odds always seemed to tilt in Lange's favor, in whatever he did. The guy had everything. A smooth, strong chin and star-quality looks to match his size and baseball skills. When he smiled, which was often, it broke down barriers and won him friends, including many lady admirers. His manner was open and warm, and his jokes kept everybody loose. All in all, a great guy to have on your team, both on the field and off.

Born in the Presidio District of San Francisco, Lange ran away from home in grammar school to live with his brother Harry in Port Townsend, Washington. They played a pretty good brand of ball in Port Townsend at that time, and the youngster received his early schooling in the game there. After high school he moved up the baseball ladder to Seattle in the Pacific Northwest League, his first professional team. The tougher competition improved his game. His body filled out, and the man at the plate grew more intimidating.

When the Pacific Northwest League went out of business the Seattle club folded with it, throwing the twenty-one-year-old outfielder out of a job. But not for long. Shortly after returning to the Bay Area, he signed with the Oakland Colonels to spin late-season magic for a team in dire need of some.

In the weeks following the arrival of Lange and the other new recruits, the revitalized Oakland club began to make up ground on first-place Los Angeles, which had also strengthened itself with some recent additions. The year before, the league had passed a rule forbidding such signings, but the teams ignored the rule and recruited new players anyway. Investigating the matter further, league officials found that fans did not mind if teams strengthened their cause by bolstering their rosters in September and October, and the rule was then quietly scrapped. This freedom of movement, along with the fact that the

California League played games well into November, drew Eastern major leaguers to the West after the close of their season. Their presence infused the stretch run with glamour and excitement.

In adopting what was known as the National Agreement, the National League and other leagues around the country had sought to maintain organizational control over professional baseball. Among other things, the agreement restricted the ability of players to jump from team to team. Throughout its history, however, the freewheeling California League had an on-again, off-again relationship with the National Agreement. In defiance of organization men in New York and Chicago it often allowed players with signed contracts with other leagues to join its teams, if only for brief stints. For this reason the California League was branded an "outlaw" league and censured for operating outside the rules of organized baseball.

To illustrate how wild and woolly things could get in outlaw California, National League star George Van Haltren signed in November with Oakland with less than ten games to go. Almost immediately Colonel Tom loaned him to San Jose for a crucial season-deciding series against Los Angeles. If San Jose swept this series it would boost the chances of the Colonels, who were then in second place but running out of time.

The gambit failed. San Jose and Van Haltren did not get the job done, and Los Angeles held off Oakland to win the pennant by a comfortable three games. The winners of the second half of the season were named co-champions with San Jose, winners of the first half.

Though they came up short in the end, Colonel Tom's ringers played with passion and skill to win thirty-six of their last fifty games. Bill Lange delivered a solid performance at the plate and ran down line drives in the outfield. Many others on the Colonels contributed too: guys like Billy Brown, Charley Irwin, Marty McQuaid. Long after age had wrinkled their skin and dimmed their eyesight and rendered their once-supple limbs brittle and weak, long after other people had ceased to care, people who had not played and felt the feelings they did, these men would look back on this pennant race and know that this was the best time of their lives, when the most important thing in the world, the only thing that mattered, was chasing a ball across fields of green.

The next season saw Bill Lange and the California League go in opposite directions. One up, the other down.

After his brief stint with Oakland, Lange received an offer to try out with Chicago of the National League. Chicago offered train fare to come east; Lange would not budge until the club guaranteed round-trip passage. If he did not make the team Lange wanted a way back to California. But he made it, all right, stepping up another rung in his ever-rising career.

The California League season began in its usual fashion with one city dropping out (San Jose) and another taking its place (Stockton). G. A. Vanderbeck departed as the Los Angeles owner. Some factionalists from northern California wanted to get rid of the Los Angeles club altogether, but a late compromise saved it from extinction.

The league moved the pitching distance back to sixty feet, six inches—the modern standard—in a bid to increase scoring and fan interest. But bad economic times plagued baseball. Attendance continued to fall, and the Oakland Colonels appeared in danger of collapse after only a month of play.

Colonel Tom's club was in more than its usual state of turmoil. When he could not meet his payroll expenses, his players refused to take the field against Stockton. His detractors accused him of skimming from game proceeds to line his pockets. It was later revealed that the Colonel regularly doled out more than one hundred free game passes to his close personal friends. To make matters worse the *Oakland Tribune* published an investigation questioning his military record. It said it found nothing to indicate any service at all, let alone service that would have merited the rank of colonel. An offended Colonel Tom replied that he had done his duty with the California National Guard. In the end, nothing could save him, and he was forced out as owner of the Oakland team.

Another casualty of the downward-spiraling league was longtime league president John Mone, who was fired in June. Mone had fought against the evils of gambling and booze in baseball, but none of that mattered now.

The lone bright spot occurred the next month when Athletic Park in Los Angeles hosted what may have been the first night game in California. Arc lights strung between poles lit the diamond, and a man in the grandstand beamed a searchlight on the individual players. The less-than-impressed *Los Angeles Times* derided the stunt as "burlesque baseball."

By August it was lights out for everybody. Sacramento and Los Angeles squabbled over financial arrangements, and when they could not agree, both teams pulled the plug on their operations. Oakland and San Francisco were still hanging on, but two teams make only a game, not a league. Organized professional baseball in California was dead, and it would be years before anyone could figure out how to revive it.

Fortunately, the demise of the California League did not mean the demise of baseball in California. All around the state children were playing the game. One of them, Frank Leroy Chance, lived in the Central Valley community of Fresno. He would grow up to become one of the most famous baseball personalities of the early 1900s and the first California-born resident of the Hall of Fame.

Chance's parents were William and Mary Chance. Missourians by birth, both came to California with their families when they were children. William was eleven when his father died, forcing him to go to work to help support his mother and family. When he got older he rented some land near Stockton and planted crops. Farming was hard work for little reward, but when William moved to Stanislaus County he had saved enough money to buy land of his own. Stanislaus was where he met Mary, whose family had come west in a covered wagon pulled by oxen, settling first in Oregon before heading south to the farming-rich Central Valley. Mary and William married and later settled in Fresno County in 1877, the same year Frank was born.

The Fresno *Daily Evening Expositor* sponsored Chance's first organized baseball team. It played against other youth teams from Visalia, Merced, Madera, and Tulare. Frank's position was first base. Though only twelve, he held his own against boys who were sixteen and older.

By this time his father had moved out of farming and ranching and into business, becoming vice president of the First National Bank of Fresno and one of its largest stockholders. But his health deteriorated and he died at the age of forty-six, leaving Mary and six children. Frank turned sixteen the year after.

Chance attended Fresno High, although, according to his biographer Gilbert Bogen, it is not clear if he graduated. The conventional stories about Chance say he attended Washington University at Irvington (now Fremont), where he was studying to be a dentist. While Chance may have attended Washington, his main purpose in being there was probably to play ball. Colleges during this era often allowed high school–age students to go to classes and play on their athletic teams.

Whatever his formal schooling, Chance's baseball education continued. In 1897, the robust twenty-year-old became the slugging star of the Fresno Republican Tigers, his position in the field switching from first base to catcher.

Fresno Daily Evening Expositor *youth baseball team, 1889.*
Boy reclining at left is Frank Chance. Fresno Historical Society

Six feet tall, one hundred ninety pounds, he was as hard-nosed as they come. William Chance knew the value of hard work, and so did his son. Only Frank's tools were not a rake and a plow but a bat and ball.

Toward the end of that year the *San Francisco Examiner* held a statewide amateur baseball tournament. Teams from as far south as Bakersfield and Los Angeles journeyed to San Francisco to compete against the best from northern California. The winner received a trophy and a thousand dollars in shiny gold coins.

The Republican Tigers entered the tourney and although they did not capture the gold, their star catcher won an even better prize: a ticket to the big time. Chance knocked the ball all over the lot and made eyeballs pop. This was the scene of his big breakthrough as a ballplayer, the moment of his discovery, although there is some controversy over who spotted him first. The president of the Chicago club, James Hart, who ultimately signed Chance to his first major league contract, claimed that his team had been following the youngster for some time. Long retired from active play but still keeping his hand in the game, Cal McVey has also been mentioned as the possible talent scout. Other accounts give the credit to a star major leaguer, an outfielder with Chicago who made his off-season home in San Francisco. In the stands during the tournament, he recognized what a find Chance was and tipped off his club. The name of this player was Bill Lange.

★   ★   ★   ★   ★

From Colonel Tom Robinson to Bill Lange to Frank Chance—it's a thumbnail history of baseball in nineteenth-century California. Colonel Tom was a quirky, colorful local figure, much like the game itself. But in the person of Frank Chance, the formerly provincial game emerged into national prominence.

Chance reported to spring training camp for Chicago, not having spent one day in the minors. The star of the Fresno Republican Tigers started his career in the major leagues as a backup catcher, filling in whenever he could. It would be several seasons before he switched to first base and broke into the Cubs' starting lineup. Joining him in the infield were shortstop Joe Tinker and second baseman Johnny Evers. Thanks to a piece of doggerel written by sportswriter Franklin Adams ("These are the saddest of possible words, / Tinker to Evers to Chance, / Trio of Bear Cubs fleeter than birds, / Tinker to Evers to Chance . . ."), they formed the most storied double-play combination in baseball history. Two years after becoming a regular for the Cubs, Chance became their player-manager, and big achievements, for the team and himself, followed. Under his leadership Chicago won four pennants and two world championships.

Gilbert Bogen believes that Chance's success as a manager was due in part to those years he spent on the bench, watching, learning, studying everything that went on in a baseball game. One of the players he watched in his first two years was his teammate Bill Lange, the man who may have recommended him to Chicago in the first place.

In the 1890s Lange was one of baseball's elite players. After departing the California League for Chicago, his career swiftly turned sensational. In his second season he hit .328; the next year his average was a gaudy .389. Then came seasons of .326, .340, .319, .325. Not only did he hit for average, he ran the bases too. In 1897 he stole a National League–leading seventy-three bases. His speed made him a top-notch center fielder; Albert Spalding and others who saw him play ranked him as one of the all-time best outfielders. While playing on teams that never finished higher than fourth place, Lange competed as if everything was at stake every moment, though it almost never was.

Then it all came to an end. At the end of the 1899 season Lange shocked baseball with the news that he was retiring from the game after only seven seasons, with a career average of .330 and one stolen base shy of four hundred. He was twenty-eight years old, in the prime of his career. No one had ever heard of a star of his caliber quitting the game so abruptly at such an early age.

To entice him to change his mind Chicago offered him a reported $3,500 salary, which would have made him the highest-paid player in baseball. But Lange turned it down flat; his decision was final.

One hundred years after the fact, it is difficult to say exactly why Lange walked away from a game in which he excelled. The story that has been handed down is that he did it for love—that he quit in order to marry. While this version certainly holds romantic appeal, it may only be partly true. This much we know: Bill Lange was in love when he quit baseball after the end of the 1899 season, his last in the major leagues. The woman he loved was a San Franciscan. So was her father, an established businessman with holdings in real estate. Playing baseball was nothing like being a landowner; it was a risky, low-paying job of dubious value to society. Ballplayers in those days were regarded as a rough and disorderly lot, representing a lower class of people. The woman's father may not have been comfortable with a ballplayer courting his daughter and opposed their marriage.

This put Bill Lange in a bind. Should he continue playing baseball, or marry the woman he loved and join her father in new, potentially lucrative ventures in real estate? Lange chose the latter, and the career of one of the era's greatest stars came to an early end.

After retiring from active play Lange did indeed go on to successful real estate ventures in San Francisco and Millbrae, where he owned a summer home. He also ran his own insurance business for a time. Throughout his life he remained in touch with baseball, briefly coaching at Stanford University, attending Pacific Coast League games in San Francisco, and keeping a personal scrapbook from his days as a player. (Lange's nephew, George Kelly, was a Hall of Fame first baseman and a native San Franciscan.) His generosity was also well known; he gave money and assistance to ex-players and sportswriters who had fallen on hard times.

But Lange was less lucky in love. It did not work out with the woman he quit baseball for and their marriage ended in divorce. A second marriage also failed. He was married a third time, this time happily, and had a son. When Lange died, a Millbrae elementary school named its playing field after him.

A Brand
New
Ballgame

SATURDAY, MARCH 22 — 2:15 P.M.
SUNDAY, MARCH 23 — 2:15 P.M.
— 1947 —
ABLISHED PRICE - - $3.33   Total $4.00
ERAL TAX - - - - .67
THIS PORTION OF TICKET NOT GOOD FOR ADMITTANCE
DETACH SEPERATE COUPONS FOR INDIVIDUAL GAMES

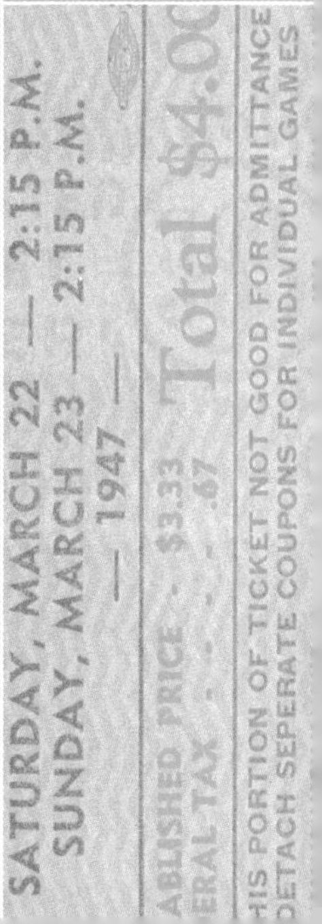

San Francisco–born pitcher Charlie Sweeney was one of the bad boys of early California baseball, as rowdy and rebellious as he was talented. One year, while in the midst of a game, he walked off the field for no reason and never came back, causing him to be kicked off his team and out of the California League. Such errant behavior might have put a crimp in a lesser man's career. But baseball owners and managers tend to ignore a player's shenanigans if he can produce for them on the field. Such was the case with the hard-throwing right-hander, who reappeared that same season on the other side of the country in the American Association, then a major league. In 1884, while pitching for Providence, Sweeney struck out nineteen Boston batters in a game, the first nineteen-strikeout game in major league history.

But trouble followed him like a shadow. After quarreling with his manager and getting kicked off Providence, he bounced around the majors for a few years before returning to his California League stomping grounds. In the winter of 1887 a visiting member of the New York Giants hit a home run in an exhibition game at the Haight Street Grounds, only to suddenly leave town on a train. One of the stories making the rounds was that the Giant had licked Sweeney in a fight and that Sweeney, in retaliation, had gone to fetch his pistol, causing the Giant to flee. There may have been some truth to this story because seven years later Sweeney shot and killed a man in a barroom brawl. Convicted of manslaughter, he served four years in San Quentin Prison on the graceful northern shores of San Francisco Bay.

His health failing, Sweeney received a pardon from the governor and a release from prison in the late 1890s. Though finished as a pitcher, he returned

Charlie Sweeney, 1880s.
The Haggin Museum, Stockton, CA.

Gilt Edge team of Sacramento, 1897.
California Historical Society

to the California League in the unlikely role of umpire. But his old ways soon caught up with him again.

In August, after officiating a Santa Cruz–Fresno game, Sweeney received word that Fresno's catcher did not agree with some of his calls. Such criticism did not sit well with him, and he physically attacked the catcher for his impertinence. After being arrested and then bailed out of jail, Sweeney immediately fled to another city where a local sheriff tracked him down. While waiting to return to Fresno, he and the sheriff decided to sample some alcoholic beverages. The sheriff may have been a fan who enjoyed hearing about Charlie's exploits in baseball, because after one drink they had another. And another. Getting drunk gave Sweeney the chance to sneak away to freedom. California League historian John E. Spalding says Sweeney may have never answered for those Fresno assault charges.

His poor health eventually did catch up to him, though, and he died four years later, at the age of thirty-eight, from tuberculosis.

The same year of Sweeney's comeback as an umpire, 1898 was a milestone season for the California League. After five years of being out of business it resumed operations, merging with another league to field teams in Sacramento, Oakland, San Francisco, and San Jose, as well as in cities never before represented in organized baseball: Fresno, Watsonville, and Santa Cruz.

The champion of the inaugural season of the reformed league was Sacramento's Gilt Edge, which had polished its game as a semipro club for years. Its owner, local gambling and horse racing raconteur Edward Kripp, also ran the Buffalo Brewing Company, which produced Gilt Edge Lager. His ball club doubled as an advertisement for his premium beer.

After winning its first title, Gilt Edge faced a stiff challenge the following season from the Beachcombers of Santa Cruz. Bringing professional baseball to Santa Cruz was the idea of civic-minded entrepreneur Fred Stanton. Like Kripp, his reasons for owning a club were partly commercial: he wanted to promote the virtues of the small resort community on the sunny beaches of Monterey Bay. The Beachcombers played their home games at Dolphin Park across from what is now the Santa Cruz Beach Boardwalk, established years later by Stanton himself. His club roared into first place early in the season, but after he sold his best player, twenty-one-year-old hitting and pitching sensation Mike Donlin, to the major leagues, a wave of losses broke over the team, allowing Sacramento back into the race. The Gilt Edge added power-hitting short-stop Truck Eagan to a potent lineup that included its own dual pitching and hitting threats, Demon Doyle and Silent Harvey, and cruised to its second straight title.

The next season the Edge's edge over the rest of the league grew more pronounced with the signing of a genuine major league ace, Jay Hughes. A Sacramento native who made his off-season home there, Hughes had won a National League–leading twenty-eight games for Brooklyn in 1899, on top of a twenty-three-win season the year before. But his wife did not like living on the East Coast and wanted to stay in California. Hughes agreed to her wishes after a group of Sacramento businessmen matched the money he would have been paid back East. With the right-hander racking up twenty-plus wins, the Gilt Edge rolled to its third consecutive (and final) California League crown.

One of many major league players who crisscrossed between California and the Eastern leagues during this era, Hughes went back to Brooklyn in 1901. Some Californians preferred life—and baseball—in the West and chose not to go back to the majors after spending time there. Others, like Hughes, used the threat of staying home as a bargaining chip to win a higher salary from their clubs in the East. (Then, and in the decades to come, some talented players chose not to leave California in the first place. They received higher pay for playing ball than they would have back East. This, plus the appeal of living in the state, made some Californians remain close to home throughout their careers.)

All players gained slightly more leverage in their dealings with management with the formation of the American League in 1901. Originally a competitor of the National League, the American challenged the older, more established circuit for fans, money, and players. It also created opportunities for umpires. One of the first umpires hired by the new league, Jack Sheridan, hailed from San Jose.

The first year of the new century saw the return of Los Angeles to organized baseball after an absence of eight years. Once the unwanted stepchild of the California League, its status had grown with the continued growth of the city. Long the major railroad hub of its region, Los Angeles had become the state's second largest city and a beehive of commercial and industrial activity. Oil flowed from the City Field. Work had begun a few years earlier on San Pedro Harbor, the major seaport the area had lacked. A web of electric railway lines carried passengers around the city and to outlying areas, and plans were being hatched to expand the system still more. Fielding a club in Los Angeles was no longer an option for league officials, a thing to be considered; it *had* to have one there.

Owned by James Morley, the Angels or "Looloos," as they were affectionately called, played their home games at Chutes Park on Washington Street. Named after an amusement park across the street that featured children's rides, Chutes originally held only five thousand spectators. But after fans went loopy for the Looloos, the park got bigger in a hurry, nearly doubling in size after a mid-season expansion. In its first year back in the league Los Angeles sold almost as many tickets as San Francisco, the perennial attendance leader. In the embryonic stages of what would become the state's grandest baseball rivalry, SF nosed out LA for the 1901 title.

When Los Angeles entered the California League this second time, it joined three other cities: San Francisco, Oakland, and Sacramento. Other communities had dropped out in previous years, winnowing the number of clubs to this core group of four. In 1860 San Francisco and Sacramento had hosted the first organized baseball games ever held in California. Oakland had been playing for nearly as long, and Los Angeles represented the rising power to the south. After Oakland claimed the 1902 California League pennant, baseball men from these four cities decided to break from the past. Looking north, beyond California's borders, they reached out to Portland and Seattle, each with a long baseball tradition of its own. Together they formed a new minor league that spanned three states and the West Coast of the United States. The name of their enterprise was the Pacific Coast League.

This new creation would become California's dominant minor league for the next fifty-five years, the beating heart of organized baseball in the state. But the California men who created the Coast League had no idea if what they were proposing would actually work. It was a gamble. But heck, they were all veterans of the old California League, so they knew all about gambling. And

Los Angeles ball team of the California League, Chutes Park, 1902. Hall of Famer Rube Waddell, a member of the club, sits in the center-left of the balloon with striped stockings. Doug McWilliams Collection

you don't become a baseball owner in the first place if you don't have some of a gambler's instincts. Along with Jim Morley, they were Henry Harris, Mike Fisher, and Cal Ewing.

Henry Harris was a survivor. Not a character, not colorful, but when you needed a job done in baseball, he was your man. For more than twenty-five years he had seen all there was to see in San Francisco baseball. In 1886 he had owned and managed the Haverly's theater team to a California League pennant. The next year "Casey at the Bat" creator Ernest Thayer, then a reporter with the *Daily Examiner,* was hanging around the Haight Street Grounds, watching the sprint for the championship flag between Harris's club and the winning Pioneers.

Harris sold the team a couple of seasons after that, leaving for Portland, but he did not stay away for long, returning to the league as one of its reigning Wise Men who admitted Los Angeles into organized baseball for the first time.

Harris knew everybody in the small society of California League baseball, and everybody knew him. One year on Opening Day he shared a ride to the ballpark with Colonel Tom Robinson. San Francisco was meeting Oakland in the season opener, and according to the custom of the time, the two managers and their players promoted the game by riding in horse-drawn carriages across the city. It was hoped that people on the street would see the ballplayers ride by in their uniforms and follow them to the park.

Like other baseball men, Harris had endured the long blackout that occurred after the California League went dark. But when the league bounced back he was right there with it, helping to usher in a period of record profits and overflow crowds.

Still, despite this success Harris felt strongly that the time had come for a change. For many years he had argued for expansion into the Northwest, saying that it would widen the fan base, promote regional as well as local rivalries, and increase revenue. He and others engaged in secret discussions over the summer, reaching a final agreement in December of 1902. The season, they announced, would begin the following March. And when it did Henry Harris would be part of it, riding through town on Opening Day.

Mike Fisher of Sacramento was another man with deep roots in the game. His baseball past stretched back to the early days of the California League and possibly beyond. It has been speculated, though never clearly established, that his father was John M. Fisher, one of the early pioneers of California baseball who founded San Francisco's first club, the Eagles, and played in the first organized game ever held in the state.

While living in San Francisco, Fisher, who did not have a middle name and so adopted "Angelo" to fill the void, starred in the outfield for the Altas of Sacramento. Since league rules at the time required that players live in the home city of their team, Fisher moved to Sacramento, where he took a job in a machine shop for the Southern Pacific Railroad. He joked that when the Altas won, his fellow workers gave him all the cushy jobs and treated him like a king.

But when they lost nobody would look at him or talk to him. "I'd get the toughest, meanest job the master mechanic could dig up for me," he recalled.

After leaving the machine shop Fisher became a detective with the Sacramento police department, winning high marks for his skill as a sharp-shooter. After the Gilt Edge's championship reign ended, he returned to the Sacramento professional baseball scene as an owner and manager. His popularity, enlivened by his storytelling abilities, helped sell the new league to Sacramento fans. In 1908 Fisher led a contingent of players to Japan, one of the earliest American baseball tours of that country. He would lead several more Japanese tours before retiring from the game.

The story of the other California founder, Cal Ewing, will be told in the next chapter. But it should be noted that his stature was such that his colleagues asked him to be the league's first president, a position he turned down in order to concentrate on running his Oakland club and other business affairs. The job instead went to another California League veteran, James T. Moran, who co-owned the Greenhood and Moran clothing shop that had sponsored a team years earlier.

Capitol City Wheelmen baseball team, Sacramento, 1906. California Historical Society, FN-40038

Pacific Coast League Opening Day, Tenth and K Streets, Sacramento, 1903. Doug McWilliams Collection

Opening Day for the spanking new Pacific Coast League was March 26, 1903. It was a big baseball event all over the state. Los Angeles hosted and whipped Seattle. At Recreation Park in San Francisco, the home club beat Portland before a large crowd that included Moran. The biggest celebration of all was in Sacramento, where many businesses shut down early in the afternoon in excitement over the game. The busiest establishment in town was the State House Hotel at the corner of K and Tenth Streets, one block from the state capitol. The State House advertised itself as "the best family hotel in the city," charging twenty-five cents for a meal and from six to ten dollars a week for lodging. Players from Sacramento and visiting Oakland met at the State House for the traditional pre-game ride across town. Women in the second-story rooms leaned out of the windows to see the men, all decked out in their uniforms and ball caps, as they left for the park. These players had taken part in Opening Day "tallyhos" for years, but this truly was a new era; this day they drove through the streets of the city in open-air automobiles.

One car broke down on the way to the park, temporarily delaying the players. But an old-fashioned horse and wagon arrived to save the day, and everybody made it to the opening ceremonies on time. A brass band played patriotic music, and Governor George Pardee threw out the first pitch. Sacramento beat Oakland, 7 to 4, and the first pennant race in league history was on.

The arrival of the Pacific Coast League finished off the old California League. With the departure of all its franchises, the league collapsed like a table without legs. Still, smaller towns around northern California—Stockton, San Jose, Vallejo, Petaluma—wanted to participate in organized baseball, as did semipro clubs from Oakland and San Francisco. This group of six formed a spin-off called the California State League and cobbled together a patchwork schedule, aware that its product on the field was nothing like it had been only the year before. How could it? All their players had walked off and taken the fans with them.

Adding to the confusion was the creation of yet another league, the Pacific National League. Seattle and Portland had been considered the territory of the Pacific Northwest League and thus off-limits to other leagues under rules established by the National Association of Professional Baseball Leagues. The National Association governed minor league baseball, determining league territories and setting tough prohibitions against players breaking their contracts and jumping between teams. Although the Coast League joined the association in its second season, in its first it refused, incurring the wrath of the national body, which censured it with a tag familiar to the old California League—"outlaw." What's more, the Northwest-based Pacific National League set up rival new baseball franchises in southern and northern California. Suddenly three organized leagues were competing in a state that could barely support one.

Away from these tussles, stirrings of another kind were taking place. In 1903, a young Japanese immigrant named Chiura Obata arrived in San Francisco. Born in Sendai, Japan, Obata loved the arts, training as a young boy in sumi (ink) brush painting. Rebelling against his father, who threatened to send him to military school, he ran away to Tokyo where he served an apprenticeship to a painter. Then, at the age of eighteen, he decided to pursue his schooling overseas and come to America.

In San Francisco he studied English and worked as household help, living in Japantown. He dropped out of the Mark Hopkins Institute of Art, preferring

Fuji Athletic Club, circa 1903. Its founder, Chiura Obata, sits at far right. Courtesy of George Aratani. From Through a Diamond: 100 Years of Japanese American Baseball, *by Kerry Yo Nakagawa. NBRP (Nisei Baseball Research Project)*

to paint on his own, and gradually found work as an illustrator for Japanese-language publications and as a commercial artist.

Besides art, Obata's other passion in life was baseball, which had been growing in popularity in Japan since an American schoolteacher, Horace Wilson, introduced the game to the country in 1872. Baseball was seen as having both physical and spiritual benefits to the Japanese students who played it. By the turn of the century, crowds of sixty thousand or more were showing up for big games between Japan's leading university teams. Obata himself had become a player and fan, and the year he came to California he formed the Fuji Athletic Club, the first Issei baseball club on the mainland United States. (Issei means "first generation"—the first generation of Japanese to immigrate to America.) Obata's artistic flair merged with his love for the game, and he designed a stylized "FAC" logo on his club's jersey.

The year after the Fuji Club formed, another Issei team, KDC, began play in San Francisco's parks and sandlots. The "K" stood for Kanagawa, the area in Japan where the team's players came from; the "D" was for "doshi," a Japanese word for "a bunch of guys" or "together"; the "C" was for club. This club of a bunch of Kanagawa guys was put together by Frank Tsuyuki, who was in his early twenties when he came to the States. Like Chiura Obata, Frank was an Issei with a thing for baseball.

The KDC and the FAC played whenever and wherever they could rustle up games. They played against each other and other Issei teams in the city. They played against school teams, youth teams, and merchant teams composed mainly of whites.

The Issei competed hard against the white players, some of whom did not relish the idea of losing to Japanese immigrants. If they were beating a white team, KDC's players quietly began to pack their gear in the late innings so if they won, they could make a quick escape after the game was over and not risk a fight with the whites.

Despite their racial differences, the whites and Issei bore many similarities. Some of the whites were neighborhood guys, just like them. There were the Irish from the Mission, the Italians from North Beach. Some of them were German, others had Spanish last names. Nearly everyone who played was in his teens or twenties. Like the Japanese, many of the whites were also born in other countries. And if they were not born across the pond, their parents and grandparents and maybe some of their brothers and sisters were. Many of these immigrant families spoke in their homes a language other than English.

But while the doors of organized baseball remained open to the white players, they were closed to Obata, Tsuyuki, and other Japanese immigrants. For the unwritten rule that kept blacks and dark-skinned Hispanics out of the Pacific Coast League also applied to them. They too were forced to walk a different path, and their journey was only beginning.

A Ballpark
Blooms in
San Francisco

SATURDAY, MARCH 22 — 2:15 P.M.
SUNDAY, MARCH 23 — 2:15 P.M.
— 1947 —

ABLISHED PRICE - - $3.33
ERAL TAX - - - .67

Total $4.00

HIS PORTION OF TICKET NOT GOOD FOR ADMITTANCE
DETACH SEPERATE COUPONS FOR INDIVIDUAL GAMES

Rinaldo Angelo Paolinelli was a city boy, a street-tough San Francisco Italian. "A son of Caesar," some people called them, although if you made a crack about Rinaldo's heritage he'd fight you. As hard as three-day-old sourdough, he knew how to use his fists. None of the other boys messed with Rinaldo when he got mad, which was often. He had, in his words, "firecrackers" in his blood.

His father, Raphael, was a grocer. His mother, Ermida, ran the house and took care of Rinaldo, his sister, and two brothers. Like the other families in the neighborhood, they did not have much but they got by. They made do.

Near where they lived was Hamilton Park Playground at Post and Steiner Streets. All the neighbor kids played ball there. In spring and summer, practically

Babe Pinelli, later in life. California Historical Society, FN-40019

from first light until it was too dark to see the ball anymore, the sounds of boys and girls playing were as constant as the chirping of birds. Most days you could find Rinaldo there, chirping away with the rest of them.

Little Rinaldo was always dogging his brother Lando and the older boys to let him play ball with them. When Lando told him no, Rinaldo threw a stink— oh man what a stink, you could hear it a block away. He bawled and bawled like a big baby. And that was the nickname the kids in the neighborhood gave him: Babe.

Babe, who later shortened his last name to Pinelli, grew up to become one of the earliest Italian Americans to play in the major leagues. After retiring as a player Babe Pinelli switched to umpiring, and at the end of his long career he called the balls and strikes for the only perfect game in World Series history.

But his father saw none of this, did not live to see the man his son would become. On the morning of April 18, 1906, Raphael Paolinelli was walking to his grocery store on Fillmore Street. It was early in the day, still dark outside, when the ground beneath his feet moved abruptly and without warning. Everything in the world that was seemingly permanent and solid revealed its true nature. A telephone pole fell over and hit Raphael, killing him.

The earthquake that killed Raphael Paolinelli struck at 5:13 a.m. When the shaking started, the clock on the Ferry Building at the foot of Market Street stopped—and one wall of the building fell into the bay. Buildings all over the city crumbled and collapsed, and hundreds of people lost their lives. People died while asleep in their beds in the supposed safety of their homes. Those who were outside on the street died from falling debris. The sides of buildings, and sometimes entire buildings, crashed down on them.

After the earthquake came the fires. The intensity of the jolt—an estimated 8.3 on the Richter scale, one of the largest earthquakes in history— flattened chimneys and knocked over wood- and coal-burning stoves that heated homes, many of which contained gas lamps. Fires erupted, leaping between damaged timber-built homes and spreading across whole blocks. The biggest fire, the famous Ham and Eggs fire, started when a woman tried to light her stove to cook breakfast for her family. The flue of the stove was cracked, and burning cinders jumped across to the wall and set it aflame. The fire grew and merged with others, all blown by the indifferent winds. These blazes roaring out of control could not be stopped because the quake had ruptured the water mains and drained the hydrants, rendering the city's firefighting capabilities impotent.

"Curtains of flame," in the telling words of historian Dan Kurzman, swept across the city. Everything in their path—hospitals, churches, libraries, brothels, boardinghouses, Nob Hill mansions, the Grand Opera House, the Palace Hotel, banks, businesses of every kind—was fuel for the fire. The flames devoured both sides of Market Street and moved relentlessly into Chinatown and North Beach, producing smoke so thick it blotted out the daylight. The sun, a sickening red in color, glowed eerily behind the canopy of gray.

Hundreds of people died in the fire, possibly thousands. The exact death count is not known, in part because of the fire's murderous efficiency. It burned city offices to the ground and destroyed the documents inside—birth records, tax and property rolls.

Those who survived fled the devastated burn areas for the open spaces of Golden Gate Park. Thousands upon thousands were injured or burned, often seriously. Nearly everyone who came to the park saw their homes and their neighbors' homes reduced to rubble and ash. They lost everything they owned.

If people could get out of the city, they did. Fishing boats came from all around San Francisco Bay to lend aid. The boats not being used to fight the fires carried the refugees away to safety.

Amidst such devastation, few thought about baseball, but it was decimated by the earthquake as surely as was everything else in the city. San Francisco

Ferry Building, San Francisco, after the earthquake. San Franicsco History Center, San Francisco Public Library

served as the headquarters for the Pacific Coast League, and the fires destroyed league offices and every piece of paper in them.

Recreation Park, the host of the Pacific Coast League's inaugural game in the city, was gone. So were Central Park downtown and the storied Haight Street Grounds next to Golden Gate Park. All of them disappeared so fast it was as if they had never existed at all.

Smaller pieces of baseball history were lost too. After winning the state's premiere baseball tournament in 1860, the Eagles brought back to San Francisco the championship trophy, which contained a silver ball from the Comstock Lode in Nevada. The trophy was never found, probably succumbing to the firestorm, whose temperatures reached up to 2,200 degrees Fahrenheit.

The Great Fire finally sizzled out Saturday morning, three days after its terrible birth. Almost immediately the hard work of rebuilding began. Temporary barracks sprung up to house the countless refugees whose homes and lives lay in ruins. Food, water, and medical supplies poured in. The sick and injured received treatment, and the grim task of clearing bodies from the rubble-strewn streets and burned-out buildings got under way.

Whole communities within the larger community of San Francisco were shattered. The losses were so great and yet how could people recover without jobs? Virtually every business in the city had been put out of commission, and it was going to take a long time for them to come back, if they ever did.

One of the businesses in jeopardy was the baseball business. The quake caused the suspension of all Pacific Coast League games, less than two weeks after Opening Day. Some questioned whether the league itself could survive. Los Angeles owner Jim Morley said he planned to disband the Angels because he did not expect the league to last another week. Northwest baseball people were talking about making room on their rosters for the former Coast League players who were expected to be looking for jobs once the league folded.

But Cal Ewing, one of the founders of the league, was not quite ready to give up. He and too many others had worked too hard to simply let their creation die.

Growing up on the streets of Oakland, Ewing was as crazy about the game as a boy can be. His boyhood team, the Merry Macks, drew its name from his Mack Street neighborhood. In his twenties Cal played some semipro baseball, but he found that his real talents lay in management. He knew how to lead people and operate athletic teams. His financial acumen—he worked as an auditor—rounded out his resumé. And in 1898, the revival year of the California League, he became the owner-manager of the Oakland club, quickly rising to a leadership position in the league hierarchy.

Cal loved to compete, off the field and on. He once lodged an official protest over an Oakland loss because the opposing pitcher wore dark pants; this, said Cal, gave him an unfair advantage over the hitters.

After helping to get the Pacific Coast League up and running, he turned down an offer to be its first president, but his influence continued to grow as the new league struggled to survive amidst competition and hard economic times.

In its first year of operation the Coast League beat back a challenge from the Pacific National League, which had organized rival clubs in California and elsewhere. Although the insurgent league died before season's end, a continuing competitive challenge came from the California State League, which fielded teams in San Francisco and Oakland as well as smaller cities around northern California. (The California State League also suspended play in the immediate aftermath of the quake.)

When the Coast League formed, its owners believed that expanding into the Northwest would strengthen their business, but the results did not meet their expectations. In only his second year in the league, Mike Fisher shifted his club from Sacramento to Tacoma, Washington. After two years there he brought it back to California, only this time to Fresno. His operation struggled to make money wherever it went.

Attendance at times dropped to ridiculous lows. One story has it that only one fan showed up for a game in Oakland against visiting Portland. The umpire, it is said, announced the starting lineups before the game by turning to the grandstand and saying, "Dear Sir…" The Oakland club had to go on the road in the Central Valley to find people willing to pay to see its games.

Pacific Coast League scorecard, 1906. California Historical Society, MS 4031/129

The three-year-old Coast League had survived these and other troubles but the earthquake was its worst crisis by far. The San Francisco club had no ballpark, uniforms, or gear. With the league's strongest club in limbo, the other team owners appeared ready to act on Jim Morley's threat and disband. All were on shaky financial footing and could not afford any more losses.

Cal Ewing, however, had money, and he used it to save the league. Ewing, who had purchased the San Francisco club about a week before the earthquake, turning his former team of Oakland over to a trustee, became the financial angel for both these clubs as well as just about every other in the league. He loaned money to Mike Fisher in Fresno to help him make ends meet. Los Angeles and Seattle received green aid from Cal, and it kept them in the league as well.

This infusion of capital made the difference. Pacific Coast League historian Dick Dobbins writes, "The San Francisco Earthquake could have been the final blow to a struggling Pacific Coast League. Without Cal Ewing's efforts, the league would not have survived."

Play resumed Wednesday, May 23, 1906. Clad in new uniforms, San Francisco returned to action against the Fresno Raisin-Pickers in Oakland's Idora Park. Since it was a team without a ballpark, San Francisco played this game and the rest of its home games that season in Oakland, which suffered damage from the quake but nothing resembling the apocalypse that struck across the bay. San Francisco edged the Raisin-Pickers, 4 to 3.

Gradually the familiar rhythms of everyday life returned. People eased back into the things that gave them comfort and joy. One of those things—one of the things that signifies continuity in American life—was baseball.

Los Angeles and the other Coast League teams returned to the field of play along with San Francisco and Fresno. Both the National and American Leagues sent gear and money on top of Ewing's largesse. The league shifted its offices to Oakland, pared its schedule, and limped through the summer and fall. San Francisco, which had been in first place before the earthquake, finished far behind champion Portland. At the end of the season the Fresno and Seattle franchises were beyond saving, and the two clubs called it quits.

Reconstruction in San Francisco continued at a rapid pace throughout the year, evoking memories of the Gold Rush pioneers who had quickly rebuilt after fires ravaged the waterfront. New homes rose where old ones had burned. Office buildings appeared with new businesses inside them, once-dead neighborhoods thrummed with vitality, parks and playgrounds popped up anew. Carpenters, steelworkers, masons, and laborers found plenty of demand for their services, as did architects and engineers. Stone by stone a new city was born.

Like so many other families in the city, the Paolinellis were recovering from their enormous losses. Raphael was gone and the future seemed dark. Just getting by was going to be harder than it had been before. It was decided that Babe needed to quit grammar school and get a job to help the family. He was ten years old.

After the quake, Chiura Obata, founder of the Fuji Athletic Club, lived for six months in a refugee camp in Lafayette Park. He eventually managed to scrape up a job and a place to live, and he remained in San Francisco.

Others in the Issei community had to leave the city because there was no work for them. KNC founder Frank Tsuyuki headed into the Central Valley, hiring on at a farm in the Lodi area. Setsuo Aratani, Obata's Hiroshima-born teammate, went south, ultimately settling in Guadalupe near San Luis Obispo. He also went into farming, over time acquiring thousands of acres of land and establishing a large vegetable-growing operation that sponsored a semipro baseball team, the Guadalupe Packers.

Tens of thousands of people escaping the horror of the fires found temporary refuge in Oakland. Many ended up staying permanently, and the city's population jumped. Because some of these transplanted San Franciscans were fans of the game, the East Bay baseball scene received a boost too.

In the spring of 1907 the Pacific Coast League was an empty shell of a baseball operation. Losing two clubs had reduced the number of teams to a shaky four: San Francisco, Oakland, Los Angeles, and Portland. The job of Cal

Postcard of Recreation Park, San Francisco, 1911. California Historical Society, FN-40030

Ewing, the league's new president, was to prevent any further team collapses and restore the baseball business to health. It seemed a large task indeed. His dreams and the dreams of the other founders to create a dominant West Coast league seemed to belong to a simpler time.

Still, there were signs of hope. The city's reconstruction included a new home for baseball, Recreation Park. It had the same name as the old park but with a different address on Valencia Street in the Mission. Ewing put up $90,000 to finance the park, which featured a covered grandstand behind home plate. While the dimensions were a little wacky—the right field fence was 235 feet from home plate—the designers remedied the problem by installing a fifty-foot-high chicken wire screen on top of the fence. Batters had to put plenty of lift on the ball to hit a home run.

In late March the famous John McGraw and his New York Giants rode the train out to San Francisco to play in an exhibition series to inaugurate the new park, but a storm hit the Bay Area at the same time, causing the games to be cancelled. After a few days of hard rain McGraw and the Giants headed south to Los Angeles without ever playing in the park.

The rain delayed everything, including putting on the final construction touches. Workmen were still applying paint to the bleachers and fixing up the infield days before the opening.

The big day finally arrived April 6, 1907, less than a year after the earthquake and fires had destroyed the city. Ten thousand people showed up to see the unveiling of the new Recreation Park. San Francisco's John Hickey pitched a complete game victory over Portland, and local fans went away happy. A missing piece of their lives had been restored. They were playing baseball again in San Francisco.

The Los Angeles Mix, Winter 1908

SATURDAY, MARCH 22 — 2:15 P.M.
SUNDAY, MARCH 23 — 2:15 P.M.
— 1947 —

ABLISHED PRICE - $3.33
FERAL TAX - - - .67
Total $4.00

HIS PORTION OF TICKET NOT GOOD FOR ADMITTANCE
DETACH SEPERATE COUPONS FOR INDIVIDUAL GAMES

In January of 1908 John McGraw left New York City to take a vacation in Los Angeles. Not only did the New York Giants manager love the year-round warmth of southern California, but he loved to gamble at the racetrack. Playing the ponies under the warm California sun was one of his favorite ways to relax after the grind of a long baseball season.

The 1907 season had been an especially long and bad one for McGraw, whose club had finished in fourth place well behind the pennant-winning Chicago Cubs. Ah, those Cubs, those infernal Cubs. Having won back-to-back pennants and a World Series the last two seasons, they were the chief nemesis of McGraw's Giants.

But there's a grand thing about the game: you get to start over every year. Wipe the slate clean, begin fresh. The Giants, McGraw felt sure, were on their way back to the winner's circle.

Which brings up another reason why he liked to escape in the off-season to California: it was away from all the pressure. "The Mastermind," as the sportswriters called him, was the most famous baseball personality in New York, which made him the most famous baseball personality in America. Celebrities sought out his company, Giants fans idolized him, and the press generally gave him the royal treatment. But all that fame brought high expectations, and those high expectations became a burden. Getting away to the West Coast gave McGraw a chance to rest and reinvigorate himself for the battles that lay ahead.

Also in California, holed up in Glendora, north of Los Angeles, was McGraw's arch-rival, Frank Chance. Chance, the player-manager of the Cubs, was the most famous man in baseball after McGraw. New York vs. Chicago, Cubs vs. Giants, Chance vs. McGraw. When those two men from those two cities met, all of America took note. Reporters never lacked for good copy at a Cubs-Giants series. Reviled in New York, beloved in Chicago, baseball fans called Chance "the Peerless Leader," a testimonial to his proven managerial skills and success in building champions. Nobody could match his toughness, on the field or off.

But when his season finished in the East, Chance returned home to southern California to a place he called Cub Ranch, where he lived with his wife, Edythe, his childhood sweetheart. When they went to Fresno High together young Frank carried Edythe's books home for her, and they fell in love. Edythe, whose maiden name was Pancake, had eleven siblings, and one brother, Carl Pancake, a former sportswriter, helped run Cub Ranch with its acres and acres of orange groves. At the ranch they sold oranges for one dollar a crate.

Chance built Cub Ranch as a retreat, a place to lick his baseball wounds, of which there were many. He once got into a fight in a café with Gentleman Jim Corbett, the former heavyweight boxing champion. Afterward Corbett called him the best amateur fighter around. At the plate, Chance was the frequent target of beanballs—pitches thrown at a batter's head to intimidate him and move him off the plate. To get on base to help the Cubs, as well as to give a lesson in toughness to his players, Chance stood his ground when pitchers threw beanballs at him. Although baseballs then were softer than they are today, batters did not wear helmets, and some beanballs knocked Chance out cold. He suffered chronic headaches from the repeated beanings and over time his left ear—the ear that faces the pitcher when you bat right-handed as Chance did—lost its hearing.

During the off-season of 1907, the Cubs player-manager was nursing an injury of a different kind, though no less potentially serious. According to one news report, his doctors in Los Angeles said he was suffering from neuritis in his left foot, a painful nerve condition. The rumors flew around baseball, and everyone speculated as to what this might mean. One New York newspaper said the problem was so severe that the toughest man in baseball might be forced to quit playing.

This baseball off-season, in the first decade of the last century, coincided with the dawn of southern California's beach culture. South of Santa Monica, a tiny coastal development sprung up by the name of Venice, California's version of the ancient Mediterranean seaport, complete with gondoliers rowing boats on canals past Italian-looking buildings. Down the coast from Venice at another tourist haven, Redondo Beach, a huge, Moorish-style pavilion attracted swingers from all over. Hundreds of couples danced on its vast second-floor ballroom to the tunes of a live orchestra. Getting to Redondo, Venice, and other spots on the coast was a breeze on the Pacific Electric Railway; you could ride twenty miles on it for only a nickel.

Along with orange trees and horse racing in winter, the beach scene was part of the mix, part of the appeal of southern California. Baseball was yet another ingredient. The Los Angeles Angels and other Coast Leaguers, semi-pros from industrial and company teams, local schoolboys eager to make a good impression, hotshots from around the country who had migrated to the area, guys who weren't going anywhere in the game but loved to play—they were all there, hitting and catching and chucking the ball around, their caps tugged down on their foreheads to keep the sun out of their eyes, working up a sweat under mostly cloudless skies. And in the off-season, big-time major leaguers like Frank Chance and John McGraw were in the mix along with everyone else.

Both Chance's Cubs and McGraw's Giants had strong Los Angeles connections. The Cubs had held spring training there for a couple of years, practicing near the beach in Santa Monica. The New York Giants skipper was well known around town too. One winter he personally saved two women from injury by stopping a team of rampaging horses on a Los Angeles street. That year his club held spring training at Chutes Park, where the Angels played their home games.

Whenever McGraw came to town he spent considerable recreational time at the racetrack. But that was not all he did. He kept himself in baseball shape by playing catch and hitting balls around with local players. This also allowed him to keep an eye out for talented prospects he might like to sign for the Giants.

While at practice one day in February, McGraw asked a group of guys if any of them knew a kid named Freddy Snodgrass. The previous season, when the Giants were in town for spring training, McGraw had umpired a game between his club and St. Vincent's College (now Loyola Marymount University), where Snodgrass played catcher. He did not like the calls being made by the man behind the plate, and the two of them—the hot-tempered young Californian and the pugnacious, sarcastic New Yorker, who was nicknamed "Little Napoleon" for his small size and authoritarian ways—bickered back and forth the entire game. Their encounter made such an impression on McGraw that a year later he wanted to see more of Freddy.

Sure, we know him, said the players.

Tell him to give me a call, said McGraw. I want to talk to him.

Fred Snodgrass baseball card, circa 1912. From
The Day the New York Giants Came to Oxnard,
by Jeffrey Wayne Maulhardt

Fred Snodgrass was born in Ventura, a small farming community up the coast from Los Angeles. When the summons came from the great McGraw, he was, as he put it, "a headstrong, quick-tempered twenty-year-old kid." Growing up in rural California, he paid little attention to what went on in the faraway majors; he could not have named all the clubs in the National and American leagues.

When his friends told him the Giants manager wanted to talk to him, Snodgrass wasn't sure what to do. So he asked his parents, who said it could not hurt to see what the man had to say. Given their blessing, Fred went to see the New Yorker in the lobby of his hotel.

"Are you thinking about playing baseball?" he asked Fred when they met.

"A little bit," replied Fred. "But not too seriously."

Snodgrass was no longer playing for St. Vincent's. His current club was sponsored by Hoegee Flags, which advertised its sporting goods store by placing a flag emblem on the back of each player's jersey. He mentioned that he had received an offer from Peoria in a Midwest minor league.

The man from the big city pulled a major league contract from his pocket and handed it to the startled youngster. The New York Giants were willing to top Peoria and pay Snodgrass $150 a month if he made the club. Suddenly things had gotten very serious.

"Talk it over with your mother and father," McGraw told him. "If you think you ought to try baseball, our train leaves for spring training in four days."

The wooing of Freddy Snodgrass by a club from the East, however brief and abrupt it may have been, was hardly an isolated event. Plenty of young members of the informal fraternity of southern California ballplayers were being bird-dogged by major league talent scouts. Three other notable ones from this era were Walter Johnson, Chief Meyers, and Gavy Cravath.

They called Walter Johnson "the Big Swede," although he was not of Swedish ancestry. His people were from the plains of Kansas. His father and mother, Frank and Minnie Johnson, were farmers whose own parents were farmers. But at the turn of the century, a drought across Kansas and the Midwest caused farmers to question their commitment to the land they had worked for generations. As Johnson wrote as an adult, "There is nothing like a drought that makes a farmer think of moving to another part of the world to try his luck."

The impetus to leave came from Minnie's brother Cliff Perry, who lived and worked in the oil fields of southern California. Returning to Kansas for a visit, he talked to his brother-in-law, Frank Johnson, who agreed to move west, where he quickly found a steady job. Soon after this, Minnie and their five children, including fourteen-year-old Walter, left behind the parched lands of their farm and rode the Santa Fe Railroad to their new home.

Frank Johnson had found a place to live in the town where he worked, Olinda, in the oil fields south of Los Angeles. He was a teamster, driving a horse and wagon that carried supplies for the Santa Fe Oil Company, which was a partnership between the railroad and the Brea Canyon Oil Company founded by E. L. Doheny, the man who made the big oil strike. The Johnsons lived on the main street of Olinda in a house owned by the oil company.

Compared to the hardships they had experienced on the farm in Kansas, the Johnsons found this to be a good life, abundant even, with family nearby and other amenities. They had indoor plumbing, electric lights, gas heat. Nobody wanted for food, and people raised chickens and livestock in their backyards. "The nearby foothills of the coastal range mountains were full of rabbits, squirrel, quail, even deer and bear at the high altitudes," writes Henry W. Thomas, a Johnson biographer. "Warm sunshine came down through clear blue skies onto the velvet green hills, and when the orange groves in Placentia were in blossom a sweet fragrance blanketed the area for miles around." Every Saturday the Olinda town hall held a dance, and when the children went to bed at night they fell asleep to the sounds of oil wells pumping in the darkness outside.

The game of choice for the boys and men who worked in the oil fields was baseball. They played at the end of the day after they got off work or on Sunday, the day of rest. The oil company hired some men as "weeders" to hack away the brush around the wells and keep down the fire hazard, but weeding was not their main occupation; their real job was to play baseball on the company teams. The best of these teams was the Olinda Oil Wells, which took on the Los Angeles Owls and other semipro clubs from around the area.

Since Olinda lacked a ballfield of suitable quality, the Oil Wells traveled a couple of hours south to play their home games in Anaheim at the newly constructed Athletics Park. Anaheim at the time was the only city in Orange County that could legally serve alcoholic beverages on Sundays, so taverners in the area drummed up business by sponsoring games there. The players put on their uniforms in the back rooms of the saloons while the men in front placed bets on the outcomes of the games to be played.

Frank Johnson and his son Walter attended some of these games. Walter played ball himself, although he was an awkward teenager, a little uncoordinated with his unusually large hands and feet. But he could always do one thing better than any other kid and, later, better than almost anybody in the entire history of the game: throw a baseball real, real hard.

On the Olinda Elementary School team, Walter liked playing catcher best of all. But Frank, noting how well his son threw the ball, suggested he try pitching. Walter, who as both a boy and an adult was always known for his polite good manners, obediently went along with his father's wishes, although he was not sure if he enjoyed being a pitcher all that much.

Then came a game between the boys from the orange groves and the boys from the oil fields. The orange grove batters were pounding the oil field pitchers until Walter's teammates prevailed on him to take a turn on the mound. Walter became the pitcher, and the pounding instantly stopped. He struck out twelve batters and found that he enjoyed the sensation of throwing three ferociously hard strikes past an outmatched hitter.

Walter started pitching more, and pretty soon he became the talk of the oil fields. Joe Burke, a Santa Fe Railroad shopkeeper who could spot a live right-handed arm when he saw one, set up a tryout for Johnson with the top slugger for the Olinda Oil Wells, Jack Burnett. Walter's fastball burned Burnett just as it had the orange grove boys, sparking Burke to set up another tryout in an actual game with the Los Angeles Eurekas. The sixteen-year-old took the hill for the Oil Wells, and three innings later, six batters had gone down on strikes.

Even with this early success Walter thought he could do better. While helping his father by driving the family's horse and wagon, he carried around a pile of cans. During his lunch break he set the cans up in a row, stepped off a certain number of paces, and threw rocks at them to improve his accuracy.

In the fall of 1904 Walter entered high school in nearby Fullerton, then a tiny town of seventeen hundred people. Though Fullerton Union High consisted of only sixty students, it still fielded a baseball team. (Besides Johnson, another future Hall of Famer attended Fullerton Union in a later era: Arky Vaughan, an infielder with Pittsburgh and Brooklyn in the thirties and forties.) But Walter threw so hard none of the players could catch his pitches. So Fullerton recruited Grover Collins, a grammar school student who played for the Oil Wells, to be the catcher for the team.

Fullerton was not good—a Johnson curse. His twenty-one-year major league career was spent on mostly poor and mediocre teams for the Washington Senators. Nevertheless, the high school's best pitcher recorded some high moments, throwing fifteen scoreless innings and striking out twenty-seven batters in a game against Santa Ana High. After whiffing on three pitches,

Walter Johnson with Washington, 1916. © Bettmann/CORBIS

one disgusted Santa Ana batter returned to the bench, sizing up Johnson's stuff for his teammates: "He ain't got a thing but a fastball."

On Sundays Walter did his thing for the Olinda Oil Wells, often performing in his street clothes with his shirttail hanging out and his unbuckled pants hitched up above his knees. Though he may have looked disheveled, his quick, compact pitching motion was a model of efficiency. A reporter from the *Whittier News* described him as "a graduate in the science of delivering the ball." One of the teams he faced featured Fred Snodgrass. "If people think Walter was fast later on, they should have seen him then," Snodgrass told baseball historian Lawrence Ritter years later. "Whew! Most of the time you couldn't see the ball."

In the final game of the 1904 season, one thousand people crowded into Athletics Field to see a day-night doubleheader between the Oil Wells and

San Diego Pickwicks, 1907. Second and third from the left: Walter Johnson and Chief Meyers.
San Diego Historical Society Photograph Collection, www.sandiegohistory.org

a Sioux Indian all-star team touring the country from their reservation in South Dakota. Johnson struck out ten in the first game, which was won by the Oil Wells, but the Sioux came back to take the nightcap.

By this time Jack Burnett, the former Oil Wells slugger who had served as a guinea pig in one of Johnson's first tries at serious pitching, had gone to play for Tacoma in the Northwest League. On his recommendation, Tacoma signed Johnson, who rode the train from Los Angeles to Washington carrying a satchel full of sandwiches made by his mother. Minnie also insisted that her son take a new suit with him because she felt it was important for him to make a good impression when he met his employers.

Even with the suit, Walter got bounced out of Tacoma fairly fast, and he moved over to another club in the Idaho State League. His fortunes improved there, but after the season ended he returned home to pitch in the semipro Southern California League, which then consisted of the Anaheim (formerly Olinda) Oil Wells and clubs from San Bernardino, Pasadena, Los Angeles, and San Diego. That winter Walter went over to watch the New York Giants practice and play at Chutes Park. He was too shy to approach John McGraw to ask him for a pitching tryout, and he left without saying a word.

The next spring in Idaho, Walter's fastball did his talking for him, as he threw eighty-five scoreless innings and struck out 166 batters in twelve games. By July Washington had signed him, and he soon began to dazzle American League hitters. Minnie and Frank's once-awkward boy had grown into a commanding athlete. With light brown hair, blue eyes, and a sculpted facial profile, he stood six feet, one inch tall and a solid 175 pounds. *Sporting News* declared him "sure to be a star."

Returning once more in the off-season to California, Walter signed to pitch for five dollars a game for Santa Ana in the new California Winter League. But before the league started he joined the San Diego Pickwicks of the Southern State League, yet another local semipro circuit. Sponsored by a theater company, the Pickwicks played their home games at Athletic Field at Twenty-sixth and Main Streets in San Diego. After claiming the Southern State championship, they had issued a challenge to the Los Angeles Angels, winners of the Pacific Coast League pennant, to determine the 1907 champion of the West Coast. The Pickwicks decided it would probably not hurt their cause to bring in Johnson. But unlike Walter's old Fullerton Union High team, the Pickwicks did not need to recruit a catcher who was good enough to handle his fastball. They already had one on the roster: Chief Meyers.

The Pickwicks posed for a team picture that season, its twelve members standing in a row on a ballfield with their uniforms on. Johnson, in a jacket, stands second to the left with his hands clasped behind his back. On his left is Chief Meyers, about the same height as Johnson but thicker and wider.

The Chief's given name was not Meyers but Mayer—John Tortes Mayer. An error in grade school caused his name to be changed to "Meyer"; this became the accepted spelling, and later an "s" was attached to the end. It is not known when he picked up the nickname of Chief, but it was a common tag applied to Indian ballplayers of that era.

Similar confusion surrounds the Chief's birthplace. Meyers told Lawrence Ritter that he was born on the Cahuilla Indian Reservation in the San Jacinto Mountains of southern California. On another occasion he told an interviewer that his birthplace was Riverside. Henry Koerper, an authority on Meyers who has done extensive research on his background, tracked down his birth records and found that he was right the second time: he was born in the family home behind his father's saloon in downtown Riverside.

His father, John Mayer, was a Civil War veteran of German descent who operated the Riverside saloon until his death. His son John, the second of three children, was still a young boy when his father passed away. Meyers's Indian heritage comes from his mother, Felicite. She was a Cahuilla, one of the tribes in the group known as the Mission Indians. Before her marriage she wove baskets for the tribe. After her husband died she worked as a maid in Riverside to support herself and her children.

For a time Meyers lived with his family on the Santa Rosa Indian reservation, attending Sixth Street Grammar School, where he learned to play ball, warming to the game like nothing else he did. Baseball stirred other Cahuillas too, and they formed a Santa Rosa tribal team that competed against Indian and white clubs.

After leaving Riverside High, Meyers went to wherever the jobs were, going north to Fresno to work for a raisin company. While there he played on the company team. In 1903 the Pacific National League, bidding to compete with the newly formed Pacific Coast League, placed a team in Los Angeles, for which Meyers played before the league's swift demise.

The unwritten rule that banned blacks and other minorities from organized baseball did not apply to Native Americans. Although fans called them "redmen" and issued mock war whoops from the stands, Meyers and other Indians could play with whites in the minor and major leagues. But he said he never felt truly accepted: "In those days, when I was young, I was considered a foreigner. I was an Indian."

The Sherman Institute, a Riverside County boarding school comprised mainly of American Indian students, sponsored a baseball team whose players largely hailed from the Cahuilla tribe. During his youthful rambling days, Meyers starred for the team.

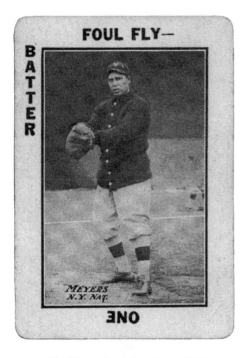

Chief Meyers baseball card, circa 1912.
Courtesy of Henry Koerper

In the spring of 1905 the Sherman Institute hosted a traveling squad from Japan's Waseda University, which was beginning a goodwill exhibition tour of the United States, the first baseball tour of the country by a Japanese university. Waseda had already played three games against Los Angeles High, attracting large crowds for each contest. But its game against the Cahuillas of the Sherman Institute, held at Fiesta Park in Los Angeles, pulled in the biggest crowd to date. "For the first time a Base Ball game was played by teams whose players were from two races that have adopted a sport heretofore distinctively that of the white man," wrote a reporter for *Sporting Life* magazine, a national baseball publication. "And victory rested with the men from across the sea because of their all-around superiority in every department of the game." The reporter went on to praise A. Kono, the winning "twirler," neglecting to mention the pitcher's first name or the final score.

A year later Chief Meyers entered Dartmouth College in New Hampshire. The original mission of Dartmouth, which was first called Moor's Indian Charity School, was to educate Native Americans, and he attended on a scholarship. But his mother soon became ill, forcing him to leave Dartmouth and return home to California.

Despite feeling like a foreigner in his own land, Meyers kept doing his work, taking his cuts, digging balls out of the dirt, making his throws to second and third, running hard, and keeping his game in competitive shape. Then came the winter of 1907, when he hooked up with the San Diego Pickwicks and Walter Johnson. With Walter throwing fastballs that mortal men could not see and the Chief receiving them, the Pickwicks looked to have a fair shot at whipping the biggest ballclub on the California block, the Los Angeles Angels.

The Angels had run away with the 1907 Pacific Coast League pennant, finishing in first place by eighteen games. This was no great shakes for them; they had won three of the first five championships in the league's short history. On the mound they threw nothing but aces, and their batting lineup packed power and plenty of it. Then there was this fella, the one with the funny name. What was it? Oh yeah, Cravath. Gavy Cravath. What kind of name was that?

Born in Escondido, north of San Diego, Gavy's birth name was Clifford Carlton Cravath. How he came by his nickname, unusual even by baseball's colorful standards, is anybody's guess. Baseball analyst and historian Bill James says that Gavy was short for "Gaviota," which is Spanish for seagull. But why would he be named after a seagull? Nobody knows. There is no debate, however, about his power at the plate. In his middle twenties, just under six feet tall with broad, strong shoulders and stovepipe arms, he could hit the dead bird that passed for a baseball in those days farther than almost anyone else. Cravath played in what is known today as the Dead Ball Era, when the ball was softer and not as lively as the current standard.

Cravath may or may not have participated in the showdown between the Angels and Pickwicks. He surely could have, for he was one of the Angel stars who might actually have been able to get around on a Johnson fastball. The best-of-five Coast Championship began with Johnson outdueling Sleepy Bill Burns of the Angels, 1 to 0. Johnson went all nine innings, striking out sixteen and allowing three hits and a walk. Chief Meyers handled the catching duties, throwing out three runners trying to steal and contributing offensively with three base hits. Shocked by the day's events, the Angels nevertheless came back to win three of the next four games and claim bragging rights as the unofficial state champions.

The end of the 1908 winter baseball season found many of the individuals discussed in this chapter heading in different directions.

Gavy Cravath made his hometown proud by joining the Boston Red Sox and becoming the first Escondido native to reach the major leagues. It would be years, however, before he was known for something other than his funny name. As an outfielder for the Philadelphia Phillies, he led the National League in home runs six times. While his slugging totals look meager by today's standards, home runs in his day were rare, and he was one of the best power hitters of his era.

After pitching for the San Diego Pickwicks and Santa Ana in the California Winter League, Walter Johnson developed a severe ear infection that caused him to miss the start of the 1908 American League season. Rejoining Washington in June, he went on to win forteen games that season. But his greatest years were yet to come. Beginning in 1910, these were his victory totals for each of the next ten seasons: 25, 25, 33, 36, 28, 27, 25, 23, 23, 20. All told, he chalked up 417 Ws, the second most ever.

Gavy Cravath, Philadelphia Phillies, circa 1915. San Diego Hall of Champions

Chief Meyers, Johnson's teammate on the Pickwicks, had to wait another season before his major league break came with the New York Giants. Meyers, who swore that Johnson never struck him out in all the times he batted against him, teamed up with him again a few seasons later on a winter barnstorming club.

Meyers never made the baseball Hall of Fame, but he did earn a place in the American Indian Hall of Fame. His .291 batting average over nine years in the majors was the highest for a catcher during the Dead Ball Era. Tough and durable, often playing with swollen and bleeding fingers, he played in four World Series, three with John McGraw's Giants and one with Brooklyn. In the 1911 Series he batted .300 and threw out twelve runners trying to steal, a Series record that still stands. While with the Giants he caught for Christy Mathewson and Rube Marquard, both Hall of Famers, and roomed with Olympic gold medal champion Jim Thorpe in his first years in professional baseball. Thorpe, a Sac and Fox Indian, and Meyers are two reasons why the years before World War I have been described as a golden age for Native American athletes in this country.

Owing to his success as a ballplayer, his Cahuilla heritage, and his gift for storytelling, Meyers was a popular and colorful figure on the New York scene. He even appeared in a vaudeville show with Mathewson. But his best performances may have been in front of sportswriters, spinning tall tales about himself and playing practical jokes. Once he dressed up in a headdress and posed for photographers, explaining that he always wore this traditional Indian garb in the off-season—something, in fact, that Cahuillas never did. A baseball general manager once received a gift of "sacred" Indian stones from him, for which the executive was flattered and humble. The Chief did not tell him that the stones actually came from his basement.

In his lair at Cub Ranch, Frank Chance was beginning to stir from hibernation. The newspaper report describing his neuritis as potentially career-threatening was wrong, the wishful musings of a New York writer hoping for better times for his hometown Giants. Chance was coming back, oh yes he was, for another season of managing and playing. Doctors had crafted a special shoe for his left foot that would allow him to fulfill his responsibilities at first base and as cleanup hitter for the Cubs. Now entering his eleventh season in the major leagues, the thirty-one-year-old Chance confidently predicted another world championship for his club—a prediction, as it turned out, that proved accurate.

But the famous and bitterly fought 1908 pennant race was Chance's last as a regular. His playing time gradually diminished as injuries and age wore him down. He stayed on as Cubs manager, though, leading them to another pennant in 1910. His run with the team ended two years later, about the same time he underwent surgery for blood clots in the brain, possibly the result of all those beanings he received as a player. After managing the Yankees for two seasons, he steered the Los Angeles Angels to the 1916 Pacific Coast League title as manager and part-owner.

Eight years later, at the age of forty-seven, Chance summoned his old infield mates, Joe Tinker and Johnny Evers, to his death bed at Good Samaritan

Hospital in Los Angeles. The trio of Bear Cubs once fleeter than birds talked about old times before their leader slipped out of consciousness. In 1946 the Hall of Fame inducted all three men as a group.

As for young Freddy Snodgrass of Ventura, given a choice between the Hoegee Flags and the New York Giants, he chose the latter, accepting John McGraw's offer to take the train east to the club's 1908 spring training camp in Texas. Fred hardly did anything that year, and not too much for the next two years, but after Chief Meyers joined the Giants and settled in as their regular catcher, Snodgrass switched to the outfield where he excelled. Being young and playing center field for the Giants, he said, was the happiest time of his life.

Schoolboys

SATURDAY, MARCH 22 — 2:15 P.M.
SUNDAY, MARCH 23 — 2:15 P.M.
— 1947 —

ABLISHED PRICE - - $3.33   Total $4.00
ERAL TAX - - - - .67

HIS PORTION OF TICKET NOT GOOD FOR ADMITTANCE
DETACH SEPERATE COUPONS FOR INDIVIDUAL GAMES

As a young man Joe Hooper was a rambler, bouncing from place to place in his native eastern Canada and the northeastern United States. But in 1876, the nation's centennial year, he decided to come west, spurred on by letters he had received from his brother and sister who were living in the Santa Clara Valley. The valley at the southern end of San Francisco Bay advertised itself as "the Garden of the World," an exaggeration perhaps, but not that much of one to Mary Hooper and her brother Bill, who had made a home for their families amidst the fruit orchards and gentle rolling hills. Joe paid seventy-six dollars for an emigrant class ticket on the Union Pacific–Central Pacific line, riding for two weeks from Maine to California. After accidentally leaving his money pouch back home, he arrived in San Francisco without a cent to his name. Luckily, some people he met on the train gave him the fare to Gilroy, where Mary and Bill lived. Joe found his way to the tiny farming community south of San Jose, in no time caught on as a hired hand at the farm, and soon had money of his own in his pocket.

Mary Keller worked as a housekeeper at the farm. Born in Frankfurt, Germany, she immigrated to this country as a young girl. Now she was no longer a girl, but an attractive young woman, a fact Joe Hooper noticed immediately. The two took a fancy to each other and within months were husband and wife. They rented a nearby piece of land and started a family. They had four children, their youngest named Harry.

When Harry was a baby the Hoopers moved to Merced County in the San Joaquin Valley. They packed up for a different part of the valley a few years later. It was not easy making a living from the land, and they struggled to pay the bills. The victories seemed small and incremental whereas the losses were overwhelming. When Harry was ten his only sister caught meningitis and died at age thirteen.

Not long after his sister's death Harry accompanied his mother on a trip to Pennsylvania, where Mary had grown up and her mother and other relatives still lived. They left in June after Harry's grammar school had let out for the summer. Still in mourning, still reeling from their loss, both the woman and boy saw the trip as a way to ease some of the hurt they felt.

This was the summer Harry discovered baseball; at a Fourth of July picnic his relatives invited him to join them in a game. Harry played and played and played—and never really stopped for the next twenty years. That summer his Uncle Mack, his baseball mentor, took him to New York to see the Brooklyn Bridegrooms, providing Harry with his first look at a major league park. As a parting gift Mack gave him a ball, bat, and glove.

Harry returned home after this life-changing summer and settled back into days of school, farm chores, hunting, horse riding, and baseball. "What a boyhood," he recalled as a grown man thinking back on his childhood in the Central Valley circa 1900. "I rode horseback to and from school, six miles each way. I had a rifle and a shotgun, and there was plenty…of deer, pheasant, geese and quail. Best of all, I had a baseball, bat and a glove." Uncle Mack's ball, bat, and glove.

But a teacher at school, Mary Sullivan, recognized Harry's aptitude with the books and wanted to see him do more in that realm. She recommended he continue up the academic ladder at St. Mary's College (then located in Oakland and now in nearby Moraga). Tuition for the year was $520, which represented a financial stretch for Mary and Joe Hooper. But they felt, and Harry's brothers agreed, that at least one Hooper should have a chance to leave the farm and get a higher education. Thus began a new chapter in the boy's life.

Originally founded during the Civil War, St. Mary's College was run by the Christian Brothers, a Catholic order established in France in the late 1600s. The founder of the order was St. John Baptist de la Salle, the patron saint of teachers. The primary mission of the Christian Brothers was to educate poor people and, in the United States especially, poor immigrants. But the tiny liberal arts school of about two hundred students was known not just for its academics. It also boasted a big-time college baseball program, one of the best in the West.

St. Mary's first began sponsoring baseball teams in the heady years following the building of the transcontinental railroad, when people and ideas streamed back and forth between East and West with greater ease than ever before. In 1876, the year Joe Hooper came west, a Bay Area all-star team headed in the other direction, competing in a national amateur tournament in Philadelphia. The Centennials, as they called themselves, won six of seven games in the tourney. Four members of this club hailed from the St. Mary's Base Ball Club, nicknamed the Phoenix.

Bare-handed third baseman Jerry Denny, one of the first California-bred players to reach the majors, received some of his early schooling in the game at St. Mary's. He is one of more than fifty St. Mary's men to suit up in the major leagues. (According to baseball historian Doug McWilliams, beginning in 1881 St. Mary's has had alumni playing in the major leagues 102 out of 188 years, through 1999.)

Another early standout was pitcher Joe Corbett, whose big brother, Gentleman Jim Corbett, knocked out James L. Sullivan to win the 1892 heavyweight championship of the world. That same year Joe pitched St. Mary's to the Pacific Amateur baseball title. Five years later he won twenty-four games with Baltimore in the National League. The next season, insulted by the salary offered by the Orioles, he walked away from the majors, working, among other jobs, as a sportswriter for the *San Francisco Call*.

St. Mary's owed some of its success in baseball to its policy—one not uncommon for colleges of the time—of allowing its student-athletes to moonlight on pay-for-play teams. It and other colleges may have paid some of their players as well. The old English ideal of amateurs playing sports purely for joy and unsullied by monetary reward held no truck with the Christian Brothers; this was America, and they saw nothing wrong with a boy making some dollars at his craft. Members of the Phoenix played college games during the week and semipro ball on the weekends.

The head baseball man on campus was Brother Agnon McCann. A man of immense learning and vitality, he taught virtually every subject in the curriculum, from mathematics to the metaphysics of St. Thomas Aquinas. Brother Agnon—members of the Christian Brothers order prefer to be called only by their first names—also organized the baseball program, raising money for the teams, coordinating the boosters, setting up the schedule, supervising the players on road trips, and coaching. He believed that athletics, and baseball in particular, was part of the college's educational mission, helping teach Christian values to undisciplined young men and turn them into responsible members of society. And if a St. Mary's boy happen to stray from these values, Brother Agnon snapped him back into line.

Phelan, Brother Agnon, and Eddie Burns, St. Mary's Phoenix, 1903.
From the College Archives Collection of St. Mary's College of California, smcaii1563a

"The venerable mentor was no respecter of persons," writes Brother Matthew, a fellow instructor and member of the order. "More than one prominent attorney, fresh from a triumph at the bar, returned to the campus with a reprimand on the mispronunciation of a word. Baseball heroes, with the cheers of crowds still ringing in their ears, likewise, were told the errors of their ways." Very little slipped past Brother Agnon, who taught at the school nearly forty years. When St. Mary's alumni returned to campus for a social occasion, he instantly recalled their names despite not having seen them for years.

It was not uncommon in those days for colleges to admit high school–age students for pre-college studies. The fifteen-year-old Harry Hooper fell into this category, and being only an ounce or two above one hundred pounds, he joined St. Mary's Midgets, its team for younger players. His original position in the field was pitcher, but because he was such a little guy he had a hard time putting much fast on his fastball. Brother Agnon, observing Harry's speed afoot and stop-on-a-dime reflexes, shifted him to a different position. There, in the wide open spaces of the outfield, he flourished.

As his grammar school teacher might have expected, Harry also thrived in the classroom. He received all As in math and science in pursuit of a degree in engineering. In his spare time he played viola and horn in the band and won the school's handball championship.

Hooper's senior year at St. Mary's marked the culmination of his collegiate baseball career. Having long outgrown the Midgets and moved up to the varsity, he became the brightest light on a team filled with bright lights. The 1907 Phoenix won twenty-six games, lost none, tied one, placing first in both the California-Nevada and Midwinter Intercollegiate Leagues. It took on a group of Pacific Coast League stars, as well as the visiting Chicago White Sox, and thumped them both. Near the end of this season Hooper accepted an offer to play professional baseball for Alameda in the California State League, thereby beginning his professional career. Soon after that he graduated from college, the first in his family to do so.

In the judgment of baseball historian Paul J. Zingg and other experts, the 1907 St. Mary's Phoenix was one of the best college baseball teams of its time. Every member of the club went on to draw a paycheck in professional baseball, and four of them, including Hooper, pursued their higher horsehide education in the majors. The ace of the Phoenix staff, San Francisco–born left-hander Harry Krause, won eighteen games for the Philadelphia Athletics in 1909 with an American League–leading 1.39 earned run average. Charlie Enwright of Sacramento roamed the outfield alongside Hooper at St. Mary's but lasted only a few games with the St. Louis Cardinals. Eddie Burns, a pint-sized catcher who started at St. Mary's as a mascot and worked his way up to varsity, played seven seasons in the majors, six of them with Philadelphia. The 1915 World Series between Philadelphia and Boston featured four former St. Mary's men: Burns, with the Phillies, and Hooper, outfielder Duffy Lewis, and pitcher Dutch Leonard, all with the Red Sox.

St. Mary's Phoenix, 1907. Harry Hooper is top row standing, far right. Hal Chase is seated, far left.

The coach of this stellar Phoenix club was a twenty-four-year-old major leaguer named Hal Chase. His regular gig was as the starting first baseman for the New York Highlanders (now Yankees), where he was gaining a reputation as one of the game's rising stars, a smooth-fielding glove man who stole bases and hit for a high average. But in the off-season he had returned to his native Bay Area, picking up some extra money playing baseball and coaching at St. Mary's. It was Brother Agnon's policy to bring in top-tier professionals to teach the game to his players.

The learned Brother Agnon and Hal Chase—they shared a passion for baseball but little else. Chase, although one of the most gifted talents of this era, was as crooked as Lombard Street, a petty thief, a liar, a gambler, and a master at the age-old art of hippodroming, or throwing baseball games.

Numerous writers and baseball historians have combed Chase's background for clues as to why he became "baseball's biggest crook," in the words of one. His most notorious exploits occurred in New York and other major league cities of the East. But his boyhood home—and the place he returned to as an older man, a penniless alcoholic whose career had ended in disgrace—was California.

Like Harry Hooper, Chase's birthplace was the Santa Clara Valley, whose lush farmlands drew Josiah and Stephen Hall Chase from the East Coast in the late 1850s. But the Chase brothers did not become farmers; instead, with so many people moving into the area and building homes, they found employment as lumbermen, establishing the S. H. Chase Company lumber mill on Summit Road, where they processed redwood trees from the Santa Cruz Mountains. The demand for redwood was so high that in time the brothers added seven more mills in the area. The company, which operated for nearly a century, provided lumber for many mansions in the valley, including what is now the Winchester Mystery House tourist spot in San Jose.

Other Chases came west to join the family business, and one of them was Edgar Chase, who managed the Alviso mill. He and his wife Mary lived on University Avenue in Los Gatos and had six children, one of whom was Hal.

A neighbor remembered Hal always throwing balls or rocks or apples at fences, practicing his aim. Sometimes he targeted moving objects. While working for three dollars a week at a fruit stand, Hal liked to liven things up by pitching apples or pears at passing horse-drawn wagons. Getting hit by a flying object sometimes caused the horse to spook, shake off his harness, and run away, to the delight of Chase and his pals.

On a diamond, though, with a baseball in his hand rather than an apple or rock, he was anything but a nuisance. He starred for Los Gatos High and on the weekends earned money on the semipro Soquel Giants, whose members consisted of ranch hands and loggers. Handsome and clear-eyed, the strapping seventeen-year-old had left behind the fruit stand for a job as a day laborer at a lumber mill.

But clearly, his future was not in the family business. Santa Clara College (now University), a Jesuit college in the valley with a strong baseball program of its own, recruited him for its team. The coach when Chase arrived was Joe Corbett, the former Oriole and St. Mary's ace, and after Corbett left, Charlie Graham, then a professional catcher with Sacramento, took his place. At the beginning of a career in baseball that would span half a century, Graham later managed and owned the San Francisco Seals.

The reason Chase went to Santa Clara was to play baseball, and he seldom, if ever, attended class. He was, in the vernacular of the time, a "ringer" or "deadhead" or "baseball bum." These baseball bums (and Chase was hardly alone in this regard) sometimes jumped from college to college, much like professional players moved between teams, depending on where the best deal was.

In later years Santa Clara and other colleges revised their rules to prohibit paying players.

Since Santa Clara already had a good first baseman, Chase, a left-hander, claimed second base, going against conventional baseball wisdom. Left-handed second basemen are thought to be at a disadvantage because it is harder for them to make the pivot and throw to first base when they receive the ball from shortstop or third on a double play. But Chase made second base look like his natural position. Graceful as a dancer, he never appeared awkward or out of place, pouncing on ground balls and easily making all the throws. (In the majors he occasionally played second, shortstop, outfield, and pitcher.)

Cal baseball team, early 1900s. Orval Overall is second from left, top row.
University of California Sports Department

With Chase patrolling second base, Santa Clara competed against local semipro teams as well as squads from Stanford and Cal. One game against Cal featured a matchup between two future major league pitchers, Santa Clara's Bobby Keefe, who spent some time with New York and Cincinnati, and a six-foot-two-inch hunk of a man named Orval Overall. Born in Farmersville, California, "Ovie," as he was called, started on Cal's varsity football team all four years he was there. Three of those years he also pitched on the baseball team. After graduation he became one of the best power pitchers of his time, winning twenty-three games with a league-leading eight shutouts for the 1907 world champion Chicago Cubs. The next year he won two games in the World Series as the Cubs repeated as champions.

After his first season with Santa Clara, Chase left his home state for the first time ever, traveling to Canada to play for a semipro club. While there, he declined offers from pro teams in the Northwest, choosing instead to return to college for another season. But he did not remain a schoolboy for long.

In March, Santa Clara went on a road trip to Los Angeles to meet St. Vincent's College, winner of nineteen straight games. In the first game of the series the visitors put an end to the streak, 13 to 8, and Chase nicked three hits, stole three bases, and scored three runs. A reporter from the *Los Angeles Times* called "the second baseman for the victors the fastest ever seen in an amateur game in Los Angeles."

The umpire of the game was Los Angeles owner Jim Morley, who was equally impressed by what he saw. Afterward he took Chase aside and signed him to a contract of seventy-five dollars per month. Santa Clara swept St. Vincent's in all three games, but the last two wins came without their star second baseman. Chase had turned pro, and his college days were done.

Events proceeded rapidly after that. His Angels debut occurred later that month, and he immediately earned rave reviews from the national press and major league scouts. Bill Lange and George Van Haltren both thought he had the goods to make it back East. The New York Highlanders swooped in, and Chase, after being converted to first base, made his maiden appearance in the Big Apple less than a year after leaving Santa Clara.

Thus began a pattern that repeated itself over the next several years—Chase spending the regular season in the big city, with all its temptations and distractions, then returning in the late fall and winter to bucolic Santa Clara Valley. After his rookie year in New York he played in the off-season for the San Jose Prune Pickers of the California State League. In the spring, before he headed back East, in a ceremony held at Cycler's Park in San Jose, the local Women's Club gave him a gold watch to show their appreciation.

His next season in New York—.323 average, second in the league in steals and runs batted in—stamped him as one of the game's young elites. Again returning to California in the off-season, he combined his appearances on the Prune Pickers with his coaching duties for the champion St. Mary's Phoenix. This was where Chase crossed paths not only with Brother Agnon but also with a young Harry Hooper.

Hooper observed years later that Chase "just wasn't all there" as a manager, which may be understandable considering these were local California kids and Chase was starting to move with a pretty fast crowd in the nation's largest city. More troubling to Hooper was his recollection that Chase stole cigars and other small items.

Chase returned, as usual, to New York in the spring, but it would be years before Hooper joined him in the American League.

CHASE N. Y. AMER.

Hal Chase baseball card. From The Day the New York Giants Came to Oxnard, *by Jeffrey Wayne Maulhardt*

After playing briefly for Alameda near the end of his senior year at St. Mary's, Hooper switched teams and joined Sacramento largely because of his desire to work for the railroad. As an engineer for the Western Pacific—his survey work included the B Street Underpass and an American River bridge—he earned seventy-five dollars a month. But as an outfielder in the California State League, he topped his railroad pay by making eighty-five dollars a month.

His manager in Sacramento was Charlie Graham, who doubled as a scout for the Boston Red Sox. Graham tipped off Boston's owner, John Taylor, who personally came to Sacramento to meet Hooper at Hooper's favorite saloon on Eighth and J Streets in order to get the twenty-one-year-old's signature on a contract. The youngster signed for three thousand dollars, more than Taylor expected to pay, but a monster of a bargain in baseball terms.

Although he sat out most of his rookie season, Hooper broke into Boston's starting lineup in his second year and became its regular right fielder. A fellow Californian, Duffy Lewis, a stylish, rifle-armed graduate of Alameda High and a former St. Mary's man himself, joined him in the outfield. With Lewis in left, Tris Speaker in center, and Hooper in right—of the three, only Lewis is not in the Hall of Fame—they formed what was called "the Golden Outfield," a defensive outfield trio second to none. The Golden Outfield's years were indeed golden for the Red Sox, who won four World Series titles between 1912 and 1918. Hooper played on all four of those championship teams.

Hal Chase's career arc stands in decided contrast. In his last year in the major leagues, he found himself near the center of the Black Sox Scandal, the most outrageous gambling episode in the game's history, and his story will resume in Chapter 13.

Playgrounds

SATURDAY, MARCH 22 — 2:15 P.M.
SUNDAY, MARCH 23 — 2:15 P.M.
— 1947 —
ABLISHED PRICE - $3.33
ERAL TAX - .67   Total $4.00

HIS PORTION OF TICKET NOT GOOD FOR ADMITTANCE
DETACH SEPERATE COUPONS FOR INDIVIDUAL GAMES

Built with pioneering resolve in the grim aftermath of the Great Earthquake and Fire, Recreation Park on Valencia Street in San Francisco steadily slid into shabby disrepair. Sports columnist Abe Kemp, who covered games there, called it "a ramshackle two-by-four ballpark." Locals referred to it as "Old Rec," a pun that succinctly described the shape it was in.

Behind home plate at Old Rec was a field-level section known as the Booze Cage. A bleacher seat in the park cost a quarter, but it took forty cents to gain admittance to the Cage. For this extra money they gave you a shot of whiskey or beer or a ham-and-cheese sandwich. In the Booze Cage, men—no females dared enter there—sat behind a chicken wire screen drinking and yelling and drinking and yelling some more. "Christ the guys in there were tough, particularly on umpires," said Kemp. "They were all drunks. They got on everybody."

Old Rec, San Francisco, 1920. The Booze Cage is under the Bar sign.
California Historical Society, FN-40031

Cold and blustery Ewing Field, circa 1914. California Historical Society, FN-40051

They gambled in the Booze Cage, of course they did, but the place appealed mainly to serious drinkers. The gamblers sat in their own section in the upper grandstand along the first base line. Gambling was against the law, but that did not stop anyone from doing it.

San Francisco owner Cal Ewing, who saved the Pacific Coast League from collapse after the earthquake and helped build it up from a shaky four clubs to a more solid six, put up the original financing for Old Rec. But he no longer wanted any part of it. He wanted out, and he wanted to take his ballclub, now known as the Seals, with him. But where? With no other suitable places to play in the city, he and his business partner, Frank Ish, decided to build a new ballpark, resolving to make it the finest minor league showcase in America.

Ewing and Ish found some land they liked off Geary Boulevard near Golden Gate Park, and the project broke ground in the fall of 1913. Planners expected it to be done by Opening Day of the next season, but March and April passed by with the hammers still pounding away. The *San Francisco Chronicle* sent a reporter to assess the progress at the site. "The only possible drawback to the location is the possibility of meeting with bad weather conditions," he noted. "Wind and fog may be experienced in the afternoon."

The grand unveiling of Ewing Field came in the middle of May, and most everyone agreed it was worth the wait, a vast improvement over that glorified woodpile in the Mission. Behind home plate were covered grandstands—and no Booze Cage or anything like it. Furthermore, every one of its eighteen thousand seats, it seemed, had a splendid view of the field. The *Chronicle* prophesied it would be "the home of the Seals for the next twenty years." The Oakland Oaks supplied the only downer of the day by shutting out the hometown boys, 3 to 0.

The weather that day—sunny with a few light winds—may have been the best all summer, for the observation of that first *Chronicle* reporter turned chillingly true. Wet, fog-bearing winds from the Pacific Ocean whipped across the park almost daily, much to the displeasure of the shivering customers and players. The fans in the grandstand said on some days the fog was so thick they could not see the outfielders.

People stayed away from Ewing Field in droves, complaining that it was too cold, too windy, and too foggy to watch baseball comfortably. Fifty years later similar complaints would be heard about another San Francisco baseball landmark, Candlestick Park.

Although able to save the Coast League, Cal Ewing could not save himself from this mistake. Attendance crashed, burying him in red ink and forcing him and Ish to sell their interest in the team. After only one season the Seals abandoned Ewing Field and returned to splintery Old Rec, which was at least in a sunnier part of town.

★　　　★　　　★

The year 1915 was an auspicious one in the life of the city. The first transcontinental telephone call from San Francisco to New York united the country in a new way, and the recently completed Panama Canal made going the long route around Cape Horn no longer necessary for ships traveling between the East and West Coasts. To trumpet its virtues as a port and trade center, San Francisco held the Panama-Pacific International Exposition. (San Diego sponsored a similar expo the same year in Balboa Park.) One purpose of the fair was to show the world that the city had come all the way back from the devastation of the '06 quake, and millions of people visited attractions such as the Tower of Jewels and the Palace of Fine Arts, which still stands in its original Marina District location.

It was also a big year for the hometown Seals, despite the embarrassment of returning to Old Rec and having to once again hear the catcalls from the patrons in the Booze Cage. The club featured two "swing hitters" in their lineup, Harry Heilmann and

Harry Heilmann, 1915. California Historical Society, FN-40013

Ping Bodie. A swing hitter, in the parlance of the day, was a fellow who swung hard, not looking for singles or cheap contact hits but really trying to powder the ball. Neither Heilmann nor Bodie was fast afoot, nor were they particularly graceful in the field, but when they connected with a pitch, both Harry and Ping could hit the ball a long, long way.

A native of San Francisco, Heilmann had played his school ball at Sacred Heart, which led to his first big break in the game. After graduating he got a job keeping the books for a biscuit company. One Saturday at work he happened to run into an ex–high school teammate who was managing Hartford in the San Joaquin Valley League. One of his players had dropped out unexpectedly, leaving him with a hole to fill for a big game against rival Bakersfield. You interested in stepping in for him? the manager asked. Harry shrugged. Sure, why not?

The next day Heilmann's clutch eleventh-inning hit to beat Bakersfield made him an overnight sensation in Hartford. A scout from the Northwest who was in the stands signed him on the spot, ending his short-lived accounting career. After a stint in Portland, the big free-swinger of German descent ascended the golden baseball staircase to the Detroit Tigers.

But Heilmann struggled in the East and the Tigers sent him back to the Coast League to get some of the rawness out of the raw-boned twenty-year-old. That was where he hooked up in the same batting order with Bodie, a short, stout Italian of limited skills and apparently limitless ego. A slugger with a big ego—not the first and hardly the last.

Ping Bodie's given name was Francesco Stephano Pezzolo; his Americanized name was Frank Stephen Bodie. Though perhaps apocryphal, the story of how he chose his new last name is as colorful as the man himself. Located in Mono County on the northeastern edge of the state, Bodie was a frontier mining town that put the wild in Wild West. There was law in Bodie but not much of it and never around when you needed it. The miners there behaved much like the rowdy fans at Old Rec, drinking, cursing, and fighting. The whorehouse district in town provided them with another recreational outlet. Looking to put a little prosperity in his pocket, Frank's father worked the Bodie mines for a time. The big strike never materialized for him, but years later, when his son was looking for a name with an all-American ring to it, the one he came up with was Bodie. The "Ping" reportedly stemmed from the sound the ball made when it struck his hard-swinging bat. And this became his baseball handle: Ping Bodie.

At the start of his career Ping earned some paychecks in the California State League—which, coincidentally, went out of business after the 1915 season, killed off by competitive pressure from the bigger, stronger Coast League—before hitching up with the Seals. When he hit thirty home runs in a season, more than anyone else in organized baseball, minors or majors, local boosters proclaimed him "the World Champion of Home Runs." His good press caught the notice of the Chicago White Sox, who brought him up to see if he could duplicate his feats in the major leagues. The journalist David

Halberstam has observed that "baseball was the first great American opportunity for Italian immigrants," but fans of the 1911 White Sox, seeing Bodie's name in the lineup, may not have even known that Francesco Stephano Pezzulo was actually making history as the first Italian American to play in the major leagues.

After a solid rookie season in Chicago, his production slid steadily over the next three years and the White Sox cut him adrift. History-making or not, Bodie was just another out-of-work ballplayer when he came back to California and signed on for his second hitch with the Seals.

With Bodie and Heilmann swinging from their heels, and sometimes connecting, the Seals pounded their way to the 1915 Coast League crown. Though missing part of the season due to illness, Harry smoked one of the longest home runs of his career—a shot off Sacramento's Lefty Williams that cleared the cigarette sign in center field at Old Rec. The Tigers may have seen the makings of greatness, for they brought him back to the big club where, this time, he stuck. In fifteen seasons in Detroit (and two more in Cincinnati), he pounded the ball at a prodigious .342 lifetime clip. In 1923 his .403 average won the second of his four batting titles. His slugging feats later earned him membership in the Hall of Fame, and after retiring from the game he became a popular broadcaster with the Tigers.

His former Seals teammate, Ping Bodie, did not immediately return to the majors like his younger counterpart. He remained in San Francisco for a few more seasons of abuse by the denizens of the Booze Cage, though he was popular with most everyone else. If, as has been written, Bodie changed his name to avoid discrimination due to his Italian heritage, the fact of who he was did not hurt him any in his hometown. The Italians who came out to see him were not fooled by his adopted name, even if others were. They knew the name his mama and papa gave him, and some may have even known him as a youngster. They had heard about his accomplishments and read about him in the newspapers, and they saw what a big man he was with the Seals—a point that Bodie did not dispute.

It was during these years that Bodie's five-year-old son wandered through the stands at Old Rec asking various fans the same question: "Who is the best hitter in the Pacific Coast League?"

"I don't know," the spectator invariably replied. "Who?"

"My father," said the boy proudly, explaining that his father was Ping Bodie.

Puzzling over this a moment, the spectator then asked, "What makes you think he's the best?"

"Because every night at supper my father tells me he's the best hitter in the Pacific Coast League."

In 1917 the self-proclaimed best hitter in the Pacific Coast League returned to the promised land of the majors.

★   ★   ★   ★   ★

Ping Bodie, 1923.
California Historical Society,
FN-40032

One person's throwaway is another's treasure. What seems useless and without value to one can be full of meaning to someone else. So it was with Ewing Field—cold, foggy, windswept Ewing Field.

Cal Ewing's apparent boondoggle actually proved to be a boon for baseball in San Francisco, for when the Pacific Coast League vacated the park, it created an opening for other people, other groups to come in. One of these groups was the Japanese.

Semipro and amateur Issei teams played at Ewing Field, Golden Gate Park, and elsewhere around the city. When they did, their families and friends came to the games to watch from the sidelines, as did the families and friends of other teams. At these games the Japanese met and mingled with white people, with whom they ordinarily had little contact. "Community ballparks were used by many diverse immigrant groups," writes baseball historian Kerry Yo Nakawaga. "For the Issei, this was their chance to finally reach outside of the inner circle of their Nikkei [Japanese American] community and establish new ties to white society."

But there remained considerable distrust between whites and Japanese. Japanese fans did not tend to go to Pacific Coast League games, in part because there were no Japanese players to watch, but also because they were not welcome, and so the mixing that occurred at Old Rec between Germans, Italians, Irish, and other ethnic groups did not involve them. Like blacks, they were rarely seen.

Additionally, in many cities as well as small towns along the coast or in the Central Valley, community ballparks used by whites were off-limits to the Japanese, which meant that if the Issei wanted to participate in the game, they had to create their own playgrounds.

Around California, particularly in the valley, where so many Issei settled and found work on farms, they built ballfields of their own in the sections of town away from where the white majority lived. First they cleared a field of weeds around their church or in an empty lot, scratching out a diamond in the dirt. Families pitched in, children included. Those who did not work brought food. At first the carpenters may have built only a wooden backstop to stop the balls the catcher missed, but that did not do for long. Most everybody in the community wanted to see the games, so up went bleachers for them to sit on.

Sunday afternoons were set aside for baseball. "Baseball Crazy Day," they called it. The Issei men and women laughed, chatted, cheered, clapped, cursed, and laid bets on the action on the field. Baseball Crazy Day always included a picnic and social get-together. The teenage girls put on pretty dresses and the boys pretended not to notice.

Seated in bleachers they had built with their own hands, often dressed formally in suits and ties, the Issei elders watched their sons play the game. These youngsters—known as Nisei, or the second generation, those who were born not in Japan but in America—were forming teams of their own, taking up where their fathers had left off. But the old men could be tough on this new generation. When a boy made a nice play he might hear "yoki sobi mashita"—

Fans at Baseball Crazy Day. From Through a Diamond: 100 Years of
Japanese American Baseball, *by Kerry Yo Nakagawa. NBRP (Nisei Baseball Research Project)*

you did well—from his father. But if the boy's team lost or he fared poorly, he received only the silent treatment. In the father's view, respect was not a thing to be given out lightly; it had to be earned. The Nisei understood this and took it to heart. Playing baseball, and playing it well, was a way for them to earn respect. And in the coming years they would attempt to do that—earn respect not only from their fathers and the elders in the community but from white Americans who viewed them with suspicion and fear.

A Left-hander for the Oaks

ZEE-NUT
SERIES
1916
CLAXTON
OAKS

SATURDAY, MARCH 22 — 2:15 P.M.
SUNDAY, MARCH 23 — 2:15 P.M.
— 1947 —

Total $4.00

ABLISHED PRICE - $3.33
ERAL TAX - - - .67

HIS PORTION OF TICKET NOT GOOD FOR ADMITTANCE
DETACH SEPERATE COUPONS FOR INDIVIDUAL GAMES

Oakland was one of the original cities of the Pacific Coast League. Like two other originals—San Francisco and Los Angeles—it remained a dependable partner in the league, always fielding a club although its population was less than either of those cities. Its team, which came to be known as the "Oaks" in recognition of the coastal and live oaks that brightened the landscape of the city and the surrounding hills, played home games at Freeman's Park on the western flatlands.

From its earliest years in the Pacific Coast League and even before then, Oakland's natural rival—in baseball and everything else—was San Francisco. The city of cable cars was everything Oakland was not: big, rich, slick. Oakland served as a railroad hub for the region, the end of the transcontinental line, but travelers from the East usually kept right on going to San Francisco, ignoring Oakland except as a transfer point for catching the ferry across the then bridgeless bay.

Oakland residents, especially those who followed baseball, countered that yes, living in San Francisco offered many advantages, but the weather was miserable. Sitting comfortably in their seats under the mild East Bay sunshine, ball fans at Freeman's Park chuckled in amusement at the fog-bound miseries of Ewing Field.

Oakland won its first Coast League flag in 1912, beating Vernon to the wire in a near–photo finish. Heady with this success, Oaks ownership decided to replace aging Freeman's Park with new, larger digs off San Pablo Avenue in Emeryville, a small town bordering Oakland. From first nail to final board, it took six weeks to build 11,000-seat Oaks Ball Park. Opening Day was a triumph; people loved its clean, simple lines and intimate views. At day's end, as after all the games played there, fans left the park by walking across the outfield grass.

While Oaks Park met with success, the team the Oaks put on the field did not. The Acorns, as they were also known, finished dead last in their first season in their new park, and last again the year after. In 1915 Jack Ness of the Oaks hit safely in forty-nine consecutive games to set a Coast League record, but his teammates did little else than look on in envy, and the club finished in the lower division. With Ness departing the next year to take a crack at the major leagues—it did not go well for him there; two abbreviated seasons and he was gone—the lowly Oaks looked around for new players to rescue them.

In late May the Oaks hired a new pitcher, James E. "Jimmy" Claxton. Every ballclub always needs good, live left-handed arms, and Claxton, an American Indian from the plains of Nebraska, qualified on that score. Probably in his mid-twenties, he was a lefty with good stuff.

Claxton took the mound for the opening game of a Memorial Day doubleheader. Possibly suffering from the jitters, understandable since this was his first game with the team and he no doubt wanted to make a good impression, he did not remain long before being removed for another pitcher. But he came back in the second game in relief. His nerves perhaps having calmed down some, he made a better showing and recorded the final outs of the contest.

Comic trading cards for the Oakland baseball team. Doug McWilliams Collection

But the fans in the park and the players and coaches noticed something different about Claxton. He was what people called "light-skinned," but his skin was darker than anyone else's in the park. An Indian, this guy? Rumors swirled. This guy was not an Indian, people said. He was black.

Those upset about Jimmy Claxton's presence in an Oakland Oaks uniform would have used the words "Negro" or "colored" to describe him. Some would have surely resorted to coarser epithets to express their displeasure and anger. In truth, Claxton was not a Native American, nor was he from Nebraska. He was a black man, and the Coast League prohibited blacks from playing on its teams.

The provision banning blacks from organized baseball could not be found in any rule book. It was understood, the way things were. And it was enforced. The fact that it was not written down did not rob it of its practical power; it formed a kind of invisible wall that kept blacks from competing in the same arena as whites.

The unwritten rule had kept black players out of the major leagues since the mid-1880s. An early California minor leaguer, Horace Wilds, had also felt its harsh effects. Described by the *Oakland Tribune* as "the colored beauty," he played with whites on amateur teams before joining the Pacific Base Ball League. But this league, a rival to the then-dominant California League, folded quickly, leaving him without a baseball job. Stopped from continuing his career in white baseball because of his color, Wilds joined an all-black team.

This was true of other blacks of his time. They formed their own teams, cadged together what equipment and uniforms they could, and held games on rock-strewn fields in another part of town.

Major newspaper coverage of these games was predictably sparse, although the *San Francisco Chronicle* made an exception for a contest between black employees from San Francisco's Pacific Hotel and Oakland's Union Club. "The game," said the *Chronicle*, "was a great deal better than some of the championship contests [of the California League] and several brilliant plays were made."

In the rapidly growing southern part of the state, the *Los Angeles Times* noted how "a hard-hitting colored man" named Lane (no first name given) had cracked the Los Angeles High School lineup. Some years later the black-owned *California Eagle* described a meeting between the city's "Colored YMCA" and Manual Arts

Fresno Cubs, Fink-Smith Playground, Fresno, circa 1914. Fresno Historical Society

Jimmy Claxton, Zee-Nut baseball card, 1916.
Doug McWilliams Collection

High. "This is the first time so far as I can remember that a colored team of any sort has had a game with the first team of any of the leading high schools," observed the *Eagle*. Around this time a game between whites and Mexicans at a local recreation hall also earned a mention in the *Times*.

The Los Angeles White Sox, a black semipro team, played at White Sox Park in the Boyle Heights District of the city. There were two parks with this name; the first White Sox Park was near the railway yards about a mile from City Hall. It had a brief life before giving way to another White Sox Park between Compton and Ascot Avenues. Nearby was the White Sox Café and Chili Parlor. "After the game, see us," it advertised. Players and fans could feast on barbecue, homemade pies, waffles, and hotcakes. Its proprietor was D. C. Knox, who charged thirty-five cents for the luncheon plate. But if you wanted your meal delivered, D. C. insisted that the order be at least fifty cents.

The first all-black baseball team in Fresno was called the Fresno Cubs. They played their home games at Fink-Smith Playground in the city, traveling around the valley and state to find competition.

In organized white baseball, Eastern major leaguers traveling to California infused the local game with talent and energy. Negro Leaguers traveling through the state did the same, although they visited less frequently than their white counterparts. Black baseball pioneer Rube Foster, the founder of the Negro National League, the first organized black league, brought his powerhouse club, the Chicago American Giants, on barnstorming tours of California and the Northwest. Foster, the six-foot-four Texas-born son of an elder in the Methodist church, who called everyone "darlin'" whether they were a man or woman, insisted that his club ride in a private railroad car, the same way the white major leaguers traveled.

While in California, Foster and his players met with resistance and hostility from locals who would not let them stay in hotels or eat in restaurants frequented by whites. Some Pacific Coast Leaguers (although not all) refused to play against them, objecting to a mixing of the races. Blacks and whites were not equal, they believed, and should be kept separate in all areas of society, including, and especially, baseball.

Certainly this was the case in the Pacific Coast League when Jimmy Claxton was trying out in Oakland. Biographical details about Claxton are sketchy. He was born in British Columbia, Canada. He pitched semipro baseball in the Northwest before coming to Oakland, where he played on a local black team. This may have been how some fans recognized him and knew he was black, not an Indian as advertised.

For that Memorial Day doubleheader, a photographer from Zee-Nuts trading cards showed up to take pictures of the Oaks players. Zee-Nuts were a popular candy; inside each package was a picture card of a Coast League player. The photographer snapped Claxton's picture in his uniform, same as the other players. The left-hander appears to have just released the ball, at the end of his follow-through. The card, which was later issued by Zee-Nuts as part of this series, may have been the first time a black man appeared on a professional baseball card.

But this would have provided little consolation to Claxton, whose first day on the Oaks was also his last. The Oakland club had no intention to challenge organized baseball or the powerful dictates of the unwritten rule and they released him.

The Oaks finished last again that season. Jimmy Claxton showed up a few years later on the roster of the Shasta Limiteds, an all-black team of railroad workers from the north of the state. With Claxton as one of their pitchers, the Limiteds won the California state semipro championship.

There Was a
Crooked Man

SATURDAY, MARCH 22 — 2:15 P.M.
SUNDAY, MARCH 23 — 2:15 P.M.
— 1947 —

ABLISHED PRICE - $3.33
ERAL TAX - - - .67

Total $4.0

HIS PORTION OF TICKET NOT GOOD FOR ADMITTANCE
DETACH SEPERATE COUPONS FOR INDIVIDUAL GAMES

Spider Baum and Ralph Stroud were saying it, and that did not make it true, but what they were saying was shaking up people all around California and the Pacific Coast League. They said two fellows had tried to bribe them to throw a game.

One of the accused was Vernon pitcher Babe Borton, who denied everything while tossing out some charges of his own. Founded in the early 1900s, Vernon is a tiny industrial city south of Los Angeles. But except for a brief interruption, it hosted a Pacific Coast League team from 1910 until the early 1920s. According to baseball historian Bob Reis, Vernon was known for its nightlife and gambling. Hollywood celebrities liked to go there, and actor-comedian Fatty Arbuckle nearly bought a piece of the ballclub. In 1919, led by Borton, the Tigers won the Coast League championship. But it was during this season that he gave two thousand dollars to players on Salt Lake and other clubs to deliberately lose games to help Vernon win the pennant.

Coast League President William McCarthy, an attorney by trade, who had long fought against the corrupting influence of baseball betting by authorizing sweeps of ballparks to chase the gamblers out of the grandstands, immediately launched an investigation, after which the league banned or released a half-dozen individuals, including the Vernon pitcher. One of the people banned by McCarthy was Hal Chase, the former Santa Clara College and Los Angeles Angels star who had just finished a noteworthy, albeit controversial, fifteen-year career in the major leagues. Viewed by his peers as one of the most gifted players in the game, "Prince Hal," as people called him, had been involved in a string of questionable incidents. The buzz about him was that he was a gambler—worse still, a gambler who might lay a wager against his own team and then boot a ground ball at first base or make a poor throw at an inopportune moment to cost his club the game. While his team may have lost, Chase walked away a winner.

The National League had conducted an inquiry into his behavior but, citing a lack of hard evidence, exonerated him. (Critics later called this decision a whitewash to hide baseball's corrupt underside from the public.) In 1919 Chase played for the New York Giants, and once again suspicion trailed him like a bad odor. The Giants cut him loose at the end of the season, and the talk was that his gambling and throwing games were the reasons for his release.

By the spring of the following year Chase had settled into a new home in Los Angeles. While his major league career was over, he was still in demand as a player, particularly in the San Jose area, where he was born and raised and where his family's lumber business still thrived. He signed a contract with San Jose of the independent Mission League, agreeing to play for the team on Sundays, then returning home during the week to Los Angeles.

In August the Baum-Stroud charges hit the newspapers, fingering Chase as one of the two men who had tried to bribe them. As with other incidents in the past, he denied the accusations and claimed his innocence. But McCarthy did not believe him. "If reports are true," McCarthy said, while issuing a decree banning him from entering any Coast League ballpark, "Chase has done more

HAROLD CHASE

FIRST BASEMAN OF THE NEW YORK (A. L.) CLUB

SPORTING LIFE × PHILADELPHIA
"THE PAPER THAT MADE BASE BALL POPULAR"

*Sporting Life magazine advertisement featuring Hal Chase, circa 1917.
From the College Archives Collection of St. Mary's College of California, smcaii1561a*

to discredit baseball than any single individual." The Mission League president barred him as well.

Chase, who was hitting .442 at the time for San Jose, hired an attorney—a San Franciscan by the name of James P. Sex—and threatened to sue the Coast League president for defamation of character. "So Hal Chase is suing me for defamation of character," responded McCarthy. "I never knew he possessed such a thing."

In defiance of the Mission League ban, Chase, whose good looks and base-ball skills had made him popular on both coasts, appeared in uniform at a game in San Jose against Hollister. The crowd cheered when he trotted onto the field and, it is presumed, booed when the umpire, acting on league orders, told him to leave. San Jose remained adamant about keeping Chase around, which caused it to forfeit the game to Hollister.

Chase eventually dropped his lawsuit, and the ban against him held. But two months later he found himself in a much stickier situation. In October 1920 a Chicago grand jury issued indictments against thirteen people for their alleged involvement in a conspiracy to fix the previous year's World Series between the Cincinnati Reds and the Chicago White Sox. One of the unlucky thirteen was Chase.

Although the 1919 Series took place in two Eastern cities, Californians followed the games through the magic of telegraph wires, which were first strung completely across the United States during the Civil War. Telegraph operators in the East relayed play-by-play accounts of the Series to the West. As these electronic messages came in, receiving operators around California posted the events of the game on a large board that contained a representation of a baseball diamond. Miniature figures on the board were then moved around the diamond according to what occurred in the game. Well before the advent of national radio broadcasts, fans gathered in large numbers in hotels, assembly halls, and sometimes on city streets (with the diamond board posted on the side of a building) to follow the game as it happened. It was, said fans, the next best thing to being there. The telegraph also relayed play-by-play accounts to news-papers, which published special editions to keep their readers up to date on the latest events in the game.

No doubt many of these fans placed wagers on the Series, which ended with a major upset: the Reds beating the heavily favored White Sox. But the games were not on the square. Gamblers had paid members of the White Sox to lose the Series. One year later the Cook County Grand Jury handed down indictments on the eight White Sox players and five gamblers who, it said, engi-neered the fix. Then in April 1921, Illinois authorities issued warrants across the country for the arrest of these men.

Detective Ray Starbird arrested Chase as he was walking out of a San Jose theater. Bail was set at three thousand dollars, which Edgar Chase, Hal's father, posted. His son denied involvement in the scandal: "If I thought they had any-thing on me and I thought there was a chance of going to jail, don't you think I'd be in Mexico now?"

One of the gamblers indicted, Abe Atell, did, in fact, go to Mexico or Latin America to escape arrest. Atell, a former San Franciscan, was an ex-featherweight boxing champion who liked to be referred to as "the Little Champ." After his sporting days ended the Little Champ had become a gambler and developed some nifty footwork around New York underworld circles. His boss, mobster Arnold Rothstein, bankrolled the fix and is widely considered to be the man most responsible for poisoning the Series.

Contemporary accounts of the fix usually identify former White Sox and Reds player Sleepy Bill Burns, who was also indicted by the grand jury, as a

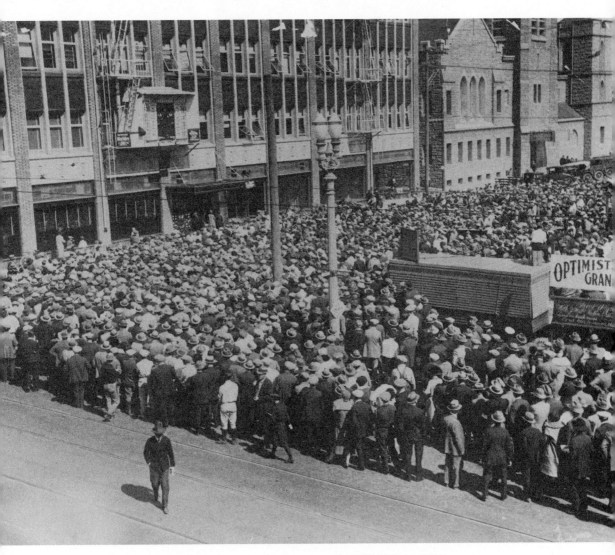

San Francisco fans gather on Market Street to watch the World Series, 1921.
California Historical Society, FN-40039

Chick Gandil. National Baseball Hall of Fame Library, Cooperstown, N.Y.

gambler. Like Chase, he too had California ties. After helping pitch the Los Angeles Angels to the 1907 Coast League pennant, the southpaw had faced the young Walter Johnson, then earning some off-season money as a member of the San Diego Pickwicks in a series in Los Angeles to decide the unofficial West Coast champion. The next year he and Johnson became teammates with the Senators in Washington.

But while Johnson ascended to greatness, Burns became a journeyman who bounced from team to team. While with Cincinnati he met Bobby Keefe, a pitcher with the Reds who was a former Santa Clara College teammate of Chase's. It has been speculated that Keefe introduced Chase to Burns, unwittingly bringing together two of the figures implicated in the scandal. Burns would later testify at the trial that was held about the conspiracy.

The day after Hal Chase was brought into custody in San Jose, Los Angeles law enforcement officials arrested Arnold "Chick" Gandil, the "ringleader" of the White Sox players, as he is so often described in accounts of the scandal. Born in Minnesota, Gandil ran away from home as a teenager, wandering west to California. A rangy first baseman with power and size—baseball historian John E. Spalding describes him as "a big, rough-hewn man, tall and muscular with deep, brooding eyes"—he played briefly in the Coast League for Fresno and Los Angeles. After that came more wanderings, through Texas and the Southwest, where, in addition to baseball, he found work as a club fighter and a copper miner. He later resurfaced in California, agreeing to a contract with Fresno of the California State League. But before he took the job, Sacramento of the rival Coast League offered him a more lucrative deal. His bolting for Sacramento caused bruised feelings in Fresno, which accused him of stealing a uniform and walking off with its advance money. Charges were filed, and Gandil was arrested. Sacramento had to pay restitution to Fresno and bail Gandil out of jail before he could play one inning for the team.

After a year in Sacramento, Gandil went up to the major leagues but retained his ties with his adopted state. In 1919, after the crooked World Series, he returned home in the off-season to Los Angeles, where he lived with his wife and daughter.

Rumors of a possible fix had circulated before, during, and after the games. The rumors had focused on Gandil and several of his teammates. Even as he publicly denied published reports about a fix, White Sox Owner Charles Comiskey hired private investigators to follow Gandil out to the West Coast, figuring that if he profited illegally from the Series, he might blow his cover by acting like a big shot and throwing money around.

Chick's finances had indeed taken a sharp turn for the better. Snooping around his bank records, the dicks found that he was perhaps thirty-five thousand dollars in the black, far more than a ballplayer with his salary could expect to have saved. He had bought a new house and a diamond ring for his wife. Investigators also saw him sporting around Los Angeles in a brand-new automobile.

The last game Gandil ever played in the major leagues was the final game of the 1919 Series, the one that clinched it for the Reds. The next season, he stayed in California, marking baseball time for a semipro club in Bakersfield. When they arrested him he was working for a Los Angeles lumber company.

San Francisco was the home of another member of the tainted White Sox, Charles August "Swede" Risberg. Risberg, a native of the city, learned his ball on North Beach playgrounds. Like Gandil and three others accused in the conspiracy—infielder Buck Weaver, pitcher Lefty Williams, and reserve Fred McMullin—he had once played for a California team in the Pacific Coast League.

His club was Vernon, and in one game in Oakland he had punched an umpire in a dispute over a call. "The Swede," said Shoeless Joe Jackson, his sweet-swinging White Sox teammate who was also named as a co-conspirator by the grand jury, "was a hard guy." After the 1919 season Risberg declared his unhappiness with baseball—all the White Sox involved in the scheme drew salaries miserably low compared to their peers around the league—and expressed his desire to open a restaurant in San Francisco. He did not follow through with this pledge, however, returning to Chicago for one more season before the grand jury indictments began the series of events that ultimately ended his big league career in disgrace.

It is beyond the scope of this book to examine in detail the Black Sox Scandal. But what is pertinent to this story is that Californians, and people with California dust on their shoes, left their tracks all over it. Although Hal Chase did not play in the Series, the grand jury wanted to speak to him because it felt that since he was a gambler with ties to Sleepy Burns and the Black Sox, he might have information pertinent to the case.

Chase never had to testify about his part in the scandal, however, because in late May a California judge ruled that the arrest warrant issued by the Illinois state attorney general's office was invalid. Therefore, Chase could not be extradited; he was a free man.

Chase himself said that he offered to go to Chicago for the trial as long as Illinois authorities paid him five hundred dollars in appearance money and travel expenses. When they turned him down, he said he figured they must not have wanted to hear his testimony all that much, so he stayed home. Others have suggested a more sinister explanation—

News clipping, 1919
Black Sox scandal.

WORLD SERIES 'SOLD,' DECLARES SPORTING KING

Startling Revelations Made by Billy Maharg; Says Chicago "Threw"

PHILADELPHIA, September 28.— The first, second and final games of last year's world's series were "thrown" to Cincinnati by eight members of the Chicago Americans, according to revelations said to have been made by Billy Maharg, former boxer and well known in local sporting circles.

Maharg's story, as printed today in the Philadelphia North American, says that he and "Bill" Burns, former American League pitcher, were the first to be approached in the conspiracy.

"I received a wire from Burns from New York the middle of last September, inviting me to take a hunting trip with him down on his ranch in New Mexico," said Maharg. "We were to take Bill James, one of the White Sox pitchers with us. James had nothing to do with the subsequent events, but while we were there in the room talking, Cicotte came in and started to talk in a low voice to Burns.

First Suspicion Aroused On First Game of Series

"I heard enough to know that he said that a group of prominent players of the White Sox would be willing to 'throw' the coming world's series if a syndicate of gamblers would give them $100,000 on the morning of the first game.

"When Cicotte left, Burns turned to me and repeated Cicotte's conversation, part of which I had heard. Burns said, 'Do you know any gamblers who would be interested in this proposition?'"

"I said I would go to Philadelphia and see what I could do. Burns said he would have to go to Montreal to close an oil deal and that he would wire me about the progress of the deal.

"I then went to Philadelphia and saw some gamblers there, they told me it was too big a proposition for them to handle, and they recommended me to Arnold Rothstein, a well-known and wealthy New York gambler.

that Arnold Rothstein did not want Chase testifying at the trial, so Rothstein's attorney arranged to keep him away from Chicago.

According to Eliot Asinof, the author of *Eight Men Out,* the definitive book on the scandal (a movie of the same name starred John Cusack), Chase knew about the scandal almost from its inception. Approached by Sleepy Burns and another gambler for advice, he recommended that they talk personally to Rothstein. Burns thanked him for the advice and asked Chase if he wanted anything out of the deal.

Nah, said Prince Hal. Just the chance to bet.

A former Giants teammate said that Chase won forty thousand dollars in wagers placed during the Series.

The accused members of the White Sox appeared in Chicago to face the charges against them. After a controversial trial, all were declared not guilty. Nevertheless, they were permanently banished from organized baseball, and not one of them ever played a big league game again.

In the years that followed, several of the Black Sox ended up in California. Fred McMullin, who only pinch-hit a couple of times in the Series and played only a bit part in the drama, worked in the United States Marshals Office in Los Angeles. Lefty Williams operated a nursery in Long Beach. Swede Risberg ran a bar in Red Bluff. Chick Gandil lived quietly in the Napa Valley, working as a plumber.

Hal Chase drifted from place to place around California and the Southwest, where his fame as a ballplayer could still earn him paychecks in outlaw leagues not affiliated with organized baseball. At various times he reportedly ran a chicken ranch and prospected for gold in the Sierra Nevada. In Colusa, suffering from health problems related to alcoholism, he stayed with friends. During World War II a company hired him to be a welder's assistant in the Alameda shipyards, but apparently he never reported for work, possibly due to his failing health.

Chase's reputation today is firmly established as a baseball crook and a cheater. But a 1940s-era poll of sportswriters, players, and others ranked him as the second-greatest first baseman of all time, behind only Lou Gehrig. To his deathbed he denied any involvement in the Black Sox infamy.

The Pride of
Their Community

SATURDAY, MARCH 22 — 2:15 P.M.
SUNDAY, MARCH 23 — 2:15 P.M.
— 1947 —

Total $4.00

ABLISHED PRICE - $3.33
DERAL TAX - - .67

HIS PORTION OF TICKET NOT GOOD FOR ADMITTANCE
DETACH SEPERATE COUPONS FOR INDIVIDUAL GAMES

Willie Kamm was about as scrawny as a ballplayer could be and still be called a ballplayer. Mom and Pop Kamm did not quite reach five feet tall. Their son eventually grew to be nearly a foot taller than they were, but it took him a long while to do it.

The Kamms lived in a San Francisco neighborhood close to a cemetery, which was where you could find little Willie a lot of the time, forever tossing a ball against the headstones. Throw a ball straight against a headstone and it bounced back on the ground, Willie moving swiftly to get his glove down and scoop it up. Toss it just in front of the stone and it rebounded up into the air, Willie snagging it on the fly. Someone walking by on the street may have seen a child playing by himself amidst the gloomy silence of the dead. But Willie's ears were filled with the roar of the crowd.

As Kamm grew older his ballgames became more communal. After finishing with his paper route in the afternoons he headed over to Golden Gate Park, where there were always games going on, always guys to play with. These guys were almost always bigger and stronger than him, but Willie had nonstop desire, which can overcome a lot of disadvantages, and pretty soon the old man of Golden Gate Park baseball, Spike Hennessy, took him under his wing.

Hennessy was a coach, surrogate father, guidance counselor, nurturer of young talent. He was, said Kamm, an "old gentleman…a rough and ready man, very poor, he just barely existed, but he devoted his whole life to kids." A later Hennessy pupil, Dom DiMaggio, who, like Kamm, succeeded in the major leagues, said, "Spike was a big man in a blue baseball cap and a heavy overcoat, and nobody knew exactly what he did for a living or even what he did." What he did was teach baseball.

Spike took a liking to Willie and worked with him. The kid could handle a glove, for certain. And his hitting? Well, it was coming along. Spike saw enough promise in the runty teenager to recommend him to the Coast League club in Sacramento, which quickly released him after a brief tryout.

But this was 1918, and being cut by a ballclub was not the worst thing that could happen to an eighteen-year-old kid, not even close. Germany, where Mom and Pop Kamm came from, was waging war against the French and English in the bloody trenches of Europe. After formally entering the war the year before, the United States had issued a "work or fight" order to all able-bodied draft-age men. Either join the military or work in a job that directly supported the war effort.

Local draft boards around the country, however, did not apply the order uniformly. Many major leaguers received exemptions and continued to play during the war while others did not. Some Coast Leaguers moved up to fill openings on big league rosters caused when players went into the service or war-related work. Other ballplayers worked in the shipyards to fulfill their obligation, which was what Kamm did. But on the weekends, when they did not need him on the job, he and others played in a shipyard baseball league.

The Pacific Coast League, citing a lack of fan interest, shut down during the summer of 1918, after playing only half of its scheduled games. The majors shortened their season too, holding the World Series in early September. With millions of Americans in uniform, and so many of them fighting and dying overseas, baseball did not seem so important.

After the war ended, in November of that year, Kamm returned to life as normal, which mainly consisted of baseball and more baseball. One day at a game at Old Rec, while playing for the semipro Union Iron Works, he captured the attention of another mentor of young baseball talent, Charlie Graham.

Graham, who came to be known as "Uncle Charlie" for his kindly, avuncular ways, had once coached both Hal Chase and Harry Hooper, and he knew a ballplayer when he saw one. And Kamm was a ballplayer, albeit a scrawny one.

Seals owner Charlie Graham, circa 1920s. California Historical Society, FN-40018

"You're going to be our regular third baseman," Uncle Charlie, who managed the Seals and owned a piece of the team, told the youngster.

"Oh no," said Willie, who weighed one hundred and forty pounds soaking wet and was not exactly overflowing with self-confidence. "I'm not that good."

In the beginning Kamm was right: he really wasn't that good. His batting average was higher than his weight, but not by much, and the balls hit at him when he was stationed at third base flew a lot faster than the ones he used to bounce against headstones. He made errors by the bushel and his self-esteem shrunk to practically non-existent. But Uncle Charlie stood by him and kept him in the Seals' starting lineup.

Still, it was sometimes painful to watch. Mom and Pop Kamm did not know a thing about baseball, but they came out to support their son. In one of her first games at Old Rec, Mom sat in the grandstands, watching the mysterious events unfold on the field and listening to the comments of the men seated around her, some of which were directed at Willie and not complimentary in nature. She was appalled. "I don't think you should go to that place anymore," she told her son at home that evening. "The people there, they talk very peculiar."

Willie's play gradually improved, though, and Mom and Pop became Old Rec regulars. Her nickname was "the Babe"; his was "the Kid." While the Babe was an unconquerable enthusiast, cheering for her son on every play, whether good or bad, the Kid's approach—Kamm described him as "an old-fashioned German father"—was more world-weary. After a big hit Mom would yell, "Willie got a triple! Willie got a triple!" To which her husband would gloomily reply, "Ach, the guy should've caught it."

Willie kept growing, and after he had his tonsils removed as a teenager, he started to put on weight. His errors became a thing of the past and he turned into the good glove man Uncle Charlie and Spike Hennessy always knew he would be. His hitting was still a work in progress, but he listened to his coaches and played winter ball, and each successive season with the Seals his batting average ticked higher. "The once despised weakling," as one sportswriter put it, "is tearing the cover off the ball."

Then in June 1922 Kamm was walking down Market Street when his life changed. Imagine this: your life changing, in a single moment, and the one who tells you about it is a boy hawking newspapers.

"Willie Kamm!" the boy shouted. "Willie Kamm!" But that was not all the boy was saying as held up the papers he was trying to sell. He was talking about a major league team, the Chicago White Sox, and he was talking about money too. Big money, more money than the twenty-two-year-old Kamm could imagine: one hundred thousand bucks! But wait, there was more he was saying. The boy was connecting all those things into one continuous sentence and yelling it again and again at the corner of Market and Powell: "Willie Kamm...sold to the Chicago White Sox...for one hundred thousand dollars."

Willie Kamm, little Willie Kamm, could not believe his ears. He walked over to buy one of the papers the boy was peddling. Maybe if he saw it in print with his own eyes it would make sense. But then the newsie recognized him. "Hey, it's Willie Kamm. It's Willie Kamm!"

Willie really did not know what to do then. The idea of first, a newsie shouting his name on the street and second, being sold for a record amount of dough to a major league club—well, it was only reasonable that he would start running as fast as he could to get away from the boy.

But when Willie looked behind him he saw not only that one newsie, but a whole *pack* of newsies running after him. Other boys had heard the first one hollering and they trotted over to see for themselves what a one-hundred-thousand-dollar ballplayer looked like. When Willie started running, they all took off after him.

Willie was too fast, though, and ditched them by ducking into a movie theater. This gave him the chance to catch his breath and absorb the news. As startling as it was, as crazy as it seemed, it was true: the Chicago White Sox had purchased his services from the Seals, and he was going to the major leagues. The next spring he reported for his rookie season in what would turn out to be a distinguished thirteen-year big league career. With the White Sox and later the Cleveland Indians, Kamm became one of the top fielding third basemen of his era while delivering clutch hits and knocking in runs.

When Kamm played for the Seals, his best friend on the team was Jimmy O'Connell, a solid-hitting outfielder from Sacramento. O'Connell was an

Willie Kamm, circa 1919. California Historical Society, FN-40014

open, bright-faced, smiling kid. You can see why he and Kamm got along so well—Jimmy outgoing and good with people, Willie quiet and held back, the two personalities complementing each other. Their destinies as ballplayers were intertwined as well. The White Sox paid a bundle for Kamm at the same time the New York Giants acquired O'Connell's services. The two pals reached the majors in the same year.

The challenge facing O'Connell, however, was far more daunting. The White Sox were a second-tier club in need of help, but the Giants under John McGraw were as good as it gets, winners of two World Series in a row and the smart bettor's choice to make it three. The left-handed-hitting O'Connell could not crack their formidable lineup and in his rookie season watched the Giants lose to the Yankees in the Series mainly from a seat in the dugout.

The next season Jimmy's world fell on top of him. In September he approached Phillies infielder Heinie Sand, a San Franciscan and a former Coast Leaguer, offering him five hundred dollars to throw a game. Sand told him to shove off, but the story reached the office of the newly appointed Commissioner of Baseball, Kenesaw Mountain Landis, whose main job after the Black Sox Scandal was to rid baseball of gambling and crooked players. He kicked O'Connell out of organized baseball. For life.

Jimmy tried to explain that it was all a misunderstanding—that he was only doing what his coach, Cozy Dolan, told him to do. (Landis banned Dolan too.) Because the order came from the coach, O'Connell did not think there was anything wrong with it. (Another version of events has some older teammates on the Giants playing a practical joke on O'Connell, urging him to talk to Sand. Young and gullible and wanting to get along with the vets, Jimmy took them seriously and committed his blunder.)

Back in the Bay Area, people expressed shock at the news and complained about the hard justice delivered by the commissioner. Alfie Putnam, the Seals co-owner who signed O'Connell to his first contract, told the papers he did not think the boy was capable of cheating. A former manager described the twenty-three-year-old as "a swell kid…a conscientious ballplayer admired by every one of his teammates." A comment by American League president Ban Johnson particularly galled local sensibilities. Perhaps in a veiled reference to Hal Chase, Chick Gandil, and others involved in the Black Sox conspiracy, Johnson accused Californians and Westerners of being more prone to gambling and throwing games than players from other parts of the country.

A sorrowful Jimmy O'Connell told reporters, "I know now that I did wrong. But I didn't think it was wrong when I did it." The incident ended his major league career, but he later played outlaw baseball in the Southwest with Chase, Gandil, and other Black Sox refugees.

Although Jimmy O'Connell's major league dreams turned into a nightmare, his problems did not stop other young men from dreaming similar dreams. One of these dreamers was a nineteen-year-old Oklahoma outfielder named Paul Waner.

Waner was spotted and signed to his first professional baseball contract by former Seals manager-turned-scout Nick Williams, who happened to stumble onto him while on a trip to Oklahoma. Waner was, in his own words, "just an ol' country boy" when he reported to Seals spring training camp on his first trip to California in 1923.

He was, Waner admitted, still a little rough around the edges. When his train arrived in Oakland he had no idea that the next thing he had to do was take the ferry to San Francisco. The ticket, after all, only mentioned the train trip to Oakland, nothing about a ferry. After getting that straightened out he boarded the ferry for the ride across the wide waters of San Francisco Bay. There were no bridges on the bay then, and Waner had never seen in person a boat as big as the ferry.

That season Jimmy O'Connell and Willie Kamm were working out at Seals camp before reporting for their rookie year in the bigs. Waner first thought they were green minor leaguers like him. When he found out the truth he was amazed. Major leaguers! To a youngster from Oklahoma they were as impressive a sight as San Francisco Bay.

When the two rookie major leaguers took batting practice, the rookie minor leaguer happily shagged balls in the outfield for them. Waner did this for about a week, shagging balls for other players too, but not once did anyone on the Seals give him a chance to hit. This was how it went for rookies in those days. The veterans mostly shunned the younger players until they proved themselves to the rest of the team. Waner finally got a chance to prove himself when someone let him take some swings in the batting cage.

A carpenter was working on the roof of a house beyond the right field fence at Old Rec. One of the first balls off Waner's bat—he swung from the left side—cleared the fence and landed on the roof, nearly hitting the carpenter on the head. When a second ball almost hit him again, the carpenter set down his hammer, took a seat on the roof, and like Waner's new teammates on the Seals, watched as the kid from Oklahoma put on a hitting show.

It still took a little while but Waner did eventually earn the respect of his teammates—and pitchers all around the Coast League. The 1925 pennant-winning Seals, featuring the hard-hitting Waner and other stars, is regarded as one of the best teams in league history. The next year he joined the Pittsburgh Pirates to begin a twenty-year career that ended in the Hall of Fame. Waner's little brother Lloyd also broke into professional ball briefly with the Seals, becoming "Little Poison" to Paul's "Big Poison" in Pittsburgh, and earned a plaque with his name on it in Cooperstown too.

Paul Waner's rookie year in Pittsburgh was also the rookie year of another Hall of Famer, Joe Cronin, a native San Franciscan born in the year of the Great Earthquake who learned his baseball at Excelsior Playground in the city. "I all but lived on that playground," recalled Cronin in his later years. A gifted all-around athlete, he played all sports at Mission High and Sacred Heart High, Harry Heilmann's old school. (Sacred Heart is one of four high schools in the state with two former students in the Hall of Fame. The others are Frank Chance and Tom Seaver of Fresno High, Walter Johnson and Arky Vaughan of Fullerton Union High, and Eddie Murray and Ozzie Smith of Locke High.)

After Sacred Heart, Cronin turned down a college baseball scholarship to take the fast track to the major leagues, reaching the Pirates before his twentieth birthday.

But his career stalled over the next few years. He slumped in Pittsburgh and moved over to Washington, D.C., where, after another bad year, he entertained thoughts of quitting. But he built his body up in the off-season and turned himself into a shortstop with real home run pop in his bat. Then, after rising to stardom as a youthful player-manager of the Senators, he went to the Boston Red Sox, where he attained the status of icon, among many other achievements managing Ted Williams in Ted's early years with the team. He later became a general manager and American League president.

Willie Kamm, Jimmy O'Connell, Paul Waner, Joe Cronin—these are only four of the many gifted ballplayers who passed through San Francisco in its golden baseball years of the 1920s and 1930s. Some of these players, like O'Connell and Waner, came from outside the city. But a whole bunch of them were like Kamm and Cronin: neighborhood guys who were born and raised in San Francisco. And a high percentage of these neighborhood guys were the sons of immigrants. Truly, this was a New World, for a man could make money and become famous playing a child's game.

George Kelly, the son of a San Francisco policeman, was a lanky power-hitting first baseman for the New York Giants who made the Hall of Fame. His teammate on the Giants, Oakland-born Emil Meusel, was as German as wiener-schnitzel but answered to the name of "Irish." Irish's San Jose–born brother Bob Meusel pounded out home runs and extra base hits as a member of the New York Yankees' famed Murderers' Row. Two of Bob's teammates on that club were San Franciscans—Mark Koenig, a high-strung shortstop who unwound off the field by playing classical piano, and Tony Lazzeri, a slugging second baseman who launched his first moon shots at Jackson Playground on Portrero Hill. When Lazzeri, who is also in the Hall of Fame, played for the Yankees, his skills and Italian heritage brought new Italian fans out to the Bronx.

Another Italian from San Francisco, Frankie Crosetti, was born in the city, but its cool, damp climate did not agree with him. He was sickly as a child, and his parents moved to Los Gatos, near San Jose, to help restore his health. Working on his family's vegetable farm, the boy flourished in the warm summers of the South Bay. At fifteen Frankie returned to San Francisco and enrolled at Lowell High. But his attention to bookish matters easily strayed, and most days if you wanted to find him you looked not in a classroom but on a ballfield.

After developing his game for the hometown Seals, Crosetti moved up to the Yankees, playing shortstop to Lazzeri's second base and forming an all–San Francisco double-play combination. As a player and later as a coach, Crosetti became a walking monument to the Yankee dynasty, participating in seventeen world championships. His off-season home was Stockton, California, where, in keeping with his personality, he led a reserved and quiet life until his death in 2002.

In 1928, when the young Crosetti was breaking into pro ball, although the talent was clearly there, the Seals decided that he was not quite ready to be a full-time regular. So they decided to platoon him at third base with Babe Pinelli, a veteran of the minor and major leagues and a fellow Italian who, it was felt, could show the younger man a few things and give him the benefit of his years.

Pinelli was a survivor. After his father was killed in the '06 Quake, the ten-year-old quit school to sell papers on the street and work other odd jobs to support the family. When he got older he made money as a prize fighter, boxing in clubs around the city, but his future wife, Mabel McKee, pushed him to get out of the fight racket and chase his dream, which was baseball. And so he did: working his way up from the semipro North Beach Outlaws through the Coast League and onto the Chicago White Sox as a late-season fill-in. Quick to anger, Pinelli struggled with his temper as much as his hitting, and he yo-yoed between the minors and majors before finding a home on the Cincinnati Reds, where he anchored third base for several seasons.

Left: Tony Lazzeri, circa 1925. California Historical Society, FN-40040
Middle: Ping Bodie, left, and Babe Pinelli, right, at Ping Bodie Day, Recreation Park,
San Francisco, 1929. California Historical Society, FN-40015
Right: Frankie Crosetti, 1929. California Historical Society, FN-40017

The year Pinelli joined the Seals to help groom Frankie Crosetti, his big league days were done. But like many another ex–major leaguer before and after him, the Coast League gave him a chance to keep earning paychecks in professional baseball and stretch out his playing career a few years more.

This was what Francesco Stephano Pezzolo—Ping Bodie—had done after the major leagues said they did not want him anymore. He came back to the hitter-friendly environs of the Coast League and found employment, stringing out his career for another half-dozen years until, at age forty-one, figuring perhaps that he had cheated time long enough, he announced his retirement from the game.

In recognition of this, Old Rec sponsored "Ping Bodie Day" during his farewell season in San Francisco. Although it was Ping's day, the ceremonies honored both him and Pinelli. It seemed all of North Beach turned out to shower them with gifts, including garlands of peppers that were draped around each ballplayer's neck. People from the old neighborhoods and around the city had followed their success in the national game and identified with them. Though they were only ballplayers, and flawed ones at that, at their best they seemed to embody the finest qualities in all those who watched them from the grandstands. Their losses were everyone's losses and their victories, which thankfully outnumbered the losses, were shared by everyone too. They were the pride of their community.

MOVIE LAND
WELCOMES
my Babe

Babe Ruth in California

SATURDAY, MARCH 22 — 2:15 P.M.
SUNDAY, MARCH 23 — 2:15 P.M.
— 1947 —

Total $4.00

ESTABLISHED PRICE - $3.33
FEDERAL TAX - - .67

THIS PORTION OF TICKET NOT GOOD FOR ADMITTANCE
DETACH SEPERATE COUPONS FOR INDIVIDUAL GAMES

It was an island paradise, a land of green mountains and extreme beauty off the coast of Los Angeles. Juan Rodríguez Cabrillo, the first European ship captain to lay eyes on it, sailed there in 1542. Another Spanish explorer, Sebastían Vizcaíno, named the island, in his native tongue, after Saint Catherine. With California's entry into the Union, Santa Catalina and the three other islands of the Catalina chain became an American possession. A succession of businessmen developed it into a tourist resort, improving the harbor, building a hotel and other amenities, and promoting it as a haven for deep-sea fishing. Then, in the aftermath of the Great War, William Wrigley Jr. bought the island—harbor, hotel, mountains, and all—reportedly without ever having set foot on it.

Wrigley, the owner of the chewing gum company of the same name, was one of the wealthiest and most successful businessmen in the country. Ebullient and personable, a natural salesman, he was also a baseball man, the owner of the Chicago Cubs. A couple of years after his purchase of Catalina, Wrigley added to his baseball holdings (and his holdings in southern California) by paying $150,000 for the Los Angeles Angels. This was a sizable sum in those days for a minor league club, but Wrigley and his camera-shy son Phillip, whose influence in his father's business rose as he grew older, had big plans—and the Coast League club fit right into them. They could see, and Angel fans could see it too, a baseball pipeline being established between Los Angeles and Chicago, with players shuttling back and forth between the two clubs, depending on the needs of each at any given time.

After gaining control of the Angels, William Wrigley made another move that strengthened the connection between the two cities and fostered his business interests. The Cubs switched their spring training site from Pasadena, where they had been for several seasons, to the tiny, picturesque town of Avalon on Catalina Island. The presence of the Cubs brought attention to the island, promoting it particularly in the Midwest as a place for tourists to come. Midwesterners of an earlier era had already transformed Los Angeles from a sleepy village into a thriving city, and it was still a popular place for them to visit and live.

The Wrigleys made an even larger commitment to the growing southern California market with the construction of a new home for the Angels at Forty-second Place and Avalon Boulevard in Los Angeles. Built at a cost of $1.3 million, Wrigley Field was made not of wood, but steel and concrete. Nearly all minor league parks built in this era consisted of only a single deck of seats; Wrigley Field featured a curving double-decked grandstand. The clock tower in the front of the park became a neighborhood landmark as soon as it went up.

When it opened in 1925, Wrigley Field in Los Angeles was the only Wrigley Field in America; Cubs Park in Chicago had not yet changed its name. As usually happens, the bell tolling for the opening of a new park also sounds the demise of an older one. In this case the one to go was Washington Park, which hosted its last Coast League game in late September 1925. Two days later more than eighteen thousand people attended Wrigley's premiere, a match between the Angels of Los Angeles and the Seals of San Francisco. The Angels won the slugfest, 10 to 8.

Almost immediately, both fans and players noticed something unusual about the field. In most ballparks, center field and the power alleys in left- and right-center are the hardest places to hit home runs because they are farthest from home plate. At tiny Wrigley Field, however, the fence for the power alleys stood only 345 feet away from the batter's box, about the same distance as directly down the lines. Not only that, the fence slanted toward the playing field, not away from it as is the norm. The owner of the island paradise of Santa Catalina had created a hitter's paradise.

Although dwarfed by the major league stadiums of the East, Wrigley Field represented a city on the move, a city on its way up. Los Angeles had already surpassed its rival to the north, San Francisco, in population, and the trains kept bringing in newcomers daily. Everybody seemed to be from somewhere else, and all of them appeared to be tootling down the road in a Model T Tin Lizzy.

Wrigley Field postcard, 1928. California Historical Society, FN-40050

A *New Republic* correspondent described Los Angeles as "a completely motorized civilization….Nowhere else in the world have human beings so thoroughly adapted themselves to the automobile." In the earliest photographs of Wrigley Field one can see lines of cars parked in lots along the left field grandstands and beyond the bleachers in right.

The year after Wrigley Field opened, the Vernon club relocated to San Francisco, but its spot was soon filled when the Salt Lake City franchise abandoned Utah for the more glamorous climes of southern California. Calling itself the Hollywood Stars, this new club in town played its home games at Wrigley Field too, establishing an instant rivalry with its co-inhabitant, the Angels.

Not only a symbol of a rising Los Angeles, Wrigley Field put a new face on the entire Coast League, which had expanded to eight teams, with six of them based in California. With so many teams in the state, local and regional rivalries flourished—Los Angeles Angels vs. Hollywood Stars, San Francisco Seals vs. San Francisco Missions (formerly Vernon), Oakland Oaks vs. anybody from San Francisco, and the Bay Area vs. southern California. Sacramento, a Coast League charter city that had slipped in and out of the league in its early years, jumped back in before the glory ride that was the 1920s. The Senators loved to beat the stuffing out of teams from the Bay Area.

This era also saw the appearance, in increasing numbers, of a new breed of baseball fan. With the passage of the Nineteenth Amendment women had gained the right to vote, the same as men. Younger women were stepping outside the traditional female roles of mother and homemaker and taking jobs, earning money, living independent lives. These burgeoning feelings of independence and

Oaks outfielder Buzz Arlett accepting the gift of a car from fans during "Buzz Arlett Day," Oaks Park, Oakland, 1927. California Historical Society, FN-40006.

Buzz Arlett's baseball card. Doug McWilliams Collection

equality found expression, among other places in society, at the ballpark. "It wasn't a feminist matter," writes journalist and historian Richard Ben Cramer. "There was no parallel interest in a women's league, or girls teams at school. In fact, the ballpark was alluring, especially, as a male place—as smart and stylish for a girl-about-town as smoking (over highballs!) at a table near the dance floor." (The previous amendment to the Constitution, the National Prohibition Act, outlawed drinking alcohol at the ballpark or anywhere else, but both sexes evaded this ban by sipping bootleg gin in soda cups.)

For years the Chicago Cubs had offered reduced ticket prices to their female customers. The Wrigleys adopted this policy in Los Angeles too and are credited with helping to popularize the game for a generation of southern California girls and women.

What all these fans saw, both male and female, was a crazy, wonderful, gorgeous spectacle—not up to major league quality perhaps, but vastly entertaining. The Coast League was not primarily a pitcher's league; its marquee names were big boppers such as Smead Jolley and Ike Boone, who were forever launching cannon shots out of Wrigley and the other cozy hitters' parks up and down the Coast.

Buzz Arlett, the pride of Elmhurst, California, was another marquee slugger of this era. Brawny with curly hair, he was, said a sportswriter, "built on heroic lines, as handsome as most movie stars are supposed to be but aren't." The pitcher-turned-outfielder never made much noise in the major leagues, but they loved him in Oakland, where he starred for the Oaks. During its championship 1927 season Oakland held a day in his honor, presenting him with a new car at a ceremony at Oaks Park. To show his gratitude Buzz took the mound for the first and only time that season, pitching a complete game victory.

A teammate of Arlett's on that '27 Oaks club was a twenty-six-year-old second baseman named Jimmie Reese. He was no big thumper, rather he earned admiration for his smooth, stylish glove work. In the years to come Reese would become one of the most enduring figures in California baseball, a person with an uncanny knack for showing up at auspicious moments in the game's history.

A native of New York City, Reese came to Los Angeles as a child with his mother and sister. Born James Herman Soloman (or Solomon; spellings differ), sometime during grade school his last name became Reese, the name of a family friend. Everybody liked little Jimmie. How could you not? Always hustling, always willing to do for you, the kid had a permanent grin plastered on his face. A newsie who hawked papers on street corners in Los Angeles, he caught a break one day when his circulation boss assigned him to the Navy submarine base at San Pedro. The sailors played lots of baseball, which drew Jimmie to them, and after selling out his papers each day he would shag flies and chase balls for them. Before long he was living on his own at the base, going to school at San Pedro High, working in his spare time and sending money home to Mom. Every other waking minute was spent playing ball.

Nobody figured Jimmie would ever do much of anything in the game. Not big enough—can't hit—can't throw. A sweet kid, but a ballplayer? Come on. But he kept his head up and his ears open and absorbed baseball the way a sponge absorbs water. On Sundays he worked as a batboy for the Angels, for which he received a dollar and a baseball in payment. All this time he kept playing and playing, and growing a little, and pretty soon people began to notice that while he did not have much of a throwing arm, his glove found every ground ball that came near it.

Reese tried out for the Seals, got cut, then went up to Eureka and took his frustration out on the pitchers there. The Oaks liked what they saw and brought him down to Oakland to play alongside their whiz-kid shortstop, Lyn Lary. The spinning and leaping double-play combination of Lary and Reese helped the Oaks win the '27 pennant and attracted the notice of the New York Yankees, which paid $150,000 in a package deal for both players. The former batboy and his infield mate were ticketed for the big time.

Unfortunately for Reese, his big league career went nowhere. The Yankees already had an All-Star second baseman in Tony Lazzeri and a bulldozer was not going to move him out of the lineup, so Reese had no future with them. After a brief appearance in pinstripes he went to the Cardinals, who also soon told him to pack his bag. (Lary met with somewhat better success in New York, earning the starting shortstop's job before being replaced. He played for an assortment of teams over a twelve-year major league career.)

After being let go by St. Louis, Reese was through as a major league player but not through with baseball. Here begins a long period of him popping up at pivotal points: as a starter on the 1934 Los Angeles Angels, considered one of the finest teams in minor league history; a few years later, with the San Diego Padres, which featured a young outfielder by the name of Ted Williams; then, a world war and a decade after that, this time as a coach, also with the Padres, the first integrated team in Pacific Coast League history.

In his years as a player and coach, Reese developed a skill with a fungo bat that few have ever matched. According to baseball historian Doug McWilliams, Reese did not use the customary thin-handled, thick-barreled fungo bat used by most. Instead he cut off one side of a regular bat, which left him with a flat half-sided bat. He then wrapped medical adhesive tape found in the trainer's room around the barrel. Reese's control with this self-created fungo was uncanny. During outfield practice, fielders stood perhaps two-hundred feet away from him. But they only had to move a step or two to catch the flies hit by Reese, who could even *pitch* batting practice with a fungo, delivering ball after ball with speed and control. One bullpen catcher for the Padres warmed up Reese, who was pitching with a fungo: "All strikes and over the plate," said the catcher in awe. "It was unbelievable."

In 1972 Reese fulfilled a lifelong dream to become a major league coach when he joined the Anaheim Angels, where he remained for two more decades. At the 1992 All-Star game in San Diego, the American League named him an honorary captain. He died two years later.

Jimmie Reese, left, and Lyn Lary. California Historical Society, FN-40007

But back in 1927, Jimmie Reese was still a novice in the professional game, an unknown second baseman for the Oakland Oaks who was thrilled, absolutely thrilled, to appear at an exhibition game that October at Oaks Ball Park in Emeryville. Everybody, in fact, was thrilled to be there, not just Jimmie—men, women, children, other ballplayers, *everybody*. Even people who did not classify themselves as baseball fans had stirred themselves to get out to the park that morning in order to see the one and only Babe Ruth.

George Herman Ruth frequently visited California in the off-season. The most famous player transaction in the history of baseball occurred when the New York Yankees purchased his services from the Boston Red Sox, changing the destinies of those two franchises as well as the game itself. Ruth in fact first learned he had become a Yankee while vacationing in California.

His western trips were a mix of pleasure and business. Like other prominent major leaguers, he found he could earn money by making off-season public appearances. In 1924, on a tour of the state, he traveled up to Weed, in the shadows of Mount Shasta, where he broke his bat in a game. He also appeared in San Francisco to raise money for the city's Christmas Cheer Fund.

During this same trip he went to Stockton's Oak Park, where a photographer snapped him in a pose with a local dignitary and two boys. This was Ruth at the height of his powers—late twenties, athletic and fit, enormously successful and popular. Clad in the uniform of his employer, the New York Yankees, he stood with his arms around the boys while the dignitary and the people in the grandstands looked on in admiration.

In so many photographs from this time, when he appears with other people, Ruth can be seen touching the other person or persons in the picture, shaking hands or resting his hand on a shoulder in a gesture of warmth. This was, by all accounts, the way he was: a man who loved people, who loved being with them. People responded by showering him with the sort of acclaim reserved for a benevolent king.

His great fame, his charismatic personality, his unparalleled achievements in baseball, his ticket-selling powers—all of this made him catnip to the cats in

Babe Ruth with Hollywood starlets, 1927. Security Pacific Collection/Los Angeles Public Library

Hollywood. With his round, doughy face and hammy personality, he was a showbiz natural, happy to pose with starlets in goofy promotional photographs cooked up by the publicity departments of the studios. The Babe was game for everything; this was another part of his personality people loved.

Ruth played the lead in a 1927 star vehicle called *The Babe Comes Home*, his first movie made in Hollywood, produced by First National Pictures. His character, named Babe Dugan, loves to chew tobacco and horse around with the fellas, but the pretty young maid who cleans his tobacco-stained uniform resolves to change his ways and make him a better man. Although she succeeds and the pair falls in love, the fortunes of Babe Dugan and his team turn sour. Realizing her error, the girl urges him to go back to his dirty old habit of chewing and spitting. Thus revived, he smacks a home run to win the big game for his team.

The Babe Dugan character was loosely based on Ruth himself, a man of large appetites in all areas of life. So, too, were the lead characters in two other baseball movies, also released in 1927: MGM's *Slide, Kelly, Slide,* featuring Mike

Babe Ruth in Hollywood, circa 1927. Security Pacific Collection/Los Angeles Public Library

Donlin in a supporting role with Bob Meusel, Irish Meusel, and Tony Lazzeri appearing as themselves, and a remake of *Casey at the Bat* starring comedian Wallace Beery. In both movies the lead character borrows heavily from the Ruth persona. Beery's slapstick Casey, for instance, is a bit of a lush who, in one scene, advances to the plate carrying a sudsy pitcher of beer. He is also fond of the ladies and is a big overgrown child, much as Ruth was perceived to be.

Ruth was the best and most famous player in baseball. The second-best, and one of the most famous, was his self-effacing Yankee teammate, Lou Gehrig. At the end of the '27 season—a season in which Ruth hit sixty home runs, Gehrig pounded the ball with equal intensity, and the Yankees swept the Pirates in the World Series—the two of them went on a cross-country tour of America, playing in front of an estimated 250,000 people in eighteen states. Baseball fans in the West had read about them in the papers and seen pictures of them in newsreels in theaters, but for most, this was their first chance to glimpse them in action.

Mayor James Rolph personally greeted the pair when they arrived in San Francisco on the first stop of the California leg of the tour. "The eminent home run specialists," as the *Chronicle* called them, attracted over thirteen thousand people for their appearance at Old Rec.

Next they went to Sodality Park in San Jose and as was true wherever they played, the event was a community celebration. Ruth played on a team called the Bustin' Babes; they wore dark uniforms with white knee-high stockings. Gehrig's team, the Larrupin' Lous, wore white uniforms with dark socks. California major leaguers home for the off-season, local Coast Leaguers, and semipros fulfilled personal fantasies by playing with the great Yankee stars.

On Sunday morning the tour made its stop at Oaks Park in Emeryville, attracting another big crowd despite the early hour. The Larrupin' Lous featured Jimmie Reese and Babe Pinelli; San Francisco favorites Lefty O'Doul and Smead Jolley performed for the Bustin' Babes. The Elks Lodge band woke everybody up, the St. Mary's College Midget baseball team showed up in their uniforms, and the Knights of Columbus presented floral bouquets to the men of the hour. When Ruth or Gehrig hit a ball into the outfield, boys jumped the fence and ran onto the field to grab the souvenir. The outfielders gracefully stepped back to let them have it. The game ended before the regulation nine innings with the fans spilling out of the grandstands onto the field, eager to shake hands with Babe and Lou, or perhaps just to stand near them, to make sure they were real.

Departing the Bay Area, the caravan stopped at Sacramento's Moreing Field before moving on to Fresno on a Saturday morning. Again, as in Oakland, the early hour did not stop people from coming out; thousands showed up to meet Ruth and Gehrig at the train station. Inside their car Babe gave a quarter to a newsboy to get him to go out the door first. The newsboy agreed, and when the door opened, the crowd burst into cheers, thinking it was the Great One. Instead it was the boy, with Ruth having a big laugh inside.

From left, Johnny Nakagawa, Lou Gehrig, Kenichi Zenimura, Babe Ruth, Fred Yoshikawa, and Harvey Iwata, Fireman's Park, Fresno, 1927. Frank Kamiyama Collection. From Through a Diamond: 100 Years of Japanese American Baseball, *by Kerry Yo Nakagawa. NBRP (Nisei Baseball Research Project)*

The guests of honor traveled by motorcade to Fireman's Park, whose overflow crowd of five thousand people was the largest in the history of Fresno baseball. Local stars rounded out the roster for each team. Fresno-born outfielder Alex Metzler, fresh from a gangbusters season with the Chicago White Sox, was there. So were Coast Leaguers Moose Cano and Howard Craghead. But on this day, the Bustin' Babes and the Larrupin' Lous had a somewhat different look, for four of the players were of Japanese descent: sluggers Johnny Nakagawa and Harvey Iwata, catcher Fred Yoshikawa, and a man who occupies a central role in the story of Nisei baseball in America, Kenichi Zenimura.

Born in Hiroshima, Zenimura emigrated as a boy from Japan to Hawaii. There, he learned the American—and increasingly Japanese—game of baseball. But Kenichi was tiny (as a grown man he stood under five feet tall), and his parents, worried that he would be hurt by the bigger boys, ordered him not to play. But he sneaked off to games without their knowledge, hiding his glove and bat when he returned home so they would not find them. Later his parents discovered the truth about their son, as did the entire Islands when he led his high school to the Hawaii prep baseball championship.

Leaving Hawaii for the mainland, Kenichi arrived in Fresno when the first notes were being sounded for the Jazz Age. This was a time of gathering tension between whites and Japanese immigrants. Fearing that the newcomers were taking jobs away from them, the white majority passed laws stopping immigration to the United States from Japan and depriving those Japanese already in the country of basic rights. But Kenichi found work in a restaurant and as a mechanic and in his spare time pursued his passion of baseball, founding in the early twenties the Fresno Athletic Club, which comprised the best Nisei players in the area. Zenimura played shortstop and captained the team and, since the Nisei could not play in parks reserved for whites, he supervised the building of a ballfield near the Fresno city dump.

As every good baseball team must, the Fresno Athletic Club took on all comers, one year beating the Salt Lake City Bees, 6 to 4, behind the pitching of Al Sako. It claimed the Japanese American state championship three consecutive years in the early 1920s. During this time it met a touring team from another disenfranchised group in American society, the Philadelphia Royal Giants of the Negro Leagues, edging them 3 to 2 in Los Angeles.

In 1924 and again in 1927, the Fresnans traveled overseas to play teams in Japan. On its second trip the club included three white players: Charley Hendsch, Jud Simons, and Al Hunt, all collegians from Fresno State. This mixing was not unusual; the Nisei frequently played with and against whites. This integrated team ran up an undefeated record against Waseda University and other Japanese college teams. The Philadelphia Royal Giants were also touring Japan at this time and making hash of the local opposition. The two clubs staged a rematch at Meiji Jungu Stadium in Tokyo, and this time the Royal Giants prevailed, 9 to 2.

Fresh from their success in Japan, Zenimura and his three Fresno Athletic Club teammates received invitations to play in the big game at Fireman's Park. Their selection carried great significance in the local Japanese community: four of their own were taking the field with the two best white players in America. The Japanese did not treat it like an exhibition; they played hard, to show they belonged and deserved to be there. Zenimura collected a hit and a stolen base, Nakagawa a single, and Yoshikawa a run-producing double for the Larrupin' Lous, who won easily.

In the evening Ruth and Gehrig attended a banquet in their honor at the Hotel Fresno. The event, a fundraiser for Monsignor J. J. Crowley's local diocesan campaign, cost one dollar and fifty cents a plate.

The California tour included stops in Los Angeles and San Diego before the Yankees headed back East. The next season they led New York to another World Series triumph. Ruth also added another Hollywood credit to his resume, appearing as himself in the Harold Lloyd comedy *Speedy*.

An Experiment in Sound and Light

SATURDAY, MARCH 22 — 2:15 P.M.
SUNDAY, MARCH 23 — 2:15 P.M.
— 1947 —
ABLISHED PRICE - $3.33
ERAL TAX - - .67   Total $4.00

HIS PORTION OF TICKET NOT GOOD FOR ADMITTANCE
ETACH SEPERATE COUPONS FOR INDIVIDUAL GAMES

The five Moreing brothers were valley men, born and bred. Growing up on the family ranch on Waterloo Road outside Stockton, they worked and played ball, worked and played ball. After leaving the ranch four of the brothers took their interest in baseball into the professional ranks.

Cyrus and Will, the twins, were among the founders of the California State League, which, in the years before World War I, gave the city boys of the Pacific Coast League a run for their money. The Coast League, with a few exceptions (Sacramento being one), was just that—a baseball circuit for coastal cities. The Moreing twins intended their league to be for people like themselves, people who lived on farms or in the country and who wanted to wash up and watch a game after working the land all day. Will played outfield for Stockton, while Cy managed the club and developed a powerful say in league affairs.

Led by Cy Moreing, the California State League made money, attracted sizable crowds, and featured blue-chippers such as outfielder Harry Hooper. State League partisans argued that their brand of ball could match the Coast League, and the owner of the Stockton Millers backed up this claim with his own money, challenging Oakland to a winner-take-all series. The Valley versus the Bay Area, said Cy Moreing, and the winner walks with five thousand dollars. Citing restrictions imposed on it by the National Association, Oakland declined the offer.

The National Association, the governing body of the minor leagues, did not want one of its members playing against the State League, which did not belong to the association nor subscribe to its rules and was therefore an "outlaw" in organized baseball. Apparently, this did not much bother Cy Moreing, for he hired one of the biggest baseball outlaws of all, Hal Chase.

During the 1908 off-season, when Chase returned to California from New York, Cy paid him one thousand dollars to handle first base for the Millers, the four-time defending State League champs. Down in San Jose, Al Jarman, manager of the local Prune Pickers, objected strenuously to this move because Chase had played for his club the year before and rightly belonged there, in his opinion. "Thief" was one of the words Jarman used to describe the Stockton owner, who nevertheless prevailed in the dispute and retained Chase's services for the season.

The next year, with Chase as his chief gate attraction, Cy threatened to move his club to San Francisco, challenging the Coast League in one of its stronghold cities and thereby sticking a thumb in the nose of organized baseball. This, however, turned out to be a bluff, although Cy remained loyal to his renegade star. In 1920, after Chase's major league career ended, Moreing, who ultimately left baseball for the construction business and became a San Joaquin County assessor, offered him a job at the Sperry Flour Company for three hundred dollars a month. But Chase, a drifter at heart, turned it down to keep playing baseball in the semipro leagues.

About this same time, two other Moreing brothers, Lew and Charles, entered professional baseball, buying a piece of the Sacramento franchise of the Pacific Coast Legue, Cy's former rival. Although the Senators performed poorly on the field and annually lost thousands of dollars, the Moreings felt they could turn the team into a winner, and they soon enlarged their stake in the club to become sole owners.

Charles, the behind-the-scenes man, handled the books and the financial operations for the club, leaving the messy, attention-getting baseball side of the business to his brother.

Pictures of Lew always show him in a suit and tie, his craggy features hidden under a broad-brimmed hat. Like Charles, he was not the chatty type; he prided himself on being a doer, not a talker. Talking was only worthwhile if it led to action—a deal. After becoming the top man for the Senators, he approached his hometown with a proposal: the Senators would play in Stockton every Sunday as long as the city guaranteed him one thousand dollars per game. Stockton agreed, and a new city tradition—Sunday morning Coast League baseball—was born at Oak Park.

The biggest item on Lew's punch list was Sacramento's creaky fixer-upper of a ballpark, Buffalo Field. Built by onetime beer and baseball mogul Edward Kripp, the home field of the Senators needed an overhaul. The city had such a small population—the smallest fan base in the league—the club had to attract every possible warm body out to its games. It could not afford to have a ballpark that turned people off. Recognizing this, Lew sunk one hundred thousand dollars of his wheat ranch money into a complete facelift. The newly transformed and renamed Moreing Field may have been the first park in the Coast League with restrooms for women.

Moreing put some money into making Oak Park fan-friendly, too. People in Stockton and Sacramento responded to these improvements, and when the play on the field became more competitive, the Senators became a hot ticket across the delta. They won the second-half championship of the Coast League's 1928 split-season while running up club-record attendance numbers.

Lew Moreing, circa 1930. Courtesy of Kay Roper

Tony Freitas, Sacramento Senators, circa 1929. Courtesy of John E. Spalding

Being a small market owner with a slender wallet, and yet competing against the likes of William Wrigley with his deep pockets, Moreing had to be creative to succeed. He could not afford to pay big salaries to his players, so he consequently put his money into developing local prospects who attracted lots of ink in the papers but did not ask for, nor expect to receive, budget-busting salaries. Pitcher Tony Freitas of Mill Valley broke in with the Senators. When his career ended in the 1940s he had collected more wins than any other left-hander in minor league history. One of those talented Italians from San Francisco,

Dolph Camilli, got a second chance with Lew Moreing's club after being released by the Seals. When he moved up to the majors Camilli became an All-Star first baseman with the Brooklyn Dodgers. Moreing's best find was Stan Hack. A Sacramento native who worked as a bank clerk before suiting up for the Senators, he played sixteen years with the Chicago Cubs and ranks as one of the best third basemen of his era.

But after their success in 1928, the fortunes of the Senators disintegrated the next season. As their losses mounted on the field, tragedy struck off it. Charles Moreing, who had been a quiet, steadying influence on the team for nearly ten years, died at age fifty-two. Depressed perhaps by his brother's loss and alarmed by mounting financial losses due to a drop in attendance from the previous season, Lew announced that he was putting the Senators up for sale. If there were no takers, he said he would junk the team rather than operate it another year. Amid these rumors of an impending sale, possibly to a buyer in southern California, events of a far larger magnitude, emanating from the other side of the country, shook the world.

It started small and quickly turned gigantic. When the stocks of mighty industrial giants suddenly plummeted in value, Wall Street traders reacted in panic. Panic selling fueled more panic, and the value of these and other companies kept falling and falling, creating a financial meltdown across America. After Black Thursday came Black Tuesday and many dark days after that. In a matter of days and weeks people lost what they had taken a lifetime to build. The stock certificates they held, signifying a share of ownership in these once-formidable companies, were suddenly worth much less, and in many cases they were worth nothing at all. Lacking money or the ability to obtain credit, businesses both big and small went bankrupt. Tens of thousands of people, rising to hundreds of thousands and millions, lost their jobs. Those lucky enough to hang onto their jobs suffered pay cuts or involuntary reductions in their hours, pay cuts in another form.

An age of plenty swiftly became an age of not enough. Banks failed, and the people who had savings accounts in these banks lost every penny they owned. Seeing this, other Americans pulled cash out of their banks and hid it under their mattresses at home, inadvertently contributing to the failure of more banks. People scrimped to pay for the basics of food and rent, and they cut back wherever they could.

At the beginning of the Depression many in baseball considered their industry immune to the ups and downs of the economy. No matter what, people have to have fun, right? They need a break from the daily heartache, a means of escape. Six months after the stock market crash, baseball opened its 1930 season pretty much as usual. Then something occurred that changed how people viewed the game.

In early May, Des Moines hosted Wichita in a minor league game. A game of this type would have drawn little national interest were it not for the fact that it was being played at night, under fixed lights. Negro League barnstormers and others had used temporary lighting for years, rigging them for the game and then packing them up afterward. But this was different. These lights were not temporary and moveable; they were attached to poles anchored in the ground. For this reason the Des Moines game commanded national attention. Baseball Commissioner Kenesaw Mountain Landis came to see it in person, and NBC Radio broadcast it live to homes around the country.

Out in California, Lew Moreing may have listened to this broadcast, the first national broadcast of baseball over the mass medium of radio. The bid from that possible southern California buyer for the Senators had fallen through, and despite his qualms about operating a baseball franchise in Sacramento, he had saddled it up for another season. And now, here was a way to help both his club and himself.

He had been thinking about installing lights for some time. The cauldron of fire that was summer in Sacramento made day baseball an endurance contest for fans and players alike. But the evenings—ah, they were so warm and pleasant, it was a joy to be outdoors after dark. Night baseball and the Central Valley were a perfect match, Moreing felt, and certain to attract loyal fans as well as the merely curious, those excited by the novelty of it. He would welcome them all to his park, and happily so, because even if baseball had thus far escaped the country's economic miseries, selling tickets to games was clearly going to get much, much harder.

With night baseball (and night World Series games) long a staple of American sports life, it may be hard to fathom the criticism that Moreing's plan encountered. But many experts of the time, in California and elsewhere, thought baseball under the lights was a gimmick that would not fly.

Workmen erected four poles around Moreing Field, ten lights per pole. The total illumination consisted of 180,000 watts of electrical power, but was it enough to do the trick? Would the batter be able to see the ball in flight once it was released from the pitcher's hand, and would the fielders see it once the batter hit it? It was an experiment and, like all experiments, it needed to be tested first. With the regular Senators away on a road trip, some practice players helped conduct the experiment. The honor of turning night into day was given to Moreing, who flipped the switch at precisely 8:31 p.m., bathing the infield and the great green outfield in light.

The batter did indeed see the pitcher's first pitch, getting the fat part of the bat on it and driving it on a line into center. "The ball was visible from the time it left the pitcher's hand until it fell smack against the center fielder's glove," wrote *Sacramento Union* sports editor Steve George, who witnessed that first pitch and all the ones after it that evening. Lew Moreing's "$10,000 gamble," as George called it, was ready for its premiere.

The first night game in Pacific Coast League baseball occurred in early June 1930, five weeks after the showcase event in Des Moines. As in Iowa, the fixed nature of the lighting—as permanent as a thing could be in a world that rapidly seemed to be falling apart—made it different than what had come before and caused a flurry of excitement around the state. More than ten thousand people jammed Moreing Field, bidding up the price of a reserved seat

Lew Moreing, center, and his Sacramento Senators at Moreing Field, 1922. Courtesy of Kay Roper

from its normal one dollar and fifty cents to ten dollars for the evening. And there were plenty of takers. Sportswriters from the coastal cities, Pacific Coast League President Harry Williams, a former sportswriter himself, and a trainload of bigwigs all came to Sac Town to be eyewitnesses to history.

Adding to the evening's excitement was yet another new element: radio. The McClatchey family, publishers of the *Bee* newspaper chain in the valley, owned Sacramento's KFBK, which had been on the air a handful of years but not once broadcast a baseball game. The buzz surrounding the night game caused the station to try a little experiment of its own, and it broadcast the game and the festivities beforehand across a Pacific Coast network that included KHJ in Los Angeles, KFRC in San Francisco, and three Northwest stations. Broadcaster Ernie Smith hosted the coverage and *Bee* sports editor Rudy Hickey provided the color commentary.

The game—oh yes, the game. Sacramento's Ed Bryan pitched a five-hit 8 to 0 shutout over visiting Oakland. It was lights out for the Oaks and lights on for professional baseball in the state.

In the years to come, Lew Moreing would lose control of the Senators. Failed investments in other areas of his business caused the banks to foreclose on him, and he had to give up the team. Soon after losing the Senators he left

Sacramento for the Mojave Desert, where a fruitless mining scheme busted him. When he died he left his wife, who was known as "Mrs. Lew," alone and indigent. Sacramento baseball people held a charity game in her behalf, raising three thousand dollars to help support her.

Though things did not end well for Lew Moreing, his gamble on night baseball proved visionary. Over sixty thousand people packed Moreing Field for the first two series under the lights, and the Senators quickly became one of the league's attendance leaders. Wrigley Field in Los Angeles and Oaks Park in Oakland soon erected permanent lights of their own, and their ticket sales increased too. Five years before the major leagues played their first night game, baseball under the lights was so popular in Los Angeles that the Angels eliminated all their weekday games at Wrigley and made them week*night* games.

The lights came on in San Francisco in 1931 with the completion of the Seals' new baseball palace, Seals Stadium. Perched at the corner of Sixteenth and Bryant Streets in the city, the graceful steel and concrete stadium was the city's answer to Wrigley Field and in itself a $1 million statement of faith and permanence with the future seeming so uncertain. Its opening marked the end of the line for Old Rec as a Pacific Coast League park, and most fans agreed that a change was long overdue. The first game at Seals occurred in March; the next month, lights went up in the park.

Another new feature of the stadium was its public address system. The home plate umpire no longer needed to use a megaphone to yell out the starting lineups to fans in the grandstand. An announcer delivered the names of the players over amplified loudspeakers that could be heard by everyone in the park. Hard times had come to California and more were on the way, but people could now watch baseball games enriched by new technologies of sound and light.

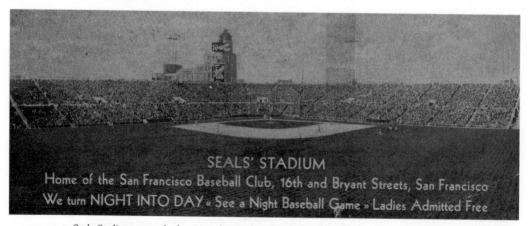

SEALS' STADIUM
Home of the San Francisco Baseball Club, 16th and Bryant Streets, San Francisco
We turn NIGHT INTO DAY « See a Night Baseball Game » Ladies Admitted Free

Seals Stadium postcard advertising the novelty of night baseball. California Historical Society

Barnstormers

SATURDAY, MARCH 22 — 2:15 P.M.
SUNDAY, MARCH 23 — 2:15 P.M.
— 1947 —

ABLISHED PRICE $3.33   Total $4.00
EDERAL TAX .67

HIS PORTION OF TICKET NOT GOOD FOR ADMITTANCE
CH SEPERATE COUPONS FOR INDIVIDUAL GAMES

From out of the East they came, riding on trains, buses, and automobiles. They were baseball stars in the tradition of the original Cincinnati Red Stockings, who rode the newly built transcontinental railroad across the plains and mountains to wow the locals with their diamond prowess and style. These men inspired similar curiosity, excitement, and awe among those Californians who came out to see them, for they were every bit as good, and sometimes better, than major leaguers. But they were different from the Red Stockings and all the other major leaguers who had passed through California over the years. They were different because they were black.

During the spring and summer, these men played professional baseball for Negro League teams primarily in the East and Midwest. But come fall and winter, when the weather turned cold in those areas of the country, they headed for sunnier climes.

Black players sometimes came to California with their teams, such as when Rube Foster brought his Chicago American Giants across the West, riding in a private railroad car. Other times they formed all-star touring teams. Hard-hitting catcher Biz Mackey and speedy outfielder Oscar Charleston led an all-black squad against the Sacramento Senators in the inaugural year of Moreing Field. Touring black professionals also played Nisei semipro and club teams. The Philadelphia Royal Giants met Kenichi Zenimura's Fresno Athletic Club in a game in Los Angeles, followed up the next year by a rematch in Tokyo.

Negro Leaguers frequently took to the road (even in summer), owing to how hard it was to make a buck at their trade—a task made harder by the prejudice they faced as black men and the accompanying legal and other restrictions imposed on them by white society. They sometimes played two, three games in a day, traveled all night on a bus over rough backcountry roads, then woke up to play again the next day in a strange new town. They needed to keep on the move because they had to go where their customers were, where people would pay to see them. And this was not only in the cities but also in small farm towns where the arrival of a Negro League team was a big occasion, something to see. People took the afternoon off from work and filled the bleachers at the local diamond to see how their boys stacked up against the out-of-towners.

"Barnstormers" is the term we use today to describe these Negro Leaguers and other traveling ballplayers like them. The practice of barnstorming now has a romantic aura, but the term was originally an insult. It applied to strolling players of the theater, not baseball athletes. These on-the-road entertainers would perform anywhere people would let them, often in barns, and they used an exaggerated style of acting that became known as "barnstorming." The term evolved to describe other types of theatrical performers on tour, politicians going from town to town making stump speeches in a campaign and, most vividly, daredevil airplane pilots. Barnstorming pilots usually performed in front of spectators outside of town in a field, dive-bombing a barn before pulling up and out of their death spiral at the last second.

From its earliest uses barnstorming has always contained an element of theater, a feature that carried over into baseball. When baseball barnstormers rolled into town they played a game, yes. But they also put on a show.

All barnstormers, whether white or black, understood that part of their job was to entertain fans. They were not only players and competitors, they were showmen. And the greatest baseball showman of all time, and one of the most famous barnstorming attractions of his day, was a Negro League pitcher named Leroy Robert "Satchel" Paige.

Born in Mobile, Alabama, early in the 1900s—his birth date has never been accurately established—Paige was the sixth of eight children. At age twelve he was nearly six feet tall, as long as he was skinny. He put on a few more inches before he stopped growing, but he remained lean and wiry, with a fastball that buckled the knees of the batters who faced him. Over time the right-hander developed an assortment of breaking balls to complement his high hard one, and he became not only a star in the Negro Leagues, but well known and respected among white major leaguers as well.

Fans of both races wanted to see him pitch. Being of an obliging nature, and not opposed to making money in the off-season, Paige formed, in the winter of 1931, a traveling all-star team of fellow Negro League luminaries. Since official records were not kept for barnstorming teams, not much is known about this club and others like it. But we do know that from one year to the next the Satchel Paige All-Stars included slugger Josh Gibson, Paige's battery-mate on the Pittsburgh Crawfords, clutch-hitting third baseman Judy "Sweet Juice" Johnson, and the fleet-footed Cool Papa Bell—men whose talents, were it not for the color barrier, would have landed them a starting job on any team in the major leagues. (Like Rube Foster and Oscar Charleston, all are in the Hall of Fame.)

With Satchel as its headliner and top gate attraction, this glittering assembly of baseball talent set off in search of the sun. And if barnstorming was partly show business, there was one place in the United States they had to visit. Where else? Hollywood, California.

By the 1930s Hollywood was long-established as the motion picture capital of the world. As early as 1910 the *Los Angeles Times* bragged that "most moving pictures made in America are produced in Los Angeles." This occurred in part due to the simple accident of warm, dry weather; people could conceivably make motion pictures in southern California every day of the year. In yet another westward migration, theater people and other creative types from New York, the traditional center of popular culture in America, went to Hollywood to make movies, and the film industry flourished.

With its inherent drama and wide popularity, baseball remained a natural subject for the movies. Babe Ruth, the greatest star in the game, appeared in movies as himself and also served as a kind of role model for fictional baseball characters. But the ballplayer who truly found a home in Hollywood was a former teenage drifter named Mike Donlin.

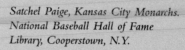

Satchel Paige, Kansas City Monarchs.
National Baseball Hall of Fame
Library, Cooperstown, N.Y.

Originally from Illinois, Donlin grew up in an orphanage following the death of his young mother. After getting out on his own he wandered the country, ending up in the place where most wanderers find themselves sooner or later: California. The California League served as his gateway into professional baseball, and he pitched and played outfield for San Jose, Watsonville, and Santa Cruz. The sterling play of Donlin, then twenty-one, led Santa Cruz into first place when, in mid-season of 1899, the Beachcombers sold his contract to St. Louis of the National League. While Santa Cruz never recovered, falling out of first and losing a shot at the pennant, Donlin went on to the major leagues, beginning an odyssey that eventually landed him on the New York Giants.

Donlin became a favorite of New York fans not only because of his hitting and outfielding (he gave up pitching), but because of his skills as a showman. He was a sharp-looking dude, eye candy to the ladies, and from his strut you could tell he knew it. Cocksure as a rooster, he liked to give the paying spectators their money's worth, give them a show along with the game they came to see. That was how he came to be known as Turkey Mike: from the way he bird-walked on the field in full view of the grandstands. It was all part of his act, and the fans loved it.

His theatrical flair, coupled with his fame and accomplishments as a ballplayer, gave him a second career on the vaudeville stage. His wife, Mabel Hite, was a New York actress, and they starred together in their own vaudeville act. But after she died of cancer Donlin's interest in baseball, which had been flagging for some time, grew cold. He retired from the major leagues after the 1914 season and moved to California, becoming, in the words of film historian Rob Edelman, "the original baseball basher–turned–Hollywood actor."

The following year Donlin had the title role in one of the earliest baseball silents, *Right Off the Bat*, produced by Arrow Film Corporation. He played himself, as did his former manager John McGraw. In his next movie Donlin appeared with John Barrymore in the crime caper *Raffles*. By playing a character in the film, not himself, his fledgling acting career gained a legitimacy it did not have before. For the next twenty years Donlin would find steady work in both baseball and non-baseball movies and, unlike some of the most famous stars of the silent film era, he made a smooth transition into talkies, providing technical assistance for the first baseball movie with sound, *Fast Company*, released in 1929 by Paramount.

For Donlin, who died of a heart attack in his sleep four years later at the age of fifty-five, his best non-baseball role as an actor was as a Union officer in the silent Civil War classic *The General*. The star and director of *The General* was Buster Keaton, himself a huge baseball buff.

The great silent screen comedian featured the game, to comic effect, in a film called *College,* in which the University of Southern California baseball team appeared with its coach, Wahoo Sam Crawford, the retired Detroit Tigers outfielder and future Hall of Fame honoree who lived in the area. Harold Goodwin, an actor and friend of Keaton's who appeared in several of his movies, said that actors interviewing for jobs at Buster Keaton Productions were asked two fundamental questions. The first was, Can you act? The second was, Can you play baseball? If you answered yes to either question, the job was yours.

Keaton employees needed to be familiar with baseball because their boss sometimes stopped shooting in the middle of a scene to play a game. "The Keaton Production Company was in fact an ever-ready baseball team, prepared to start a game on a moment's notice," said Goodwin. "That moment would often come whenever a production problem arose that seemed to defy immediate solution. Buster would officially declare that a game was in order. If someone had an inspiration halfway through it, the shooting would resume."

Fast Company, the first baseball talkie, was based on the Broadway play *Elmer the Great,* which was co-authored by Ring Lardner, the former sports reporter turned short story writer and playwright. When Hollywood decided to make a new screen version of the play, using the original name, it tabbed Lardner to write the script. The star of *Elmer the Great* the movie was Joe E. Brown, a wide-mouthed comic actor with a noisemaker of a voice.

Brown, a former minor league ballplayer, made three baseball movies in the early years of the Depression. In the first, *Fireman, Save My Child,* he plays a pitcher who devises a cap that works like a fire extinguisher, dousing out flames. While playing for the Rosedale Roses, Brown's character must leave in the middle of a game to put out a fire in town. His teammates and the opposing players politely wait for him to return, at which time the game resumes.

After *Elmer the Great,* the final installment in the Brown baseball trilogy was *Alibi Ike,* loosely based on a short story of the same name by Lardner. Brown plays the title character, who makes his entrance in the movie by smashing his Model T car through a ballpark fence. The park where this scene took place was in Riverside, the spring training site for the Hollywood Stars. Several of the Stars players, dressed up in Cubs and Yankees uniforms, made cameo appearances in the film.

While making his fictional baseball creations, Brown frequently attended real-life games at Wrigley Field in Los Angeles. His appearances there were not purely for public relations as they might have been for other celebrities; he genuinely enjoyed watching the Stars and Angels play. He also sponsored an annual charity baseball game in which movie stars teamed up with Coast League players. Brown pitched in these games, delivering the ball with a comic windmill windup.

At an Angels game at Wrigley, Brown would have surely noticed the club's smooth-gliding, sharp-fielding second baseman. As a real fan and a guy who schmoozed with the players personally, Brown may have even known some of his back story—that he was a local kid, out of San Pedro High and, get this, a former Angels batboy. Wasn't that something? A batboy who grew up to be a ballplayer. Sounded as corny as something you'd see in a movie.

After his abbreviated major league career ended in disappointment, Jimmie Reese came back to Los Angeles and found a spot in the starting lineup on the hometown Angels. And, as far as baseball jobs go, it was pretty good. Wrigley Field was a hitter's dream, Groucho Marx and William Powell called themselves

Turkey Mike Donlin, left, with Jack Oakie on the movie Fast Company, *1929. Courtesy of University of Southern California, on behalf of the USC Special Libraries and Archival Collections*

fans, and the club he played on was the Coast League equivalent of New York's Bronx Bombers: too good for the competition.

Reese batted second in the Angels lineup behind leadoff hitter Jigger Statz, a speedy, pint-sized center fielder who snagged fly balls using a fielder's glove

Jigger Statz shows off his slide at spring camp. Security Pacific Collection/Los Angeles Public Library

with a hole in its palm. Statz cut the hole in the leather because he said it gave him a better feel for the ball. Jigger, whose real name was Arnold, played eight seasons in the major leagues, but his greatest success in baseball came in Los Angeles, where his hitting, speed on the bases, and fine outfield work with that crazy hole in his glove made him a local legend. When he retired in 1943 his eighteen seasons for the Angels set the record for longevity with one team in the minor leagues.

Statz had something in common with many of his Angel teammates: at one time or another they all wore the uniform of the Chicago Cubs. Some played before they arrived in Los Angeles, some played after. This connection was due, of course, to the Wrigley family's joint ownership of both teams. With the passing of his father William, Phillip K. Wrigley assumed control of the baseball operations as well as the family's substantial business and real estate holdings.

The president of the Angels for many years was Joe Patrick, a big favorite of the players. After an Angel made an outstanding play in the field or a clutch hit to win a game, Joe would call him up to his box seat at Wrigley and, as a reward, tell him to go downtown to buy a new suit for himself. And, Joe Patrick never failed to say, put it on my tab. The Angels won the Pacific Coast League championship in 1933, Patrick's last as president. The next year the Angels repeated as league champions, winning 137 games against 50 losses and finishing 35 1/2 games ahead of the second-place club. (The Coast League was known for its long seasons, playing an annual schedule of 180 to 200 games.) Baseball experts consider this Angels club to be one of the greatest in minor league history. Everywhere you turned, somebody was doing something fabulous—Statz, Reese, slugger Frank Demaree, twenty-game (or more) winners Fay Thomas, Louis Garland, and Emile Meola, and a whole bunch of other guys. It was a good thing Joe Patrick left the club when he did, because with all the new suits he would have been buying for the Angels, it might have busted him.

★   ★   ★   ★   ★

A few years after the turn of the century, a southern California dairy farmer named Arthur Gilmore sunk a drill into his Rancho La Brea property. Instead of finding water as he expected, Gilmore hit something else, something black and sticky. His accidental discovery of oil made him and his family a fortune. After his death, his son Earl built the Farmer's Market at Third and Fairfax Streets in Hollywood on the site of what had once been Rancho La Brea.

As part of this development, Earl also constructed Gilmore Stadium, which sported a football field encircled by a midget car-racing track. But it featured other sports and attractions as well, and in 1934, following the Angels' record-setting Pacific Coast League season, it may have hosted the greatest pitching duel of the segregated era.

Because the duel occurred in a barnstorming game, it is not entered in any official record book, but that does not mean it did not happen. It most certainly did. Bill Veeck, then a young college dropout working for Phil Wrigley's Chicago Cubs, sat in the stands following every pitch. Veeck, who became a pioneering major league owner and witnessed thousands upon thousands of baseball games in his lifetime, described it as "the greatest pitchers' battle I have ever seen."

On one side was Dizzy Dean, swinging through Hollywood as the headliner of his own barnstorming troupe. Born in Arkansas, the son of an Oklahoma sharecropper, he was a self-professed hillbilly who had just come off a thirty-win season for the world champion St. Louis Cardinals. Then in his early twenties, in his pitching prime, he was widely considered to be the best right-hander in organized baseball. Their farmlands having turned to dust, tens of thousands of displaced families from Dean's part of the country—Kansas, Oklahoma, Arkansas, Texas—abandoned their homes during this period, tied their belongings onto the roofs of their beater Fords, and headed west. Mostly poor and white from rural backgrounds, they faced discrimination, poverty, and

Dizzy Dean, St. Louis Cardinals. National Baseball Hall of Fame Library, Cooperstown, N.Y.

severe hardship when they crossed the California state line, often being herded into migrant camps. These Dust Bowl migrants and others around the country saw Dean as a hero at a time when heroes and hope were in short supply.

The man he faced in this duel may have been the best pitcher in all of baseball, organized or not. After their successful trip in the winter of 1931, Satchel Paige brought his traveling band of Negro League All-Stars back to California for the next three off-seasons, culminating with their showdown with the Dizzy Dean All-Stars.

Like all baseball barnstormers, Paige was a showman at heart, but when he and his fellow Negro Leaguers faced white major league competition, they became very, very serious. The journalist Richard Donovan, who interviewed Paige late in the pitcher's career, writes, "The games against big leaguers were of tremendous importance to Paige and the others. They knew, the sportswriters knew, and many of the fans knew that many of the Negro stars were better ballplayers than some of the high-salaried, internationally famous men they faced. Yet they were denied a shot at the big fame, big money, big records and big company. Paige burned with quiet resentment....The bigger the major league stars, the more Paige bore down."

In their matchup in Hollywood, Paige bore down against Dean, and Dean bore down against Paige—two great pitchers, throwing inning after inning after inning of shutout baseball. Finally, in the thirteenth, the Satchel Paige All-Stars pushed across a run to break a scoreless tie and win, 1 to 0. Dean struck out fifteen batters and pitched all thirteen innings. Paige did the same, only he struck out seventeen. After the game Dean said the better pitcher won, though both men walked off the field with honor.

In the Shadows
of War

SATURDAY, MARCH 22 — 2:15 P.M.
SUNDAY, MARCH 23 — 2:15 P.M.
— 1947 —

TABLISHED PRICE - $3.33
FEDERAL TAX - .67

Total $4.00

THIS PORTION OF TICKET NOT GOOD FOR ADMITTANCE
DETACH SEPERATE COUPONS FOR INDIVIDUAL GAMES

Francis Joseph "Lefty" O'Doul came from Butchertown, the meatpacking district of San Francisco. His father, Eugene, was a butcher. His uncles were butchers. When Lefty was born in 1897 his family expected him to grow up to be a butcher too.

Butchertown, now Bay View–Hunter's Point, was a tough neighborhood. Many of the families who lived there were Irish, and some of them did not like the Italians. Sometimes the Irish boys of Butchertown challenged the Italian boys of North Beach with fists and rocks. Lefty, it is said, joined these rumbles alongside his Irish brothers.

In his teen years Lefty met the woman who changed his life, Rosie Stoltz, a seventh-grade teacher at Bay View Grammar School and its baseball coach. The left-handed O'Doul played sandlot ball like all the other boys in the city, whether they were Irish, Italian, or you name it. But Rosie believed that if you were going to play the game, you needed to play it *right*. "[She] taught me the essential fundamentals of the game," said her former pupil years later. "She taught me to pitch, field, and hit." With Lefty pitching and Rosie calling the shots from the sidelines, Bay View swept to the city championship.

The next year Lefty quit school to work in his father's trade. He butchered meat six days a week at the slaughterhouse, taking a break on Sundays to play in the city leagues. His father must have realized that his son was not cut out to be a butcher, for he urged Lefty to join a team sponsored by the Native Sons of the Golden West. Lefty took his father's advice, and when he led the Native Sons to an undefeated season it piqued the interest of the San Francisco Seals. With the city's large Irish population, the Seals were always on the lookout for talented young Irish prospects, and it is hard to find a more Irish-sounding name than O'Doul. After spending some time in the bush leagues, Lefty joined the Seals and pitched impressively, causing a flurry of interest from another city with a fondness for players with Irish surnames: New York. The butcher's son had found a new trade.

But O'Doodle—that was what the sportswriters called him in New York—hurt his arm in a 1919 spring training throwing contest and only made token appearances for the Yankees before being sent back to San Francisco. Once more he pitched well enough with the Seals to earn a second look in New York. But he flopped again, and after a similar failure in Boston his major league prospects appeared to be dead.

As hard as it is to succeed in major league baseball, it is harder by far to be a butcher in Butchertown. Lefty knew the truth of this from personal experience, which gave him the motivation to return, once again, to San Francisco and retool his game. The workshop where he switched from pitching to being a full-time outfielder was the Pacific Coast League, and by 1927, after pounding pitchers for a .378 average, his transformation was complete. In a ceremony at Old Rec, Lefty received a one-thousand-dollar cash prize as the Coast League's first-ever Most Valuable Player, and in gratitude he remembered his old form and pitched a two-hit shutout for the Seals that day. Afterward he handed out free baseballs to the fans. Not long after that he was back in the big leagues.

"Lefty," said a journalist, "had the gift of greeting life with a glad heart." He was known as "the Man in the Green Suit" because wherever he went in public he wore a green suit—a tribute, he said, to his Irish roots. He bought his first green suit the year of his first batting title in Philadelphia. After wearing it to a game and collecting three hits, the next day he put on a green shirt to match his coat and pants. Then he got four hits. Figuring the suit was his lucky charm, he added green socks to the ensemble and, so the legend goes, green underwear. Nobody could miss Lefty when he walked into a room, and nobody wanted to because a good time always walked in with him.

Lefty O'Doul accepts the 1927 MVP Award for the Pacific Coast League. California Historical Society, FN-33874

By 1931 O'Doul was a big enough name to be invited to tour Japan with other major league stars. The tour, sponsored by Japanese publisher Matsutaro Shoriki, featured future Hall of Famers Lou Gehrig and Frankie Frisch and other top attractions in the American game. Passage across the Pacific on an ocean liner took two weeks, and to kill time the baseball stars played cards, dice, and other games of chance. The streetwise Butchertown boy consistently walked away from their games with his pockets full of dough.

During the tour the Americans played seventeen games in front of sellout crowds at every stadium they appeared. But for Lefty, those two weeks turned out to be more than just a barnstorming trip; they began a decades-long involvement with Japan and her people. He became friends with Shoriki, who asked him if he could possibly persuade Babe Ruth to come on a future tour. The most famous baseball player in the world had not come on that trip reportedly because he was making a movie in Hollywood. O'Doul, who had once been a teammate of Ruth's on the Yankees, said he would talk to him about it.

Beyond his friendship with Shoriki, O'Doul enjoyed working with young Japanese players. "I like people who you're not wasting your time on, trying to help them," he said. "The American kid knows more than the coach." The Japanese were skilled fielders, he noticed, and showed real savvy running the bases. But they acted like wimps with bats in their hands. O'Doul, who hit .398 to win the 1929 National League batting title and won it again three years later, figured he could be of service in this area. If there was one thing he knew how to do, besides playing poker and dice and holding his liquor with any man alive, it was hit a baseball.

★   ★   ★   ★   ★

In late 1931, shortly before Lefty O'Doul's first trip overseas, the Japanese Army invaded Manchuria, a province of China, and seized control of it, installing a puppet regime run by Tokyo. When the Chinese resisted, the occupying army bombed Shanghai, killing tens of thousands of people. Resentful of the worldwide criticism it received for the bombings, the increasingly isolated Japanese government withdrew from the League of Nations, a world body that was a predecessor to the United Nations.

Some historians consider these events to be the beginning of World War II in Asia, although their effect on California and the rest of America seemed remote at the time. No one could know then what darkness lay ahead.

But the turmoil created a kind of opportunity for Kenso Nushida, a Nisei pitcher who played in the Japanese leagues in the Central Valley while working at a hardware store in Stockton. Stockton was also the hometown of Sacramento Senators owner Lew Moreing, and Nushida decided to approach him about a job with his club.

Nushida kept a scrapbook with newspaper clippings and statistics he had collected about himself. The sportswriters called him "the Boy Wonder" because of his exuberant, outgoing nature. He played ukulele and sang songs from his native Hawaii to his teammates and friends. When on the field, he got charged up playing the game. The people in the stands saw this—saw that his joy was real, not a show staged for their benefit—and Nushida attracted crowds wherever he went. Given all this, and no doubt interested in selling tickets to the large and growing Japanese population in the valley, Moreing agreed to give him a shot.

In July 1932 Nushida became the first American of Japanese descent to play in the Pacific Coast League and one of the earliest in organized baseball. The Sacramento papers listed his age at twenty-four, but that was inaccurate. The Boy Wonder was less of a boy and more of a man, probably in his early thirties, but being older would have hurt his chances to make the club, so he may have sliced a few years off his listed age.

Even so, the five-foot-one-inch, 110-pound right-hander saw only limited duty with the Senators, or Solons, as they were also known. His best performance came against Seattle when he took a no-hitter into the seventh inning before losing, 3 to 1. Even in defeat he remained a happy warrior. "The Solons needed a few more like Nushida to boost the morale of the team," said a reporter from the local *Bee*. As he had in the past, Nushida proved a popular gate attraction, which inspired Moreing and his counterpart in Oakland, Cookie Devincenzi, to devise a late-season plan to boost attendance for their teams.

Oakland had a number of Chinese residents, nearly all of whom were mad at Japan for seizing their homeland. Nushida and other Nisei obviously had no say in the affairs of the Japanese government; nevertheless, tension existed between the Japanese and Chinese communities in the United States. With the idea of exploiting this rivalry on a baseball field, the Oaks owner recruited a Chinese American pitcher, Lee Gum Hong. Hong against Nushida, China against Japan. Their duel was scheduled at Oaks Ball Park for the last week of the season.

Lee Gum Hong was an American-born member of Oakland's Chinese community, which for many years largely viewed baseball as a waste of time, contributing to sloth and personal indulgence. But gradually the game gained approval as a way to keep

Kenso Nushida, 1932.
Doug McWilliams Collection

youngsters out of trouble and divert them from gambling and other pleasures. As a pitcher for the Oakland High Wildcats, Hong's strength was his fastball. He and other members of his family also starred for the Wa Sungs, the best Chinese team in the East Bay, and Hong doubled as coach.

Hong, possibly the first American of Chinese descent to appear in the Pacific Coast League and organized baseball, held the Senators to one hit through five innings. His opposite number also pitched well until being chased from the game in the fifth, trailing by a run. The Senators came back to win, 7 to 5, hanging the loss on Hong.

Three thousand people, one of Oakland's largest crowds of the year, came out to see the Hong-Nushida rematch on the last day of the season, the second game of a Sunday doubleheader. This time Hong came out on top, pitching the Oaks to an easy 7 to 1 win over Nushida's Senators. After leaving the park Chinese fans set off firecrackers in the streets in celebration.

Lee Gum Hong, 1932.
Doug McWilliams Collection

If the Hong-Nushida matchups represented a tiny crack in the wall of organized baseball, it was quickly patched over. The Oaks and Senators promptly released both men, and neither played in the Coast League again.

Not long after the games in Oakland, the major league season ended in the East and Lefty O'Doul left for Japan for the second time. But, unlike his previous visit, he went alone to hold instructional clinics and see more of the country. His biographer Richard Leutzinger said that Lefty "had fallen in love with the country from the beginning." He ate sushi while he was there and took a real stab at learning the language. Being a famous baseball player, his travels received newspaper coverage, and the Japanese fans appeared to enjoy him as much as he enjoyed them. "O'Dou-san," as he came to be known, made twenty visits to the country in his lifetime.

In 1934 O'Dou-san went back to Japan on another all-star barnstorming tour, this time, to Shoriki's delight, with Babe Ruth. The public response was enormous. More than one million people crowded into downtown Tokyo to catch a glimpse of the aging Ruth and the other Americans in a welcoming parade.

Shoriki wanted the Japanese to be as good as the Americans in baseball; this was a major reason why he sponsored the tours and instructional clinics by the major leaguers. To this end, Lefty suggested to his friend another way to improve the quality of play in the country: add an economic incentive. From these conversations sprung Japanese professional baseball, which thrives today. The Tokyo Giants, Japan's first professional club, had the same nickname as the New York Giants, Lefty's team at the time.

On the tour with Ruth or soon thereafter, O'Doul learned that his old friend Charlie Graham, the owner of the San Francisco Seals, had purchased his contract from the Giants. Being named as player-manager of the Seals signified the end of Lefty's major league career but once again brought him back to his hometown, where he was as popular as the cable cars.

Lefty O'Doul accepting an award from the Tokyo Giants, 1935. California Historical Society, FN-33868

Over the next twenty years Lefty managed in several Pacific Coast League cities, but San Francisco remained his town. His cocktail lounge near Union Square was the city's equivalent of Toots Shor's in New York: a watering hole for jocks, politicians, celebrities, and their hangers-on. "You'll Meet Everybody Who's Anybody at Lefty's," crowed an advertisement for the bar. At the center of this crowd, at the center of most every crowd he was in, was the Man in the Green Suit, who told his players that if they ever saw him drinking at a bar they could not leave until they stopped by his table and shared a glass with him.

Before games he often stopped in at his favorite North Beach eatery and went back into the kitchen to fix pasta con picelli for his lunch. Always a soft touch around kids, he gave away baseballs and gear at Seals Stadium, held free instructional clinics at playgrounds around the city, and after a game slipped the batboys a dollar apiece so they could see a picture show.

O'Doul's arrival on the Seals was one of the best breaks Joe DiMaggio ever got. The New York Yankees had already signed DiMaggio, but kept the twenty-year-old on the West Coast for more seasoning. All the raw skills were there, but they lacked polish. O'Doul applied the polish, showing Joe how to turn on a fastball and pull it down the left field line—a necessity for success for a right-handed hitter in spacious Yankee Stadium, where long, deep fly balls into left-center or center field ended quietly in an outfielder's glove. Under Lefty's tutelage, Joe hit .398 for the Seals, making the jump to instant stardom in New York the next season. Additionally, Lefty showed Joe a thing or two about how to conduct himself in public, how to handle his business when every eyeball in the joint was fixed on him and every move he made set tongues wagging. These lessons also proved handy in New York.

In the spring of 1935 the Tokyo Giants visited San Francisco to play and practice with the Seals. O'Doul and Shoriki had arranged the visit—the first by a Japanese professional team to America—as part of their ongoing baseball exchange. But relations between Japan and the United States were deteriorating. The political climate had only grown worse in the years since Japan's invasion of China. When Lefty made plans to go back to Japan two years later, the trip never left shore. And it would be another decade before he could return.

As for Kenso Nushida, after his partial season in the Coast League, he kept playing baseball, one year leading a Nisei team from Watsonville to the semifinals of a national semipro championship tournament in the Midwest. A couple of seasons later he served as an assistant coach on a barnstorming team that featured Nisei players from around northern California. Its coach was Kenichi Zenimura of the Fresno Athletic Club.

These Nisei barnstormers traveled to Asia, playing games in Japan, Korea, and occupied Manchuria. When the tour was over four of the team's stars decided to remain in Japan to pursue professional baseball careers there. Nushida, Zenimura, and the others came home to California. It was the last baseball exchange trip between America and Japan before the bombs started falling.

Joe, Ted, Jackie

SATURDAY, MARCH 22 — 2:15 P.M.
SUNDAY, MARCH 23 — 2:15 P.M.
— 1947 —
TABLISHED PRICE - $3.33
FEDERAL TAX - - - - .67   Total $4.00

THIS PORTION OF TICKET NOT GOOD FOR ADMITTANCE
DETACH SEPERATE COUPONS FOR INDIVIDUAL GAMES

Giuseppe and Rosalie DiMaggio lived on a tiny island off the coast of Sicily, Isola delle Femmine, where they scraped by on what Giuseppe, a fisherman, made from the sea. When relatives living in America wrote them letters saying that the fishing was better in their new country and life was not so hard, Rosalie, though pregnant with their first child, urged her husband to leave Sicily and go to America too, which he did. In 1898, he came to Pittsburg, California, where his relatives had settled, then moved a few miles downstream to Martinez, a small fishing village on the Carquinez Strait, a strip of water connecting the Sacramento River with San Francisco Bay. After five years Rosalie and their daughter Nellie joined Giuseppe on North Berellessa Street in Martinez in an area near the wharf known as Portuguese Flats. A creek passed through their backyard, and the Southern Pacific Railroad tracks ran close by. In their cabin Giuseppe and Rosalie began to raise a large family of girls and boys; their eighth child arrived in the year the Great War broke out in Europe. His name was Joseph Paul DiMaggio.

Now, to a different family in a different part of the state. The father of this family was Sam Williams, who as a teenager had enlisted in the Rough Riders, the United States Army cavalry unit once led by Teddy Roosevelt. At the end of his tour of duty in the Philippines, while returning to the States, Sam stopped in Hawaii. There, he fell in love with an energetic and passionate eighteen-year-old Hispanic girl named May Venzer, a lieutenant in the Salvation Army who had worked for the Christian charitable organization for years. Sam asked her to marry him and, in what must have been a hard decision for her—he did not belong to the Salvation Army and she was not supposed to marry outside the organization—she said yes. The new couple moved to San Diego and after a few years of marriage May gave birth to a boy at Sunshine Maternity Hospital. His name was Theodore Samuel Williams.

Once more, this time to a family in another part of the country. This family lived in Georgia, and they were black. Jerry Robinson, the father, raised chickens and hogs and grew cotton, potatoes, and peanuts on a farm outside Cairo in the southern part of the state. The land he farmed was owned by a white man who provided housing, seed, fertilizer, and tools in exchange for much of what Jerry grew. Jerry was allowed a share of his crops, and the owner considered him a strong worker and a steady earner.

Mallie Robinson, Jerry's wife, was the daughter of slaves. She met Jerry when she was a teenager, and a year after their wedding they had their first child, Edgar. Then came two more boys and a girl. Their fifth child, a boy, was born in Grady County. Mallie named him Jack and, in honor of former president Theodore Roosevelt, who had recently died, she chose Roosevelt to be his middle name. His full name was Jack Roosevelt Robinson.

Six months after Jack was born, his father told Mallie he was going to Texas. This was a lie. Instead he took up with another woman and deserted his family. When the landowner who profited from Jerry's labor found out he was gone, he accused Mallie of getting rid of her husband, and in retaliation he threw the family off his property.

After being kicked off the farm, Mallie and her children—the oldest, Edgar, was eleven, and the youngest, Jack, was sixteen months—rode a horse and buggy to Cairo, where they stayed in the home of a relative. But they did not intend to be there for long. Mallie had a half-brother named Burton Thomas, a well-dressed, nice-talking man who lived in Pasadena, California. This was where Mallie planned to go, but she could not simply buy a ticket and board the train. Georgia authorities discouraged blacks from leaving the state because landowners needed cheap labor to work their farms. When the police saw black travelers boarding a train they often tore up their tickets and bullied them into leaving the station.

Mallie and her children, accompanied by friends and family, arrived at the Cairo station before midnight. Mallie had sold everything she owned except what she was carrying in her scuffed and weathered bags. Three dollars, which was all she had left after buying her train tickets, was sewn into her undergarments for safekeeping.

The police stopped and questioned her at the station. They checked her tickets, kicked her bags. But they ultimately let her and her children board the train, which caused a whole mess of emotion, everyone crying and hugging and carrying on. Her friends and relations in Cairo knew, as did Mallie, this was probably the last time they would ever see her and the kids. The No. 58 train slowly chugged out of the station, leaving Cairo behind in the darkness.

Jackie Robinson. Ted Williams. Joe DiMaggio. Each man occupies an esteemed place not only in the history of baseball, but in the history of the country. If the national pastime had a Mount Rushmore, the likeness of Robinson—the first black man to play modern major league baseball, one of the greatest all-around athletes of his or any time, the first and only player to have his number (42) permanently retired by all major league teams and posted at parks around the country—would certainly be on it. But both DiMaggio—arguably the greatest center fielder and all-around player of his time, a cultural icon and "the first Italian superstar," in the words of David Halberstam—and Williams—the best hitter of his time and the last man to hit .400 or above in a regular season, a skilled outdoorsman and a decorated Marine pilot who flew combat missions in two wars—would be on the shortlist of candidates to accompany him.

Williams starred for the Boston Red Sox, DiMaggio for the New York Yankees, and Jackie Robinson for the Brooklyn Dodgers. But before they took their place on the national stage they were boys, all growing up in the same state at basically the same time, hanging out at their neighborhood haunts and playing ball. Beginning with the oldest and ending with the youngest, here are their stories:

When Joe DiMaggio was a baby, his family moved from Martinez to North Beach in San Francisco. As journalist Ron Fimrite points out, North Beach then was hardly the chic neighborhood it is today. Many who lived there were poor Italian immigrants like the DiMaggios. Giuseppe was a crab fisherman whose boat was too small to go onto the open waters of the ocean, where the fishing was best. Consequently he had to stay inside the Golden Gate in the more protected and heavily fished waters of the bay. The catch was never as good there, and paying the bills and putting food on the table—their ninth and last child, Dominic, was born in San Francisco—was a continual struggle.

The DiMaggio family home was on Taylor Street, not far from Fisherman's Wharf, where Giuseppe docked his boat (and where, after joining the Yankees, Joe started a restaurant with his brother Tom). Fisherman's Wharf is at the foot of Columbus Avenue, the main artery of North Beach, which leads up to Washington Square, where old Italian men in worn suits drank espressos and discussed the issues of the day in their native tongue. Sts. Peter and Paul Church, where the DiMaggios worshipped, adjoins the square, and the service for Joe's first marriage, to Dorothy Arnold, was held there.

Another major neighborhood landmark, also on Columbus, was North Beach Playground. This was where the DiMaggio boys learned their ball—most notably Joe, older brother Vince, and younger brother Dom. When they played the outfield at the playground, particularly in deep left-center, they had to watch their step because that was where the Golden State Dairy grazed its horses in the afternoons after they were done pulling the milk wagons for the day.

Vincent Paul DiMaggio—all the boys had the middle name of Giuseppe's favorite saint—was the first of the brothers to take up the game seriously, sneaking out of junior high to play with his friends. He had a long, sweet face, a full head of thick black hair, and a likable personality. He loved to talk—and sing. Once he thought he might want to become an opera singer, using the money he earned from baseball to pay for voice training. An opera career never came to pass, but he did sing arias while standing in the outfield waiting for the next pitch.

When Vince was a teenager a semipro club from the northern part of the state offered him a job to play on its team, but Giuseppe told him flatly no, he could not go. In Giuseppe's view, a man who did not work was a "maga-bonu"—a bum. Baseball was a silly game, a stupid game, a game for children. Who could make a living at such foolishness? Tom and Mike, the oldest sons, had followed their father into fishing, and this was what Vince should do too, in Giuseppe's strongly worded view.

But Vince had other ideas. This was not Sicily, and he refused to follow his father's path. He forged Giuseppe's signature on the playing contract—he was underage and needed parental consent—and ran off to the north woods. To make matters worse, Vince married a girl without his father's permission, yet another challenge to Giuseppe's authority. Years would pass before Giuseppe would speak to his son or permit him and his wife to visit the Taylor Street house.

Vince's vision of himself, not his father's, was the true one. He became a professional ballplayer, later catching on with the hometown Seals and other Pacific Coast League teams before making the majors. Too much of a free-swinger to ever be a strong hitter—"He'd swing at balls two feet outside," said one sportswriter—he played ten seasons in the outfield for the Braves, Pirates, and other clubs.

But Vince is remembered mainly not for what he did on a baseball field, but for the role he played in getting Joe started on the Seals. With three games left in the '32 season, Seals outfielder Prince Oana and shortstop Augie Galan (a Berkeley native who later became a major league All-Star) announced they were leaving on a barnstorming junket to Hawaii. This created the opening for Vince, who was on the Seals, to suggest his brother as a fill-in at shortstop. Manager Ike Caveney said all right, he'd give the kid a look, thus beginning Joe's professional career.

Joe was only seventeen at the time and untested in organized baseball, but it would not be accurate to say he was unknown. "There may never have been a time when DiMaggio was not, in one way or another, famous," observes Ron Fimrite. "The future Yankee Clipper was, because of his athletic prowess, a boy apart in the neighborhood, a hero to the other kids even then." In the neighborhood they called him "Coscilunghi," which is Italian for "long legs." He was not good-looking like Vince, and definitely not an extrovert. Shy, quiet, withdrawn, aloof, sullen—these are all words used to describe him. But his great athletic gifts made him stand out from the other boys. There was Joe—and there was everybody else. This did not much change after he became one of the most famous men in America.

Joe DiMaggio and Frankie Crosetti, Fisherman's Wharf, San Francisco, 1936.
California Historical Society, FN-40026

He could always pound the ball, just pound it. Legend has it that Joe learned to hit using a sawed-off oar from his father's fishing boat. You know this could not be true because Joe hated fishing even more than Vince did—hated the smell of it, hated everything about it. But he never had to fight the battles with his father that Vince did, in part because his mother would not allow it. Rosalie was as strong as Giuseppe, stronger perhaps. She cooked, cleaned, washed clothes, sewed, ran a household of eleven. A strong Catholic, she told stories to her children about how the power of belief made miracles happen for poor people like themselves. One of her sons had already been cut off from the family, and she was not going to let it happen again. She stuck up for Joe (and Dom), and helped calm her husband down when he became angry at them.

Joe's September stint with the Seals led him to be invited the following spring to a tryout for the club's regular-season roster. The tryout was held at Seals Stadium. One of those present was Seals co-owner Charlie Graham, who was so delighted by his new prospect's potential that he could overlook the teenager's occasionally wild throws from shortstop. "I'll say one thing about the kid," said Uncle Charlie after an errant DiMaggio throw sailed over the head of the first baseman and landed near him in the seats. "He's got a hell of an arm!"

Besides DiMaggio, about twenty players participated in the tryout, including a sharp-looking shortstop, Tony Gomez. He moved real nice, fielded his position with skill. He and another top local prospect, Eddie Joost, a San Francisco–born infielder who went on to have a seventeen-year career in the majors, played American Legion ball together. With Joost at second base and Gomez at short, their club had won a local championship sponsored by the veterans' organization.

Everything checked out with young Tony except the color of his skin. His skin was dark, his hair black and curly. He was of Hispanic descent but white people looked at him and saw a black man, and that was not acceptable under baseball's racial code.

When Gomez appeared on the field, some people in the stands yelled dirty names at him. A coach cleared the other players off the infield and began to hit ground balls at him, one right after another, and hard. Gomez fielded them, most of them anyhow, and made his throws to first the way he was supposed to. But then his leg cramped up and he sat down to rest it. DiMaggio went over to him and said, Stand up, you can't sit down now, not with all these people watching. But Tony's leg hurt too much, and he could not play anymore that day.

The early promise shown by Gomez never came to fruition in organized professional baseball. He remained in camp for a week before the Seals cut him. No team in the Coast League ever hired him. He continued to play on semi-pro teams around California, Nevada, and Mexico.

Although DiMaggio was never blackballed from the game like Tony Gomez, he encountered prejudice and stereotyping because of his Italian heritage. A few years after his arrival in New York, *Life* magazine published a feature on him, noting how well he and other Italians did in sports: "Italians, bad at war, are well-suited for milder competition, and the number of top-notch Italian prize fighters, golfers and baseball players is out of all proportion to the population." But Joe, the magazine went on, was different from those others: "Instead of olive oil or smelly bear grease, he keeps his hair slick with water. He never reeks of garlic and prefers chicken chow mein to spaghetti....[DiMaggio's] rise in baseball is a testimonial to the value of general shiftlessness."

To those who had suffered similar insults, or worse, DiMaggio represented more than just a ballplayer. "For Italian Americans," writes the novelist and journalist John Gregory Dunne, "he was a magnet of ethnic pride. The pride was shared by made men as well as shoemakers and lawmakers, doctors and politicians." And this pride surfaced almost as soon as Joe put on a uniform for the Seals, switched from shortstop to the outfield, and began to pound the baseball.

On May 28, 1933, he hit a single in four trips to the plate in the first game of a doubleheader against Portland. In the second game he produced a double. Joe spread six hits across the next two games and at least one more in each of the five after that. This was the way it went: day after day, game after game. And when his streak reached twenty-five...thirty...forty...and kept

The DiMaggio brothers: Vince, Joe, Dom. Doug McWilliams Collection

on going, all sorts of people, not just Italians, started to pay attention. Big crowds filled Seals Stadium, and fans from Los Angeles to Seattle paid to see this new teen sensation do what he had once done, for free, with only his pals and some dairy cattle in attendance.

Joe blew past the old Pacific Coast League consecutive-game hitting record of forty-nine, set twenty years before by Jack Ness of Oakland, and headed into uncharted territory. Fifty...fifty-five...sixty. Finally Oakland's Ed Walsh Jr., the son of the Hall of Fame right-hander, held Joe hitless in five plate appearances and the streak ended at sixty-one—a forerunner of DiMaggio's major-league record fifty-six-game streak with the Yankees that captivated a nation on the brink of world war.

One of Joe's biggest fans during the streak was his father Giuseppe, whose view of baseball had changed considerably since his son signed his first professional contract with the Seals. They were paying his son $225 a month, which was more than Giuseppe made in one month of fishing. Not only that, Vince was earning a paycheck too. After being cut by the Seals a few games into the '33 season, he eventually landed a paying job with the Hollywood Stars. Clearly Vince was no magabonu, and he and Giuseppe repaired their relationship.

Every day Giuseppe rose before the sun came up to buy a copy of the morning *Chronicle*. He first pulled out the Sporting Green (the *Chronicle* published its sports pages on green newsprint then). Although he could not read or write, he had learned to decipher a baseball box score, and he looked to find his son's name; sportswriters at first incorrectly spelled it "De Maggio." If the box score showed a hit, Giuseppe rushed home to tell Rosalie, who was still in bed. Joe's streak caused her sleep to be interrupted many times.

It was also during the streak that Dom DiMaggio's name first appeared in the newspaper, on a Boys Club team. Giuseppe's view of the game had changed so much that he started riding his youngest son at an early age, asking him when he was going to play baseball like his two brothers.

Whether it was on his father's fishing boat or on a ballfield, Dominic wanted to prove that he was every bit the equal of his older and bigger brothers. But the game did not come easily to him, not like it did to Joe anyhow. He went to Galileo High (where Joe also attended) and in his senior year hit for a high average despite his small size. A greater liability was his poor eyesight. His eyeglasses, unusual for ballplayers in those days, contributed to his frail-looking schoolboy image. (Berkeley's Chick Hafey, whose Hall of Fame career was ending at about the same time as Dom was getting started in pro baseball, was another early ballplayer who wore glasses.)

But Spike Hennessy, the old Golden Gate Park baseball man who had tutored Willie Kamm and many other San Francisco players, moved Dom from shortstop to the outfield and, in an effort to increase his assertiveness and leadership skills, made him umpire some games. Dom also got a job at the Simmons Bed Company, and hauling and lifting mattresses all day long helped build up his body. At age twenty Dom tried out for the Seals and made the club, quitting the mattress factory to become a full-time player.

After a few years with the Seals, Dom graduated to the Boston Red Sox, hitting .298 lifetime over eleven seasons while roaming center field next to Ted Williams in left. Critics dogged him early in his career, saying the only reason he had a job in baseball was because his brother was Joe DiMaggio. But some modern experts believe he deserves a place in Cooperstown next to his brother and his former outfield mate.

Like Vince, Dom played in the shadow of his famous brother, who was always It, the natural, the guy other guys longed to be. Joe's reputation, his fame, this sense of being tapped on the shoulder by Destiny, only grew stronger after his first season with the Seals. What ballplayer could hit safely in sixty-one straight games? Who could do that? Joe DiMaggio, that's who.

From left, Joe DiMaggio, Tony Lazzeri, and Frankie Crosetti, 1937.
California Historical Society, FN-40027

Then Joe's career almost ended just as it was getting started. It happened the season after the streak, in late May, when Joe fell stepping out of a taxicab in San Francisco. "Down I went, as though I had been shot," he said. "There was no twisting, just four sharp cracks at the knee, and I couldn't straighten out the leg. The pain was terrific."

An injury to the city's leading sports star was big news. As Richard Ben Cramer recounts the story, the *Examiner* assigned a reporter to do some digging about the incident. The paper said it occurred around midnight on Market Street, and DiMaggio fell while getting *into* his car, not out of it as he claimed. Since then other reports have said that he had been drinking and sought to hide the facts because of the potential harm to his public image.

Whatever the true story, this was undeniable: the can't-miss prospect had suddenly become a risky bet.

First Joe tried to play with torn ligaments—no dice. He could not even pinch-hit. His leg went into a cast and his season was done. This was scary stuff for a ballplayer; surgical repair of torn knee ligaments did not exist then. Would he come back at all and, if he did, what kind of shape would he be in? Nobody knew.

Bill Essick was a scout with the New York Yankees. He knew the DiMaggio family, having lived on the same block in North Beach with them, and they trusted him. He secretly took Joe to an orthopedist for a medical evaluation of his knee. The prognosis could not have been rosier. The orthopedist felt confident the knee would recover fully, there would be no lingering problems, and that over time the patient would regain full strength and mobility. Essick and the Yankees did not bother to share this information with the other major league clubs also interested in possibly signing DiMaggio. Rather, they offered the Seals $25,000 for his rights—considerably lower than the $100,000 his sale might have brought before the injury—with the understanding he would play one more year on the coast before venturing east. A disappointed but realistic Charlie Graham had no choice but to accept the offer.

In Joe's last season with the Seals, his knee recovered as the orthopedist predicted, and he grew stronger than ever. Lefty O'Doul, the club's new manager, taught him about hitting and life, and after a season of destroying Coast League pitching he was ready for the only place in America big enough to hold him: New York.

In the spring of 1936, two other San Francisco Italians on the Yankees, Tony Lazzeri and Frankie Crosetti, gathered up DiMaggio for the cross-country ride to training camp in Florida. Back then only a few cars had radios, air conditioning meant rolling down the windows, and all the roads were two lanes. Tony started out behind the wheel in his new Ford, Frankie rode shotgun, and the twenty-one-year-old DiMaggio sat silently in the backseat, watching the miles roll by. This was his first trip east.

★   ★   ★   ★   ★

In his autobiography Ted Williams said he would have encountered prejudice, both growing up and as a ballplayer, if he had used the maiden name of his mother, May Venzer, who was of Hispanic descent. "If I had had my mother's name," he recalled, "there is no doubt I would have run into problems in those days, the prejudices people had in southern California." But Ted's last name was Williams, he was a skinny white kid with a sweet batting stroke, and he never had to face those problems.

Still, he had unique challenges of his own as a boy, mainly involving the relationship (or non-relationship) of his parents and the unusual nature of his mother's work and her complete commitment to it.

"Salvation May," as she was known, was a highly visible personality in San Diego. Her soft round face, short-cropped dark hair, and horn-rim glasses gave her a maternal appearance even as a young woman. She never failed to appear in public in her Salvation Army uniform, perhaps with a bonnet tied at her neck and a tambourine in her hand. She preached at rallies, marched in parades, tirelessly raised money by ringing her Salvation Army bell on street corners, played cornet in the band, worked late at night in the soup kitchen, and regularly walked the streets of the city's red-light district, hoping to lead the women and sailors she met there away from lives of sin. Her missionary work extended across the border to Tijuana, where her acts of kindness became local legend. Another name for her was "the Angel of Tijuana."

After Ted was born she had another son, Danny, and a few years after that the family moved to Utah Street in the North Park section of town. Their modest one-story home, which still stands, was where Ted lived until he signed with the Boston Red Sox and went back East. "Modest" describes their family finances as well. They could not afford to buy their home, which was given to them by a person wishing to support May's charitable activities. The Williamses were supposed to pay rent but did so infrequently for the simple reason that they did not have it.

Owing to the tension between him and his wife, Sam Williams, who ran a photography shop downtown, did not come home much, and when he did it was late at night, much like May. "The more his wife manifested her religiosity," writes David Halberstam, "the less likely he was to come home; and the less often he came home, the more religious she became." One consequence of their sad dance of avoidance was that they frequently left their two boys at home by themselves. Many an evening Ted and Danny sat on the front porch of their house until well after dark, waiting for one of their parents to come home.

Danny got into trouble a lot when he was young. Several schools expelled him for non-attendance or bad behavior or both. He stole things from his mother in his own house. His behavior eventually caught up to him as an adult, and he served time in prison.

Ted took a different path in his life, becoming absorbed with doing one thing—hitting a baseball—and doing it better than anyone had ever done it before. John Lutz, who lived across the street from him, remembered Ted showing up on his doorstep at the age of five or six, dragging a bat. Nobody was home at his house, said Ted, and he wanted a grown-up to pitch to him. Lutz said sure, as he did many times after that.

Leila Bowen, Ted's fifth-grade teacher at Garfield Elementary, described him as "a skinny, tempestuous ten-year-old" who was always first out the classroom door when the bell rang for recess. "First ups!" he shouted in a mad dash for the playground. If another kid beat him to the spot and Ted did not get his wish to be first up in the game, he threw his cap on the ground and broke into tears.

Most days in the fifth grade Ted made breakfast for himself and his brother and then tore off to school early in the morning to be the first to get the balls and bats at the playground. At noon he ran home, filled up a sack with leftover fried potatoes, and raced back to school to play some more before classes resumed after lunch recess.

Whatever he ate, however much he ate, it never seemed to add a pound to his long, gangly, all-arms-and-elbows frame. Some boys called him "Birdlegs," which he hated. But those same boys, even then, regarded him with a kind of awe, for none of them could hit a baseball like Ted. Nor did they possess anything close to his determination to do that, and only that, day after day after day.

This desire to hit a baseball—this obsession, this burning love—drove him like nothing else in his life, and other men besides John Lutz came forward to help. Rod Luscomb, the playground director at North Park Playground, which was only a short block and a half away from Ted's house, hit balls with him for hours, just the two of them, with no one else around. Ted pitched and Lusk, a former minor leaguer, hit. Then they switched roles and Ted hit. And hit. And hit. And hit. And hit.

Another early mentor, Wos Caldwell, the baseball coach at Hoover High— Ted thanked both Luscomb and Caldwell in his Hall of Fame acceptance speech—was doing the pitching when Williams tried out for the school team. On the first pitch Ted saw, he hit the ball farther than anybody had all day. "What's your name, kid?" the coach asked. Ted told him, explaining that, technically, he was still in the eighth grade and would not graduate until Friday. The Monday after graduation Ted returned to Hoover, and Caldwell threw him batting practice.

Les Cassie, who was already on the Hoover High team, attended this tryout and soon became friends with the whippet-thin slugger. In Ted's endless quest to bulk up, the two of them often pounded down malted shakes at Doc Powelson's drugstore.

Les lived on Thirty-sixth Street, and Ted started showing up at his house to eat dinner and hang out with his family. Les Sr. was another of the men who befriended him; he loved to fish and Ted showed an interest, and on Friday nights they drove down to the beach at Coronado Island. Arriving in darkness, they waded up to their waists in water and fished under the stars till dawn. Ted showed the same kind of dedication to fishing that he did to his hitting, practicing his casts in his front yard in the evenings, in time learning to send his line as far out into the surf as the men.

The boy who would grow up to be one of the most famous outdoorsmen of his time also learned to hunt, taking day trips to Mexico with John Lutz and others, shooting jackrabbits and quail in the Rancho Penasquitos area, and stalking the Mission Valley woods using a Model 12 Winchester rifle given to him by his mother.

Hoover High—named after Herbert Hoover, the first native Californian to become president of the United States—opened in 1930, the year before voters turned him out of office. Being a new school with fewer than one thousand students, Hoover provided only meager competition to the traditional prep powerhouse in town, San Diego High. But its baseball team took a step up in class after Salvation May's son entered the picture. In his junior year almost nobody could get him out. He batted close to .600, pitched and played the outfield, and the Cardinals thumped San Diego to win the Bay League championship.

A shy, high-strung, nervous type who constantly chewed his fingernails, Ted felt awkward around girls and never dated in high school. He did not drink or party or smoke cigarettes. What he did was practice his hitting so much the palms of his hands bled. He and a buddy, Wilbur Wylie, played hitting contests for hours at the handball courts at North Park. When the cover of the ball came off, they wrapped it with black tape and kept playing. When the bat handle broke, they applied more tape and kept playing.

In high school (and later with the San Diego Padres), Ted paid younger kids to shag balls for him when he hit. (One of the kids who shagged for him was a future major league All-Star, San Diego native Ray Boone, whose son Bob Boone and grandsons Aaron and Bret Boone all became major league All-Stars.) Ted paid twenty-five cents, his lunch money, to anyone who would chase balls for him. But when he kept showing up at school with no money to buy lunch, Hoover officials called his mother, who said yes, of course, she gave him a quarter every day. Questioned later by his mother about what he was doing with this money, Ted said he was giving it to poor kids in school, an explanation, he felt, that would make her feel good.

Ted played pickup games at North Park Playground, American Legion games for the local "Fighting Bob" Post, and semipro games for a merchant team that paid him three dollars every time he came out, plus a milkshake and hamburger. In his senior year in high school, when he hit over .400 and the Cardinals swept undefeated through the Bay League, Hoover traveled to Pomona, east of Los Angeles, to compete in a regional championship tournament. In a sign of the gathering strength of southern California youth baseball, three future Hall of Famers made the all-tourney team at this championship. One was Williams. Another was Bob Lemon of Wilson High in Long Beach, who, after World War II, became one of the top right-handed pitchers of his generation, winning 207 games lifetime, all with the Cleveland Indians.

The other all-tourney performer and future Hall of Famer was Jackie Robinson of Pasadena.

San Diego in the 1930s was, in the words of sportswriter Earl Keller, who lived and covered games there, "a little hamburger town." On two occasions the Pacific Coast League had refused to put a club there, citing its lack of population, inadequate playing facilities, and the increased costs of travel to its out-of-the-way location. But all this changed when Hollywood Stars owner Bill Lane decided to pack up his ballclub and move it south.

Ted Williams described Lane as "a tough, gruff old guy," fitting for a man whose nickname was "Hard Rock." After striking it rich in the goldfields of Alaska, Hard Rock went into the baseball business, purchasing the Coast League's Salt Lake City operation. When he grew disgruntled with Utah, he shifted his club to Hollywood and renamed it the Stars. More disgruntlement followed. Lacking a ballpark of their own, the Stars played their home games

Ted Williams, Hoover High, 1936. San Diego Hall of Champions

at Wrigley Field in Los Angeles, which forced Hard Rock to reach into his own pocket for rent. He did not like that. Poor ticket sales and poor play on the field only increased his desire to get out of town and make a fresh start.

The town fathers of San Diego were only happy to accommodate his wishes, and in January 1936 Lane signed an agreement to move his club—newly renamed, after a poll of fans, "the Padres," a reference to the eighteenth-century Spanish priests who established the first California mission there. (Coast League fans in Los Angeles did not have to wait long before another team filled the void caused by Lane's departure; in two years the San Francisco Missions relocated to southern California, reviving the name and putting the Hollywood Stars back in business.)

Though it now had a ballclub, San Diego still had a little problem: no ball-park, or none that was up to Coast League standards at any rate. But in less than three months, with the assistance of the Works Progress (later, Projects) Administration, a federal building program designed to spur employment during the Depression, old Sports Field on the Pacific Coast Highway between the

Construction of Lane Field, San Diego, 1936.
San Diego Historical Society Photograph Collection, www.sandiegohistory.org

railroad yards and San Diego Bay morphed into the refurbished and rebuilt Lane Field, and the Padres had a place to call home.

San Diego welcomed Pacific Coast League baseball for the first time on March 31, 1936, with an Opening Day parade down Twelfth and Broadway that ended at Lane Field. About eight thousand fans watched as the home-towners whipped the Seattle Indians, 6 to 2. But this was more than just a baseball game; it was a coming-out party for the entire city. Los Angeles, San Francisco, Oakland, and Sacramento all had Coast League teams. San Diego, at long last, had joined their ranks.

About this same time schoolboy legend Ted Williams was shopping around for a place to begin his professional baseball career. Actually his father, Sam Williams, who appeared in his son's life whenever money was being discussed and contracts were about to be drawn up, was the one doing the shopping, contacting several Coast League clubs to see if they were interested in his son. They, and a posse of Eastern major league scouts, expressed enthusiastic interest, and a few made serious offers.

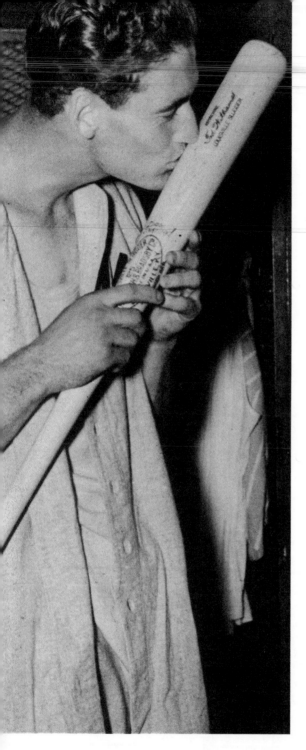

Ted Williams, circa 1941.
San Diego Hall of Champions

But local politicians and baseball fans clamored for him to stay in town with the Padres, which was what his mom wanted too. To sweeten the deal Bill Lane told May (or so she said anyway) that he would keep her son in San Diego until he was twenty-one and that when he sold him to the majors she would receive 10 percent of the sale price. With Wos Caldwell being a friend of Lane's and throwing in on the side of the hometown club, that sewed it up. In June, while still a student at Hoover High, Williams signed with the Padres for a salary of one hundred fifty dollars a month.

In his first game, a benefit exhibition for the Naval Relief Fund, Ted got a hit. The following Monday the Padres headed north, giving him his first extended trip away from home and his first look at the rest of California and the Northwest. "It was like a fairyland to me," he recalled later. "Everything was new." Including the menu in the railroad dining car, which baffled him at first. The only places he had ever eaten out in San Diego wrote their menus on a mirror or wipe board.

Still skinny as a walking stick—he stood six feet, three inches tall and weighed under one hundred fifty pounds—Ted ate constantly while on the road. When he exceeded the $2.50 daily meal money limit for Padres players, Hard Rock Lane docked a portion of his pay. Another favorite road pastime was pinball. Ted spent so much money on it that his mother asked Lane to send her son's paychecks directly to her.

His roommate that first year was former Yankee outfielder Cedric Durst, a veteran who clued Ted in a little bit and showed him how things were done. Another steadying influence was Padres manager Frank Shellenback, a former spitball artist who remains to this day the winningest pitcher in Pacific Coast League history. Also on this club were Vince DiMaggio, in his last minor league season before entering the majors, and two teenagers from Los Angeles,

Bobby Doerr and George McDonald, who were playing professional baseball while other kids their age were still in high school.

Both Doerr and McDonald were students at Fremont High in Los Angeles when they starred on an outstanding American Legion team that later sent five of its players to the major leagues. The pair then dropped out in the eleventh grade and turned pro, signing with the Hollywood Stars and going south when the Stars became the Padres. When the free-spirited McDonald signed his contract, he spent the money on a single-seat Chevy coupe. Doerr was more conservative, investing in the phone company where his father worked.

Doerr, who is in the Hall of Fame, came from a baseball family. His father, Harold, had wanted his sons to play professionally, giving permission to his oldest son, Hal, to quit high school to sign with the Portland Beavers. Thus, when Hollywood came calling and Bobby, at the age of sixteen, asked to do the same thing, Harold could hardly say no. The first thing father and son did after Bobby signed was drive down to the Sears and Roebuck store. They figured Bobby was going to be on the road a lot with the team and would need a new suitcase.

Doerr was such a baby face the clubhouse security guards often refused to let him in the door because they thought he was too young to be on the team. First in San Diego, and later with the Boston Red Sox, where they played together for many seasons, he formed a deep friendship with Williams, a friendship that extended well after their years in baseball ended. Doerr was the steady and quiet one, in contrast to the always moving, shark-like energy of his friend.

It was Doerr who inadvertently put the Red Sox onto Williams in the first place. In July 1936, Eddie Collins, Boston's general manager, went to Portland to observe Doerr and another prospect. But his attention quickly shifted to the youngster with the quick bat who had been with the Padres less than a month. The Padres traveled next to the Bay Area, and Collins, a former American League infielder and future Hall of Famer himself, tagged along for further observation. While in San Francisco he told Bill Lane that he wanted to make Doerr a member of the Red Sox. And oh yeah, he added, we'll take that Williams kid too. Hard Rock and Eddie shook hands on the deal, although a year and a half would pass before they formally drew up a contract.

The Padres finished in a tie for second and attracted big crowds in their smash rookie season in the Coast League. After Ted's rookie season with the club he returned to Hoover to finish his senior year and get his diploma. In the Hoover High yearbook the seniors stated what they wanted to do with their lives after graduation. Ted's wish for the future was summed up in a single word: "Baseball."

This intense yearning to be the best, to be able to walk down the street and have people say, "There goes the greatest hitter who ever lived," consumed him always. At night in his backyard on Utah Street, he swung a bat, again and again and again, taking his cuts. On the road with the Padres it was the same thing: up every morning at six, swinging a rolled-up newspaper in front of the mirror in his hotel room, worrying out loud that his eyes were going bad and that it was affecting his hitting. (Several years later, at his military induction physical, his eyesight was judged to be 20/10.)

While his understanding of hitting (and pitchers) grew, he never understood his mother, who remained a source of pain and humiliation for him. When Salvation May rang her bell on street corners she talked about her son to passersby in order to solicit money from them. Ted asked her to stop this practice but she continued to do it. May saw her son play only a half-dozen times in her lifetime and never when he was in the majors. At one of the few Padres games she attended, she roamed the stands in her Salvation Army uniform, identifying herself as Ted's mother and asking for donations.

In his second year in San Diego, Ted led the league in home runs and the Padres sold more than two hundred thousand tickets on their way to their first pennant. That winter, the Red Sox announced his signing, although May was not happy about it. She felt betrayed by Lane, saying she had turned down better offers than his when Ted was in high school based on the understanding that her son would stay in San Diego until his twenty-first birthday. Hard Rock denied making this agreement with her as well as her contention that he promised to give her 10 percent of the sale price. Money straightened out these tangles in the end. The Red Sox paid Lane $35,000, May received $2,500 in compensation for her son departing San Diego, and Ted earned $3,000 for his first year in the Red Sox organization.

The architect of this deal, Eddie Collins, rode the train from the East Coast to San Diego to meet with May and Sam and get Ted's signature on his contract. But strangely, Ted did not stand to shake Eddie's hand when the old man entered the living room on Utah Street. In fact, he did not get up the entire time Collins was there. The Red Sox executive shrugged it off as the behavior of a nervous nineteen-year-old, later learning that Ted did not get up because there was a hole in his chair and in his embarrassment he did not want the man from Boston to see it.

Torrential rains hit southern California in early 1938. Floods knocked out many roads and power lines, and Doerr and Williams, who planned to take the train together to Red Sox training camp in Florida, could not reach each other by phone. So Doerr hired a pair of ham operators to send a message to Williams to meet him in the Imperial Valley. Word reached Williams, and he hooked up with his buddy for the ride to his first major league spring training camp.

But the greatest Red Sox of them all did not immediately make the club. He spent a season in the minors before arriving in Boston in 1939. That same year Sam and May Williams obtained a divorce.

★   ★   ★   ★   ★

Ted Williams's boyhood years ended with a trip to a major league training camp to take the next step in his baseball career. Joe DiMaggio's early California years ended much the same way. But baseball's unwritten rule prevented Jackie Robinson from playing in either the major leagues or the Pacific Coast League.

It was Robinson, of course, who broke the color line in organized baseball when he signed with the Brooklyn organization in 1945. Taking the field for the Dodgers two years later, he became the first black man in the modern era to play in a major league game. Baseball then was the biggest professional sport in America. New York City, where the game was born, was the nation's media capital. What happened there mattered. That a black man, the grandson of slaves, was playing with and against whites in America's national game—few could miss the significance of this event. Some historians argue that Robinson's breakthrough marked the beginning of the civil rights movement; after him came other breakthroughs in law, politics, and society. *Time* magazine named him one of the one hundred most influential people of the twentieth century.

Robinson's story, like DiMaggio's and Williams's, is too big for any one city or state to claim. He was born in the South, trained in the Armed Forces in the Southwest, played a year of Negro League ball in the Midwest, and his big league home was Brooklyn. But he grew up and came to manhood in California, and these years are essential to his story.

Dodger president and general manager Branch Rickey chose Robinson to carry the burden and honor of being the first black major leaguer for a number of reasons. The obvious one was his talent. Another was the fact that Robinson had gone to school his entire life with whites: he had played on integrated sports teams both in school and after school. He was also educated—college-educated. Additionally, he was a churchgoing man of principle and earnest purpose who was devoted to one woman. All of these facts, which are intertwined with his upbringing, helped form his character, which was probably the fundamental reason for Rickey's choice and certainly why Jackie succeeded in his ordeal.

After leaving on that midnight train from Georgia, Mallie Robinson and her five children arrived in Los Angeles in June 1920. In a letter to her relatives back home, she described it as "the most beautiful sight of my life." The train took them beyond Los Angeles to nearby Pasadena, where her half-brother, Burton Thomas, lived. Mallie found an apartment near the railroad station and, the day after she arrived, went looking for work. A white family in town hired her as a maid for eight dollars a week. After they moved away she hired on with another white family, the Dodges, for whom she worked for the next twenty years.

Situated at the base of the San Gabriel Mountains, Pasadena was a wealthy, largely white residential community originally settled in the 1870s by Midwesterners. Orange Grove Avenue in the city was nicknamed "Millionaire's Row" for its mansions and large estates. The city drew national acclaim for its gardens, the most famous of which belonged to Adolphus Busch, the Midwest beer manufacturer whose heirs now own the St. Louis Cardinals. Pasadena also prided itself as a seat of education and culture: the California Institute of Technology, founded in the late 1800s, and the Huntington Library and Art Gallery, which were formed after the First World War, still thrive in the area.

Two years after the Robinsons arrived, Pasadena opened the Rose Bowl, one of the biggest and best college football stadiums in the country. Across a length of land from the Rose Bowl are the baseball fields of Brookside Park. Both are in northwest Pasadena, which was where the small number of blacks lived in town and where Mallie eventually bought a home on Pepper Street. Jackie lived in this home from the time he was in diapers until his early twenties.

Mallie and her children and another family were the first blacks to live on Pepper Street, and some of their white neighbors did not want them to be there. If they saw a Robinson walking down the street, they went inside their house and closed the door. A few tried to buy Mallie out to get her to leave. Failing this, they took more direct action, burning a cross onto her front lawn. The police made frequent visits to the Robinson house, responding, they said, to complaints from the neighbors about the children making too much noise. But Mallie and the other blacks on Pepper Street considered these visits another form of intimidation to get them to leave the neighborhood.

Mallie prayed every night on her knees, and every Sunday she took her family to services at Scott United Methodist Church. "God watches what you do," she told her children, warning them not to respond to the provocations of whites. "She didn't allow us to go out of our way to antagonize the whites," Jackie said, "and she still made it perfectly clear to us and to them that she was not afraid of them and that she had no intention of allowing them to mistreat us." At the end of the week a bakery in town gave its day-old bread to the Robinsons. After feeding her family, Mallie gave the leftovers to her white neighbors, many of whom were hurting for money and grateful for the help. The whites grudgingly came to accept the presence of the Robinsons on the block.

Jack's first experience with open racial prejudice occurred at the age of eight. A girl neighbor on Pepper Street saw him sweeping the sidewalk outside his house and started yelling, "Nigger! Nigger!" He responded by calling her a "cracker," an insult for whites he had learned from one of his brothers. The girl's father charged out of the house to join in the shouting match. He and Jack started throwing rocks at each other until the man's wife came outside and shamed her husband back inside.

As the youngest of five children, with three big brothers, Jack (the sportswriters gave him the name of Jackie; when he was growing up he was known simply as Jack) learned to stand up for himself at an early age. Despite his mother's warnings he did not always hold his tongue with whites, especially those in authority. This tendency got him into jams and earned him a reputation, unfair or not, as a troublemaker. Angry with one of his white neighbors on Pepper Street, Jack and a few of his friends spread tar across his lawn. When Mallie learned about this she made her son go back and clean it up, standing over him to make sure he did the job right.

In his early teens Jack hooked up with a gang of boys—"blacks, Japanese and Mexican kids," as he described them in his autobiography, but young whites with a nose for trouble ran with them too. The Pepper Street gang stole things from stores, threw dirt clods at passing cars, swiped golf balls off a nearby golf course in order to sell them later. More seriously, a sheriff caught Jack swimming in the Pasadena city reservoir, an activity that was forbidden, and he unholstered his gun and pointed it at the boy to make him get out of the water.

Being told what to do with the barrel of a gun staring at him was one more reminder, if reminder was needed, that life for blacks in Pasadena was different than it was for whites. When the Brookside Plunge, the municipal swimming pool, opened in 1914, it was for whites only. Under a storm of protest the pool's managers agreed to open it for one day a week to blacks and other minorities. "International Day," as it was called, was still city policy when Jack Robinson lived nearby. On hot days in the summer he stood outside the fence watching white kids splash in the pool. He felt justified about taking a dip in the reservoir because on most days the plunge was off limits to him.

Other Pasadena establishments placed restrictions on blacks as well. Blacks could sit in only one section of the movie theater. The Pasadena Playhouse left seats open between white and black patrons to create a physical separation between the races. Schraft's Drug Store hired blacks to work in the kitchen but would not let them eat out front with the whites. At Kress Soda Fountain a black youngster wishing to buy an ice-cream cone might be ignored entirely and not served.

Looking back as a grown-up, Robinson admitted he might have become "a full-fledged juvenile delinquent" were it not for his mother and two influential men who provided guidance to him at critical points in his life. One of these men, Carl Anderson, a car mechanic whose shop was near Pepper Street, did not talk down to Jack the way some adults did. Not scolding, not patronizing, he said that anyone could follow the pack but it took guts to stand apart from the crowd, to go your own way. For Jack Robinson that way was clear, and it led in one direction: sports.

"He was a special little boy," said Willa Mae about her younger brother, "and ever since I can remember, he always had a ball in his hand." Jack excelled at all of the major sports at Pasadena's John Muir Technical High School and a few of the minor ones. He was the playmaking and top scoring guard on the basketball team. He led the Terriers to a regional high school championship baseball tournament against the likes of Wilson's Bob Lemon and Hoover's Ted Williams. On the track team he jumped 23 feet, 1 inch to win the southern California prep title. At the Pacific Coast Negro Tennis Tournament, he walked away with the junior boys title. In football, probably his best sport, he played quarterback, running and throwing the Terriers to an undefeated season until the last game of his senior year. In the big showdown with rival Glendale High, some defenders gang-tackled him and broke three of his ribs. With the best prep athlete in southern California on the sidelines, Glendale won the league title.

An intense competitor, Jackie broke into tears if his team lost or if he performed below his expectations. He was not moved to tears often. In the summer he played shortstop on an all-black team in the Owl League, a night softball league that held its games at Brookside. It was commonplace for him to reach first base on a single or walk and then steal around—second, third, and

Jackie Robinson, Pasadena Junior College, late 1930s.
Security Pacific Collection/Los Angeles Public Library

home. "That isn't stealing," said Pasadena *Post* columnist Rube Samuelson, "it's grand larceny."

As skilled as he was, though, Jackie was not considered the best athlete in the family. This honor belonged to his older brother Mack, whose sport was track. In 1932, when the Summer Olympics came to Los Angeles, Brookside Plunge hosted the swimming events. It was an exciting time for sports in the area and Mack got swept up in it, vowing to become a member of the American track and field team and participate in the next Olympics. Four years later, at the Games in Berlin, Germany, he won a silver medal behind Jesse Owens in the 200-meter dash. Back in Pasadena the Robinson family listened to the race on the radio.

When Jackie enrolled at Pasadena Junior (now City) College, Mack, who also attended school there, was a legend on campus. In his freshman year Jackie long-jumped 23 feet, 9 1/2 inches, surpassing his high school best. But Mack had set the national junior college record with a jump of more than 25 feet. Mack also set national junior college records in the 100-yard and 200-yard sprints, and later attended the University of Oregon, where he also ran track.

After his college days ended, however, Mack found more bitterness than glory. The best job he could get in town was on the night shift sweeping the streets. He carried a broom and pushed around a cart and, on cold nights, he wore his USA Olympic jacket to keep warm. Some Pasadena residents were offended by this, saying that an Olympic jacket should not be worn by a street sweeper and he should take it off. But Mack said he did not have another coat to wear and it was the warmest piece of clothing he owned. After several years he left this job and drifted off to others.

The prejudice and disillusionment experienced by Mack Robinson was nothing new to him or other blacks. His younger brother felt it too as his athletic career progressed. Shig Kawai was a boyhood friend of Jackie's who played with him on the Pasadena Junior College baseball and football teams. "A lot of the time you would hear 'Get that Jap' and 'Get that nigger,'" said Kawai, recalling what opponents said to them. Several of Jackie's white teammates once refused to play with him and the other blacks on the squad until coach Tom Mallory called the whites into his office and put an end to their protest.

One night a patrolman stopped Robinson and a friend as they were walking home from a movie. Jackie and the cop exchanged words, and Jackie was taken to jail, where he spent the night. Later he received a suspended ten-day sentence, a more lenient treatment than other blacks might have received, partly because it was his first offense and partly because of his prominence as an athlete.

The arrest proved to be a pivotal moment for Jackie, for it was around this time that he met another significant figure in his life, the Reverend Karl Downs, the new pastor of the Methodist church where Mallie Robinson worshipped. Being in his twenties, Downs was open to young people and interested in involving them in the activities of the church. "Those of us who had been indifferent church members began to feel an excitement in the belonging," said Jackie, who never backed down athletically, never walked away from a sporting challenge. This new faith in God gave him another frame of reference for his battles on and off the field.

Restaurants sometimes refused to serve him and other blacks on the Bulldog baseball team on road trips. Some hotels would not allow the team to stay there because of the presence of black and Japanese players. When they were on the road Shig Kawai sometimes roomed with Jackie and, after turning out the light at night, he would hear his teammate get out of bed. Then Jackie would kneel in the darkness and softly say a prayer.

On a day in early May 1938, at a track meet in Pomona, Jackie Robinson jumped 25 feet, 6 1/2 inches to establish a new national junior college record, breaking the mark set by his brother. That same afternoon Pasadena Junior College was facing Glendale in a pivotal league baseball contest. From the track meet Jackie hustled over to Glendale, where, despite entering the game late, he got a hit and stole a base in a Bulldog win. For the season he hit .417 and stole second and third seemingly every time he touched first, earning Most Valuable Player and All-Southland honors.

Earlier in the spring Jackie starred for the Pasadena Sox, a youth team with whites and blacks. In a game with the major league Chicago White Sox, who were holding spring training at Brookside Park, Robinson collected two hits, stole second, and triggered a double play with some flashy glove work at shortstop. "Geez," White Sox manager Jimmy Dykes reportedly said, "if that kid was white I'd sign him right now."

Over the spring and summer Jackie again played softball under the lights at Brookside. His games attracted as many as five thousand spectators, an attendance

Jackie Robinson on the Pasadena Junior College Bulldogs, late 1930s.
Security Pacific Collection / Los Angeles Public Library

unheard of for the Owl League. But it was no mystery why the crowds were coming out: they wanted to see Jackie do his thing.

Reporters called him the greatest Pasadena athlete ever. On a football field he was a magician of a runner, dazzling huge crowds at the Rose Bowl, where he had sold hot dogs as a kid to earn money. More than forty thousand people saw him and his Bulldog teammates play Compton, then the largest crowd ever to see a junior college game in the United States.

Watching from the stands that day, probably with his father, was a boy named Edwin Snider. Not yet a teenager, Edwin was already showing signs of athletic prowess. His father had come to California from Ohio and was a fan of the Cincinnati Reds. Ward Snider knew that the right field fences of ballparks tended to be shorter than those in left, so he taught his son to bat left-handed and aim for those shorter fences. The young Snider learned his lessons well. After Compton High he enrolled in the junior college, where, it was said, he could throw a football seventy yards in the air. Pete Rozelle, the future commissioner of the National Football League, played with him on the basketball team. But Edwin liked baseball best of all, and this was the game he pursued professionally, signing with the Brooklyn Dodgers.

Edwin "Duke" Snider's first season with the Dodgers, 1947, was also the rookie year of Jackie Robinson. As a native of Los Angeles who had watched Robinson fake out Compton defenders on the floor of the Rose Bowl, Snider knew the Dodgers were getting somebody real special. The Duke turned out to be fairly special himself, teaming with Jackie on the great Brooklyn teams of the 1950s. The writer Peter Golenbock described Snider as "the first of the California surfer types, the young, sun-bleached blondes with the earthy good looks and the healthy complexions." In New York in the fifties, fans of the city's three major league teams hotly debated which center fielder was best: Willie Mays of the Giants, Mickey Mantle of the Yankees, or the sun-bleached Californian of the Dodgers. All three are in the Hall of Fame.

In describing Jackie Robinson's years in Pasadena, one biographer, Arnold Rampersad, writes, "Whites as well as blacks bowed to his gifts; indeed, most of Jack's classmates seemed able to like and accept one another easily, without much anxiety about differences in race or social standing. He and other gifted young athletes in Pasadena, black or white or Asian American, competed against one another without allowing race to drive a permanent wedge of hatred or resentment between them. After the democracy he had known as a boy, among boys and girls in Pasadena, nothing could convince Robinson that Jim Crow in any sport—or in any other aspect of American life, for that matter—was right or natural."

On the playing field, Jackie Robinson and his classmates may have been creating a vision of the future, a way things could be. But away from the playground the hard fist of reality—the way things were—kept sticking itself into his face.

In the first days of 1939 two white policemen hit and knocked down Jackie's oldest brother, Edgar, in a scuffle along the Tournament of Roses Parade route. They demanded that Edgar produce a chair rental permit (licenses were needed to sit along the parade route), but when he reached into his pocket for his license, one of the officers hit him. He ended up with a black eye and bruises on his arms, although when he went for treatment at a local hospital the medical staff refused to see him because he was black.

The protest by the Pasadena chapter of the National Association for the Advancement of Colored People met with official silence, which added to the outrage felt by Edgar's family. This was one of many incidents that left Jackie with bitterness toward his hometown. "I've always felt like an intruder, even in school," he said once. "People in Pasadena were less understanding, in some ways, than Southerners. And they were more openly hostile."

With his junior college career nearing an end, Robinson began to look at his next step: a four-year university. Many colleges of this time, however, did not accept blacks, and the ones that did often allowed them only token participation in the life of the university. A black student might be permitted to play on the football team, for instance, but have to sit on the bench. Jackie wanted no part of this, and so he chose the University of California at Los Angeles, whose white football coach, Babe Horrell, was a longtime Pasadena man known for his fairness to black players. Also, UCLA's campus in Westwood was only a short drive from Pasadena, so Jackie could remain close to his mother and family.

As he did in high school and junior college, Robinson earned four varsity letters at UCLA—not just playing but starring in football, basketball, track, and baseball. In his debut game for Bruin baseball, he got four hits with four stolen bases, including a trademark theft of home. Because of his baseball commitments, he did not compete in track during the regular season, joining the team only for the conference championship meet, but his winning long jump of 25 feet, second-longest in the nation that year, set a conference record. He later won the National Collegiate Championship in the event.

Jackie Robinson at the University of California, Los Angeles, circa 1940. Associated Students of UCLA

By this time Jackie had matured as an athlete and as a man. He was less shy, more confident in social situations. Lifting weights for football had filled out his shoulders, added muscles, flattened his stomach. Well known around campus, he began to adopt a certain style, nearly always wearing white shirts with the collar open at the neck. The effect, for a black man of this time, was dramatic, for it highlighted his dark skin tones.

These qualities—his self-confidence and his pride in his color, as shown by the vivid contrast of those white shirts—captured the interest of a seventeen-year-old coed named Rachel Isum. A graduate of Manual Arts High in the city, Rachel was a well-dressed, well-put-together freshman who was serious about pursuing a career in nursing. Ray Bartlett, an old friend of Jackie's who also attended UCLA, introduced them. Of course, she knew who he was—everybody on campus knew who Jackie Robinson was—but at first those white shirts put her off. "I thought to myself, Now why would he do that?" she asked herself. "Why would anybody that dark wear a white shirt?"

Each was intrigued by the other and they saw each other regularly until, in the spring of 1941, Jackie decided to quit college after his athletic eligibility ran out. Rachel tried to talk him out of it. So did Reverend Downs and Mallie Robinson, who wanted her son to finish and get his degree. But Jackie saw no point in it; he wanted to earn money to help his mother financially, and he could not do that while still in college. Besides, he was done with school, ready to be out on his own.

The campus newspaper reported that a semipro basketball team and the Mexican baseball leagues had each approached Jackie about a possible job. If true, he turned them both down, instead working as a summer camp director for troubled youths in Atascadero in central California. Then, in the fall, after the camp closed, he traveled to Hawaii to play football for the Honolulu Bears in a semipro league there.

On December 5, 1941, after the season ended, Jackie boarded a ship in Honolulu to return home to California. Two days later he was playing poker with some fellow passengers when members of the crew started to paint the windows of the ship black. Everybody was told to go on deck, where the captain broke the news: Pearl Harbor had been bombed. The United States and Japan were at war. For the rest of the voyage the *Lurline* moved in and out of the sea lanes to avoid being spotted by Japanese warplanes, traveling at night with its lights off. Although it was a passenger ship with no military purpose, no one could be certain it was safe from attack. All on board felt relief when the coast finally came into view.

Before moving onto the war that changed everything, it is worth noting the many traits held in common by these three players—Joe, Ted, and Jackie—the best of their generation. Each was a loner, a man set apart from people even in the midst of a crowd. Each was singled out for his gifts and achieved prominence at an early age. Despite this, or perhaps because of it, each was socially awkward at first and shy around the opposite sex.

All had strong mothers of deep religious faith. Robinson and Williams essentially grew up without a father. Even Giuseppe DiMaggio, who worked long hours to support his large family, was probably not around the house much when Joe was a boy.

All their families struggled to pay the bills and make ends meet. This surely affected all three men. Their hunger to prove themselves and to improve their families' lot in life as well as their own pushed them toward achievement.

Of the three, only DiMaggio closely identified with his hometown, living in San Francisco during the off-season and coming back to stay after his Yankee days were over. Williams's connection with San Diego, though also close, was complicated by his troubled relationship with his mother. Robinson's estrangement with Pasadena was near total. (The city, however, has sought to make amends, several years ago erecting two monumental busts of Jackie and Mack in downtown Centennial Square.)

Another connection among the three, already alluded to, was their shared California boyhood. How much did their surroundings and early experiences contribute to their achievements later in life? It remains an open question. But one thing is certain: greatness had already found them before they ever left the state.

War Games

SATURDAY, MARCH 22 — 2:15 P.M.
SUNDAY, MARCH 23 — 2:15 P.M.
— 1947 —
ESTABLISHED PRICE $3.33   Total $4.00
DERAL TAX   .67
HIS PORTION OF TICKET NOT GOOD FOR ADMITTANCE
DETACH SEPERATE COUPONS FOR INDIVIDUAL GAMES

Donald Barnes was the owner of the St. Louis Browns, a perennial American League doormat that trailed their National League rival in town, the Cardinals, in every meaningful category: championships, stars, tradition, attendance. A dwindling number of fans went to see the Browns play at Sportsman's Park, which Barnes also owned a chunk of, and the club was a money loser.

But Barnes had a daring plan to revive his franchise: move it to Los Angeles. No big league team played in California or anywhere else west of St. Louis, so he knew he would need to do his homework if he expected to sell his plan to the other American League owners, whose approval was required before the move could take place. He checked into train schedules between California and the rest of the country, figuring that ballclubs would be on the road more, criss-crossing between East and West, and travel costs would be higher. He cobbled together a sample schedule of games to show how a Los Angeles franchise would fit into the overall scheme of things.

How did he plan to pay for such a big move? The owners would naturally want to know, and Barnes had done some hard thinking on this subject too. First, sell Sportsman's Park. Then, unload—for a fee—his territorial rights in St. Louis to the Cardinals, who would never have to worry about another baseball competitor in the city again. With the money he made from these deals he planned to buy Wrigley Field in Los Angeles and the Coast League Angels from Phil Wrigley. The Angels would then leave town, clearing the way for the major leagues to begin play in Los Angeles by Opening Day of 1942.

Timing, in baseball and life, is everything, and Barnes's timing could not have been worse. The winter meeting of the owners took place December 8, 1941, the day after Pearl Harbor. Roughly twenty-four hundred American servicemen had been killed and others wounded. The president of the United States had declared war. People across the country feared that the next place on the Japanese hit list was California, and there was widespread doubt whether baseball—any baseball—would be played during the war. One report says the owners did not bother to read Barnes's proposal and tabled it without discussion. Another says they quickly voted it down.

In any event, the Browns stayed put. After the war there was some talk about reviving the idea of moving them to Los Angeles, but it remained just talk. Early in the 1950s they relocated to Baltimore and became the Orioles.

Everybody's plans across America suddenly changed after Pearl Harbor. This was true for nineteen-year-old Mel Atwell, who learned the game playing with his brothers in the front yard of their house on Linda Rosa Street in Pasadena. The Atwells lived on the north side of the tracks in a nothing-fancy house, they were just scraping by like every other family they knew, but their front yard was huge and the pickup games they held there drew kids from all around the neighborhood.

One reason why their games were so popular was that they had bona fide baseball gear at their house. Nobody could afford to buy anything new; they scrounged around for whatever they could find and they played with it, no matter how wrecked and ripped up it was. But Bud and Dick Atwell, Mel's older brothers, both played professional baseball, and when they came home they brought balls and bats and gloves that everybody could use.

Bud played in the minor leagues in the Midwest, while Dick traveled all around with the House of David barnstorming team. The Israelite House of David, based in Michigan, sponsored several barnstorming teams, and for a time Dick Atwell was their highest-paid performer. To play for the House of David you did not have to subscribe to its religious beliefs, which Dick did not,

House of David baseball team, 1932. Dick Atwell is standing, fourth from the left. Millie and Mel Atwell Collection

but you did have to grow a beard, which Dick did. The bearded Davids traveled across Canada and America, down through Mexico and Latin America, playing exhibitions against local clubs and entertaining fans with their whiz-bang pre-game trick-throwing and -catching routines. In the off-season, when not on tour, Dick went back to Pasadena and worked as a prop man for Republic Pictures, also playing on the studio's semipro team.

When Dick and Bud came home, they spent lots of time at Brookside Park, which was only a bicycle ride away from their house. Little brother Mel tagged along with them, shagging balls and playing catch and breathing the same rarefied air as these older guys, some of whom were way bigger stars than his brothers. Fat Freddie Fitzsimmons, a pitcher for the Giants and Dodgers, hung out there in the winter. So did Max West, a National League (and later, Coast League) slugger.

Then there were the guys Mel's age, the guys he hung out with: Irv Noren, who grew up to play outfield for the New York Yankees, and Ralph Kiner, a powerhouse home run hitter with the Pittsburgh Pirates who reached the pinnacle, the Hall of Fame. But in the late 1930s Ralph was just a big kid from Alhambra with uncombed hair who was looking for a game like everybody else. What made him stand out, at least to Mel and the others, was his car. They all piled into Ralph's car and he drove them around to games in the area. Bob Lillis, who went on to be a major league shortstop, coach, and manager, was only a kid at the time, but he made himself useful as batboy on Mel's semipro team.

Mel was a catcher and infielder, not big or fast, but he played with Jackie Robinson on the Pasadena Sox youth team and made money of sorts on the semipro Merchants. During the game someone would pass a hat around the stands, and the fans would chip in whatever they could. First the owner took his cut, then the players split what was left. On a Sunday Mel would walk away with a dollar and change in his pocket, which was not half bad considering you could buy a cold soda for a nickel and you earned it playing ball.

Mel had his sights set on professional baseball. Not on the majors or the Coast League—his skills were not up to that level—but maybe some club in Idaho or Nebraska, the way his brother Bud did. But after Pearl Harbor these dreams got set aside. In this way he was like millions of other young men who left behind their boyhood fantasies to do the awful work that needed to be done. Mel saw duty on over a dozen ships in the war, participating in the Battle of Okinawa and other major battles in the Pacific. After six years in the service, his best baseball well behind him, he returned to Pasadena grateful to be alive and glad to be done with the fighting. He bought a house, started a family with his wife, Millie, and became a firefighter with the Pasadena Fire Department, where he served for decades before retiring.

In January 1942 President Franklin Roosevelt issued his famous letter about baseball, permitting the game to continue during the war. "I honestly feel that it would be best for the country to keep baseball going," he wrote. "There will be fewer people unemployed and everybody will work longer hours and harder than ever before….Here is another way of looking at it—

if 300 teams use 5,000 or 6,000 players, these players are a definite recreational asset to at least 20,000,000 of their fellow citizens—and that in my judgment
is thoroughly worthwhile."

P.P.F.

January 15, 1942.

My dear Judge:-

Thank you for yours of January fourteenth. As
you will, of course, realise the final decision about the
baseball season must rest with you and the Baseball Club
owners -- so what I am going to say is solely a personal
and not an official point of view.

I honestly feel that it would be best for the
country to keep baseball going. There will be fewer people
unemployed and everybody will work longer hours and harder
than ever before.

And that means that they ought to have a
chance for recreation and for taking their minds off
their work even more than before.

Baseball provides a recreation which does
not last over two hours or two hours and a half, and
which can be got for very little cost. And, incidentally,
I hope that night games can be extended because it gives
an opportunity to the day shift to see a game occasionally.

As to the players themselves, I know you agree
with me that individual players who are of active military
or naval age should go, without question, into the services.
Even if the actual quality of the teams is lowered by the
greater use of older players, this will not dampen the
popularity of the sport. Of course, if any individual
has some particular aptitude in a trade or profession,
he ought to serve the Government. That, however, is a
matter which I know you can handle with complete justice.

Here is another way of looking at it -- if
300 teams use 5,000 or 6,000 players, these players are
a definite recreational asset to at least 20,000,000
of their fellow citizens -- and that in my judgment is
thoroughly worthwhile.

With every best wish,

Very sincerely yours,

Hon. Kenesaw M. Landis,
233 North Michigan Avenue,
Chicago,
Illinois.

*President Franklin Roosevelt's famous "Green Light Letter," permitting baseball
to be played during the war, 1942. National Archives and Records Administration*

While the president offered broad approval for baseball, specific authority for the Pacific Coast League fell under the jurisdiction of United States Army Lieutenant General John DeWitt, who oversaw the Western Defense Command covering California and other states. By spring the fears of a Japanese attack on the mainland had lessened, and General DeWitt gave the go-ahead for the Coast League for its 1942 season, which included night games until they were banned in August. But the Army lifted this ban after the next season because night games had become a popular source of recreation for workers in defense industries, who could go out to the ballpark after the day shift ended.

Because of the influx of men into the Armed Forces, the best baseball played in America during the war was on service teams. The military saw baseball as a way to improve the fitness of its soldiers, boost morale, and build pride. Service teams competed against one another and civilian and college clubs. In the spring of 1943 Joe DiMaggio was gliding around center field for the Santa Ana Air Base team in Riverside. Two other San Francisco major leaguers played on this Army Air Corps club in Riverside: St. Louis Browns outfielder Wally Judnich, and Dario Lodigiani, a gifted infielder for Philadelphia and Chicago in the American League.

The stars of this team later transferred to Hawaii, where more baseball talent joined them: Charlie Silvera, another San Franciscan, who became a reserve catcher with the Yankees; first baseman Ferris Fain, a graduate of Roosevelt High in Oakland who won back-to-back batting titles with the Philadelphia Athletics in the early 1950s while fielding his position peerlessly; second baseman Jerry Priddy, who played eleven big league seasons; and Joe Gordon, who, like Priddy, hailed from Los Angeles. The acrobatic-fielding Gordon, for the Yankees and Indians, stands with Bobby Doerr as one of the two best second basemen of their era.

With so many fine players away in the service, organized baseball suffered a steep decline, both in fan interest and quality of play. Hole-pluggers—guys who were there only because the regulars were not—filled the rosters of the Pacific Coast League. Too young to wear the uniform of the United States Army, fifteen-year-old Bill Sarni of Los Angeles wore the uniform of the hometown Angels and filled in as catcher. Sarni had real talent, though, and years later punched a time card with the St. Louis Cardinals. Some grizzled baseball veterans, easily old enough to be Sarni's father, got to hang around the game a while longer because their younger competition was overseas. They included ex–major leaguer Charlie Root, who, at forty-four, won fifteen games as pitcher-manager of the Hollywood Stars, and Herm "Old Folks" Pilette, who baffled wartime hitters on the Coast until a year shy of his fiftieth birthday.

Two years before Pearl Harbor, a minor league club from Ogden, Utah, held a tryout in San Pablo, a small town in the East Bay. Players from all around northern California attended the tryout in hopes of making the team.

Two of the players, Billy Hebert, a Stockton second baseman, and Pete Deas, a shortstop who lived in San Francisco with his parents, were good friends who had gotten to know each other kicking around the semipro circuit in the area. Both were eager to show people they could make it in organized baseball.

Billy made the grade, all right, and signed a contract, his first as a professional. But his buddy had to wait two weeks until the end of camp to learn that Ogden had *two* new starting middle infielders—Hebert at second, Deas at short.

In Ogden, which was a Cincinnati farm team, Deas and Hebert became even closer friends than before, close enough to know the other's quirks. "What a mess," Pete said about Billy. "I never saw a ballplayer who had such a dirty uniform. He chewed tobacco and he'd spit tobacco juice on his hands and rub it on the front of his uniform."

In addition, Deas discovered, Billy was one of the most superstitious ballplayers he ever saw. In those days, after they retired the side, fielders did not carry their gloves with them into the dugout; rather, they tossed them on the grass near their positions. But to Billy if a glove landed with its palm up, it was bad luck. Another sign of bad luck was when two gloves lying on the ground touched each other. In those cases Billy made sure not to touch the other glove when he picked up his, otherwise the bad luck would rub off on him. And he always stepped on second base when running off the field at the end of an inning. That was good luck, he said.

It is not clear how long Billy played for Ogden, but the 1941 season was his last in professional baseball. In August of the following year, he entered combat in the Battle of Guadalcanal. The Japanese were building an air base at Guadalcanal, an island in the Solomon Islands chain, for use as a launching pad for attacks against American ships. The Marines invaded and won a hard-fought victory in which nearly eighteen hundred Americans lost their lives. One of those killed was Hebert.

Pete Deas was serving in Milne Bay, New Guinea, when he learned of his friend's death. His parents sent him the newspaper clipping about it. Deas survived the war to become a San Francisco firefighter. Today, the Stockton Ports of the California League play their home games at Billy Hebert Field.

★   ★   ★   ★   ★

The Los Angeles Nippons were one of the best Japanese American teams of their era. The Nips, as they called themselves—some players had the name sewn on their uniforms—competed against the San Fernando Aces, the San Pedro Skippers, and other Nisei teams. The Nippons, who sometimes featured whites on their roster, also played against white semipro teams in southern California.

On the afternoon of December 7 or December 8—the exact day is not clear—the Nippons were playing in Los Angeles against a studio team from the Paramount movie lot. During the game FBI agents arrived at the field and watched from the sidelines. They did not interfere with the game, waiting until it was over before taking the Nisei players away for questioning. They were later released.

What happened that day to the Los Angeles Nippons happened to Nisei and Issei all around California, which had (and still has) the largest population of Japanese Americans of any state in the country. Authorized to do so by the president, law enforcement authorities rounded up all persons suspected of possible sabotage against the United States. This sweep focused on those of Japanese descent, and over the next weeks they faced a series of restrictive and punitive measures that culminated, on February 19, 1942, with the harsh dictates of Executive Order 9066, which called for the detention of all persons who posed a potential threat to the American war effort.

Executive Order 9066 broadly applied to Americans of German, Italian, and Japanese descent as well as to foreign nationals from those countries. But it was left to the Western Defense Command to determine specifically how the order was to be enforced. In February congressional hearings in Los Angeles, San Francisco, and two Northwest cities considered a proposal by General DeWitt to evacuate all three of these groups from the West Coast and detain them in isolated inland camps during the war. But German Americans, who had suffered prejudice during the first world war, successfully sought to be excluded from the order. Italian Americans also argued for an exemption, citing, among other reasons, the case of Giuseppe and Rosalie DiMaggio. Neither was an American citizen, but, their attorney argued, forcing the parents of Joe DiMaggio to leave their home would hurt the country's morale. In the end it was decided that Executive Order 9066 should not apply to the Italians either, and the hammer fell on the Japanese (although other groups were still the targets of intimidation and restrictions).

Japanese in California had to leave their homes, sometimes with only a day's notice or less, and report to assembly centers where they were held until more permanent relocation. Kenso Nushida, the former Sacramento Solon pitcher and "Boy Wonder" of Nisei baseball, fled the state rather than be interned. He returned to his native Hawaii, which did not have such camps.

Chiura Obata, founder of the Fuji Athletic Club, the first mainland Japanese baseball club, was living in Berkeley with his wife, Haruko, and their three children when the order was signed. By the spring of 1942 he had long since moved on from his youthful passion of baseball to become an artist and a professor at the University of California. He felt he had no choice but to submit to the camps, but his youngest son, Gyo, an architecture student at Cal, did not see it that way.

It is wrong, he told his father. It is against the Constitution, and I will not go.

Chiura agreed to help his son. If they could find a college for him outside California, he could escape the camps and continue with his studies. But most universities refused to accept Nisei students because of the war. Finally, Washington University in St. Louis said it would accept Gyo as a transfer student. All he had to do was get there.

Because of travel restrictions on the Japanese, Gyo needed special permission to go to San Francisco to plead his case at Army headquarters. He received an okay to go to the city but not the answer he wanted to hear there: he could not leave the state for any reason. Chiura then got involved, calling on a friend and former student, attorney Geraldine Scott, who worked for General DeWitt in his office. With Scott on his side, Gyo got a second hearing and won permission to leave, but only if he was on a train by midnight that night because the evacuation was scheduled to begin the next morning. If he remained in California, he would have to report for incarceration with the rest of his family.

All the banks were closed that day. Gyo had to leave, but he had no money. His father and Scott emptied their pockets and borrowed some more money so he could buy a ticket to St. Louis. He made it onto the train in time.

Down in San Jose, other Japanese families, like the Minetas, received their orders to report to the local railroad yards, where they would be taken to an assembly center. The Minetas had lived in the area for decades and operated a successful business. Nevertheless, they too had to go into the camps, leaving behind their home and business and bringing only what they could carry in their hands. Norm Mineta, who was ten years old, wore his Cub Scout uniform and carried a baseball bat and glove when he arrived at the railroad yards. Some of his white friends from school came with him to say goodbye to him and his family. They watched as a guard took the bat away from him because it could possibly be used as a weapon.

Kenichi Zenimura reported with his family to the Fresno Assembly Center, one of the temporary detention centers in California used to house the Japanese before they moved to camps elsewhere in the state and the West. Evicted from their home, the Zenimuras stayed in horse stalls in the converted fairgrounds. When Kenichi immigrated to Fresno in the early 1920s, he had helped build a ballpark for the Issei and Nisei in town because whites excluded them from the one they used; at the assembly center he and the other internees did the same, creating a place for them to play ball during their detention.

After a period of months Kenichi, his wife, Kiyoko, and their two American-born sons, Howard and Harvey, left California for the Gila River Indian Reservation in Arizona, one of ten internment camps operated by the War Department. Initially Kenichi expressed dismay at being assigned to Gila River because other Fresno-area ballplayers had gone elsewhere and he felt the quality of competition would be inferior there. But as soon as they arrived at Gila he and his sons began to build a ballfield, just as internees were doing at every other camp in the West.

Every camp had organized baseball leagues and teams, playing a slate of games on fields built by the internees themselves. As a rule the fields were located outside the barbed wire fences that formed the perimeter of the compound. The camps were in such isolated venues that authorities did not worry much about the Japanese trying to escape. Nor was escape on the minds of the Japanese anyway. As much as they hated being incarcerated, most Japanese went along with the restrictions imposed on them because they felt it was the best thing they could do under the circumstances.

In the Manzanar camp in Inyo County in the Mojave Desert, the internees drove out into the hills in search of rock for their ballfield. They filled up the

Camp baseball player,
Manzanar, 1942. Photo by
Dorothea Lange.
Courtesy of the Bancroft
Library, University of
California, Berkeley

truck, drove back to camp, unloaded the rock, and placed it around the dugout and bleacher areas, tamping down the dirt with shovels to eliminate the dust kicked up by the desert winds. Former San Fernando Aces catcher Barry Tamura, who worked for the camp fire department, brought over a hose and sprayed water on the dirt in a further effort to keep down the dust.

At Tule Lake in Modoc County in the northeast corner of California, one camp team ordered their jerseys from a Sears and Roebuck catalog. The name of each player was then stenciled on the back of his jersey. For pants they used heavy cotton potato sacks fitted and sewn by camp seamstresses. Another resourceful Tule Lake club used canvas uniforms made from mattress coverings.

Baseball was a staple of camp life. Intense rivalries sprung up between teams, who vied against one another for the camp championship and occasionally traveled to other camps to see how they stacked up against internees elsewhere. On Opening Day of the 1944 season at Tule Lake, clubs from Manzanar, Arizona, and the host camp competed in a tournament attended by eighteen thousand spectator-internees. It was Baseball Crazy Day all over again: a chance for people to laugh and yell and let loose with their emotions. "Without baseball, camp life would have been miserable," said internee George Omachi, who later became a coach and major league scout in the Central Valley. "There was no torture or anything like that, but it was humiliating."

Champions, Manzanar Baseball Association, 1943. Courtesy of Pete Mitsui.
From Through a Diamond: 100 Years of Japanese American Baseball,
by Kerry Yo Nakagawa. NBRP (Nisei Baseball Research Project)

The grandest of the internment camp fields was at Gila River, the wartime home of the Zenimuras. First it was just Kenichi and his sons, chopping down sagebrush, shoveling dirt, clearing rocks. Soon other internees pitched in, pulling weeds and hacking at the brush. With the field mostly cleared, Kenichi borrowed a bulldozer from camp officials and used its blade to scrape down the surface of the infield, his crew of workers following behind, meticulously clearing away every rock and pebble and patting down the dirt with shovels. No matter what they did, though, the relentless wind kept kicking up dirt. To solve this problem Zenimura and his men ran an irrigation line to the field and flooded it with water. When the water evaporated, the dirt dried solid.

Next they laid pipe from the laundry room to the field, providing it with a steady supply of water. Then they planted seeds. Over time these seeds grew into outfield and infield grass. The crew scrounged wood pieces from the camp's perimeter fence, and these two-by-fours became the makings of a backstop. One part of the camp held a lumber yard, and at night Kenichi and other internees stole across to the yard, grabbed pieces of lumber, and carried them

Camp baseball game, Tule Lake, 1944. Courtesy of the Bancroft Library, University of California, Berkeley

over to the field. Camp officials evidently knew what they were doing but looked the other way as an eight-foot-high fence, crafted by Nisei carpenters, rose around the outfield grass. When they finished the fence the carpenters built bleachers behind home plate, five rows deep, so when fans came to watch the games at Gila River Field, they had a place to sit.

They played baseball year-round at Gila River, every day they could. Close to six thousand people, half the camp's population, attended the biggest games. They passed a hat around the bleachers, and with the money they raised they ordered gear from Holman's Sporting Goods back home in Fresno. Holman's sent boxes full of balls, bats, gloves, and caps to Gila River.

The Gila River camp closed in November 1945, after the Allied victories in Europe and Japan. Manzanar also closed that month. The last of the ten camps to shut down, Tule Lake, operated in a limited capacity until spring of the next year.

About 120,000 Japanese were held in camps during the war. Upon their release, internees received three dollars in meal money and a ticket back to where they originally departed from, if they chose to go back there. Kenichi Zenimura returned to Fresno with his family, where he continued his lifelong association with the game, coaching youth baseball and playing well into his fifties. His sons, Harvey and Howard, starred on the Fresno State University baseball team and played professionally in Japan.

Kenichi Zenimura, 1930s. Kenichi Zenimura Collection.
From Through a Diamond: 100 Years of Japanese American Baseball,
by Kerry Yo Nakagawa. NBRP (Nisei Baseball Research Project)

Norm Mineta's family spent most of the war in the Heart Mountain intern-ment camp in Wyoming. He grew up to become the mayor of San Jose, a United States congressman, and Secretary of the Department of Transportation.

Chiura Obata, his wife, and two of his children stayed at the Tanforan Assembly Center in San Bruno before moving to a Topaz, Utah, camp. In both Topaz and San Bruno, Chiura taught and practiced art. In the fall of 1945 he resumed his position as a professor of art at the University of California at Berkeley.

Gyo Obata never went into the camps, continuing his studies in architec-ture in St. Louis during the war. He later co-founded the firm of Hellmuth, Obata, and Kassabaum (HOK), which has since grown into one of the largest architectural and engineering companies in the world. With Gyo as its princi-pal designer and chairman, HOK has designed some of the most beautiful ball-parks in America, including Camden Yards in Baltimore. Another widely praised HOK creation, Pacific Bell (now SBC) Park in San Francisco, opened in 2000.

In 1976 President Gerald Ford formally revoked Executive Order 9066, calling the internment period "a sad day in American history." A later president, George H. W. Bush, authorized the payment of reparations to all internment camp survivors and issued an apology on behalf of the people of the United States, although, as he said in a letter to Nisei families, "a monetary sum and words alone cannot restore lost years or painful memories."

Breakthrough

SATURDAY, MARCH 22 — 2:15 P.M.
SUNDAY, MARCH 23 — 2:15 P.M.
— 1947 —
ABLISHED PRICE - - $3.33   Total $4.00
ERAL TAX - - - .67
THIS PORTION OF TICKET NOT GOOD FOR ADMITTANCE
DETACH SEPERATE COUPONS FOR INDIVIDUAL GAMES

The convulsions of war brought sweeping changes to California. Women entered the workforce in greater numbers than ever before, taking over jobs formerly filled by the men who were fighting overseas. Women worked on assembly lines, used welding torches, soldered fittings, climbed scaffolding, hauled cable, and painted the battleships and bombers being sent to Europe, Africa, and Asia. The famous portraits of Rosie the Riveter, an idealized female factory worker clad in overalls and flexing her muscles, came to symbolize America's total commitment to winning the war over totalitarianism.

In February 1943, the sports department of the *San Francisco Call-Bulletin* faced a similar shortage of men. Newspaper staffs at that time were essentially men's clubs, and the few female reporters who worked in newsrooms almost always wrote about traditional female-oriented topics such as food or fashion, their stories appearing on what was called the "woman's page." Generally only men covered sports.

But Ernie Cope, the sports editor for the *Call-Bulletin*, was in a fix. Another of his reporters had left the paper for the service, and he needed somebody to cover that beat while he was gone. "Too bad you're a girl," he told Adeline Sumi. "Because if you weren't a girl," he added, "you could have the job."

Though a woman of twenty-one, Adeline Sumi was, in the parlance of the newsroom, a copyboy. Her job mainly consisted of minor editorial tasks and fetching things for the other, mostly male employees of the paper. She immediately protested Cope's idea that she knew nothing about sports.

Sure she knew sports—"absolutely," she said. Growing up in Nashwauk, Minnesota, she had played hockey, baseball, and football with her brothers. She had played wide receiver and caught passes on their street football teams.

Cope looked at her and said, "All right, it's yours," agreeing to give her a two-week trial covering high school baseball.

Except for the part about growing up in Minnesota and having brothers, not a word of what Sumi told Cope was true. She did not know a thing about sports. She had never seen a baseball game in her life, but this was her chance to get out of being a copyboy and into writing, which was what she wanted. The job also doubled her salary to thirty-six dollars a week.

After work Adeline headed straight for the public library to do some cramming. She checked out sports books and poured over them that night. At the paper the next day she read over old game clippings in an attempt to learn as much as she could.

Covering her first game, however, she received unpleasant news: she had to keep score, too. The reporter covering the game was the official scorer, recording the hits, errors, strikeouts, walks, and runs. No one had mentioned this to her and she had read nothing about it, so she had to figure it out on the spot.

It made sense to Adeline that anyone who made contact with the ball and knocked it onto the field of play deserved credit for a hit, regardless of whether the batter reached base or not. She was similarly forgiving about errors. She felt that even if a boy in the field had flubbed the ball, he did not deserve to receive a black mark if he had made an honest effort to catch it. The box score for her first game, if it had been accurate, would have represented one of the more unusual games in baseball history: Balboa High—2 runs, 29 hits, no errors; Lincoln High—0 runs, 23 hits, no errors.

But Sumi was a quick study, and with her editor's guidance she rapidly caught on to scorekeeping and other intricacies of the sportswriter's craft. Her knowledge of baseball increased with every game she saw, and she soon became the trivia expert on the *Call-Bulletin* sports desk. Whenever a member of the public called in with a question about sports, Sumi could be counted on to provide the answer. Her encyclopedic knowledge impressed even the old-timers in the department who were uneasy with the presence of a female in their formerly all-male enclave.

Sumi did not mention that the questions were prearranged setups. She had asked friends to phone in with obscure questions that she already knew the answers to. Displaying such expertise, she felt, would strengthen her standing among the men.

The ruse unraveled one day when a friend asked a question that varied from the script, and Sumi fumbled the answer. "Hey," she said loud enough for the men to hear, "you weren't supposed to ask that."

Since her editors felt that their largely male readership would not react well to seeing a female byline in the sports section, Adeline's name was shortened to the more manly-sounding "Del." But when Del showed up at games, her cover was obviously blown. While fans, coaches, and players were generally open and accepting of her, her male colleagues who covered the high school beat for the other papers in town were not so charmed. They inevitably stuck her with the worst games when they pooled reporting assignments.

Sumi's two-week trial as a sportswriter extended three years. By war's end her true identity was no longer a secret, and most readers knew she was a she.

In the summer of 1945 Walt Daley, the *Call-Bulletin*'s sportswriter whose position Sumi had filled, returned to San Francisco on leave from the war. On a visit to the paper he and Sumi met and they quickly hit it off. Two months after their first date, wedding bells sounded, and a year later they had the first of seven children. Walt resumed his old job on the *Call-Bulletin* sports beat, and Adeline quit the paper to raise a family. Some years later, with the children grown, she returned to newspapers to write a humor column for the *San Francisco Chronicle*.

The grim realities of war created opportunities for women like Adeline Sumi Daley as well as African Americans and other minorities. Blacks from the South and elsewhere poured into California in search of work—and in many cases they found it. The seaport cities of Oakland, San Francisco, Los Angeles, and San Diego boomed with the business of war. By itself the southern California aircraft industry—North American, Lockheed, Douglas, and other companies—produced an estimated fifty thousand combat planes during the war, with women and blacks holding down spots in the assembly lines. "Normally the aircraft industry was hostile to blacks," writes historian Arnold Rampersad, "but the suddenly vital need for military equipment and supplies

Chet Brewer, circa 1950s. Courtesy of University of Southern California, on behalf of the USC Special Libraries and Archival Collections

following Pearl Harbor had cracked the racial walls."

The social changes triggered by the war appeared poised to crack baseball's color barrier. In July 1943, Pacific Coast League president Clarence Rowland announced that a tryout was to be held by the Los Angeles Angels, at Wrigley Field in Los Angeles, of two southern California black players: Lou Dials and Chet Brewer. Dials, a former engineering student of Cal Berkeley, was working at Lockheed and playing for its semipro team. Brewer, also employed in the aircraft industry, was a six-foot-four-inch Negro League right-hander who had pitched against the likes of Satchel Paige and Smoky Joe Williams. If the twosome made the Angels, they would become the first blacks in organized baseball in the twentieth century.

But the tryout never took place because Phil Wrigley, the owner of the Angels and the major league Chicago Cubs, stopped it. Wrigley was a much admired and respected baseball man who, among his other achievements in the game, founded the All-American Girls Baseball League in 1943. This all-female league, based in the Midwest, gave women (some of whom came from California) the chance to play what was traditionally a man's game. But while Wrigley could create opportunities for women in baseball, he could not, at this time, do the same for blacks. Apparently fearing a backlash from other major league owners if he allowed the two players onto his Coast League club, he reportedly told Dials, "I know how good you are, but I don't have a place for you."

After Wrigley's rejection, Rowland took his case to Oakland owner Cookie Devincenzi, whose Oaks were in town to play the Angels. Devincenzi agreed to a tryout, but again, it got stopped before it could occur. When Dials and Brewer arrived at Wrigley Field to suit up for practice, Oaks manager Johnny Vergez told them to get out of the clubhouse. They replied that Devincenzi had personally approved the tryout and they were there on his instructions. But Vergez, a former St. Mary's man who had played against Dials at Cal, refused to let them have uniforms, and they left without ever taking the field.

The United Auto Workers Union and the Los Angeles County Board of Supervisors filed letters of protest about the incident, and picketers briefly

Los Angeles Angels (and Chicago Cubs) owner Phil Wrigley and his wife, circa 1930s.
Security Pacific Collection / Los Angeles Public Library

demonstrated outside Wrigley Field to express their unhappiness with the Angels. But organized baseball's policy regarding blacks remained intact.

Dials continued to play on Lockheed's semipro team during the war and for various teams after it. Brewer pitched in black baseball for five more years before retiring from active play. In the 1950s and '60s he became a significant figure in Los Angeles youth baseball, coaching and tutoring a number of gifted inner-city players who grew up to do what Brewer himself was not permitted to do—play in the major leagues. They include Hall of Famer Eddie Murray, pitchers

Dock Ellis and Don Wilson, outfielders Reggie Smith, Bobby Tolan, and Willie Crawford, and many more.

Pressure had been building to admit blacks into organized baseball well before the war. But the war brought the issue forward in the starkest of terms: how could a man be expected to work for his country, and fight and die for it, and yet be denied basic Constitutional rights because of his color alone? The national pastime had no answer to this question, and other people had to come forward before the breakthrough could occur.

Soon after Pearl Harbor, Jackie Robinson got a job driving a truck for Lockheed in Burbank. While living with his mother on Pepper Street in Pasadena, he felt good about earning a regular paycheck that contributed to her financial support. His relationship with Rachel Isum blossomed, and he started playing baseball again, working out with the Chicago White Sox at their training camp at Brookside Park. White Sox manager Jimmy Dykes, who had seen Robinson play in the past, said that Jackie was worth fifty thousand dollars to the major league club that signed him. But no offers were forthcoming.

In March Robinson received his orders to report for induction into the United States Army. He got his vaccinations and a physical at Fort MacArthur in San Pedro before beginning basic training at Fort Riley, Arkansas. Well known for his accomplishments in college track and football, he applied to Officer Candidate School. The Army turned him down at first, for racial reasons, but later revised its stance and accepted him and a few others, the first blacks to be admitted into officer training school in its history. Not having graduated from either UCLA or Pasadena Junior College, Robinson took pride in becoming a second lieutenant in the Army Cavalry because it showed he was making his way in the world. (Rachel was herself making her way in the world, studying nursing at the University of California, San Francisco.)

After being transferred from Fort Riley to Fort Hood, Texas, Robinson boarded an Army bus. Ordered to move to the back of the bus, the second lieutenant, knowing that Army regulations had outlawed segregation on its buses, refused to move. The military police were called in, and Robinson was later arrested and ordered to stand trial for disobeying an officer. He saw the court martial as a test of his faith in God. His defense attorney described it to the jury as "a situation in which a few individuals sought to vent their bigotry on a Negro they considered 'uppity' because he had the audacity to seek to exercise rights that belonged to him as an American and as a soldier." The trial lasted four hours and Robinson was

Jackie Robinson, United States Army Lieutenant, 1944.
USC Special Collections

acquitted on all counts. In November 1944, after three years in the Army, he received his honorable discharge.

Early the next year he returned once more to baseball, trying out, with two other blacks, for the Boston Red Sox. Both the Red Sox and the National League Boston Braves had been under local political pressure to give black players a chance. Red Sox manager Joe Cronin reportedly expressed admiration for Robinson and the others, but like so many other tryouts involving blacks, nothing came of it.

With no place for him in white baseball, Jackie joined the Kansas City Monarchs of the Negro Leagues, but the constant travel around the country wore him down. So did the indignities of being refused rooms at white hotels and not being allowed to eat at restaurants that served only whites. Nor did Robinson fit in all that well in the Negro Leagues. Many players in the league came from the South and represented an older generation of blacks. Robinson was from California, college-educated, a former officer in the Army who did not drink or smoke or chase women. And Negro League baseball was the first time he had ever played solely with and against blacks and in front of mainly black audiences.

Discouraged about never cracking the walls of white baseball, unhappy in the Negro Leagues, lonesome and homesick, Jackie considered quitting the game. He thought about going home to Los Angeles, marrying Rachel, and perhaps working with youngsters as a high school coach.

It was late August 1945. Japan had surrendered, ending the war in the Pacific. Victory in Europe had come only months before. The old order was in ruins; a new order was forming. The unlikely bearer of this news was a middle-aged Brooklyn Dodgers scout named Clyde Sukeforth.

Sukeforth approached Robinson after a Monarchs game in Chicago, explaining that he was acting on behalf of his boss, Branch Rickey, who wanted to speak to him in person. Jackie did not know why the Dodgers president and general manager wanted to talk to him, and the canny scout did not tell him. Nevertheless Jackie agreed to go to Brooklyn.

One of baseball's smartest and most innovative front office men, Rickey, a lifelong Methodist who quoted Scripture while chewing on a cigar, had a secret plan to integrate baseball. It had to be secret, he felt, because if word leaked out, opposition would surely surface to stop him. For months he had been surveying the Negro Leagues, looking for the right candidate, the man who would be first. No one else had Jackie's credentials. The Brooklyn executive himself made discrete inquiries in southern California about Robinson before dispatching Sukeforth to Chicago.

Robinson and Sukeforth went to Dodger headquarters on Montague Street to meet with Rickey. Opening the door to Rickey's office, Sukeforth said, "Mr. Rickey, here is Jack Roosevelt Robinson." The three men sat down, closing the door behind them. When the door opened again Jackie had signed a contract with the Dodgers organization, and the modern game of baseball was born.

Six months after his signing, Jackie and Rachel became husband and wife at a ceremony at the Independent Church of Christ in Los Angeles, the Reverend Karl Downs presiding. Ray Bartlett, who had introduced the bride and groom, acted as best man. Babe Horrell, Jackie's UCLA football coach, was among those in attendance.

After honeymoon night in the Clark Hotel, the happy couple traveled north to San Jose, staying at the home of Rachel's aunt. But the honeymoon had to be cut short because both of them needed to prepare for spring training, Robinson's first with the Dodgers. Branch Rickey had requested that Rachel come to Florida too. Her husband's long journey was only beginning, and she planned to be with him every step of the way.

Jackie and Rachel Robinson at a UCLA homecoming, 1951.
Associated Students of UCLA

Golden Boys

SATURDAY, MARCH 22 — 2:15 P.M.
SUNDAY, MARCH 23 — 2:15 P.M.
— 1947 —

ABLISHED PRICE $3.33
ERAL TAX .67 Total $4.0(

HIS PORTION OF TICKET NOT GOOD FOR ADMITTANCE
DETACH SEPERATE COUPONS FOR INDIVIDUAL GAMES

His name was Jackie too—Jackie Jensen. He was a white fellow born in San Francisco who moved to Oakland at the age of five after his parents divorced. His father lost touch with the family and his mother raised him and his two brothers by herself. It was not a life of plenty. She worked long hours at a warehouse in San Francisco, leaving Jackie and his brothers to fend for themselves much of the time. Jackie and the family moved sixteen times before he entered high school—"every time," he said, "the rent came due."

Despite the struggles at home Jackie excelled in sports at Oakland High, making All-City in baseball and football and honorable mention in basketball. After graduation and a year in the Navy he enrolled at the University of California at Berkeley, where he quickly became a football star, combining all-American skills as a running back with husky all-American good looks. "He was blond and broad shouldered," writes Ron Fimrite, "[and] his body looked

Jackie Jensen, 1947. University of California Sports Department

as if it had been sculpted instead of grown." For his looks, for his dazzling achievements on the gridiron, he became known as "the Golden Boy."

Jensen's best sport was football, but his talents on a diamond could match almost anybody, and in the spring of 1947 he joined the Cal baseball team as a hard-hitting outfielder and pitcher. His coach was Clint Evans, "the Clinter," as people called him, who had been a fixture in Berkeley almost since the stock market crash of 1929. For years the Clinter had been pushing the idea of a national intercollegiate baseball championship similar to the World Series, but the idea went nowhere until after the war, when the nation's best college baseball players met in an All-Star game in Boston. The event drew raves from all over, and suddenly the Clinter's scheme of pitting East vs. West in a college baseball playoff did not seem so crazy after all.

This was a time perhaps unlike any other in American university life. Millions of veterans, aided by the GI Bill of Rights, which provided educational benefits to those who had served in the war, were attending college in California and around the nation. Interest in intercollegiate athletics was surging, in part because of those same veterans who filled the rosters of university sports teams alongside other students. Former servicemen starred for Cal just as they did for Stanford and the University of Southern California, the two teams beaten by the Bears in the last two games of the '47 California Intercollegiate Baseball Association championship.

Winning its last two games meant that Cal had finished in a tie with USC for the conference title, with the champion to be decided in a one-game playoff. The winner would then advance to regional competition for the first-ever College World Series. Clint Evans named, as his starting pitcher, his hard-throwing all-American right-hander, who won twelve games and lost only two during the season.

Rod Dedeaux, 1935. Courtesy of University of Southern California, on behalf of the USC Special Libraries and Archival Collections

Cal baseball coach Clint Evans.
University of California Sports Department

Despite struggling with his control all day—he walked eight batters and hit another—Jackie Jensen did the job, stranding fifteen runners on base and helping the Bears eke out a win to move on in the tournament.

The team Jensen and the Bears beat that day, the University of Southern California, had an unusual coaching arrangement. During the 1930s Sam Barry was the head coach of the Trojans, leaving the university after Pearl Harbor to join the Navy. When he returned four years later, Barry shared duties with the man who had replaced him and became a co-coach beginning in 1946. His co-coach was Rod Dedeaux, at the start of the greatest coaching career in the history of college baseball.

Dedeaux—born in New Orleans, his given name was Raoul—earned his first letter as a player at USC in the early thirties. An infielder, he earned a blink-and-you'll-miss-it call-up with the Brooklyn Dodgers in 1935 before moving into full-time coaching. Relentlessly upbeat and positive, calling everyone he met "Tiger," Dedeaux originally joined Barry as co-coach in 1942, ran the show by himself during the war years, shared duties again with Barry for a few years until Barry left the school, then became solely in charge at USC until he retired as coach in 1986.

In Dedeaux's forty-five years at USC, his teams won a record eleven national championships, including five in a row from 1970 through 1974. He coached one of the best right-handers of all time, Tom Seaver, and one of the best left-handers, Randy Johnson—both former California schoolboys. He also coached another former California schoolboy, one of the game's greatest sluggers, Mark McGwire, who teamed with Johnson on the 1984 U.S. Olympic baseball team managed by Dedeaux. A legion of other stellar Dedeaux-tutored pupils, some from California and some not—Jim Barr, Don Buford, Steve Busby, Rich Dauer, Ron Fairly, Dave Kingman, Steve Kemp, Bill Lee,

Fred Lynn, Roy Smalley, and many more—graduated to the majors. USC under Dedeaux, wrote columnist Jim Murray only half-jokingly, was "the greatest farm club in the history of the major leagues."

But one of the greatest success stories to come out of Dedeaux's program did not play for USC or go to school there; in fact, he did not attend college at all, not one day. He was the batboy, and his name was George Lee Anderson.

George moved to Los Angeles from Bridgewater, South Dakota, when he was nine. Eight other Andersons came with him: his mother Shirley, his father LeeRoy, Grandma and Grandpa Anderson, his three sisters, and brother. As George joked, when the Andersons left Bridgewater (pop. 632), they took a good piece of the town with them.

The nine Andersons had lived together in their house in South Dakota, and they all lived together in California too, only the house in Los Angeles was bigger and there was indoor plumbing, a definite improvement. George and younger brother Billy shared one of the bedrooms with Grandma and Grandpa; his two younger sisters slept in the other bedroom with Mom and Dad; and his big sister, Beverly, folded down the pullout couch in the front room. When the boys got older they gained a little privacy by moving their beds onto the covered back porch next to the washing machine.

George (who was born on George Washington's birthday in 1934, hence his first name) was a small, skinny, light-haired kid with big ears. His mom tried to tape his ears against his head but the tape always peeled off and they kept popping back out. Finally she gave up and he learned to live with the razzing he got from the other kids on the playground, almost all of whom were bigger than he was.

"I was a little kid always playing against guys twice my size," recalled George. "There were better hitters, better fielders. Guys could throw the ball twice as hard as I could. Almost everybody could beat me in a race." What the other kids lacked that George had—at least to George's degree—was desire. When everyone else walked, he ran. When everyone else ran, he sprinted. And if they all played a game and George's team lost, he hated it, just hated it. He wanted to win every time he played, even if he was going against bigger guys, *especially* then.

The Andersons lived only a few blocks from the University of Southern California's campus in central Los Angeles. This was during the war, and they had just moved from South Dakota. One day George was walking home from school past the field where the Trojan baseball team practiced when a ball sailed over the fence and landed in a bush. Pretty soon the team's equipment manager came running out to look for the ball; unable to find it, he returned to practice empty-handed.

But George saw where it went—or maybe he just looked harder than the other guy, because he pulled the ball out of the bush. Then he followed the equipment manager's steps onto the practice field.

"Where's the boss?" he said, looking to give the ball to someone in authority.

The first man he spoke to was Rod Dedeaux, the boss. Dedeaux thanked him for returning the ball and, when the kid kept hanging around and did not leave, started talking to him. Maybe it was the charm of those big ears, or the fact that he was such a little guy without a drop of pretense to him, but the coach, then in his late twenties, took an instant liking to him. And he made Georgie—Dedeaux's nickname for him—the batboy for the team.

The deal was this: George could be the batboy and hang out with the team after school as long as he kept his grades up. George said, Sure, you got it. So he started showing up at USC every day after school, chasing foul balls over the fence, hauling out the gear and taking it back after practice was over, setting up the bases, raking the dirt around the bases, drawing the chalk lines for the batter's box, whatever Coach wanted him to do. For George, this was not work; it was being around baseball, and nothing about it resembled work.

Being able to hang out with the older guys and Coach Dedeaux was an education for George, to be sure. An education about baseball but other things too. "He taught me more than baseball," George said about Dedeaux. "He helped me become a man."

George was crazy about the game and played it all the time. After spending the afternoon at USC he would walk back home, eat dinner, and then go outside with his brother and play some more in the evening warmth. Ralph's Market across the street from their house had a light in the front that let them see well enough to hit and catch at night. Though they used a tennis ball for their games, they still knocked out that light plenty of times.

Their father LeeRoy was a former semipro catcher who loved baseball as much as his sons. When he was not working—he was a house painter by trade—he sat on their backyard patio listening to games on the radio, happy as a person can be. LeeRoy was, in George's words, "lead-pipe tough," but he always told his son to be nice to people, that it did not cost you a penny, and that if you did people would be nice to you in return and this would help you in your life. In all his years in baseball George never forgot what his father told him.

First in South Dakota, then in Los Angeles, George played pickup games almost entirely until he was about thirteen, when he joined his first organized league. Once he did, though, his diet of all baseball, all the time produced quick dividends. His Crenshaw Post American Legion team won the 1951 national championship. Lefty Phillips, then a major league scout (later a manager of the California Angels), became interested in the youngster, driving him around to games and talking baseball with him, just baseball, for hours at a time. Lefty arranged a summer job for him at a box factory in Oroville in northern California. Lifting heavy crates onto railroad box cars put some meat on George's bones and improved his strength and stamina. After his senior season at Dorsey High the second baseman had a choice: play for his mentor Rod Dedeaux, who wanted him to come to USC, or sign with another mentor, Phillips, who had since moved over to the Dodger organization. George chose the latter, and in February 1953 signed a minor league contract.

That year he played for Santa Barbara in the California League, got married, and worked at the Virtue Brothers furniture store in Los Angeles in the off-season. This was how it went for him the next few years: scuffling about the minor leagues, working a regular job in the off-season. One year in Texas a radio announcer, observing George's fiery, intensely competitive nature, started calling him "Sparky." George was at first embarrassed by the nickname, but it has stuck with him throughout his baseball days.

Sparky Anderson played one season in the big leagues before returning to the minors as a coach and manager. His first major league coaching job, with the 1969 expansion San Diego Padres, was followed the next year by his first big league managing job, with the Cincinnati Reds. He led both the Reds and the Detroit Tigers to world championships in his Hall of Fame career.

Sparky served as batboy at USC for six years, until the late 1940s. Although he probably did not attend the game, he surely felt the sting of the Trojan loss at the hands of Jackie Jensen in that 1947 playoff game against Cal, which went on to face Yale in the finals of the first-ever College World Series. Yale, led by first baseman George "Poppy" Bush, got beat

George "Sparky" Anderson, with the Angels, circa 1950s. California Historical Society, FN-40003

17 to 4 in the first game of the best-of-three series, Jensen again earning the victory. In the second game, with the score tied in the seventh, the Bears pushed across a run in the next inning and hung on to win, 8 to 7, to become the first national collegiate champions in baseball.

The College World Series has since evolved into the premiere event of college baseball. Clint Evans, the man who dreamed it up and whose club won the first series, retired after the 1954 season with a clutch of titles to his credit. Evans Diamond on the Berkeley campus is named in his memory.

In his three years at Cal, Golden Boy Jackie Jensen won all-American honors twice in baseball and once in football, leaving college early to play professional baseball with the Oakland Oaks. After less than a season in Oakland, the New York Yankees signed him amid speculation that they saw him as a potential replacement for the aging Joe DiMaggio in center field.

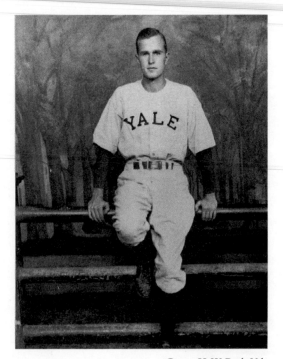

George H. W. Bush, Yale University baseball, 1945–1948. George Bush Presidential Library

But New York did not work out for Jensen, who eventually landed in Boston, where he manned the outfield with Ted Williams and won Most Valuable Player honors. After battling a fear of flying and other personal problems, Jensen retired after eleven seasons, the only athlete to play in the Rose Bowl, the World Series, a major league All-Star game, and the East-West Shrine All-Star game, then the pinnacle of collegiate football competition.

In 1948, the year after Cal won the inaugural College World Series, Rod Dedeaux and USC captured their first national baseball championship, also beating Yale, which was once again led by George Bush. After graduation Bush went into politics and later became president of the United States.

In a Corner of
the United States

SATURDAY, MARCH 22 — 2:15 P.M.
SUNDAY, MARCH 23 — 2:15 P.M.
— 1947 —
ABLISHED PRICE - $3.33   Total $4.00
ERAL TAX   67
HIS PORTION OF TICKET NOT GOOD FOR ADMITTANCE
DETACH SEPERATE COUPONS FOR INDIVIDUAL GAMES

Formed in 1879, the California League quickly became the leading professional baseball organization in the state. Ernest Thayer sat in on California League games in San Francisco before going back home to Worcester to write "Casey at the Bat." The first professional baseball franchise in Los Angeles, established in 1892, was a California League franchise. But Los Angeles lacked the population then to support a pro team, and in a matter of years the club, and the league, died.

The league reformed in 1898 and achieved some measure of prosperity, only to disintegrate once again with the arrival, five years later, of the Pacific Coast League, which usurped its former position as the state's leading purveyor of professional baseball. But Cy and Will Moreing and some other never-say-die spirits refused to give up, and they began the California State League in the early 1900s to serve baseball fans in the smaller rural towns of the state.

For a time, thanks to the play of sparkling young prospects such as future Hall of Famer Harry Hooper, the league made a go of it. But poor attendance and a shortage of cash in the bank crippled operations until it came to a stop, once more, before World War I.

This disruption in play lasted a quarter of a century until the fall of 1940, when a group of baseball men, led by Bill Schroeder, met at the Knickerbocker Hotel in Hollywood with the idea of reviving the long-dormant league. Their idea, like Cy Moreing's, was to bring baseball to cities not served by the Pacific Coast League, but in a reflection of how much the state had grown, this latest version of the California League consisted of teams in Santa Barbara, Anaheim, San Bernardino, Riverside, Bakersfield, Merced, Fresno, and Stockton. In the early years of the league, teams from northern California dominated, but that was now no longer the case.

The league survived its start-up season only to be blindsided by events outside its control: Pearl Harbor, manpower call-ups, blackouts, shortages, rationing. Four teams folded, leaving three survivors and a newcomer, the San Jose Owls, to carry on for another season. But money was tight to nonexistent. The Owls could not afford to hire a team bus for away games; instead they gave each player a Greyhound bus ticket and schedule and said it was up to them to make it to the games on time. The hitter with the lowest batting average on the team had to carry the bats, while the pitcher with the worst win-loss record brought the balls. The Owls and the three other clubs could not last the season before calling it quits, and in 1942 the California League, bowing to the inevitable, yet again suspended operations.

★   ★   ★   ★   ★

Like the California League, the origins of Hispanic baseball in the state reach back into the late 1800s. San Francisco's Vincent "Sandy" Nava may have been the first Hispanic player to reach the major leagues, making his rookie debut as a catcher with the Providence Grays in 1882. His teammates kidded him about the color of his skin, and Nava claimed his heritage was Cuban or Portuguese.

Lefty Gomez, 1929.
California Historical Society, FN-40016

About the same time Nava was breaking in with Providence, white settlers from the Midwest were pouring into Los Angeles in search of cheap land and a better life. Baseball was one of the ways in which they mixed with the Mexicans already living in the area. A rare baseball photograph from this time shows Mexican and Anglo players posing together for a team picture.

Players with Hispanic surnames pop up from time to time in early newspaper accounts, although as with black and Asian players, coverage of their activities was slim. A pitcher described as a "Mexican marvel" wowed spectators at a contest at Occidental College in southern California before World War I. Los Angeles semipro teams in the 1920s included players with such names as Gonzales and Estrada. Mexican American clubs in Los Angeles as well as smaller cities around the state sponsored teams and leagues that played with and against whites.

During the Depression the best ballplayer of Hispanic descent in America—and one of the best ballplayers, period—was Vernon Louis "Lefty" Gomez, who was born in the tiny town of Rodeo on the eastern side of San Francisco Bay and went to high school in Richmond. His nationality is listed in a 1940 baseball register as "Spanish-Irish." A tough competitor unafraid of challenging any hitter, he spent a season with the San Francisco Seals before beginning his luminous pitching career with the New York Yankees. Known for his lively wit and screwball sense of humor, "El Goofy," as he was known, is in the National Baseball Hall of Fame.

Existing alongside, and often merging with, Hispanic baseball in the state is the Native American tradition in the sport. Chief Meyers, a Cahuilla Indian who caught for the New York Giants in the days of John McGraw, played on tribal and reservation teams in the Riverside area where he grew up. John Joseph Andreas, a contemporary of the Chief's, probably competed against him in those same Indian leagues. A member of the Agua Caliente band of Cahuillas, Andreas was the patriarch of three generations of Indian ballplayers. His son Biff starred as shortstop and pitcher for the Morongo All-Indian team, which traveled around inland southern California and Arizona, playing in the blistering desert heat while wearing the heavy wool uniforms of their time. Biff's son and John Joseph's grandson, also named John Andreas, got his start in baseball in a boys' summer league sponsored by the Agua Calientes. Scouted by the White Sox and Dodgers while in high school, John never made it in organized baseball but taught the game to youngsters in his tribe and around the Banning area.

Edwin Miguel Garcia, better known as Mike, was of Mexican and Indian descent. A native of San Gabriel, he was a big, burly right-handed pitcher who learned to put his size to good use by throwing a hard fastball. The Cleveland Indians organization signed him as a teenager, and on the night of his high school graduation he boarded a train for Wisconsin to begin his minor league assignment. Then World War II intervened and Garcia had to exchange his baseball uniform for one in the Armed Forces, and he served three years as a radio communications engineer.

When he returned to civilian life, determined to resume his pitching career, he signed with Bakersfield in the newly reformed California League. At war's end the persistent Bill Schroeder had called for another meeting of baseball men from around the state. The location of this parley—Wrigley Field in Los Angeles—was different from the one in 1940, but the agenda was basically the same: bring the pro game to smaller cities around the state. This time the cities were Santa Barbara, Stockton, Fresno, Modesto, Visalia, and Bakersfield, Mike Garcia's new club.

In his one year in Bakersfield, Garcia led the league in wins and earned run average, quickly showing that he was ready for bigger things. In 1949, his first full season in the majors, he won fourteen games for the Cleveland Indians. More success followed in the years to come and, along with Hall of Famers Early Wynn, Bob Feller, and Bob Lemon, he formed one quarter of one of the era's best four-man pitching rotations. In many Latino barbershops around California and elsewhere, a photograph of Garcia, a man who made it in America's national game, hung on the wall.

The current Class C California League has been in continuous operation since 1946. Now with ten teams primarily in inland southern California and the Central Valley, it is a gateway league in which young players entering the minors begin their upward ascent to the majors (they hope). According to baseball historian Bill Weiss, for the past quarter-century one out of four major leaguers have first passed through the portals of the California League. Among these are current and future residents of the Hall of Fame: Don Drysdale (Bakersfield), Joe Morgan, Rollie Fingers, and Rickey Henderson (Modesto), Don Sutton (Santa Barbara), George Brett (San Jose), Mark McGwire (Fresno), and many more.

After playing pro ball in California, Toni Stone became one of the
Negro League's few female players. Negro League Baseball Museum

The same year of the California League revival—1946—marked the birth of another baseball league: the all-black West Coast Baseball Association. Consisting of six teams in and out of California, its rosters featured veterans of black semipro baseball in the state as well as Negro Leaguers. Toni Stone, who moved to the Bay Area during the war, played second base for the Association's team in San Francisco, the Sea Lions, and caused comment because she was a woman. She later moved onto the Indianapolis Clowns, one of a few women to play in the Negro Leagues. Lionel Wilson, a pitcher for the Oakland Larks, later became the mayor of Oakland.

Like their counterparts in the Negro Leagues, teams in the West Coast Baseball Association frequently played in the home parks of white clubs when the white clubs were not using them. The Sea Lions held their home games in Seals Stadium, for instance, and the Larks hosted teams at Oaks Ball Park in Emeryville. Although the league collapsed after only a couple of months, the Larks, who were in first place at the time of the demise, barnstormed for two more seasons around the Pacific Coast and Midwest.

Even if the West Coast Baseball Association had survived longer, its days were numbered, for the era of racial separation in organized baseball was nearing an end. In 1946 Jackie Robinson of the Montreal Royals became the first black in the formerly all-white minor leagues, a distinction followed by his major league breakthrough the next year with the Dodgers. In 1948, the Pacific Coast League accepted its first black player, John Ritchey.

Ritchey was himself a veteran of black baseball, hitting .388 for the Chicago American Giants to lead the Negro American League the year before. A line drive hitter with exceptional speed for a catcher, he often hit leadoff or in the second spot in the batting order. Like Jackie Robinson, he was an educated California man and, although he could hold his own on a ballfield with his Negro League peers, he did not fit in well with them. "He was a green-eyed ballplayer from California," said his wife Lydia. "He wasn't really accepted because he was from California."

Ritchey's home town was San Diego. This was where he grew up and learned his baseball, playing with blacks and whites at San Diego High and in youth leagues in the area. He was the quiet type, not a big talker, but he got a charge out of playing the game and it showed. His teammates called him "Johnny Baseball," a nod to his enthusiasm and passion. At age fifteen he and another black player, Nelson Manuel, starred on a San Diego American Legion team that traveled to Spartanburg, South Carolina, to compete in the Junior World Series. But neither could participate in the tournament because in Spartanburg they did not allow blacks to share the same field with whites.

The next year the Post 6 club, again led by Ritchey and Manuel, returned to the American Legion national finals, this time being held in North Carolina. Both players understood that this tournament would be different and that they would be allowed to play. They were wrong. While taking batting practice before the championship game, they were told to leave the field. They weren't even allowed to sit in the stands to watch. The boys quietly complied and left the grounds. "In those days you just did what the adults told you to do," said Ritchey, looking back on the incident as a man. Without its two stars San Diego lost the game and the national championship.

After high school, Ritchey entered San Diego State College (now University), but as with the rest of his generation, the war had other plans for him. As a sergeant in the engineering corps of the Army, he earned five battle stars in fighting during the European campaign. When the Third Reich surrendered, his unit was on the move toward Berlin, preparing to attack. Returning to San Diego State to finish his schooling, the left-handed-hitting Ritchey became one of the stars of the Aztec baseball team. But while several of his white teammates signed professional contracts, the scouts passed over Johnny Baseball because of the color of his skin. His coach Charlie Smith commented on how unfair it was, but there was nothing he could do about it. There was nothing anybody could do about it—until somebody did.

Bill Starr was a Brooklyn native who played for the San Diego Padres when Ted Williams was breaking into pro ball with the team. During Ted's rookie season, Starr actually pinch-hit for arguably the greatest hitter who ever lived. It was the ninth inning of a game against Seattle, and he made an out. After leaving baseball Starr invested in real estate, becoming wealthy enough to purchase his old club in the mid-1940s. It was Starr who signed Ritchey to break the color barrier in the Coast League.

Starr has said that he was influenced by the example of Jackie Robinson and saw no reason to continue segregation in the game. "The Coast League was lily white and had some old-timers who were very critical of Branch Rickey," he said. "I thought it was kinda stupid." Starr also said he signed Ritchey not because he was black but because he could help the Padres. A former catcher himself, Starr saw how Ritchey had torn up Negro League pitching in Chicago and figured he could do the same in the hitter-friendly Coast League.

Johnny Baseball's debut with the Padres occurred on March 30, 1948. In his first eleven at-bats he collected seven hits, including a home run. But the twenty-three-year-old was not prepared for what happened next. "All of a sudden he was thrust into the middle of all this," said Lydia Ritchey. "We were young and didn't know how to handle it." On road trips around California and the Northwest, her husband stayed in a different hotel than his white teammates. He almost never ate his meals with them or socialized off the field with them. He roomed by himself, found his way to and from the ballpark by himself. He was a member of the Padres but not a member—part of, but separate.

When a pitcher throws a beanball at a batter, the pitcher on the other team is obliged to retaliate by throwing at a hitter on the opposite side. This you-hit-me-and-I'll-hit-you-back strategy, one of the time-honored fundamentals of the baseball code, works to keep pitchers on both sides honest and protects batters from getting balls aimed at their head. But when Coast League hurlers threw knockdown pitches at Ritchey, no Padre pitcher came to his defense by throwing at batters on the other team. Their lack of response sent a message around the league that Ritchey was fair game.

Some of the balls thrown at Ritchey were intended simply to keep a good hitter off the plate. Others were racially motivated. In close plays in the field, a catcher's job is to tag out runners sliding into home and block them from reaching the plate. Ritchey said he felt that baserunners came into the plate "extra hard" on him, perhaps to test his toughness or possibly injure him. He

John Ritchey, hitting the dirt to avoid a beanball, 1948. California Historical Society, FN-40011

also heard abusive language from white spectators and other players. But he never responded to their taunts, carrying on as if he heard nothing.

Being a pioneer is a hard business. Though Ritchey batted .323 in his first season in San Diego, Jim Gleason, a teammate of his on the Padres and at San Diego State, noticed a change in his friend's personality. His once outgoing demeanor turned cool and guarded. He became more distant than before, less apt to break into a smile the way he did when people nicknamed him Johnny Baseball. The next season Ritchey's hitting fell off and he was shipped to Vancouver of the Western International League, where he later won Player of the Year honors. In time he returned to the Coast League, playing a total of seven seasons with a lifetime .282 batting average.

Jules Tygiel, author of a groundbreaking book on the integration of baseball, writes, "Jackie Robinson had endured his pioneering ordeal amidst considerable fanfare and publicity. In the aftermath of his accomplishment scores of other blacks performed in the unexposed corners of the United States, recreating his trials and triumphs. Their remarkable achievements and contributions to the cause of racial equality rarely received acknowledgment. But, at a time when segregation remained an unyielding American reality, they, like Robinson, carved out and affirmed the black man's niche in the American pastime."

Tucked away in a corner of the United States, the minor league San Diego Padres formed one of the earliest multiracial professional baseball teams, a portrait in miniature of the game to come. Bucky Harris, the former big league infielder and manager who is in the Hall of Fame, managed the club. One of its coaches was the onetime batboy-turned-fungo-whiz Jimmie Reese.

Escondido's Pete Coscarart, an ex–major leaguer and an early advocate of a baseball players' union, operated at second base. The third baseman was Al Rosen, a young Jewish slugger from the South who got his first look at San Diego as a Naval navigator during the war. He batted fifth in the powerful Padres lineup behind slugger Max West, who introduced Rosen to his first taste of Alaskan king crab at a Fisherman's Wharf restaurant in San Francisco. These whites as well as the blacks on the club helped Jesse Flores, a Hispanic pitcher, lead the staff with twenty-one wins.

Until he came to San Diego, Rosen, who later starred in the majors for the Cleveland Indians and became an executive with the Giants and other clubs, had never played with blacks. One of his Padre teammates was Minnie Minoso, who was born on a sugar plantation in Cuba and whose first baseball uniform was a converted flour sack. Coming to America, he starred in Negro baseball, then made a brief stop in Cleveland before landing in San Diego, where he stayed with a family on Imperial Avenue. His power and speed on the bases rattled pitchers and took over games, and in his two years in the Coast League he became one of its top stars. San Diego, Minoso said, "opened the door for me" in organized baseball. When the door to the majors swung open again in 1951, Minnie charged through it, going on to become one of the first Caribbean-born stars in the big leagues.

The Padres led the Coast League in signing blacks partly because they were a

From left, Luke Easter, Artie Wilson, and John Ritchey, 1949. Courtesy of Bill Swank

farm team of the Cleveland Indians, which were owned by Bill Veeck, a strong supporter of integration who endorsed the recruiting of minorities. The Indians then got first crack at bringing these players up to the big leagues.

In less than a full season in San Diego, Luke Easter became the greatest Coast League gate attraction since Joe DiMaggio. A veteran of the Negro Leagues, the six-foot-four-inch, two-hundred-forty-pounder could, to borrow an old joke, hit it out of every park except Yellowstone. It was said that the Coast League substituted its regular balls with smaller, juiced-up Japanese-made balls for his batting practice, so Luke could put on a show, which he did. According to one sportswriter who saw him, the balls he hit rose like golf balls in the afternoon sky.

Everything about Easter was big—his home runs, his personality, his luxury Buick automobile. He liked for his teammate Artie Wilson to act as chauffeur and let him sit in the back seat so that when he was driving around town people would think a big shot was passing by. A woman who knew him (and there were more than a few of those) described his free-spending, party-loving personality as "flamboyant." One night he and Minnie Minoso drove up the coast for a Hollywood party. The next day they returned to San Diego for a game, not having slept a wink, and Luke got four hits in five at-bats and was ready to go out on the town again afterward. Not so his friend, who was suffering. "I say to Luke, 'I love you,'" said Minoso." "'You are my friend, but I can't keep up with you.'"

Fans knew Easter was too big of a talent to stay on the coast for long. Coast League owners knew this too and asked Veeck not to take him up to the Indians until he had made a road swing through all their cities. The call for him came late in the 1949 season, and Luke took his big bat with him to Cleveland.

Although gifted black players such as Easter and Minoso reached the major leagues, others did not. "You know in one period you had to be twice as good," said Jimmie Reese, referring to the obstacles faced by blacks in competing against whites. "[Blacks] were handicapped to start with."

One talented black infielder who only got a brief try in the majors was Artie Wilson, another member of the '49 Padres, who moved on from there to become the first black player on the Oakland Oaks. A favorite of fans, the Alabama-born ex–Negro Leaguer slapped the ball to all fields, stole bases, and on defense used his quickness to get to ground balls that other shortstops never would have reached. In 1950 Wilson had 264 hits and scored 169 runs for Oakland, and those who saw him play say he was one of the best Coast League shortstops ever.

In those days it was unusual for blacks and whites to room together on a baseball team. Blacks roomed with other blacks and, if there were no other African Americans on the team, they normally stayed by themselves. But when Wilson came to Oakland a white member of the Oaks volunteered to room with him. This white guy, who played second base and was not quite twenty-one years old, had grown up in nearby Berkeley and had suffered a few knocks of his own in his life. It did not matter to him what Wilson's color was. The only thing that mattered was could he play or not. Artie could definitely play, and this feisty white second baseman—well, he could play, too. And if you did not think so, if you disrespected him on the field or challenged him in a way he did not like, he would call you out for it and come at you with his fists. His name was Billy Martin.

Casey, Billy, and the Yanks

SATURDAY, MARCH 22 — 2:15 P.M.
SUNDAY, MARCH 23 — 2:15 P.M.
— 1947 —

Total $4.00

ESTABLISHED PRICE - $3.33
FEDERAL TAX - .67

THIS PORTION OF TICKET NOT GOOD FOR ADMITTANCE
DETACH SEPERATE COUPONS FOR INDIVIDUAL GAMES

Looking to better his life, Nicholas Salvini left his hometown of La Brusse, Italy, to come to America, first settling in San Francisco in 1879. A couple of years after he arrived, the girl he left behind, Raefella, joined him and they were married. Soon they began having children, eventually buying a small house in Berkeley at Seventh and Virginia Streets. The house was once a stop for Pony Express riders, who watered their horses there and washed the dust of the trail out of their throats with beer and whiskey.

The home of Nicholas and Raefella, crammed with ten children, did not have indoor plumbing. During the calamitous 1906 earthquake their house remained standing but the outhouse in back tumbled over. Nicholas was so rattled by the shaking that he loaded his family's most precious possessions onto a raft and floated it on the bay near their home because he felt the water was safer than the land.

Twice a year Nicholas, who was a fisherman, journeyed north to Alaska, where a man could make good money on the salmon boats in only a few months of work. When he returned home after these trips he would pour coins onto the living room carpet to impress the children, who scrambled happily after them.

One of these children was Joan Salvini, who, when she was seventeen, married an Italian fisherman like her father. They had a boy they called "ToTo," but the marriage ended in hard feelings and divorce. Joan then met Alfred Martin, a handsome, dark-eyed man of Portuguese descent with slick black hair and a beak for a nose. He too was a fisherman, but his real passion was singing and playing the guitar in nightclubs around the area. The two were married, although not happily, for Alfred liked to play at more than music. When Joan found out he was cheating on her with coeds from the University of California, she smashed the windows of his car with a hammer.

Joan kicked Alfred out of the house, although she was pregnant with his child at the time. ToTo was a baby and her mother Raefella was living with her as well. Her second son was born upstairs in the Seventh Street house and circumcised downstairs on the kitchen table. The name on the birth certificate was Alfred Manuel Pisano, but his last name was actually Martin. Alfred Manuel Martin, who came to be known as Billy.

The year after Billy's birth, Joan married Jack Downey, a Berkeley truck driver. This time she got it right. They lived together the rest of their lives, raising three children of their own as well as ToTo and Billy, who shared a bedroom with their grandmother. If any of the children talked back to Raefella, she bit their hand.

Things were tight in the Downey household. They did not own a refrigerator or an icebox; the food stored in the pantry was cooled by air coming up through a basement grate. "I remember I ate stale bread dipped in coffee for breakfast almost every day of my life," said Billy. Maury Allen, a Martin biographer, described the west Berkeley neighborhood where Billy grew up as "mixed…[with] Italians, Irish, Mexicans, even a few blacks." Martin himself said his hardscrabble childhood gave him a better understanding of the hardships encountered by black and Latin ballplayers. "When nothing talks to nothing," he said, "they understand each other."

Not far from Martin's house was a laundry owned by the Galan family, who were famous in the neighborhood because their son, Augie, played outfield in the big leagues. Martin had newspaper pictures of Augie taped on the wall of his bedroom. In the off-season Galan, Cookie Lavagetto, Nick Etten, and other local big leaguers came home to the East Bay during the winter, practicing and playing games at James Kenney Park, another neighborhood fixture. Though only eleven or twelve and small for his age, Martin badgered the older guys to let him into their games. The pros took a liking to the brash little kid and gave him pointers and let him hang around with them.

Martin was always hanging around Kenney Park anyway, arriving early in the morning and not leaving until night chased him home. The park only had two meager lights, and even when they were on, the batter at the plate could not see beyond second base in the darkness.

Martin told the story many times—that when he was a junior at Berkeley High, a teacher gave him the book *Lou Gehrig: A Quiet Hero,* by sportswriter Frank Graham. Martin supposedly read it cover to cover in one sitting, and from then on his dream was to become a member of the New York Yankees. Nevertheless, he was only five feet, eight inches tall, one hundred and twenty pounds—too small to be considered a legitimate professional prospect despite batting .450 in his senior season. A teammate signed a pro contact after graduation, but not the supposedly undersized Martin. The scouts walked by him like he was nothing.

While in high school, Martin had played for the Oakland Junior Oaks, a development team sponsored by the city's Pacific Coast League club. If any of the young prospects on the Junior Oaks looked promising, the parent club scooped them up. Martin had made a decent enough impression while with the team but nothing happened for him until an infielder on Oakland's Class D farm club in Idaho Falls went down with a broken arm. The organization needed a body to fill his spot, and that was when somebody suggested the scrawny teen from the juniors.

One Martin biographer gives Oakland scout Jimmy Hole the credit for making contact with Billy. Another says it was owner Brick Laws and his business manager, Cookie Devincenzi, the previous Oaks owner who had a soft spot for Italian ballplayers like Martin. It may be that all of these men were in the Oaks' office when Martin showed up to sign his first professional baseball contract for two hundred dollars a month.

Do you have a suit to wear on the train to Idaho Falls? they asked him.

No, said Billy. My uncle just died, and we needed a suit to bury him in. So they used mine. It was the only one I had.

Do you have any money?

No, said Billy. None of that.

Jimmy Hole or Brick Laws then gave Martin three hundred dollars, probably an advance against his salary, to buy some clothes and a train ticket to

Idaho. It was the summer of 1946 and Martin was eighteen years old. The night before he left, his family held a big party for him in the old house where Pony Expressmen once drank and told stories about their hardships on the trail. The next morning Hole picked him up and took him to the train station, and Martin set off on his own trail.

The man who would become Billy Martin's manager and teacher is another of those famous baseball personalities who is associated in the public mind with New York but whose ties to California are long and deep. Born and raised in Kansas City, Missouri, Casey Stengel broke into the major leagues with the Brooklyn Dodgers. After six seasons in Brooklyn he bounced between teams before returning to New York, this time with the Giants. One of his teammates on the Giants was Irish Meusel, whose wife, Van, decided in the summer of 1923 to play matchmaker, introducing Stengel to a girlfriend of hers, Edna Lawson, who was visiting New York City from southern California.

Baseball historian Robert Creamer described Edna as "a tall, slim, smart young woman in her late twenties." Her father, a building contractor, had moved the family from Michigan to the Los Angeles area when she was nineteen. A stylish dancer and graceful in person, Edna was pretty enough to work as an extra in several silent films. But she also had a keen mind and later on managed her father's substantial business holdings, which included real estate properties and a bank.

Edna was the total package, and Casey flipped for her, asking for her hand in marriage two weeks after they met. She did not say yes or no, preferring to wait a while before deciding. When she returned home to Glendale later that summer she still had not given a definitive answer, though her suitor was clearly on her mind.

Stengel's most famous moment as a player occurred in the first game of the '23 World Series, when he hit a two-out, ninth-inning, inside-the-park home run to beat the Yankees. Although the Giants' happiness was short-lived (the Yanks won the Series), the drama of the moment caused a sensation that spanned the coasts. The Los Angeles papers carried coverage of Stengel's exploits, and a beaming Edna proudly displayed a sports page to her father, who had yet to meet him. "What do you think of my Casey now, Pop?" she asked him.

Pop evidently approved because after the two were married he built a house in Glendale for them as a Christmas present. For the next fifty years, that was Edna and Casey's home. He would leave in the spring, at the beginning of each season, returning to Glendale when his baseball schedule allowed. When the season ended in the fall, Casey always came back to be with his wife.

Stengel knew many of the players and personalities of the Pacific Coast League, scouting the young Ted Williams and trying unsuccessfully to sign him for the Boston Braves, the National League team he managed beginning in 1938. But his stint with the Braves was a disaster; in six seasons under Stengel they never finished higher than fifth place, and his reputation sunk as low as his team. Smart baseball people regarded him as a clown and buffoon who pulled comical stunts and talked in that funny way he had—"Stengelese," the writers later called it—that seemed to walk a fine line between sense and nonsense. When you do funny things in baseball and win, they call you a "character." But when you do funny things and lose, you're just a loser. And after being bounced out of Boston, Stengel was just a loser.

★   ★   ★   ★   ★

Oakland Oaks owner Clarence "Brick" Laws had operated a chain of movie theaters in the 1930s. If there was such a thing as a Depression-proof business, talking pictures was it. Even so, Laws and his partner Joe Blumenfeld still had to lure people out of their houses in lean times and get them to pry open their wallets and purses. To do this, they staged regular "Bag Night" promotions at their theaters. Ticket-buying patrons not only got to see the latest Clark Gable or Gary Cooper movie, but they walked away with a paper bag full of free items given to them at the theater.

Laws believed in the value of promoting your product, whether your product was motion pictures or baseball, and when he bought the Oaks he soon introduced Bag Night to Oaks Park in Emeryville. But he knew that trinkets alone would not draw fans to the park; the park itself had to be respectable. So Laws poured a few hundred thousand dollars of his theater money into new lights, new bleachers, and other amenities at "the splinter emporium," as wags called the rickety old home of the Oaks. To improve the team on the field he signed more competitive talent and then shopped around for the right manager. A well-known name would be best, with local connections perhaps, and if this fellow was colorful and a natural showman, well, that was just gravy. Laws knew he had the right man when he hired Casey Stengel to manage the Oaks for the 1946 Pacific Coast League season.

Having managed in the minors in the Midwest for a few years after his debacle in Boston, Stengel was trying to resurrect his career. He grabbed the Oaks job in part because he could be close to home and Edna. But it also represented a step up for him because during this period the Pacific Coast League was as close as you could get to the major leagues without actually being in them.

The war was over and Americans were done with tragedy and drama. They wanted normal, they wanted their old lives back, and baseball was a big part of that. The familiar players who had left their teams due to the war had come back, and the irregulars who had held their spots while they were gone had left. With the National and American Leagues still playing their games on the other side of the country, the Coast League owned the burgeoning California and West Coast markets virtually all to itself.

Upon arriving in the East Bay, Stengel was taking over a club that had long been one of the league's hardship cases, not having won a championship since the days of Buzz Arlett. But his pledge to bring a flag to pennant-starved Oakland in three years nearly proved too pessimistic, for in his first season the Oaks finished in second place, four games behind the champion Seals. Meanwhile his rambling free-association thoughts on whatever happened to cross his mind charmed reporters and fans alike. "I like the idea of bridges," he said, speaking about the Bay Bridge. "Everywhere I go they throw in a bridge as part of the service. Every manager wants to jump off a bridge sooner or later, and it's very nice for an old man to know he doesn't have to walk fifty miles to find one."

At the end of his first season with the team, Casey and Edna hosted a barbecue for the Oaks, serving steaks and cocktails at their home in Glendale.

Ernie Lombardi, 1937. California Historical Society, FN-40010

Afterward a waiting line of taxis picked up the players at curbside to drive them to the railroad station in time to make the 8:30 p.m. train back to Oakland. With the games over for the year, Casey said goodbye until next season.

Things did not go so well that next season—Oakland fell back to fourth place—but by 1948, the Oaks featured a club full of ex–major leaguers with time-tested baseball skills. One of them was a future Hall of Famer, forty-year-old Ernie Lombardi, who had begun his career twenty years earlier with his hometown Oaks. The Schnozz, as he was nicknamed for his notable olfactory organ, hit .306 over seventeen major league seasons despite being as slow afoot as a parked car. Easy and good-natured, he pinch-hit and split time at catcher for the Oaks in what would be his last professional season. When he could not backhand a pitch with his glove, he would simply reach out and snare the ball with his bare right hand. Bare-handed, said one Oaks pitcher, Lombardi could "catch the best fastball you could throw."

Other ex–major leaguers such as Cookie Lavagetto and Dario Lodigiani filled out the roster with Lombardi. Indeed, there were so many aging baseball warhorses on the Oaks—including the manager, who was in his late fifties—sportswriters dubbed them "the Nine Old Men." Not everybody was an old man, though. The teenaged Billy Martin was on the team too.

Stengel's first look at Martin actually occurred two years before the youngster joined the Nine Old Men. Martin was on the Junior Oaks, and Stengel had just taken over as Oakland manager: "I remember him coming on the field, this puny-looking, skinny kid, all lit up with his jaw stuck out like he would take over the team if you let him." But the kid needed a summer of seasoning in Idaho Falls, and then another year at an Oaks' farm club in Phoenix. Growing taller and adding nearly forty pounds of heft, the no-longer-quite-so-scrawny Martin was tearing up the Arizona League when the Oaks brought him up near the end of the '47 season to see if what he was doing in the desert was a mirage or not.

When Martin first arrived in Oakland, the club's graybeards predictably gave him a hard time. "How big are the parks down there? Big as a bullpen?" They had trouble believing that Martin could hit .392, his batting average in Phoenix. But his manager overheard what the veterans were saying and came to the kid's defense. "I don't care if he done it in Africa," said Stengel. "It's still .392."

Over the winter Stengel traveled from Glendale up to Oakland for off-season workouts and team banquets. Martin showed up at a few of these occasions, and the two got to know each other better. Come spring, they were working together on the Nine Old Men.

Stengel preferred managing veterans over younger players because the veterans did not need to be taught. They knew what to do, and Stengel knew what they could do. There were no surprises, no mysteries, and if they were the right veterans, they could win right away. A manager could not be so sure with youngsters. They took years to develop, and some never developed at all. Stengel wanted his players to produce for him *now*.

But Stengel made an exception for Martin, hitting grounder after grounder after grounder to him during infield practice. Martin never told him to quit, he always wanted to field one more, just one more. Stengel liked that. The old man also liked the fact that Martin was a smart kid, but not so smart he thought he knew it all. He listened, tuning into the mental side of the game: how all the pieces fit, the strategy of it. Stengel also could not fail to notice that Martin was not just smart, he was a smart-*ass*. He lipped off to everybody, including his manager. "He's a fresh kid ain't he?" Stengel said with a smile after being on the receiving end of a Martin outburst.

But Stengel enjoyed that about Martin too, because, well, he had been a fresh kid himself. In fact he saw a lot of himself in the youngster. This may have been why, in Robert Creamer's words, Stengel "growled at [Martin], laughed at him, bawled him out, praised him," all with the idea of pushing him toward higher achievement. They fought like family, sometimes screaming at each other. The press picked up on their close connection and referred to Martin as "Casey's boy."

As an adult, Martin said he fought a lot when he was growing up because he ran with tough kids in his neighborhood and had to stick up for himself. This philosophy of sticking up for himself every time he stepped onto a baseball field extended throughout his career, beginning with his early days on the Oaks.

One telling photograph from the '48 season shows Martin, wearing number 7 for the Oaks, talking back to an umpire. Clearly, the ump has made a call that Martin does not like. His face is turned sideways, and he is hissing a protest out of the side of his mouth. But standing between him and the umpire is Stengel, in an Oaks jacket with his cap off. He is not exactly smiling but his face wears none of the angry intensity of Martin's. Stengel is doing his job, protecting one of his players from being thrown out of the game for arguing a call, but the photograph captures so much more: who Billy was, and how the old man stood by him.

Martin played third base, shortstop, and second base for the Oaks, filling in wherever Stengel needed him. Always seeking an edge over the opposing team, Stengel moved other players in and out of the lineup too—for example, if the other team was starting a left-handed pitcher, he would stack his batting order with right-handed hitters, giving them a higher probability of success. This strategy of "platooning," which Casey later honed to perfection with the Yankees and is now an accepted commonplace of managerial strategy, received an early trial with the Oaks. Martin and the Oakland vets originally grumbled about the lack of a set lineup, wanting more playing time for themselves,

Billy Martin and Casey Stengel argue a call as Oaks coach John Babich looks on, 1948. Doug McWilliams Collection

but nobody could argue with the results. The Nine Old Men brought a championship to Oakland, just as Stengel had promised.

Stengel's success in Oakland revived his managerial career. No longer seen as a loser (though his image as a clown would take longer to erase), he was once more a hot property, attractive enough for the game's most successful franchise to come courting. George Weiss, general manager of the New York Yankees, had been a fan of Stengel's for some time. While others in the major leagues had soured on him, Weiss had not. What Stengel had done on the coast only strengthened Weiss's view of him. After the Oaks closed out the Coast League championship, followed by a parade through downtown Oakland in which their manager, riding in an open convertible, was the unquestioned star, Stengel met the press at the "21" Club in Manhattan as the new head man of the Yankees.

Back in Oakland, Casey's boy expected to follow him immediately to New York. But the call did not come and Martin returned to the Oaks for the 1949 season. Charlie Dressen, a venerable baseball hand who would later manage the Brooklyn Dodgers, replaced Stengel as manager in Oakland. George Kelly, the former New York Giant star from San Francisco, served as one of his coaches. Artie Wilson, the club's first black player, also joined the Oaks in '49, as did the Golden Boy from Cal, Jackie Jensen, the all-American football and baseball player. Although Jensen struggled at the plate with the Oaks, the Yankees purchased his contract at the end of the season.

The "so what?" part of the package to bring Jensen to New York was Billy Martin. The Yankees purchased his contract at the same time, but he was a nobody compared to Jensen and his mesmerizing potential, and the sportswriters paid little attention to him. The old man had not forgotten him, though. Martin came to the Yankees on Stengel's recommendation.

Martin, said Casey, was "a hard-nosed, big-nosed player." This was a term of endearment; he often referred to Martin as his "big-nosed player." Once Martin had posed for a comical photograph with Oaks teammate Ernie Lombardi to see whose schnozz was bigger, while Stengel held a ruler as if measuring the length of their noses. But when Martin showed up at Yankee training camp in the spring of 1950, he had a different look about him. The size of his nose had always embarrassed him, and he did not like being kidded about it. Before leaving to begin his big league career, Martin had gotten a nose job from a California cosmetic surgeon.

Billy Martin may have been Casey Stengel's pet, but that did not make him the starting second baseman for the world champion New York Yankees. That job belonged to Jerry Coleman, a former Marine pilot who had flown an F-10 Corsair, a single-engine fighter plane, during World War II and who was not about to be intimidated by some punk kid from Berkeley. Coleman was himself a Bay Area native, raised in San Francisco, who signed with the Yankees while still a student at Lowell High in the city. When he reported to Yankee training camp as a rookie he had three hundred dollars in his pocket, his earnings from an off-season salesman's job at a San Francisco clothing shop.

Coleman was another one of those guys with a ton of desire but not much meat on his bones. His father, a former minor leaguer, sent him a steady stream of inspirational letters from San Francisco during the '49 season: "Keep going," one of them said. "The way up is always rough." Despite losing fifteen pounds and being worn down in the heat of a New York summer (and a hot pennant race with the Red Sox), Coleman won Rookie of the Year honors as the Yankees took the first of five consecutive world championships. The next season, with Martin mainly watching from the bench, he won the Most Valuable Player award in the World Series.

But like Ted Williams, who was also a Marine pilot, two wars knocked a hole in Coleman's baseball career. In 1952 he left the Yankees to return to active duty in the Korean War, earning two Distinguished Flying Crosses for his service. He eventually returned to the Yankees, playing part-time for a few years before retiring and later turning to broadcasting. In the early seventies he became an announcer with the San Diego Padres, where he has since become one of the most popular personalities in team history.

Jerry Coleman was only one of many New York Yankees during this era with connections to California. Pasadena's Irv Noren won two World Series rings with the team. Frankie Crosetti of San Francisco (and later, Stockton) collected a drawer full of rings as a coach to go with the ones he won as a player. Gil McDougald, a graduate of Commerce High in San Francisco, drove a United States Mail truck in the city in the off-season while toiling away in the Yankee farm system. When he reached the big time he came in with a bang, winning 1951 Rookie of the Year honors and hitting a grand slam in the World Series. Two other San Francisco schoolboys, Charlie Silvera and transplant Bobby Brown, played with Coleman in San Francisco on the Keneally Yankees, a semipro club organized by Joe Devine, the Yankees' West Coast scout.

Instead of following the usual baseball career path and signing with a big league organization after graduating from Galileo High, Brown enrolled at Stanford University to become a doctor. During the war he transferred to UCLA to be part of its officer training program and then worked at the Naval Hospital in San Diego, in both places playing baseball while studying and practicing medicine. After the war ended the left-handed-hitting third baseman joined the Yankees, continuing to juggle baseball and medicine, often reporting late to spring training because of his medical school commitments. But war called again, and he missed part of the 1952 season and all of the next while tending to the wounded in Korea. Returning home, he decided to practice medicine full-time, informing the Yankees that he was quitting baseball after playing on four world championship teams in eight seasons. His last game at Yankee Stadium was June 30, 1954; the next day he reported to San Francisco County Hospital to begin his medical residency. He later became a cardiologist and in 1984, after only limited involvement with the game for decades, Brown became president of the American League, a post he held for ten years.

Charlie Silvera, Brown and Coleman's teammate on both the Keneally and New York Yankees, grew up on Guerrero Street in the Mission District of

The California Yankees, early 1950s. From left, Jerry Coleman, Bobby Brown, Casey Stengel, Billy Martin, Jackie Jensen, and Charlie Silvera. Not pictured: Gil McDougald and Irv Noren. The Oakland Tribune *Collection, The Oakland Museum of California. Gift of Alameda Newspaper Group*

San Francisco, blocks away from Seals Stadium. "This was our major leagues," said Silvera. "You wanted to play for the Seals." The boys on the playground nicknamed him "Swede" for his wavy blond hair, although his father, Victor, a mechanic for a dairy, was of Portuguese descent. A stout and compact catcher, Swede roomed with his good buddy Coleman in their first year together in New York. But unlike Coleman, who cracked the starting lineup, Silvera served as backup to Yogi Berra, one of the game's all-time great catchers, which meant that Charlie did not appear in many games. Still, he played nine seasons in New York and collected more World Series rings than you can wear on one hand. He later became a major league coach and served as a West Coast scout for the Florida Marlins in their 1994 championship run, for which he received yet another Series ring.

One of the greatest moments in baseball history was Don Larsen's 1956 World Series perfect game for the Yankees. Californians played leading roles in this drama too, starting with the man on the mound.

Born in Indiana, Larsen moved to San Diego when he was a teenager. Tall and lean, he excelled in both basketball and baseball at Point Loma High, where he drew the notice of major league scouts. After playing for a couple of teams he came to New York and, in his second season there, in the fifth game of the Series, he earned a permanent place in the annals of the game, retiring every batter he faced—twenty-seven up, twenty-seven down, with no hits, walks, or errors—to beat the Brooklyn Dodgers, 2 to 0, and record the only perfect game in the century-old competition between the American and National leagues. (Coincidentally, the next perfect game to occur at Yankee Stadium took place in 1998, though not during a World Series. The pitcher was Yankee left-hander David Wells, also a graduate of Point Loma High.) Larsen pitched fourteen big league seasons, including with the pennant-winning '62 San Francisco Giants, before retiring in the San Diego area.

The man behind the plate calling the balls and strikes for Larsen's masterpiece was Babe Pinelli, the San Francisco native. A former minor and major leaguer, he had moved into umpiring in the 1930s as a way to stay involved in the game after his playing days ended. By the time of the perfect game, he had overcome a once-volatile temper to become one of baseball's most respected umpires. He reportedly walked off the field after the final out and wept in the locker room. His long, distinguished career in baseball came to a close after that series.

After the last Dodger hitter struck out to end the game, a jubilant Yogi Berra ran out from behind the plate and jumped into his surprised pitcher's arms. Television footage of this moment survives to this day, and it remains the most famous single image from that game. The second most famous image is the photograph of the last pitch delivered by Larsen. His right elbow is cocked and the ball is in flight. Behind him in the far background is a scoreboard showing all those zeroes for Brooklyn. In the near background is the Yankee second baseman in the ready position, his right throwing hand resting on his right knee, his left gloved hand on his left knee. From his stance you can tell that if a ball is hit anywhere near him, he is going to get it, nothing is going to get past him. The second baseman in the picture is Billy Martin.

Martin's 1956 season was his last full one with the Yankees. The team that he had dreamed all his life of playing for—the only team he ever wanted to play for—traded him in the middle of the next season after he took part in a controversial fight at the Copacabana night club in New York City. Mickey Mantle and Whitey Ford were involved too, but blame for the incident fell on Martin, who was seen as a bad influence on the two great Yankee stars. He cried when he learned that his new team was Kansas City.

Martin blamed his longtime mentor, Yankee manager Casey Stengel, for not stepping in to block the trade. "I was hurt," he said. "I felt Stengel could have prevented it." In his anger Martin stopped talking to Stengel and refused to have anything to do with him. The two remained ostracized until the old man was himself banished from the Yankee kingdom, fired after the 1960 season despite having led New York to seven world championships.

After being let go by the Yankees, Stengel received a parade in his honor in Glendale. Marching bands played and Little Leaguers held up signs along the parade route saying, "To Heck with the A. L., Stay Home Casey" and "Don't Cry

Casey, We Need You." The parade ended at city hall, where local dignitaries awarded Casey and Edna the key to the city. Despite such blandishments Casey returned to New York two years later to manage the expansion Mets, whose teams were every bit as bad as his former Yankee teams were good. But once again his personality and charm won over fans and confirmed his reputation as one of the game's most enduring treasures.

Don Larsen throws the final pitch of his perfect game. Behind him at second base is Billy Martin. Doug McWilliams Collection

During these years Stengel and Martin patched up their feud. Stengel had never had children, and he regarded Martin as a son. Not being able to talk to him was like being cut off from his own family. Both men had so much in common, so many shared experiences, so many years together. Gradually even Billy, hardheaded Billy, could not help but bury his resentments and renew his close ties with the old man. He, too, spoke in terms of family when he spoke about Stengel: "I loved the old man. I loved him like a father."

After his playing career ended Martin moved into coaching and managing, rapidly earning a reputation as a top baseball strategist and motivator despite off-field problems with alcohol and a combative personality that sometimes clashed with players on his own team. His greatest glories (and controversies) came as the oft-hired, oft-fired manager of the Yankees, but in 1980 he returned to his East Bay roots as skipper of the Oakland Athletics. His aggressive, risk-taking style of managing, dubbed "Billy Ball," helped revitalize a then-comatose A's franchise. In his brief tenure in Oakland he also steered the early career of the game's all-time greatest base stealer, Rickey Henderson.

In all his years as manager Martin never failed to cite the influence of his onetime benefactor. "Much of what I am as a manager I took from Casey Stengel," he said. In every manager's office he occupied, including his office at the Oakland Coliseum, a picture of Casey hung on the wall.

But as Martin's managing career gained momentum in the early seventies, Stengel's life slowed down. After leaving the Mets he retired, at long last, to Glendale. A living emblem of the game's past, he was the guest of honor at

Casey Stengel and Billy Martin, circa 1949. Oakland Post Enquirer, Doug McWilliams Collection

special tributes from Yankee Stadium to Dodger Stadium. When they dedicated a field to him in Glendale, he said, "I feel greatly honored to have a ballpark named after me, especially since I have been thrown out of so many."

Meanwhile, Edna's health declined. After suffering a series of strokes she had to leave the house where they had lived for so many years and go into a nursing home. Her husband remained devoted to her, visiting her every day and pushing her around in a wheelchair. But driving there each day became an increasing challenge as Casey grew more frail and his hand on the wheel became less steady. His car was a mass of minor dings and dents. His driver's license was suspended after several traffic violations. But he could not walk all the way to Edna's, so he kept driving. When the Glendale police saw him on the road they redirected him back to his house. But after they left, Casey got back in his car and went to see his wife.

When Stengel appeared at Dodger Stadium for the 1974 World Series between Oakland and Los Angeles, those who saw him noted how weak he looked. His famous Stengelese had turned into the sad and aimless ramblings of a confused old man. In September of the following year he checked into Glendale Memorial Hospital, terminally ill with cancer.

The story is told that Stengel was lying in his hospital bed watching a baseball game on television when the first notes of the National Anthem sounded. "I might as well do this one last time," he said, climbing out of bed and standing with his hand placed over his heart. He died September 29, 1975, at the age of eighty-five. Edna survived him a couple of years before passing on.

Casey died the day after the end of the regular season. That year the Athletics, the champions of the West, were playing the Boston Red Sox, the winners of the East, for the American League title. With the first two games of the series being hosted by Boston, it was decided to postpone Casey's funeral for a week. That way, when the series shifted to California, more baseball people could attend.

Services were held at the Church of the Recessional at Forest Lawn Cemetary in Glendale, where Casey was laid to rest. The night before the funeral Billy Martin stayed at Casey's house and slept in his old bed.

For the rest of his life Martin made trips to Stengel's grave at Forest Lawn, visiting the site when he was in Los Angeles on road trips with the team he was managing or on other business. He always brought flowers and set them on the headstone. As he did he talked aloud to the old man, catching him up on the baseball news of the day and confiding in him like a son to his absent father.

CHAPTER 25

Brown Derby
Baseball

SATURDAY, MARCH 22 — 2:15 P.M.
SUNDAY, MARCH 23 — 2:15 P.M.
— 1947 —

Total $4.00

BLISHED PRICE - $3.33
ERAL TAX - .67

THIS PORTION OF TICKET NOT GOOD FOR ADMITTANCE
DETACH SEPERATE COUPONS FOR INDIVIDUAL GAMES

Joe DiMaggio opened up the sports page of the newspaper and saw her picture. He had never seen her before or even heard of her. (She was not a big name yet.) But as soon as he laid eyes on her he knew he wanted to meet her.

Marilyn Monroe was wearing a halter top, skimpy shorts, and high heels. Posing with her in the picture was Gus Zernial of the Philadelphia Athletics, showing her how to hold a baseball bat. It was a press agent's dream—a curvy Hollywood starlet and a brawny ballplayer: Beauty and the Beast. The publicity department at Twentieth Century Fox had arranged the photo to promote Monroe's upcoming movie *Clash by Night*. The movies liked being associated with baseball because of its wholesome family image, and baseball liked the movies because of their glamour. Everybody came out a winner.

Soon after the picture appeared, Zernial and DiMaggio, the famed Yankee Clipper who had just retired from baseball after a glorious career in New York, played in a charity exhibition together. Joe asked Gus about the blonde, and Gus gave him the name of Marilyn's business agent. DiMaggio's people called her people, and in a matter of days one of the most storied romances in American pop culture had begun.

Their first date took place at the Villa Nova Restaurant on Sunset Strip in Los Angeles. Marilyn made Joe wait two hours before she showed, probably because she did not want to be there at all, feeling that sports stars were crude, lewd bumpkins and not her style. She had never been to a baseball game and did not know or care who Joe DiMaggio was. But her business manager talked her into it, agreeing to bring a date of his own and come to dinner with them. Mostly Marilyn and the other couple talked while Joe sat there, hardly uttering a word but still making an impression. "I found myself staring at a reserved gentleman in a gray suit, with a gray tie and a sprinkle of gray hair in his hair," she said later. "If I hadn't been told he was some sort of ballplayer, I would have guessed he was either a steel magnate or a Congressman." When actor Mickey Rooney came up to their table and fawned over DiMaggio, that made an impression on her as well.

After that night the two went out—unescorted— several nights in a row, and Marilyn got to know and like Joe a little better each time she saw him. She noticed how men, famous men, real Hollywood big shots, deferred to him and acted almost like little boys around him. And he was not crude or rough, as she thought he might be. Rather he was a gentleman, almost Old World, silent as a statue but classy, caring, and attentive. When she had her appendix removed at a Los Angeles hospital, DiMaggio, stuck on the East Coast in his post-retirement broadcasting job for the Yankees, called her every day, several times a day, and buried her room in roses, her favorite flower.

Marilyn's physical attributes—in her middle twenties she looked, in the words of Norman Mailer, as if she were "fed on sexual candy"—obviously appealed to DiMaggio. But there was more to it than that for him. Those qualities that radiated outward off the screen to audiences watching her in the dark—her vulnerability, her innocence—got under Joe's skin as well. He wanted to protect her and take care of her.

Their bicoastal romance—Joe on the East Coast during baseball season, Marilyn mostly in Hollywood making pictures—blossomed. When he was in town he frequently stayed at her suite at the Beverly Hills Hotel. When they stepped out for the evening, wherever they went around town flashbulbs popped and gossip columnists took note. DiMaggio, a private man by nature who had had his fill of the press in New York, did not much enjoy this. Besides, his playing career was over. Monroe's, on the other hand, was on the rise. It was good for her to get out on the town and see people—be talked about, get her picture in the papers. Not only that, she enjoyed it, liked to go out and have some fun. One of the places they went, one of the places where everybody in show business went, was the Brown Derby.

The Hollywood Brown Derby was on Vine Street, a half-block down from Hollywood Boulevard, which was close enough for the restaurant to accurately list its address as the corner of Hollywood and Vine, perhaps the most famous intersection in the world in the 1930s and '40s, when the Derby was at its peak. After the restaurant's founder died, Bob Cobb took over its operation and became the owner. There were actually four Derbies—the in-spot at Hollywood and Vine; the one in the shape of a bowler hat on Wilshire Boulevard; the location in Beverly Hills; and the one in the Los Feliz section of Los Angeles—and Cobb watched over them all with a jeweler's eye for detail.

The Brown Derby, Wilshire Boulevard, Los Angeles.
Security Pacific Collection/Los Angeles Public Library

The Derbies were known for their sumptuous food—Cobb was the inventor of the Cobb salad, the signature dish of the restaurant—and unmatched people-watching atmosphere. The main dining room at the Hollywood Derby was a large open room with low-slung leather booths that allowed everybody to see everybody else who was dining there. The most prestigious seats, reserved for Hollywood's glitterati, were near the front and along the walls hung with caricatures of the most famous stars—another Derby trademark. If you had a representation of your face on the wall of the Derby, it was a sign that you had arrived in Hollywood. The waiters wore starched white linen jackets, the china and silver place settings were immaculate, and the polished copper light fixtures were in the shape of derby hats.

Cobb, a Montanan by birth, was what writers of another age might have described as dapper. His face was long with a soft chin and his wavy dark hair was parted down the middle in the style of the day. The attentiveness to detail he showed at his restaurants appeared as well in his grooming and dress. He wore tailored suits that were always immaculate, from the starched white collar of his embroidered shirt with its tie bar underneath the knot of the tie, his tie clasp, pocket handkerchief, cufflinks, even down to the cowboy-style boot heels on his handmade leather shoes. But he was no dandy, no fop; he was charming and accessible, greeting friends with a "Hiya, partner." He rode horses and ranched in his younger days, loved to eat and drink and dance, and after everyone had gone home for the night, he would pop open a bottle of his private label rum or Napa Valley wine and talk baseball with his friends.

"While my mother and the Brown Derbies were certainly his first loves," wrote his stepdaughter Peggy Cobb Walsh, "a close third was baseball." In 1938 Cobb formed a partnership to buy the Hollywood Stars baseball team, and the other members of his investment group were both patrons of his restaurants and Hollywood stars of the celluloid variety.

The CBS Radio Playhouse Theater was on Vine Street across from the Hollywood Derby, and many of the stars who ate there came from radio. One of them was George Burns, then best known as the straight man in a comedy team with his wife Gracie Allen. Burns sunk some money into the Stars with Cobb. Recording artist Bing Crosby, who also starred in the movies, was another investor. Barbara Stanwyck and Robert Taylor were two of MGM's biggest stars and, in the era before Joe and Marilyn, one of Hollywood's most photographed couples. They also threw in some dough for the Stars, as did handsome leading man Gary Cooper, who played Lou Gehrig in the poignant drama of the great Yankee star's life and death, *Pride of the Yankees*. Walt Disney, whose innovative animated movie *Snow White and the Seven Dwarfs* had opened in theaters the year before, was also part of the group. Yet another investor was cowboy recording and movie star Gene Autry, who later sold his shares in the team to Cobb. (Two decades later Autry would, however, re-enter professional baseball in a big way by founding the expansion Los Angeles (now Anaheim) Angels of the American League.)

The Hollywood Stars baseball team had two incarnations: the first, when the owner was Bill Lane, who eventually moved it to San Diego where it became the Padres; and the second, far more successful reign under Bob Cobb. One of the problems that bedeviled the Stars under Lane was its lack of a ballpark; they had to play their home games at Wrigley Field in Los Angeles. But on May 2, 1939, Cobb's Hollywood Stars began play in their own brand-new, single-deck, all-wood ballpark, Gilmore Field, located in the Farmer's Market area of Hollywood near Gilmore Stadium. Comedian and longtime baseball booster Joe E. Brown caught the ceremonial first pitch on Opening Day, and a half-dozen photographers, using box cameras, crowded around home plate to capture him in the act. In the years to come Brown would be a frequent sight at Gilmore Field (and the Brown Derby), as would a host of other celebrities, including a movie star who first came to Hollywood because of baseball. He was Ronald Reagan.

Growing up in Dixon, Illinois, Ronald Reagan loved sports, playing football, basketball, and track for North Dixon High. His father named him "Dutch" when he was a baby because he looked like a "little Dutchman." In the summers Dutch worked as a lifeguard at a beach on the Rock River, earning a reputation as a local hero by rescuing dozens of swimmers who had gotten

Advertising flyer, Gilmore Field Opening, 1939. California Historical Society

into trouble in the water. After high school his athletic career continued at Eureka College, where he played football and captained the Golden Tornado swim team. Following graduation he decided to see if he could parlay his interest in sports into a broadcasting career, traveling to Chicago to apply for a job at a radio station.

After being turned down there, he went to WOC Radio in Davenport, Iowa, which hired him to broadcast University of Iowa football games for one hundred dollars a month. This experience enabled him to move up, only a few months later, to a bigger station with a more powerful radio signal, WHO in Des Moines. WHO carried the Chicago Cubs games on its air, and Reagan acted as the announcer for the station, doing what are called "re-creation" broadcasts. Reagan did not personally attend the Cubs games at Wrigley Field in Chicago or when they were on the road. Rather he remained in Des Moines and received telegraph transmissions of what was occurring on the field, messages he then translated, in his own words, for listeners in Des Moines. Re-creations were a common practice for money-strapped radio stations during the Depression.

Broadcasting the Cubs games gave Reagan an idea. Partly in a desire to learn more about the team for the coming season, but mainly to take a vacation from the grim coldness of an Iowa winter, he proposed accompanying the Cubs to Catalina Island, where they held spring training. Watching the Cubs practice would give him insights when he called their games during the regular season, he explained to his employers, who agreed to his plan. Then in his mid-twenties, Reagan came to California for the first time in the mid-1930s, watching the Cubs practice on Catalina and also going over to see the White Sox train at Brookside Park in Pasadena.

One year when Reagan was in southern California on another spring training trip with the Cubs, a bad storm hit the area, causing high seas along the coast and blocking access to and from Catalina Island. The Cubs were holed up in their hotel on the island, and nobody was playing baseball. Freed from his broadcasting responsibilities for the day, Reagan checked into the Biltmore Hotel in Los Angeles, where he met an old friend from Iowa in the hotel nightclub. The two got to talking. His friend was a singer who had moved to Hollywood to break into the movies. Reagan confessed that he, too, had always had a secret desire to be in pictures. His friend gave him the name of an agent, who agreed to meet with Reagan the next morning.

The agent could see potential in the former lifeguard's dark-haired good looks and arranged a screen test for him at Warner Brothers. But the test had to wait for another day because the storm had cleared and Reagan had to get back to Catalina. When he finally showed up at practice, Cubs manager Charlie Grimm ragged on him for being late.

Reagan's screen test turned out to be a hit, so much so that Warners offered him a seven-year contract at two hundred dollars a week. When he said yes, it brought to a close his career in sports broadcasting and began a promising new one in the movies.

The future governor of California and president of the United States jokingly described himself as "the Errol Flynn of the B pictures," a leading man for lower-budget, less prestigious movies. Nevertheless he commanded a $1 million contract in the boom years after World War II, his peak years in Hollywood, and appeared in more than fifty movies in all. During these years Reagan (a regular at the Hollywood Brown Derby) could be seen around town at Gilmore Field or Wrigley Field in Los Angeles, or watching the St. Louis Browns spring practices at Olive Memorial Stadium (now Izay Park) in Burbank, or perhaps even making a sentimental appearance at Catalina Island where the Cubs, who had stopped coming to California during the war, had resumed spring training. He also starred in the 1952 baseball movie *The Winning Team,* in which he played

Hall of Fame pitcher Grover Cleveland Alexander. It was one of the movies in Reagan's career of which he was most proud.

The Winning Team was also notable in that its cast included a host of real-life baseball players: Hall of Fame pitcher Bob Lemon, infielder Jerry Priddy, major league veteran and Angels Camp–native Catfish Metkovich, Yankee outfielder Irv Noren, and a sharp-minded young student of the game, Gene Mauch. Mauch, a graduate of Fremont High in Los Angeles, was then a so-so major league infielder. Greater success would come to him in later years as a manager of the Philadelphia Phillies, California Angels, and other clubs. His twenty-six-year tenure as a big league manager, in which he established a reputation as one of the game's top strategists, is among the longest in baseball history.

Another noteworthy baseball film of the early fifties was *The Jackie Robinson Story,* in which Robinson starred as himself. The movie, a surprisingly candid treatment of the racial issues of its time, also stands out for another reason: some scenes show Robinson playing baseball, preserving for today's fans a glimpse of the greatness that once was.

Two popular baseball comedies of this era were *It Happens Every Spring,* in which a man becomes a successful pitcher after discovering a magic liquid that makes the balls he throws impossible to hit, and *Angels in the Outfield,* the story of an awful Pittsburgh Pirates club transformed into a champion by the assistance of heavenly spirits. Another baseball fantasy, though of a somewhat later vintage, was *Damn Yankees,* based on the Broadway musical of the same name, in which a Senators fan agrees to give his soul to the devil in exchange for becoming a baseball star. Wrigley Field in Los Angeles provided the setting for the baseball scenes.

Pat and Mike was a 1952 comedy about a female athlete (played by Katharine Hepburn) and her manager (Spencer Tracy). With cameos by various real-life sports stars, it marks the screen debut of Chuck Connors in a bit part. The Brooklyn-born Connors appeared ever-so-briefly with the Cubs and the Dodgers before being sent to the Angels, the Cubs' farm team in Los Angeles. Once in southern California, he turned his strong jaw and rugged looks into a second career on the screen, leaving baseball to star in the popular television series *The Rifleman* and later, *Branded.*

Wrigley Field, where Connors played first base for the Angels, was one of the Los Angeles ballyards where fans could spot celebrities in the grandstands. But these were down years for the franchise, largely due to its affiliation with the lower-division Cubs, and a dearth of good players combined with a glut of losing games took away some of the fun in watching the Angels. This, plus Bob Cobb's show business connections and the championship-caliber team he put on the field, made Stars games at Gilmore Field the in-spot to watch baseball in town, with some of the most beautiful and glamorous people in America in the grandstands.

Celebrity sighting was certainly one of the appeals of watching Stars games, and the promotion-minded Cobb made sure fans knew about it. Pictures of famous people, such as comedians Danny Kaye and Jack Benny posing for a gag shot eating hot dogs in their seats at Gilmore Field, appeared on the cover of game programs. The celebrities were not averse to the publicity and were generally happy to help out their friend. Night games in baseball became more common after the war, and the entrance to Gilmore Field was lit up like a movie theater marquee. For a time the club hired female cheerleaders to exhort the crowd. One year the Stars broke new fashion ground in baseball uniforms, doing away with the traditional pants and introducing pinstriped shorts for the players. Not every innovation smacks of genius, however, and after receiving considerable ridicule—"Will the Stars Shave Their Legs Next?" mocked one headline—Cobb abandoned the experiment.

Danny Kaye, left, and Jack Benny, Hollywood Stars program, 1948. California Historical Society

The Stars were the first club on the coast to televise a game. The Angels followed suit the next season, and by the late 1940s both teams were showing their home games on television.

The Stars of this era pounded the Coast League, winning three championships in five seasons. When they journeyed crosstown to Wrigley or the Angels came to Gilmore, local baseball fans, including celebrities, scrambled for tickets. The rivalry between the two clubs was real. A 1953 Angel-Star brawl at Gilmore captured headlines and a huge photo spread in the *Los Angeles Times*. In the foreground of the pictures players are throwing punches at one another on the field. In the background are all the fans in short-sleeve shirts who have jumped to their feet to get a better view of the rhubarb. Not a seat is empty; the place is stuffed with bodies. The crowded parks, the year-round sun, the surging southern California population, the celebrities, the whole baseball *scene*—it seemed only a matter of time before the major leagues caught up with what was happening on the West Coast, and eventually they did.

Casey Stengel, Joe DiMaggio, General William F. Dean, Bob Hope, and Marilyn Monroe enjoy a night at the Derby, circa 1953. Security Pacific Collection / Los Angeles Public Library

Bob Cobb died in 1970. Over time his Derby restaurants became associated with Old Hollywood, and in Hollywood old is as good as dead. The restaurants fell out of favor, the stars found new places to go, and the area he helped to mythologize, Hollywood and Vine, turned seedy. A chain took over the Brown Derbies, which were shut down for a time for earthquake retrofitting and ultimately destroyed. None of the original Derby restaurants exists today.

But in its heyday it hosted the best baseball parties around. In a pre–World War II photograph from the Derby, Joe E. Brown, his mouth opened wide in song, stands in the center of a band of revelers that includes actor Robert Taylor and aging Hall of Famers Al Simmons, Connie Mack, and Frankie Frisch. After the war, in another photo, Fred Haney, a former Hollywood Stars manager who became the first general manager of the major league Los Angeles Angels, grips one of comedian Georgie Jessel's long, long cigars, as if to show Jessel and Bob Cobb, who are also pictured, how to handle a bat.

Another photograph, possibly from the Bamboo Room cocktail lounge at the Hollywood Brown Derby, includes Casey Stengel, Bob Hope, Joe DiMaggio, and Marilyn Monroe seated on a couch. Joe is smoking a cigarette and smiling, and Marilyn, in a revealing evening dress with long formal gloves, looks radiant and happy, too. She has every reason to be. When she and

DiMaggio met, she was a girl on the make, with a few movies and magazine covers to her credit. By the time of the photograph—December 1953—she had become a superstar. *Gentlemen Prefer Blondes,* with her and Jane Russell in the title roles, had been a big hit, and she and Russell had done their star turn at Grauman's Chinese Theatre, putting their handprints and footprints into cement as a horde of photographers snapped their picture. Monroe had made a guest appearance on Jack Benny's top-rated television show, and she was receiving twenty-five thousand fan letters a week.

Her relationship with DiMaggio was holding together, although the fracture lines were already apparent. Indeed they had been there from the very beginning. One can imagine Marilyn wanting to sit at the Derby at a booth in the front, reflective of her new status in Hollywood, where she could see people and people could see her. DiMaggio's style was much different. He preferred quiet and privacy—a table in a back room would have been more to his liking. Adding to this tension was his dislike of show business people; he felt they were parading Monroe's body around on screen while making millions off her and paying her peanuts. He wanted her to take more control, be more selective about her projects. Joe, who was more than a decade older than Marilyn, also wished she would cover up more when she was in public, show less skin.

Despite fighting about these and other issues they talked seriously about marriage. "We knew it wouldn't be an easy marriage," said Marilyn. "On the other hand, we couldn't keep going on forever as a pair of crosscountry lovers."

What helped them decide was an upcoming baseball trip that Joe was going to take to Japan. They could tie the knot and have their honeymoon in the Far East. That settled it, and on June 14, 1954, the two exchanged vows in a civil ceremony at San Francisco City Hall. After making their way out of the building through a mob of reporters and photographers, they drove south down the coast in Joe's blue Cadillac. Honeymoon night was spent in the Clifton Motel in Paso Robles in central California, where they paid six and a half dollars for a room with a double bed and a television. Not long after that the most talked-about couple in the world was winging across the Pacific.

The trip overseas was arranged by Joe's best man, Lefty O'Doul, his former manager and hitting coach with the San Francisco Seals, a longtime friend and another fellow who knew how to mix baseball with good times. Lefty had traveled to Japan several times in the 1930s to play exhibitions and teach hitting, but the war had put an end to any attempts at goodwill between the two countries. It was said that he took the attack on Pearl Harbor as a personal insult, a betrayal by a country for which he had developed a genuine bond. If this was true, O'Doul did not hold a grudge for long. After going to Japan on his own the year after the war ended, he went back again in 1949, this time bringing the Seals with him in a piece of international baseball diplomacy.

Many Japanese felt resentment toward the American troops stationed in their country. Protests and riots broke out in Tokyo and other cities. General Douglas MacArthur, the American commander of Allied forces in Japan, felt, along with one of his aides, Lieutenant Cappy Harada, a decorated Japanese

Lefty O'Doul receives gifts during the Seals'
groundbreaking 1949 trip to Japan.
California Historical Society, FN-40042

Joe and Marilyn.
Security Pacific Collection/
Los Angeles Public Library

American combat veteran from Santa Maria (who later served as a special assistant and scout for the Giants), that baseball was a way to establish better ties between the two countries and lift the spirits of the Japanese in the process. O'Doul agreed. "It was terrible," he recalled when the Seals first arrived in Tokyo. "The people were so depressed."

But gradually the mood lightened, as more than half a million people turned out for the eleven-game tour, including 140,000 for two games in Nagoya played in a driving rainstorm. Never one to let a customer go away unhappy, whether at his saloon or at a ballpark, O'Doul, then in his early fifties, pitched the final game of the tour against a Tokyo collegiate all-star team, throwing two scoreless innings before leaving the game to enthusiastic shouts of "Banzai! Banzai!" from the fans.

The trip, a diplomatic triumph, "broke the postwar tension in Japanese-American relations," in the words of baseball historian Kerry Yo Nakagawa. General MacArthur lavishly praised O'Doul, who, along with Seals president Paul Fagan and vice president Charlie Graham, received an invitation to visit Emperor Hirohito at the Imperial Palace in Tokyo. The invitation and its acceptance were seen as significant gestures of goodwill, a step forward in repairing relations between America and Japan.

After this trip, the first by an American baseball team to postwar Japan, Lefty's fame overseas increased, and two years later he took an all-star band of major leaguers, including Joe DiMaggio, to the country. Then, in 1954, he returned yet again, this time with Joe and his new bride.

Both DiMaggio and O'Doul had played in front of large, passionate crowds of baseball fans, but even they were caught off guard by the Japanese response to Marilyn. So many people crowded Tokyo airport when they arrived that it took nearly an hour for them to get off the plane. Masses of fans, reporters, photographers swarmed her everywhere she went. When she took a side trip, on her own, to the war in Korea, she caused a frenzy of appreciation among the American servicemen she visited there. O'Doul said it was on this trip that DiMaggio, for the first time, understood what a huge, huge star his wife had become.

Their relationship deteriorated quickly once they came back home. In New York for the filming of her new movie, *The Seven Year Itch,* Monroe stayed with her husband in a suite at the St. Regis Hotel. The two argued and DiMaggio evidently struck her. Three weeks later she filed for divorce. DiMaggio packed up his things and moved out of their North Palm Drive house to return home to San Francisco.

But their story does not end there. Despite their differences (and another failed marriage in the meantime between Monroe and playwright Arthur Miller), the two remained close over the years. Some have suggested they were about to get back together before Monroe's death in 1962. Shattered by her passing, his face a mask of contained grief, DiMaggio arranged her funeral at Westwood Memorial Park in west Los Angeles. For years after her death he had fresh roses placed at her gravesite.

They Changed the Game

SATURDAY, MARCH 22 — 2:15 P.M.
SUNDAY, MARCH 23 — 2:15 P.M.
— 1947 —

ABLISHED PRICE - $3.33   Total $4.00
DERAL TAX - .67

HIS PORTION OF TICKET NOT GOOD FOR ADMITTANCE
DETACH SEPERATE COUPONS FOR INDIVIDUAL GAMES

Ruth Shaw was a Texas woman whose second husband, a man by the name of Frank Robinson, worked for the railroads. Ruth had ten children in all, but only one with Frank—a boy, born in Beaumont, Texas, who took his father's name. But big Frank did not stay around the house much, and he and Ruth split up when little Frank was a baby.

Frank was Ruth's youngest child and by the time of his birth only two brothers were living at home with him and his mother. Several of the older children had moved to Oakland, California, where they had found jobs in the shipyards and other places. Their letters to Texas convinced Ruth to leave her home state and go to Oakland with her boys to see if she could find steady work too.

A year or so after Ruth Shaw and her children arrived in Oakland, another family from Texas came to live in the growing city. America had not yet entered World War II, but the shipyards of the East Bay were busy and getting busier all the time. The opportunity for work drew Herman Flood, his wife, and four of their children, including their youngest, a two-year-old named Curt. They settled into a two-family apartment in west Oakland where Curt shared a bedroom with his two older brothers, each of whom had his own bed. Having your own bed was considered a luxury by the family, which scraped by to make ends meet.

Willie Stargell's family came to Oakland after the war started, when the shipyards and factory assembly lines pulsed with activity and workers were in demand. But Willie's father drank too much, and after he and Willie's mother broke up, she sent her son to stay with an aunt in Florida. They lived in the black part of town, with its dirt streets and wooden shacks. When Willie's mom remarried and brought him back to California to live with her and her new husband in the projects, it felt like a different, and better, atmosphere to him. Everybody drove cars and had their own apartment. And he saw people of all colors, not just his own.

Like Frank Robinson and Curt Flood, Joe Morgan was a native of Texas (Stargell was born in Oklahoma). But it was hard for Joe's parents to make a living in the tiny town of Bonham, and they decided to follow the lead of a couple of Joe's uncles who had settled in Oakland. The war had ended by this time, but there was still work to be found, still shops and manufacturing plants posting "Help Wanted" signs. Joe, the oldest of six children, was five years old. The neighborhood they moved into, in west Oakland not far from Oaks Ball Park, was almost entirely white, and they were one of the first black families to live there.

When these four families moved into Oakland, the racial composition of the city was beginning to change, mirroring a transformation that was taking place in downtown neighborhoods in California and across America. Whites were moving out to the suburbs, and the black (and Hispanic and Asian) population in the cities was increasing. Evidence of this growing division in American society could be found in the faces of the boys and girls who played school and league sports. Generally whites played on teams in the suburbs, and blacks played on teams in the cities.

In Oakland in the forties and fifties, when Frank Robinson was a tall, lanky teenager who could hit a baseball a mile, the city's racial makeup was changing. The Myrtle Street block where he and his family lived consisted of a row of tenement buildings. "It was a rough, mixed neighborhood," Robinson said in his autobiography, "mostly Negroes but also Mexicans and a lot of [Asians]." He added that "it wasn't a bad, Harlem-type ghetto" and he did not remember having problems over race.

If Robinson wanted to find problems, not of a racial kind but of a wrong-side-of-the-law kind, all he needed to do was walk a few blocks over to Seventh Street, where the gangs hung out and fights occurred. But he stayed clear of Seventh and mostly out of trouble because if he was not in school you could almost certainly find him over at Tompkins Street Playground, playing ball.

In 1949 Oakland's Bill Erwin Post 237, coached by George Powles, won the national American Legion championship. The next year the name of Frank Robinson was added to the roster, and the Post repeated as national champions. (The year after that Sparky Anderson's Crenshaw club won the legion's national title.) Fourteen players from those back-to-back Oakland title-winners went on to play pro baseball, and when the champs returned home after the second year, dozens of friends and family greeted them at the railroad station in celebration. But, as only one of two blacks on the team, Robinson felt distanced from the celebration and many of his teammates. Contributing to these feelings of isolation was his shyness as a teenager.

At times like this, when he was feeling down, he would go over to Coach Powles's house. "He'd invite me over to his house and I'd go in the living room and sit in a chair with my head hanging to the floor," he recalled. "I'd say hello and never look up. But then we'd start to talk baseball and it'd be all right. We'd talk for hours, maybe three or four days a week. That was a real baseball house."

A native Oaklander, Powles (pronounced "poles") was a white man—"a stocky guy with a friendly open face," in Robinson's words—and a wanna-be player who was not quite good enough to make it into the Coast League or anywhere else in organized baseball. With the pro game closed to him, he got his credential at San Francisco State College (now University) and became a science and physical education teacher and a coach. Coaching was his passion. He coached everything—school, youth leagues, American Legion, playground. He found out about Robinson by asking a group of playground kids who was the best player in their junior high. When they said, as one, "Frank Robinson," he invited Frank to a tryout at Bushrod Park and then onto his national champion American Legion team.

"Even as a kid Frank understood the game," Powles said. "He was just a natural hitter. It wasn't a question of teaching him this or that. He had it all." When Robinson entered McClymonds High, its enrollment consisted mainly of blacks, and Powles was the baseball and basketball coach. In Robinson's junior year, in addition to starring on the varsity baseball team, he played on the

McClymonds basketball squad with future college and NBA great Bill Russell. Powles coached them both.

In 1953, his senior season at McClymonds (Russell graduated the previous year), Robinson tore up Oakland prep baseball, but his .424 batting average was only second on his team. The kid with the top batting average, five points higher than Frank's, was a small, skinny sophomore who could outrun a greyhound, Curt Flood.

"We were not poor," said Curt as a grown man, remembering his childhood in Oakland. "But we had nothing." This, despite the fact that his father worked double shifts at a local hospital and his mother held down two jobs in addition to taking in sewing in her off-time. To save money Herman Flood recycled the same Christmas tree several years in a row. After the holidays were over he took the tree down, lacquered it, and hung it upside down in the basement, where it would stay until the next December when he would pull it out of storage and put it up again. Many a Christmas passed before Curt realized that other families bought a new tree each year.

Flood's memories of his old neighborhood are etched in harsher terms than Robinson's. He described it as "a conventionally squalid west Oakland ghetto" where broken glass littered the sidewalks and junk cars sat abandoned on the streets and in empty lots. Old couches and chairs were dumped outside their building. Certain doorways contained the smell of urine. Drug pushers plied their trade on street corners, not far from prostitutes waiting for customers to drive by. Nearly all the whites Flood saw growing up were in positions of authority: teachers, landlords, bill collectors, cops.

With his parents away at work so much of the time, Curt and his brothers ran the streets by day and night. When Curt was ten he stole a car and crashed it; a night in juvenile hall followed. His older brother Carl also spent a night in juvenile hall for bicycle theft. This turned out to be Curt's last brush with the law, but not his brother's. Carl in later years went to prison for armed robbery.

Along with his brother, Curt played for Junior's Sweet Shop midget baseball team in a league sponsored by the Oakland police in the late 1940s. The coach was George Powles, who invited Curt to hang out and play with the older guys on his American Legion team, which included Frank Robinson. After practices and games all the guys went over to Powles's house, where they celebrated with ice cream or maybe a hot meal cooked up by his wife. "If I now see whites as human beings rather than as stereotypes, it is because of a process that began with George Powles," said Flood. "The beauty of George was that you did not have to adulterate your blackness to win his confidence and approval. He never preached or patronized."

Willie Stargell evidently never played for Powles, though Powles probably coached against him in East Bay youth baseball. Stargell lived in a different part of Oakland and went to Encinal High in Alameda. He spent four years in the minor leagues and felt he could have probably made the majors sooner if he had received better instruction as a youngster. Much of what he learned, growing up in the projects, he learned on his own.

When he was young Stargell used to go down to the lumberyard near where he lived, find a two-by-four scrap of wood and perhaps whittle the handle down to resemble a baseball bat, then hit rocks with it. Other times he would use a broom or an ax handle for a bat. Even using a broom handle, the big lefty swinger could get good wood on the ball.

With his size, Stargell was a natural for football and he loved the game, but after hurting his knee during a scrimmage at Encinal as a sophomore, and then again the next year, he gave up the sport to concentrate on baseball, which became his ticket out of the ghetto. "I was exposed to everything an average black kid gets to see," he said. "Pimps and con men, dope pushers and gamblers. I could have easily taken the wrong road, but I always wanted to be a baseball player."

This wish received an early test in Texas in 1959, his first season in the minor leagues. Not allowed to stay with the white players in their lodging, he slept on fold-up cots on the back porches of black people's homes in the black part of town. Whites–only restaurants were off-limits to him as well. In order to get a meal at these places he

Willie Stargell on the Pittsburgh Pirates.
National Baseball Hall of Fame Library, Cooperstown, N.Y.

had to go around back and eat scraps of food on napkins given to him by the kitchen help. Nor could he avoid issues of race at the ballpark. One time before a game a white man threatened him with a shotgun, sticking it next to his face and saying he would kill him if Stargell got a hit that night.

Stargell was so discouraged when he returned home to Oakland after that season that he thought about quitting the game. He had lost weight and he felt weak, both physically and emotionally, and he never wanted to face that sort of treatment again.

Also in Oakland, Joe Morgan received one of his first lessons about race after a game of street ball with some white and black kids in his neighborhood. He got into an argument with one of the guys and when he told his mother about it afterward, he mentioned that the kid was white.

"Would you be upset if it was a black kid who argued with you?" his mother asked him.

"Yes," said Joe.

"Then why does it matter that he's white? You deal with people, not color."

But it *did* matter, at least in some ways, and Joe's mother of course knew this.

Living so close to Oaks Park, Joe and his father, who was a former semi-pro player, would walk over to see the Oaks when they were in town. They went practically every night, forty or fifty times in a season, sitting together in the stands and talking baseball and watching the game as a light breeze blew in across the bay.

When the Morgans were going to Oaks Ball Park, black stars such as Piper Davis, a quiet ex–Negro League veteran, played for the Oaks. But tensions existed between white and black players on the team. The blacks on the club were often the stars or, at the very least, above average, while the more marginal players and the men on the bench were white, as were the coaches and managers. Though the unwritten rule barring blacks from organized baseball was no more, a different sort of rule, also unspoken, had taken its place—one that required blacks to not just be good, but to excel, to be far better than whites, otherwise they would not make the club. Those blacks who managed to overcome this invisible barrier often received abuse from white fans and players. One of the Coast League's most notorious brawls occurred when a white pitcher for the San Francisco Seals, Bill Boemler, threw knockdown pitches at both Davis and Cuban-born Rafael Noble, the two black players on the Oaks, almost certainly because of their race. White players on the Oaks came to the defense of their teammates in the headline-making fight that followed.

Morgan does not refer to this incident in his autobiography, and he may not have been aware of it as a nine-year-old (although his father probably was). But as he grew older he saw other things that struck him as unfair.

Morgan went to Castlemont High in Oakland, which was then almost entirely white, but one of his teammates and best friends was a black pitcher, Rudy May. In the tenth grade, said Morgan, May had a major league arm with an eye-popping fastball. But May's bonus for signing with a major league organization was only eight thousand dollars. A white Oakland high schooler with nowhere near his skills received a one-hundred-thousand-dollar big league bonus and never got within shouting distance of the major leagues. May, on the other hand, pitched sixteen big league seasons with the Angels and other clubs.

The knock against the five-foot-seven-inch Morgan—he heard it all the time: in Babe Ruth baseball, at Castlemont, at Oakland City (now Merritt) College, where he went for a year after high school—was that he was a "good little player," emphasis on little. But Cookie Lavagetto, the big leaguer turned scout who grew up in Oakland and still lived in the area, saw a smart kid with

Joe Morgan with the Cincinnati Reds, circa 1975.
National Baseball Hall of Fame Library, Cooperstown, N.Y.

a good glove who choked up on the bat but never got cheated on his cuts. He tried to get the Mets to sign him; when they passed, Houston scout Bill Wight stepped in with a minor league contract offer.

Wight's first offer included a two-thousand-dollar signing bonus, but then Joe's father invited him over to their house to talk it over. After they shared a few beers (and a few more beers after that), Wight upped his offer to three thousand dollars, and that sounded better to everyone.

Morgan's first full season in the majors was in 1965 in Houston, and he joined a wave of young black players who were reshaping the game. These young blacks did not have to follow the path of their fathers and grandfathers into segregated baseball. Instead they were making the jump from high school or college directly into organized baseball, and their power, speed, intelligence, and all the skills they brought to the game were making it better. They made baseball more exciting, more competitive, and their presence brought black spectators out to ballparks where once only whites filled the seats.

Perhaps the greatest of this new wave of black talent, a man who never played a day in racially restricted baseball, was Frank Robinson. After winning Rookie of the Year honors in 1956 and later the Most Valuable Player award in the National League, he was traded from the Reds to the Baltimore Orioles.

Frank Robinson as manager of the Giants, circa 1981.
Ken Lee copyright 88

He then proceeded to win the American League MVP and lead the Orioles to a World Series championship. After retiring with 586 home runs, he became the first black manager in baseball history and later managed the San Francisco Giants. At his Hall of Fame acceptance speech he thanked his former high school coach, George Powles, for helping him early in life.

Bobby Mattick was the Cincinnati Reds' scout who signed Robinson out of McClymonds High. Another Mattick signee was Curt Flood, who had since transferred to Oakland Tech (the future alma mater of Rickey Henderson). It took a few years for Flood to blossom, but in 1961, now with the St. Louis Cardinals, his hitting finally began to catch up with his exemplary fielding. Too small, too skinny? Nobody was saying that about him anymore. By the middle of the decade some people thought he was a better defensive center fielder than Willie Mays. His most lasting impact on the game, however, came off the field, and Flood's challenge to baseball's reserve clause will be taken up later in the book.

Vada Pinson's family came to Oakland at the end of World War II, when he was a boy. He too grew up under the tutelage of George Powles and played with Flood and Robinson at McClymonds and in the American Legion. In youth baseball the best athletes tend to play the infield, so an outfield consisting of Frank Robinson, Vada Pinson, and Curt Flood never materialized. But if it had, it is hard to imagine a better high school outfield than that one. In eighteen seasons in the majors Pinson sparkled in the outfield but did not quite reach three thousand hits and so fell a notch or two below Hall of Fame standards.

Pinson's rookie season with the Reds was 1959, the same year Elijah "Pumpsie" Green made his breakthrough appearance with the Boston Red Sox. Unlike these other, more talented Oakland-bred players, Green was a California native. Raised in nearby Richmond in an athletic family—his brother Cornell played defensive back for the Dallas Cowboys—his dream as a boy was to suit up for the hometown Oaks or the across-the-bay Seals. The second baseman did, in fact, get his wish and play in the Coast League, but he achieved much more than that. In 1959 Boston was the only major league team without a black

Pumpsie Green, before moving up to the Red Sox, late 1950s. California Historical Society, FN-40025

player on its roster. On July 21 Pumpsie took the field for the Red Sox, becoming the first black player in club history. His appearance meant that at last every club in the major leagues was integrated and the era of separate but equal, at least on the playing field, was over. Green played five seasons in the majors, four with the Red Sox, before hanging up his glove.

After his horrific 1959 minor league season, Willie Stargell went back to Oakland and took a job at a Chevrolet plant, working during the day and playing on its winter league team in the evenings and weekends. He beefed up on his mother's home cooking, rejuvenated his spirits, and reported to spring training to give baseball another try. Stargell reached the Pittsburgh Pirates, his one and only major league team, in the early 1960s and stayed there for twenty-one seasons. Known for his prodigious power, he hit, in 1969, the first ball to sail completely out of Dodger Stadium. And four years later he did it again. Two Stargell-led Pirate clubs won world championships, but perhaps even more impressive than his Hall of Fame accomplishments was the esteem and affection in which fans and fellow players held him. At Encinal High, his alma mater, the baseball and football fields are named after him, and every year it sponsors the Willie Stargell Classic, a local prep baseball tournament.

Stargell died in 2001 at the age of sixty-one, and fellow Hall of Famer and longtime friend Joe Morgan spoke at his funeral. Morgan said he chose number 8 for his own uniform jersey because that was Stargell's number and he wanted to model himself after the big man. After beginning his career in Houston, Morgan joined the Cincinnati Reds, where he won back-to-back Most Valuable Player awards and earned recognition as one of the all-time-great second basemen on one of the all-time-great teams, the Reds of '75–'76. Toward the end of his career he joined the Frank Robinson–managed San Francisco Giants and delivered a clutch home run against Los Angeles on the last day of the 1982 season to kill the Dodgers' hopes for a division title. After retiring from active play he became one of the first black network television baseball analysts and is widely regarded as one of the best in his field, regardless of color.

Los Angeles Dodgers
vs.
San Francisco Giants,
April 1958

ROSEBORO

HERRY

SATURDAY, MARCH 22 — 2:15 P.M.
SUNDAY, MARCH 23 — 2:15 P.M.
— 1947 —
ESTABLISHED PRICE $3.33 Total $4.00
FEDERAL TAX .67
THIS PORTION OF TICKET NOT GOOD FOR ADMITTANCE
SEPERATE COUPONS FOR INDIVIDUAL GAMES

The Los Angeles Dodgers may have begun and the Brooklyn Dodgers may have ended on a pleasant October day in Los Angeles in 1956. After losing to the New York Yankees in the World Series, the Dodgers flew cross-country on their way to a goodwill baseball tour of Japan. During their stopover in Los Angeles, Brooklyn owner Walter O'Malley met County Supervisor Kenneth Hahn for a helicopter ride around the city. But their purpose was not to see the sights; they were investigating possible places to put a new baseball stadium, should the Brooklyn franchise elect to pull up stakes and move west.

The search focused on Chavez Ravine, a three-hundred acre parcel of public land north of downtown. Named after Julian Chavez, a former owner of the land and a past city councilman, the site had been a source of controversy for years. In a bitterly contested civic debate, Los Angeles voters had turned down a proposal to build public housing there. Partly on the strength of his opposition to the referendum, Norris Poulson won election as mayor a few years later.

Since taking office Poulson had tried unsuccessfully to interest various groups in the site. About the only party to express serious interest was a cemetery that wanted to use it for burial plots. Then the Brooklyn Dodgers Baseball Club entered the picture. The possibility of a major league team—and not just any team, but one of the oldest and grandest in the history of the game—coming to Los Angeles caused a stir in the mayor's office and around the city. But a major league team would need a place to play its games, and suddenly the old potter's field of Chavez Ravine had become a vital piece of the puzzle.

To give the visiting Brooklyn owner a full appreciation of the site's potential, the Sheriff's Department provided the use of a helicopter for O'Malley and his host. They could see things from the air that they could not from the ground, and there it was, the whole panorama of Greater Los Angeles in the prosperous 1950s stretched out beneath their feet. The first freeway in the state, the Pasadena Freeway connecting Pasadena with Los Angeles, had opened in the previous decade, and since then an interlocking web of freeways had spread across the region. The automobile had freed people from needing to live so close to where they worked, and this newly mobile population was moving to the suburbs. The heavily agrarian pre–World War II California way of life was rapidly giving way to the needs of a growing urban and suburban population, and housing tracts were sprouting on what were once farmlands and orange groves.

The man from Brooklyn could see all this from the air, as well as the location of Chavez Ravine near a network of freeways. The new park would be a car-friendly place, providing Dodger fans in the outlying suburbs with easy access in and out. Beyond this, O'Malley could look across the dry, brown valleys and hills and see large and growing communities that were only certain to grow larger in the future. The potential was vast.

When the helicopter set down and the tour ended, O'Malley and Supervisor Hahn shook hands—easily the most controversial handshake in the long history of baseball. Did O'Malley, as some have alleged, agree to move the Dodgers to Los Angeles at that moment and furthermore tell Hahn to keep this information secret because of the public outcry that would surely erupt if news of their pact leaked out in Brooklyn? The answer to this question, like so many others involving the move of the Dodgers to Los Angeles, is not clear. No franchise shift in professional sports history has ever engendered so much rancor and emotion. And sorting out the facts of the matter, which frequently contradict, depending as they do on the perspective of who is telling the story and the particular ax he or she has to grind, is complicated still more by the figure at the center of the controversy, Walter O'Malley. To this day Brooklyn fans accuse him of nothing less than betrayal and treachery.

Born in New York in the early 1900s, the son of a New York city commissioner, O'Malley finished first in his graduating class at the University of Pennsylvania. After obtaining a law degree from Fordham, he hung out his attorney's shingle in Manhattan, where he began to provide legal services to the Dodgers in Brooklyn. His involvement with the club grew, and he and Branch Rickey (and another individual) purchased a controlling interest in the mid-1940s. But a management team of O'Malley and Rickey, the pioneering executive who signed Jackie Robinson to break organized baseball's color barrier, was never going to work; both were commanding personalities who needed to be in charge. A struggle for control took place, and Rickey lost and left Brooklyn. By the end of the decade O'Malley had emerged the victor. They were his team; he ran the Dodgers.

This assertion—that O'Malley controlled the fate of the Dodgers, not the fans who had stuck with them over the years, dying a little with every defeat and rejoicing with every win—partly explains the acrimony that some still hold toward the man a quarter-century after his death. "O'Malley was the first to say out loud that [baseball] was all business, a business that he owned and could operate as he chose," wrote Red Smith, a New York columnist of the time.

Critics of O'Malley, particularly New Yorkers upset by the move, tend to portray him as a kind of capitalist buccaneer—arrogant, cheap, with dreams (never realized) of cashing in on a potential pay-television bonanza with the Dodgers—and certainly he looked the part in a double-breasted business suit and tie, glasses, combed-back dark hair that was graying at the temples, and a jowly chin. A photograph during this era shows him sitting probably at a Los Angeles City Council meeting with his son Peter, who ultimately inherited the Dodgers from his father. Peter, also wearing a suit and glasses, has his arms folded in a gesture of either boredom or nerves, while his father appears relaxed and confident, a man of power secure in the meeting rooms of power.

About a month after O'Malley's helicopter ride with Kenneth Hahn, the city of Los Angeles issued a study saying that yes, a baseball stadium could feasibly be built at Chavez Ravine. It recommended the appropriation of $2 million in starter money for the project, leaving unanswered the central questions of whether a privately-owned ballpark was an appropriate, not to mention legal, use of public land. Also left untouched was another hot potato political issue of what to do about the mostly Mexican American families who lived on the land.

In Los Angeles the Dodgers apparently only seriously considered Chavez Ravine as a potential site for their park, unlike in New York where O'Malley, unhappy with the club's aging longtime home of Ebbets Field, discussed with city officials several possible locations to build a new place to play. Negotiations in New York revolved around a variety of contentious issues, with each side increasingly viewing the other with mistrust. Then, in February 1957, O'Malley changed the power equation on both coasts with the blockbuster announcement of his $3 million purchase of the Los Angeles Angels and Wrigley Field in Los Angeles. The Angels had been the property of the Wrigley family for almost as long as the Wrigleys had been making chewing gum. They had built the landmark park at Forty-second Place and Avalon Boulevard and turned the Pacific Coast League Angels into perhaps the premiere minor league franchise in the country. The sale made front page headlines in Los Angeles and New York because its impact was clear: the owner of the Brooklyn Dodgers (and now, the Los Angeles Angels) was no longer merely contemplating a move to the West Coast, he now had a tangible connection to it, a foothold, and had locked up territorial rights in the area.

The next month Mayor Poulson, the leading advocate to bring the Dodgers to Los Angeles, flew with a delegation of city officials to Dodgers spring training camp in Vero Beach, Florida, to meet with O'Malley. They went armed with the virtually unanimous support of elected officials on the City Council and Board of Supervisors, the strong endorsement of business leaders and the business community at large, the editorial backing of the *Los Angeles Times* and other newspapers, and widespread popular approval. Even those who criticized the use of Chavez Ravine for a ballpark wanted to see the Dodgers come to town; their concerns, they said, had to do with the city obtaining an agreement that protected the interests of the public.

Seemingly all of Los Angeles, in short, wanted what Walter O'Malley had. An attorney, a businessman, and a tough negotiator, he held the whip hand in these discussions and was not afraid to use it. "One of our officials promised O'Malley the moon," said Poulson, "and O'Malley asked for more."

While conducting negotiations with Los Angeles, O'Malley continued to talk to New York about keeping the Dodgers in Brooklyn, engendering criticism that he was playing both sides against the other to get the best possible deal for himself. Even so, few in New York could see the business sense in moving one of the most profitable franchises in baseball out of the city. Baseball people around the country shared this view. "You had to be crazy to think a thing like that," said Dom DiMaggio, referring to the Dodgers possibly leaving Brooklyn. "And all the way to California? You had to be even crazier."

The major leagues had entertained thoughts of moving to California since before World War II. St. Louis Browns owner Donald Barnes was on the verge of proposing the relocation of his team to Los Angeles only to have his plans scuttled by bad timing. The day he planned to seek the approval of other American League owners was December 8, 1941, the day after Pearl Harbor. Obviously, more urgent war-related worries took precedence, and his proposal was tabled or quickly voted down.

Walter O'Malley, circa 1958. Courtesy of University of Southern California, on behalf of the USC Special Libraries and Archival Collections

Early in the next decade the geography of major league baseball began to shift westward. In the first major league franchise shift since the days of Teddy Roosevelt, the Boston Braves moved to Milwaukee in 1953. A team without a pulse in Beantown, the Braves found new life in their new city, emboldening the owners of other moribund clubs to launch moves of their own. The next year the Browns of St. Louis became the Orioles of Baltimore, followed next by the Athletics, who moved from their ancestral home of Philadelphia to Kansas City in 1955. If California's baseball fans naturally began to dream their own major league dreams, they could do so partly because of advances in a non-baseball arena: air transportation.

Originally used to transport military troops and cargo during World War II, the propeller-driven Douglas DC-6 and Lockheed Constellation, both engineered and built by California companies, had become the workhorses of commercial air travel, flying regular passenger service between the coasts. A trip from Los Angeles to New York took twelve hours, shorter by days than the same distance by train. The advent of jet aircraft reduced travel times still more. By 1958, the year the Dodgers and Giants began play in California, the Boeing 707 entered into commercial transcontinental service, bringing East and West closer together.

Technological advances of a different kind were changing the game in other ways. With the formation of the Mutual Radio network, fans all over the country could listen to major league games taking place in the East and Midwest. While this increased the popularity of the major leagues in California, it steadily undermined the Pacific Coast League's traditional hold on the state. If you could listen to the big boys on the box at home, why go out to the park to see the local minor leaguers play? For obvious reasons minor league baseball cannot compete with the major leagues, and when the Dodgers and Giants arrived it blew the bolts off Coast League baseball in the state. The Los Angeles Angels, Hollywood Stars, and San Francisco Seals all transferred out of California. A founding member of the league, the Oakland Oaks, had already packed up and gone to Vancouver, which left teams hanging on only in Sacramento and San Diego.

★   ★   ★   ★   ★

The movement to bring a major league team to San Francisco began in the early 1950s with the formation by the San Francisco Board of Supervisors of a major league search committee composed of leading citizens. As in Los Angeles, public opinion strongly supported their efforts. Voters approved a $5 million bond measure to build a new stadium in the city, and Mayor George Christopher made bringing a major league ballclub to San Francisco one of the top priorities of his administration.

Horace Stoneham. National Baseball Hall of Fame Library, Cooperstown, N.Y.

With the state's two major cities now both in the hunt for a big league team, Christopher called Poulson in early 1957 to discuss their common interests. It was an exciting time full of promise. Poulson related how the Dodgers were seriously considering a move to Los Angeles, and he asked Christopher to support his bid for the team. Christopher said he would and asked the same of Poulson, who readily agreed. Both men could see the logic of not just one team moving to California, but two.

On the other side of the country, New York Giants owner Horace Stoneham and Walter O'Malley were doing some talking of their own. What made sense to the mayors made sense to them too. The longtime rivalry between the Giants and Dodgers could go on, should go on, only transplanted to different soil.

The conventional view is that O'Malley wanted to move the Dodgers but, needing the approval of the other National League owners and knowing he probably would not get it if he sought to relocate only his team, he persuaded Stoneham to move to San Francisco. But the Giants owner told author Peter Golenbock that he considered leaving New York well before O'Malley: "I had intended to move the Giants out of New York even before I knew Mr. O'Malley was intending to move. I was unhappy playing in the Polo Grounds." Located in the upper reaches of Manhattan, the Polo Grounds was an ancient monument to baseball's past, and Stoneham wanted a new park for his team. Frustrated in his talks with New York officials, he began to cast about for a new city that might be more receptive to his concerns. But his first choice was Minneapolis, not San Francisco. It may be true that O'Malley helped change Stoneham's mind, but if San Francisco had not come up with an attractive offer, the Giants owner would have been much less likely to move his team there, if he would have done it at all.

In May Christopher flew to New York for a face-to-face with Stoneham. One of the things they agreed on was to talk exclusively over the phone and not to meet in person. High-profile meetings generated coverage and speculation in the press (of which there was already plenty), and they wanted to low-key it as much as possible. They talked almost every day, with the mayor acting as the Great Persuader, selling the Giants owner on the merits of San Francisco, how it had the population and prosperity to support a major league team, why it was better suited for this than Minneapolis, and how the city would build a new stadium for the team.

In early August Stoneham received a memorandum of understanding from the city of San Francisco, spelling out the terms of their agreement. The Giants board of directors voted their approval, and on August 19, 1957, Stoneham announced that the New York Giants were no more. When asked by a reporter if he felt he was letting down the children of New York by leaving the city, the owner of the new San Francisco Giants issued his now-famous remark: "I feel bad about the kids, but I haven't seen many of their fathers lately."

There are several reasons why the Giants' move to San Francisco never generated the controversy that accompanied the Dodgers. One was the personality of Stoneham, a less polarizing figure than O'Malley. Stoneham, whose father owned the Giants before him, came from a venerable baseball family, while O'Malley was seen as more of a gate crasher in

Headline, San Francisco Chronicle, *1957. "Say Hey" was the nickname of Willie Mays. California Historical Society*

Brooklyn. Nor did the Giants in New York occupy the unique niche the Dodgers did as Brooklyn's only professional sports team. Brooklyn fans identified with their Bums as fully as a city (or in this case, a borough) can identify with a sports team. Additionally Jackie Robinson, Duke Snider, Pee Wee Reese, and the other Boys of Summer were a spectacularly good baseball team, the 1955 world champions and a perennial National League challenger to the Yankee dynasty of this period.

The Giants' August 19 announcement raised the stakes for the two cities competing over the Dodgers. New Yorkers realized that a ballclub could indeed leave their city, while Los Angeles officials, feeling the prize nearly within their grasp, scrambled to craft a winning agreement that would close the deal. In

May the National League owners had unanimously approved the move of the Dodgers and Giants to California, as long as they declared their intentions by October 1. But as the clock ticked down toward the deadline, agreement seemed elusive as ever. In a tumultuous session on September 30, the Los Angeles City Council could not muster the two-thirds majority needed to approve its final offer sheet to the Dodgers. Lacking a formal resolution from the city, O'Malley would not commit to moving the team, and night passed into morning without a settlement.

Fortunately for Los Angeles, the National League owners extended their deadline, giving Dodger supporters on the council extra time to corral the votes they needed. In the end, the resolution passed, and on October 8 the Dodgers announced they were finished in Brooklyn and headed for the West Coast.

According to Neil J. Sullivan, author of the definitive book on the Dodgers move, this battle of civic wills came down to one of those intangibles that you hear about so often in sports: desire. Ultimately, he writes, "It was more important to Los Angeles politicians to attract the Dodgers than it was for New York politicians to keep the team." New York got beat in a game of power and money, a game it usually wins, and again the map of baseball had to be redrawn.

★   ★   ★   ★   ★

People had played baseball, or some form of it, in California since after the Gold Rush, but until the arrival of the Dodgers and Giants, the major leagues had never held a regular season game west of the Mississippi River. John Thorn, a leading baseball historian, says that the West Coast franchise shifts were the best thing to happen to major league baseball in the 1950s, making the national pastime truly national for the first time. "America's population had already begun the westward and southward shift that was to become so pronounced in the 1960s and '70s," Thorn writes. "The move to Los Angeles and San Francisco, rather than confirming those cities' stature as 'big league,' as is so often written, brought baseball into step with America, which had long recognized them as such. Baseball could now call itself the national pastime without apology."

Walter O'Malley and Horace Stoneham created a new industry in the state—major league baseball—and with it came opportunity. Rene Cardenas, a young Nicaraguan-born journalist living in Los Angeles, understood this immediately. And he had an idea how to take advantage of it.

Cardenas had immigrated to the city earlier in the decade, taking English classes at night and working as a stringer by day for the Los Angeles bureau of the Nicaraguan newspaper *La Prensa,* covering Pacific Coast League games and dreaming of the big leagues—"las grandes ligas." One of the writers he admired, Rudy Garcia of the Spanish-language *La Opinion,* was covering big league baseball "even though," in Cardenas's words, "the major leagues weren't in California. And I said, 'Wow. Imagine a Spanish man who writes about baseball.'"

But Cardenas's idea had to do with radio, not print. Soon after the Dodgers announced they were coming to town, he went to see William Beaton, the station manager of KWKW, then one of two Spanish-language radio stations in Los Angeles. His pitch was loaded with what every station manager wants to hear: numbers. Since World War II the Hispanic population in southern California had jumped to 1.4 million, with nearly half living in Los Angeles. Most of these newcomers hailed from Mexico, especially northern Mexico, where literacy rates were low. Unable to read Spanish, let alone the English papers, they relied on radio for news and entertainment. (Television was not yet the all-pervasive force it would become.) Said Cardenas: "They were going to broadcast games on the radio. Why not do it in Spanish?"

Beaton thought the idea had merit, but the Dodgers needed to approve it first. The club in turn passed the proposal onto its advertising agency, which essentially echoed what Beaton said: If there's a market there, we want to be part of it.

The only thing left to decide was who would be the broadcaster. Hundreds of Spanish announcers sent in audition tapes but, partly on Beaton's recommendation, the job went to the guy who dreamed it up in the first place, Cardenas, who had done play-by-play baseball broadcasts in his native country and was known there as El Chelito, "the blond one."

In the spring of 1958 the new Spanish-language announcer for the Dodgers flew to Vero Beach, Florida, to see the players in action and meet the club's number-one radio man, Vin Scully. A former New York prep schooler and a graduate of Fordham University, Scully, then in his late twenties, was making the move west to begin this new chapter in major league history. But neither he, Cardenas, or anyone else on the Dodgers—or, for that matter, the Giants—knew quite what to expect at the upcoming season opener in San Francisco. All anyone knew was that it promised to be wild.

★   ★   ★   ★   ★

April 15, 1958, was a sunny and mild day in San Francisco, a wonderful day for a ballgame. Some 23,448 people, including politicians, dignitaries, celebrities, and reporters from around the country, had squeezed into tiny Seals Stadium at Sixteenth and Bryant Streets to see the debut of major league baseball in California.

The host city had gone slightly batty for its new team. People began lining up at Seals Stadium a week ahead of time to buy tickets for Opening Day. Signs and billboards all around town proclaimed "Welcome S.F. Giants," careful not to forget the all-important "S.F." part of the message. The mannequins in the Macy's windows sported Giants uniforms and caps, and at Joseph Magnin's department store, patrons received booklets of fashion advice on what to wear at the ballpark. A group of cheering fans, including a triumphant Mayor Christopher, greeted the Giants when they arrived at San Francisco Airport from spring training. But that was nothing compared to the hundreds of thousands of people who lined downtown streets for a welcoming parade for the team. Giants players, dressed in suits and ties, rode in slow-moving open

Seals Stadium, the first home of the San Francisco Giants.
Courtesy of the Bancroft Library, University of California, Berkeley

convertibles as the fans in their enthusiasm surged forward off the sidewalk and into the street, in some cases getting so close to the players they could almost reach out and touch them.

After the parade, at a luncheon in honor of the men of the moment at the Sheraton Palace Hotel, Christopher awarded the key to the city to Bill Rigney, who stood out not only because he was manager of the Giants but because of his East Bay roots. Born in Alameda, Rigney was one of those boys who was always dragging around a bat and ball, looking for someone to play with. But when he tried out for his high school team, the coach told him to go home because he was too small. Rigney persisted, and the coach finally let him on the team. It was a wise choice because the scrawny, bespectacled youngster had talent to go along with his gumption. After Oakland High he signed with the hometown Oaks, and when World War II ended he joined the New York Giants as an infielder, moving up to manager a few years after his playing career ended. Coming back to the Bay Area represented a return to his baseball roots.

The gathering at Seals Stadium the next day was the greatest collection of baseball talent on one field in California history. It was a national and international assembly of people of different colors and backgrounds and at least two languages.

For the Giants, there were other guys besides Rigney with California ties—hardworking pitcher Marv Grissom, who grew up in Red Bluff in the north of the state; sharp-dressing left-hander Mike McCormick, a onetime schoolboy

From left, Orlando Cepeda,
Willie Kirkland, Jim Davenport.
Courtesy of the Bancroft Library,
University of California, Berkeley

wonder from Alhambra; and grizzled veteran Hank Sauer of Los Angeles. Though they both lived in southern California, neither Sauer nor McCormick had ever been to San Francisco before. The same was true of starting rookie third baseman Jimmy Davenport, an Alabama native who had never set foot in the city until stepping off the plane from spring training a few days before. The leader of the Giants, Willie Mays, was already a legend in New York for his wondrous play in center field. But his childhood roots were in Alabama too. Playing right field alongside Mays and batting behind him was Willie Kirkland, a Detroit guy who loved to kid around and have fun. Following the two Willies in the batting order was Puerto Rican–born Orlando Cepeda, a rookie first baseman who had earned a spot in the starting lineup with a springtime display of power. Watching him pound away on pitchers in Phoenix, coach Whitey Lockman said to Bill Rigney, "It's too bad he's a year away." The manager looked at him aghast: "A year away from what?" "The Hall of Fame," said Lockman.

The twenty-year-old Cepeda and another rookie on the team, outfielder Felipe Alou, a native of the Dominican Republic, spoke only limited English. But team and league officials would not permit them to speak Spanish in the clubhouse or on the field. In the years to come the National League would, in fact, repeatedly fine Alou for violating this rule. Latin players of this time also labored under a commonly held stereotype—that they were lazy and faked injuries to avoid playing when they did not feel like it. Consequently, many played hurt rather than have people think they were slacking off on the job.

Giants owner Horace Stoneham regularly made off-season scouting trips to the Caribbean, and Latin players contributed significantly to the team's early success in San Francisco. Its Opening Day battery was an all-Caribbean one—catcher Valmy Thomas, who learned the game by playing stickball as a kid in the Virgin Islands, and starting pitcher Ruben Gomez, a countryman of Cepeda's from Puerto Rico.

The game was not televised, but fans around the city and state tuned into it on transistor radios. Calling the game for the Giants were veteran broadcaster Russ Hodges, who had come from New York with the team, and a smooth-voiced radio newcomer from southern California, Lon Simmons. Also on hand was Bob Stevens of the *Chronicle,* a former Coast League beat reporter who had made the step up to the major leagues.

It was one of those days in which baseball was almost secondary to everything else going on around it. Mayor Christopher threw the ceremonial first pitch and Mayor Poulson caught it. After they cleared the field of everyone who did not belong on it, up to the plate stepped Dodger leadoff hitter Gino Cimoli, a sentimental choice because he was a native San Franciscan who grew up in the city and still lived in North Beach. But the sentiment stopped when the game began, and Gomez, who had nasty stuff all day, struck Cimoli out.

After Gomez and the Giants beat the Dodgers, 8 to 0, in the opener, the two teams split the next two games before heading south to do Opening Day all over again. Los Angeles held its welcoming parade for the Dodgers on the morning of April 18. Unlike the Giants, who dressed more formally for their parade, the Dodger players wore their game uniforms and caps, riding through

May Co. employees greet the Dodgers, Los Angeles, 1958.
Courtesy of University of Southern California, on behalf of
the USC Special Libraries and Archival Collections

Los Angeles Memorial Coliseum postcard, circa 1960.
California Historical Society, FN-40053

Dodger players receive welcoming gifts,
Los Angeles City Hall, 1958.
Courtesy of University of Southern
California, on behalf of the USC Special
Libraries and Archival Collections

downtown in open-air convertibles and waving to the throngs of fans who stood five or six deep on the sidewalks. Everybody got caught up in the swing of things. At Eighth and Broadway some female May Co. employees dressed up as cheerleaders and waved pennants and cheered. At parade's end the players sat on the steps of City Hall and received small gifts from Chicana women in traditional Mexican blouses and long skirts.

The festivities carried over into the afternoon when more than seventy-eight thousand fans poured into the Los Angeles Coliseum, setting a new National League opening day attendance mark. The Dodgers had settled on the cavernous Coliseum as their temporary home, vetoing Wrigley Field as too small and inadequate. But the Coliseum, the home of the 1932 Olympic Games, was primarily a football stadium, and adjustments had to be made to render it suitable for baseball. With the fence in left field a mere 251 feet from home plate and the power alleys in left-center not much farther, workers erected a forty-foot-high screen in left to prevent lazy pop flies from becoming home runs.

For the home team, their lineup looked similar in many respects to the great Brooklyn teams of the recent past, with shortstop Pee Wee Reese, steady first baseman Gil Hodges, and strong-armed right fielder Carl Furillo all holdovers from Ebbets Field days. Another Brooklyn holdover, outfielder Duke Snider, was a Los Angeles native and an all-sports star at Compton High who

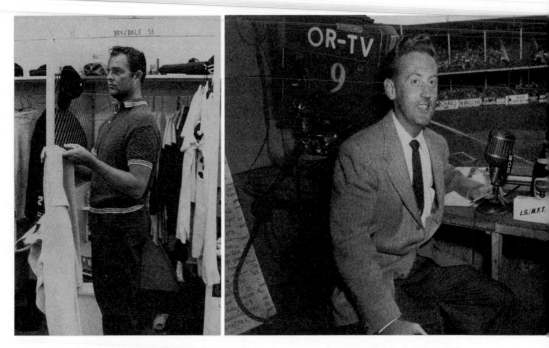

Don Drysdale. Security Pacific Collection/   *Announcer Vin Scully, circa 1955.*
Los Angeles Public Library   *Security Pacific Collection/Los Angeles Public Library*

ran an avocado ranch near Fallbrook north of San Diego in the off-season; the move west was a kind of homecoming for him. Two standouts from the Brooklyn era, however, were missing: second baseman Jackie Robinson, who retired after the '56 season rather than accept a trade to the Giants, and catcher Roy Campanella, the club's inspirational leader who was paralyzed in a car accident only months earlier.

Dodger right-hander Don Drysdale was, like Snider, a Californian who was coming home. The pride of Van Nuys was a big, rangy right-handed pitcher who was good-looking to everybody except the man facing him in the batter's box. His wife then was a Tournament of Roses princess, and a float in the 1959 New Year's Day parade was a re-creation of their wedding cake consisting of twenty-eight thousand roses and eight thousand camellias. Drysdale anchored a pitching staff that included stalwarts Johnny Podres, Don Newcombe, and Carl Erskine, and a promising young left-hander who really was from Brooklyn, having been born there, Sandy Koufax. Rookie John Roseboro was stepping into Campy's big shoes as catcher, and quietly making all the pieces fit together was Walt Alston, the manager.

On the radio, calling the game for the Dodgers in English, was Vin Scully. And at the Coliseum Rene Cardenas showed up to do the same in Spanish. Due to financial constraints at KWKW, he could not accompany the Dodgers to San Francisco, so he stayed in Los Angeles and broadcast re-creations, just as a young Ronald Reagan had done when he was a sportscaster in Iowa. Listening in the KWKW studio to Scully's play-by-play call from Seals Stadium, Cardenas gave his listeners a virtually simultaneous Spanish translation of the game's events. When the series shifted to Los Angeles, Cardenas could at last attend the games personally and call them as he saw them, with his own eyes. In Friday's home opener the Dodgers edged the Giants, 6 to 5, but the visitors came back to take the next two in the series. Cardenas called these games as he did all season long—broadcasting live and in person when they were home and doing re-creations when the Dodgers were on the road. They were the first Spanish-language broadcasts of major league baseball in America, an idea since copied by many teams.

After the flurry of excitement over Opening Day passed, the focus in Los Angeles shifted to the increasingly contentious fight over the future of Chavez Ravine and whether the Dodgers should be allowed to build a ballpark there. The previous December opponents had gathered enough signatures to put the issue on the June 3, 1958, ballot. Opinion polls on the referendum, known as Proposition B, substantially favored the Dodgers in the early months. By spring, however, public sentiment had turned against them, with a slight majority opposed to the ballpark development, and the rhetoric heated up on both sides.

Prop B supporters claimed that if the measure did not pass and the park was not built, the city could lose the team. A "Yea on Baseball" citizens committee, chaired by comedian and baseball supporter Joe E. Brown, sought to stop the slide in public opinion by emphasizing the importance of keeping the Dodgers and major league baseball in Los Angeles. Although Vin Scully never talked politics or mentioned Prop B in his broadcasts, observers feel that his immediate popularity in Los Angeles made people think positively about the Dodgers, despite their losing season on the field.

Opposition to Proposition B was financed by San Diego Padres owner Jack Smith, who feared competition from the major leagues. Apart from this, opponents contended that the city's agreement with the Dodgers was a bad one for Los Angeles and that it was unwise to commit public land and resources for a privately held business. Attention centered on the Mexican American families living at Chavez Ravine who would lose their homes if the plan went forward. Although most of these families accepted buyouts and left the land, opponents argued it was small change compared to what the Dodgers would make in their new stadium. City leaders replied that the city would earn taxes and other revenue if the site were developed, whereas it currently received next to nothing for a site with only limited commercial potential.

The larger issue in the debate was how Los Angeles viewed itself as a city and what effect, if any, the presence of the Dodgers would have on its civic identity. On the Sunday before the referendum, the *Times* urged a yes vote, arguing that in a city as spread out as Los Angeles, with so many different kinds of people living in it, the Dodgers served as a common connection for all, a unifier. "Do you, a citizen-voter, want Los Angeles to be a great city, with common interests and the civic unity which gives a great city character?"

it asked. Ronald Reagan (in an early foray into politics), Jack Benny, Groucho Marx, and other celebrities spoke on behalf of the measure at a Prop B telethon in the evening.

The next Tuesday Proposition B won the approval of a majority of voters, but that did not end the controversy. Opponents filed suit to block the agreement, beginning a lengthy legal tussle that reached the California Supreme Court. In January 1959 the court ruled unanimously in favor of the Dodgers and the city, approving the planned use of Chavez Ravine. Opponents nevertheless vowed to carry their fight to the Supreme Court of the United States.

By May the last remaining families at Chavez Ravine had left except for the Arechigas, who refused to go. Local television news stations carried the politically incendiary images of policemen carrying sixty-eight-year-old Avrana Arechiga and other members of her family off the site. Many were outraged. But public opinion quickly reversed itself after it was revealed that the Arechigas owned as many as nine homes in the area while living rent-free at Chavez Ravine, and they had a place to go; one nearby three-bedroom home of theirs was vacant at the time of their eviction.

Despite the continuing controversy over Chavez Ravine, the Dodgers' second season in Los Angeles began on a much brighter note than the first. Leading the National League at the end of April, they hosted a poignant tribute to Roy Campanella in a May exhibition at the Coliseum. The former Negro League and Brooklyn great, who could no longer walk due to the injuries suffered in his accident the year before, appeared in a wheelchair pushed by his former teammate, Pee Wee Reese, who had retired after the last season. During the pre-game ceremonies the entire Coliseum went dark and the 93,103 fans—then the largest crowd to see a major league game—lit candles to symbolize the imperishability of Campanella's spirit.

Before the season the Coliseum's playing dimensions had been made fairer to hitters. Jaime Jarrin, an immigrant from Ecuador pursuing a broadcasting career in this country, joined Rene Cardenas in the booth at KWKW, and both started broadcasting and re-creating games. The Dodgers began to take on a new look too—less Brooklyn, more Los Angeles. Infielder Junior Gilliam and several other Brooklyn carryovers were solid as ever, but new faces such as Ron Fairly, a young outfielder from USC, and future stolen-base king Maury Wills, were starting to emerge as well. (Outfield speedsters Tommy Davis and Willie Davis would make their mark in coming years for the Dodgers.) Don Drysdale, then the team's No. 1 starter, had turned things around after a bad season, and Sandy Koufax was beginning to show people why Drysdale would soon become the No. 2 starter. And then there was that July call-up from the minor leagues, pitcher Larry Sherry, an all-everything from Fairfax High in Los Angeles who had suddenly, and mysteriously, become unhittable.

The 1959 season was the first knock-down-drag-out pennant race between the Los Angeles Dodgers and the San Francisco Giants, the first in a continuing series. The Giants had taken a similar turn as their rivals, becoming less New York and more San Francisco with the addition of rookie Willie McCovey, a tall, lanky

ROSEBORO

SHERRY

Catcher John Roseboro congratulates relief ace Larry Sherry after the Dodgers
win the 1959 World Series. Courtesy of University of Southern California,
on behalf of the USC Special Libraries and Archival Collections

first baseman with thunder in his bat. In his first major league game McCovey
went four for four with two triples. "He walked into Seals Stadium a rookie," said
Chronicle sportswriter Bob Stevens, "and he walked out owning it." McCovey
joined fellow future Hall of Famers Mays and Cepeda—two more Giant Hall of
Famers, pitchers Juan Marichal and Gaylord Perry, had yet to arrive—to push San
Francisco into first place in late September with only five games to go. But the

Dodgers, boasting their own contingent of future Cooperstown residents—Alston, Snider, Koufax, Drysdale—pushed back harder, sweeping the Giants in a three-game series at Seals Stadium. The Dodgers finished in a first-place tie with Milwaukee and won the National League pennant after beating the Braves in a playoff.

The Dodgers and the American League champion Chicago White Sox split the first two games of the World Series in Chicago. When the Dodgers won Game 3 at the Coliseum, the first World Series game ever held in California, 92,394 fans set a single-game Series attendance record. For Game 4, another Dodgers win, 92,650 turned out to break the attendance record set the previous day. In Game 5, the Coliseum somehow found room for more bodies and set its third record in three days; the attendance of 92,706 is still the benchmark for a Series game. But Koufax lost a nail-biter, 1 to 0, and Dodger fans uneasily watched as the series shifted back to Chicago.

Los Angeles took the drama out of the sixth game by jumping up 8 to 0 in the top of the fourth inning, but when the White Sox scored three runs and threatened to put the drama back in, the Dodgers summoned Larry Sherry from the bullpen and the champagne corks were as good as popped. Sherry, who won two games and saved two others in the Series, shut the White Sox down the rest of the way to bring Los Angeles its first world championship. As followers of the Dodger blue rejoiced, their rivals in the north of the state, pledging fealty to the orange and black, grumbled in their beers and vowed revenge next season.

Less than two weeks after the Series, the United States Supreme Court dismissed the final appeals of Proposition B opponents, clearing the way for the construction of Dodger Stadium at Chavez Ravine.

The Last Days
of Ty Cobb

SATURDAY, MARCH 22 — 2:15 P.M.
SUNDAY, MARCH 23 — 2:15 P.M.
— 1947 —

ABLISHED PRICE - $3.33   Total $4.00
ERAL TAX - - - - .67

HIS PORTION OF TICKET NOT GOOD FOR ADMITTANCE
DETACH SEPERATE COUPONS FOR INDIVIDUAL GAMES

Like so many of the great players of his time, Ty Cobb often traveled to California in the off-season for pleasure, recreation, and business. One of his earliest trips to the state (although surely not his first) came before World War I, when the movie industry was getting rolling in southern California and he was a big enough name to star in *Somewhere in Georgia,* produced by the Sunbeam Motion Picture Company of Hollywood. Cobb, a Georgia native, plays the title role of a bank clerk who achieves his dream of making the Detroit Tigers (his team in real life), and in the process defeats some bullies, wins the girl, and becomes the hero of the big game. The film, as a reviewer from *Variety* noted, was "a production aimed at one thing and that was to present the celebrated Ty Cobb in camera action and give the small town boys a chance to see more of him."

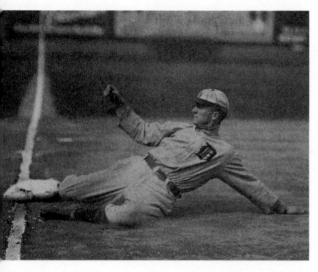

Ty Cobb in his prime with the Detroit Tigers.
©*Bettman/CORBIS*

Cobb continued to visit the state after this and established an off-season home here as early as the 1920s. A man of his abilities and reputation would be expected to be involved in local baseball, and he was. He managed Willie Kamm, then a struggling Coast Leaguer with a weak bat, for a season of winter ball in San Francisco. Cobb's guidance may have helped, for the next season Kamm broke out with a .342 average for the Seals and earned his ticket up to the Chicago White Sox.

When Cobb ended his unparalleled major league career—.366 lifetime average, 4,189 hits, 2,246 runs, twelve batting titles; the writer John Updike called him "the Einstein of average"—he was regarded as the greatest player of all time, rivaled only by Babe Ruth. A sportswriter of an earlier generation described Cobb's impact on the game in poetic terms: "Up from the South like an eagle swooping upon the baseball scene with spikes for talons" was how he put it. Modern assessments draw him with a much sharper pencil. "He was egotistical, brash, rude, thin-skinned, a racist and a bully," write the authors of *Baseball: The Biographical Encyclopedia.* "In short, he was a great player and a terrible person." But the sun shines on scoundrels as well as saints, and after finishing with the major leagues Cobb came to live year-round in northern California, where he spent the next thirty years.

One account of his retirement years says he moved to California to become a golfer. This may have been true, but golf was not all he did. He also kept a hand in the game of baseball. In April 1931, at the unveiling of new Seals Stadium in San Francisco, Cobb was one of the dignitaries whose presence added luster to the occasion. Two years later he showed up again at Seals Stadium (though he almost certainly attended games there in between) for one of the most famous moments in San Francisco city baseball history—the try-out of Joe DiMaggio. Clearly this was a big occasion because his friend Charlie Graham, the Seals owner, invited Cobb to sit beside him in the grandstands to see if the kid was as good as everybody was saying.

This tryout was also where Hispanic infielder Tony Gomez got harassed for being dark-skinned. A coach hit a succession of hard ground balls at him to make him quit, and Gomez cramped up and sat down in hurt and frustration. It is presumed Cobb saw all of this and, like Graham and the other observers, said nothing because organized baseball was then a whites-only affair and, in their view, people like Gomez did not belong in it.

As for Joe DiMaggio, Cobb liked what he saw and followed his career with the Seals. Lefty O'Doul, who managed the Seals in Joe's last year with the team, brought in Cobb as an advisor when the Yankees began salary negotiations for DiMaggio's rookie contract in New York. Cobb's services were enlisted because, in Richard Ben Cramer's memorable phrase, he was "a man who could squeeze a nickel till the buffalo on it was dead from lack of air." New York's first offer came in at $5,625—not enough, said Cobb, who drafted a letter on DiMaggio's behalf asking for more. The Yankees then upped the ante to $6,500—still not enough, Cobb wrote back (for DiMaggio). The Yankees apparently knew the identity of DiMaggio's business agent because when they presented their third and final offer of $8,500, they told Joe not to have Cobb send them any more letters.

Cobb was as shrewd and tightfisted with his money as only a rich man can be. In the early 1900s, while other players were spending their paychecks on booze and women, he invested heavily in Coca-Cola, United (now General) Motors, and other growing companies. Reportedly a millionaire while still with the Tigers, his sizable financial resources allowed him to retire comfortably to a country home in Atherton, a lovely wooded community south of San Francisco, and one of the wealthiest and most exclusive communities in the United States.

While living on the Peninsula, Cobb commuted back and forth to San Francisco to watch ballgames and even participate in them. In 1935 the Tokyo Giants of Japanese professional baseball toured the Northwest and California, playing an exhibition in San Francisco against a team managed by Cobb. Early the next year he won election in the first-ever balloting for the newly formed National Baseball Hall of Fame. Such was the esteem Cobb's peers held for him that of the five original inductees to the Hall—the actual induction ceremonies would not be held for a few more years—he garnered more votes than anyone else, including Babe Ruth. Not long after winning this honor, Cobb appeared on the field at Opening Day ceremonies at Seals Stadium and received an ovation from fans.

Cobb was admired for many reasons, not least of which was the way he played the game. Fathers told their sons to play like him because he was such a tough, hard-nosed competitor. Don't back down. Fight for everything you can get. Nobody fought harder on a ballfield than Cobb. And it is probably true that no one with his athletic skills played meaner or nastier or dirtier. Before games he sat in the Detroit dugout sharpening the spikes on his shoes, which he then used to slash at the arms or legs of fielders when he slid into a base and they tried to tag him out. Casey Stengel talked about Cobb's "wild eyes"—how, in the heat of a game, he took on the look of a crazy man, an opponent you did not want to mess with.

But Cobb, unlike so many former ballplayers, achieved great success off the field after the games were over, and this was another reason why people admired him. Many asked him for money or approached him with business offers, including Lefty O'Doul, who asked him to invest in the new tavern he was starting in San Francisco. Cobb turned him down, explaining, "He drinks more than I do." The Georgia Peach, however, did not just move in baseball circles; he socialized at the Domino Club in San Francisco and counted among his friends members of the city's moneyed elite.

Cobb lived in California during and after World War II and appeared, in a cameo role, with Joe DiMaggio in MGM's production of the original version of *Angels in the Outfield*. Then, in March 1957, he announced that he was leaving California to move back to Georgia, where he had endowed a hospital in Royston and established an educational fund to send poor children to college. Both these philanthropic endeavors needed his personal attention, he said.

"I'll hate to leave," he told a wire service reporter. "No one could live in California even a few months and not love it."

In the photograph that accompanied the article, Cobb, a bald white man who was not quite seventy years old, stands in the driveway of his home in a wrinkled double-breasted jacket with his hands in his trouser pockets. It seems appropriate, somehow, that he is looking away from the camera, a removed and solitary figure. Behind him is his mansion, on Spencer Lane in Atherton, a two-story white stucco Spanish villa with a tile roof. The second-story balcony visible in the photograph probably led to one of the seven bedrooms in the eighteen-room house. Equally impressive were the grounds—"You could have held a ball game on the grounds," observed a writer. The value of the estate in the 1950s—approximately ninety-thousand dollars—would surely be worth in the many millions today.

For whatever reason, though, Cobb did not follow through with his plans to return to Georgia; he remained in California, dividing his time between Atherton and his ten-room hunting lodge at Lake Tahoe. In the spring of 1958, in the first major league game in California baseball history, there he was again: one of the dignitaries at Opening Day ceremonies between the Los Angeles Dodgers and San Francisco Giants at Seals Stadium.

★   ★   ★   ★   ★

In many respects, the life of Seals Stadium runs parallel with Cobb's time in California. He was present for its two biggest moments: the day it opened and the day it became a major league ballpark—the home, albeit temporary, of the

Giants. Unlike the broken-down park it replaced (Old Rec), and the modern multipurpose stadium that replaced it (Candlestick Park), most everyone who went to Seals Stadium seemed to love it.

Seals Stadium was built at a time when all the ballparks were neighborhood ballparks. Its Portrero Hill neighborhood was a bustling city landscape with cars, trucks, buses, taxis on the streets, people passing on the sidewalks, walking in and out of shops, restaurants, markets, and bars—lots of bars. One of the neighborhood bars was the Double Play Tavern, which is still in business today.

The Double Play was a favorite of ballplayers who liked to drink, and that basically meant all of them. In the 1930s the Seals featured an aging pitcher named Noble Winfield "Old Pard" Ballou, who liked to wind down after a night game with a nightcap or two at the Double Play. Some nights Old Pard had a few drinks more than was perhaps wise, and on these occasions he could be found the next day sleeping it off in the Seals' bullpen. But sometimes the Seals, in need of a late-inning reliever, put in a call to the bullpen for Old Pard, who was not to be found. At these times a clubhouse boy ran down to the Double Play where, as often as not, Old Pard would be propping up a stool, partaking of the hair of the dog that bit him. Stirred to action, the old baseball warrior would put on his game face and do his duty for the Seals.

That is how the story goes anyhow, and it may or may not bear an intimate relationship to the truth. Roy McKercher, who was a batboy at Seals Stadium for many years, said he saw ballplayers go to the Double Play for a sandwich between games of a doubleheader. And although he saw players drink after a game, he never saw it happen during. But McKercher's time at Seals was the 1950s, well after Old Pard passed through, so that leaves the issue still open to question.

Seals Stadium featured a sweeping, single-deck grandstand with no second level, so the only thing between a fan's head and the sky was his hat. Two working businesses in the neighborhood were the Langendorf bakery and the Rainier brewery (later Hamm's), and the sweet smells of baking bread and brewing beer wafted across the park during games. Atop the brewery was a sign with a giant representation of a glass of beer with a creamy white head. Visible from inside the park, the glass of beer was lit up at night.

Giants vs. Dodgers, Seals Stadium, San Francisco, 1958. Courtesy of the Bancroft Library, University of California, Berkeley

Candlestick Park under construction, San Francisco.
San Francisco History Center, San Francisco Public Library

Seals Stadium hosted its final Coast League game in 1957; the next year the major leagues moved in and the Seals became a different franchise in another state. Their former home, the onetime jewel of the minor leagues, was considered too small and antiquated to be a modern major league stadium, and plans called for its destruction and the creation of a new $15 million stadium to be located in the Bayview–Hunter's Point area, the old Butchertown district of the city. It has been observed that for many fans, the era they would describe as the greatest in baseball was the one they saw as a kid growing up. For many San Franciscans, Seals Stadium was the ballpark they grew up in, where they saw their greatest era. Lefty O'Doul and *Chronicle* columnist Herb Caen, among others, argued that the old park should be saved, that its capacity of twenty-three thousand or so could be practically doubled by adding a second tier of grandstands, thus turning it into a major league park with adequate seating and revenue-earning potential. But city estimates said that renovating Seals Stadium would cost nearly as much as building Candlestick Park, which would also feature ample parking and modern amenities. Besides, said Candlestick supporters, the weather would be better there.

Although generations of baseball fans would come to view Candlestick Park as a colossal blunder, it seemed, to many at the time, like a good place for a stadium. A citizens' lawsuit to stop its construction was dismissed or dropped. A business group proposed an alternative downtown location, but it, and other suggestions for other sites, received no sustained support. In July 1958 the Board of Supervisors approved the final plans for Candlestick, and the first shovel broke ground the next month.

Predictions that Candlestick would be ready by Opening Day of 1959 proved overly optimistic. Construction delays and cost overruns, which triggered an investigation into the awarding of contracts and other financial issues, meant that the Giants would play one last season at Seals. It turned out to be a dandy, a down-to-the-wire pennant race between Los Angeles, Milwaukee, and San Francisco that ended badly for the hometown club. In the final game at the park, in late September 1959, Los Angeles beat San Francisco, 8 to 2, to ruin the Giants' pennant hopes and catapult the Dodgers to the National League pennant and world championship.

Seals Stadium met the wrecking ball less than two weeks later. H. J. Brunnier, the architect who originally designed it, served as consulting engineer for its destruction. Oaks Park in Oakland was gone. Moreing Field in

Sacramento (redubbed Edmonds Field) had burned down. Lane Field in San Diego was finished. Gilmore Field in Hollywood was going or gone. Only Wrigley Field in Los Angeles still had some life left in it, although the dooms-day clock was ticking for it too. The world in which these old parks belonged was no more, and a new world, full of its own flaws and inequities, was rising in its place.

★   ★   ★   ★   ★

Late in the inaugural season of Candlestick Park, Ty Cobb showed up there to watch a game between the Giants and the Cincinnati Reds. But Cobb was now too sick and frail to come on his own power. In fact, he had sneaked out of Stanford Hospital in Palo Alto, where he was receiving radiation treatments for cancer, with the help of a journalist, Al Stump, who was writing Cobb's auto-biography with him.

Cobb was a wreck of a human being, suffering from diabetes and a dozen other ailments in addition to the cancer. He could barely walk, though he was too proud to let anyone see him use a cane. When he fell, which was often, Stump, who was staying in Cobb's house while working on the book, had to pick him up and, if it was late at night, carry him to bed. Beset by constant fevers, chugging codeine and handfuls of painkillers, he survived seemingly on spite alone. His rages were as unpredictable as they were violent. Making mat-ters worse was his habit of drinking a quart of Old Rarity Scotch a day. Doctors told him his drinking would kill him, but Cobb returned their advice with hateful insults and ignored them.

Taking Cobb to the game was a way that Stump, wisely or not, figured he could lift a dying man's spirits. It is not clear if this was Cobb's first trip to Candlestick; in the famous magazine article he later wrote about his months with Cobb, Stump does not say. But even in deteriorating health the old man enjoyed watching baseball—"He kept coming to games, loving the sounds of the ballpark," said Stump.

Nevertheless Cobb did not think much of the modern game, and he was not afraid to say so. "Today they hit for ridiculous averages, can't bunt, can't steal, can't hit and run, can't place-hit to the opposite field, and you can't call them ballplayers," he told Stump. Although Stump does not talk about it, it is likely that Cobb did not view the presence of black and Latino ballplayers on the field with much favor either.

After leaving Candlestick Park that night (and eventually checking out of the hospital), the pair drove to Lake Tahoe. In the foothills of the Sierra they stayed at a motel in a town Stump refers to as Hangtown (probably Placerville). During the night Cobb, who carried a loaded Luger with him at all times, fired shots into the air in order to get the people in the next room to stop making noise. When they arrived in Tahoe they soon discovered his expensive Chris Craft speedboat had sunk into the lake (probably from simple neglect and dis-repair). Cobb, thinking that the same person who had sabotaged his boat was trying to get him, sat up all night with his Luger. Extreme bouts of paranoia and rage were the norm for him. In a Reno casino he took swings at a craps dealer and a bartender over perceived insults.

After Tahoe the pair flew to Georgia and then to Arizona for spring training the next March. Wherever Cobb went, along with his Luger, he packed $1 million in stock certificates and bonds in an old carry-bag. Two or three days a week he bought and sold stocks over the phone even as the cancer spread into his skull.

Next they traveled to Stump's beach house in Santa Barbara, continuing to work on the autobiography. When Cobb was a young ballplayer on the road he used to roll his pants up and place them under his pillow at night. This was standard practice for players of his time because they worried that someone might steal their stuff when they were sleeping. In Santa Barbara Stump noticed that Cobb, well past his seventieth birthday, still slept with his pants under his pillow.

Turning north, their odyssey nearing an end, they returned to Cobb's estate in Atherton, which had no lights, no heat, and no hot water. Pacific Gas and Electric had cut off his utility services because Cobb, who claimed he had been overcharged, refused to pay a sixteen-dollar bill. The millionaire Cobb (and Stump, when he was there) relied on candles for light, cooked on a camping stove, took cold baths, could not operate the refrigerator, stove, television, or electric radio, and walked to their bedrooms at night along dark hallways as if through an old haunted mansion.

And that was how Stump, who finally got enough material to finish the book, left Cobb: sitting in the darkness of his haunted house, alone with all his ghosts. "Do we die a little at a time," Cobb once asked Stump, "or all at once?" Shortly after the reporter said goodbye, Cobb went back to Georgia and in July 1961, the pieces that were left of him finally cracked apart.

Ty Cobb in Atherton, age 62, with his dog.
© *Bettmann/CORBIS*

My Life in Baseball, by Ty Cobb with Al Stump, was published later that year. In the early 1990s Ron Shelton of *Bull Durham* fame wrote and directed *Cobb,* a feature film (starring Tommy Lee Jones as Cobb) based on Stump's experience with the Hall of Famer.

The Cowboy
Rides In

SATURDAY, MARCH 22 — 2:15 P.M.
SUNDAY, MARCH 23 — 2:15 P.M.
— 1947 —

ABLISHED PRICE - $3.33
ERAL TAX   .67   Total $4.00

THIS PORTION OF TICKET NOT GOOD FOR ADMITTANCE
DETACH SEPERATE COUPONS FOR INDIVIDUAL GAMES

Steve Bilko, said a sportswriter, was "built like a packing crate for farm machinery." Of Pennsylvania stock, with a broad face and blond features, Bilko liked to wear short-sleeve jerseys that showed off his biceps and his thick upper arms, which were indeed an impressive sight. Being a big man, he liked big portions of food and drink, which made him gain weight. He regularly converted his bathroom into a temporary sauna, standing in the shower and turning on the hot water full blast in order to sweat off a few pounds.

Steve Bilko, circa 1950s.
California Historical Society, FN-40004

Bilko played first base, but nobody paid to see him wear a glove. People wanted to see him walk up to the plate with a piece of lumber in his hands, scowl at the pitcher, and swing hard, real hard. His best years as a player came with the Pacific Coast League Angels when the Angels owned the show at Wrigley Field, whose Lilliputian dimensions were made to order for a pull hitter like Bilko. The 1956 Angels, with Bilko clobbering home runs and Gene Mauch (the future big league manager, then an infielder) and a bunch of other guys having career seasons, is considered one of the best minor league clubs of all time.

It was a beautiful thing when Bilko put a ball into orbit, but he could only do it with any consistency against minor league pitching. In his years in the major leagues, when Bilko strode up to the batter's box to take his mighty hacks, as often as not he walked straight back to the dugout after being struck out. Several big league teams, including the Los Angeles Dodgers, gave him a try, but his major league career was as good as dead until his name got called in the 1961 American League expansion draft.

The draft actually occurred in December 1960, and its purpose was to stock the two new American League franchises in Washington and Los Angeles with players. Because Bilko was such a popular figure in Los Angeles, and also in the hopes that he might somehow find a way to hit big league pitching, the new major league Los Angeles Angels chose him in the draft along with twenty-seven other players from around the league. Making the selections were their new manager

Bill Rigney, the former Giants skipper who had been hired only two days before, and general manager Fred Haney, a former Coast League player and manager. Their boss, the principal owner of the Angels, was a Texas-born multimillionaire who had loved baseball since he was a boy, Gene Autry.

Baseball, said Autry, was his "boyhood passion." He played shortstop on his Tioga, Texas, American Legion team and played it well enough to be offered a one-hundred-dollar-per-month contract with a minor league club in Tulsa, a farm team of the St. Louis Cardinals. The nineteen-year-old Autry was working for the railroad in Oklahoma at the time and chumming around with the likes of Dizzy Dean, another country boy who liked baseball. Dean and Autry also shared a taste for Jamaica Ginger whiskey, and although Prohibition was in effect and alcoholic spirits were against the law, the pair knew a storekeeper who manufactured it and sold it for a fair price.

Autry turned down the Tulsa offer because it paid less than the railroad, and he could not see walking away from a steady job for the uncertain life of a professional ballplayer, however desirable it may have been. While his pal

Gene Autry, left, and Stars manager Babe Herman exchanged getups for a publicity shot.
Security Pacific Collection/Los Angeles Public Library

Dean went on to the Cardinals and a Hall of Fame pitching career, Autry did not stay at the railroad for long, pursuing a talent for singing that soon made him into a hit-making recording artist and a major country-and-western touring attraction. Hollywood beckoned, and in 1934 Autry arrived in town to see if his genial, easygoing charm (and ticket-selling powers) would translate to the big screen. But California struck him as "formless, too sprawling, too far from the rest of the country," and he left Hollywood to go back on tour after his first few movies did only so-so at the box office. The next time he returned to town he made "Tumblin' Tumbleweeds," which became a smash hit and propelled Autry—singing songs of the Old West on his horse, Champion—to movie fame on top of his recording and radio success.

Autry, the only person to have five stars on the Hollywood Walk of Fame, made more than ninety movies and six hundred records, nine of which sold over one million copies apiece. "Rudolph the Red-Nosed Reindeer," his biggest hit, sold more than twenty-five million records. But by 1960 his performing career was over and he had turned another of his talents—this one for finances—into a Bonanza-sized real estate and media empire, which included KSFO, the radio home of the San Francisco Giants, and KMPC, which broadcast the Los Angeles Dodgers.

But when the Dodgers decided to shift stations to KFI in late 1960, leaving KMPC without a team, it put Autry in a quandary. Not wanting to lose his station's sports identity, he contacted Bill Veeck and Hank Greenberg, who were all but certain to be the owners of the new American League franchise set for Los Angeles. They assured Autry that if they became the team's owners, KMPC could broadcast its games. Content with this arrangement, Autry thought—incorrectly, as events showed—that this would be the extent of his involvement with the new team.

Though they may not have discussed it at the time, Autry and Veeck had a distant baseball connection. Veeck had been in the stands for the 1934 barnstorming game in Hollywood in which Autry's friend Dizzy Dean squared off against Negro League star Satchel Paige in perhaps the greatest pitching duel of the segregated era. Autry described Veeck as "a born boat-rocker, with the sly grin of a man who is about to drop an egg in your pocket." Veeck had been dropping eggs in the pockets of major league baseball for decades. One of the game's great promoters and a pioneer of integration who hired Larry Doby as the second black to play major league baseball, he had been involved in baseball management and ownership virtually his entire adult life. Currently he owned a majority share of the Chicago White Sox, where his close friend, Hank Greenberg, also had a partial interest.

Also a highly notable name in baseball, Greenberg was the greatest Jewish slugger of all time and one of the greatest ever, regardless of religion. After his playing days ended (he spent the bulk of his thirteen-year career with the Detroit Tigers) he had entered the management side of the game with his partner Veeck and moved to southern California where, among other activities, he was a member of the Beverly Hills Tennis Club. The actor Walter Matthau was also a member. Like Greenberg, Matthau was a Jew and, as a child of immigrant New York City he, like so many boys of his generation, grew up idolizing Greenberg for his size—he stood nearly six feet, four inches tall, towering over his family and members of his community—and his prodigious power-hitting. The only reason Matthau joined the club was to meet Greenberg. "I didn't play tennis," said Matthau. "So I was there every afternoon trying to get lunch with him. Most of the time I succeeded. So I had a lot of lunches with him."

When he was not having lunch with Matthau and other star-struck admirers, Greenberg was working to acquire the new Los Angeles expansion team. He sat on the American League expansion committee and his group—which also included Ralph Kiner, a Hall of Fame slugger like Greenberg, and Arnholt Smith, the owner of the Coast League San Diego Padres—was considered to be a lock to land the team. They had already picked out a site in Los Angeles for a new park and a construction company to build it.

But the Greenberg group balked when Dodgers owner Walter O'Malley insisted on a $350,000 payment for baseball territorial rights to Los Angeles, which, in O'Malley's view, he controlled. According to Veeck, O'Malley also made other demands that did not sit well with Greenberg, who was already unhappy with the low caliber of players made available to his team during the expansion draft. Feeling like the whole deal had suddenly turned sour on him, Greenberg withdrew his bid.

This withdrawal created an opening, and Autry, who had briefly owned a small piece of the old Hollywood Stars, decided to make a run for the team. Several entertainment and media companies own baseball teams today because of what is seen as a natural business affinity between broadcasting and sports. Although not usually regarded in this light, Autry was one of the first owners to use sports as one element of an overall business and media strategy.

On a Friday afternoon he called American League president Joe Cronin and expressed his interest in buying the team. Cronin, an old friend of Autry's who had seen him perform in his traveling rodeo days, told him there was another bidder and that if he was serious he needed to deliver a $1.5 million letter of credit to Cronin's office by Monday. Autry *was* serious, and the financial guarantee arrived in time. The other bidder was a Chicago insurance man, Charlie O. Finley, who was eager to get into baseball. In December the American League owners unanimously approved Autry's bid over Finley's, and only three months after the Dodgers had dropped KMPC for another radio station, Autry and his business partner, Bob Reynolds, a strapping former Stanford all-American football tackle who owned a minority interest in KMPC, had themselves a ballclub.

In a matter of days Autry hired Haney and Rigney, who oversaw the expansion draft, their first pick being a cast-off pitcher from the Yankees, Eli Grba. Others chosen included Bilko; Dean Chance, a young Ohioan who would later win twenty games in a season and a Cy Young Award for the Angels; and infielder Jim Fregosi, a good-looking all-sports grad from Serra High in San Mateo (the future school of Barry Bonds), who went on to

Angels star Jim Fregosi, 1967. Security Pacific Collection/Los Angeles Public Library

become the team leader and an All-Star (and later, a manager of the club). The Angels paid $2.1 million, or $75,000 apiece, for their original twenty-eight players. At some point they also paid the $350,000 territorial fee owed to the Dodgers—"for what amounted to grazing rights," as Autry expressed it.

Scrambling for more players wherever they could find them, the Angels held an open tryout in Los Angeles two months before the start of the season. Of the close to three hundred players who showed up, six received contracts; one of those cut was an aspiring infielder named Charlie Pride, who, like Autry, ultimately gave up baseball to become a country music star. The Angels held spring training in Palm Springs, practicing at a field known as the Polo Grounds, which quickly became a magnet for show business celebrities, many of them old friends of Autry's. When not playing golf, former president Dwight Eisenhower, who had a home in the area, frequently stopped by to watch some ball.

With No. 1 pick Grba on the mound, the Angels opened the regular season in Baltimore with a win—a win! Considering how quickly they had pulled the team together, how much hard work it took, the obstacles (financial and otherwise) they had to overcome to do it, Autry, who owned the Angels nearly four decades, always maintained that this first-game victory was his "biggest thrill in baseball."

Angels Opening Day, Wrigley Field, Los Angeles, 1961. California Historical Society, FN-40005

For their inaugural season in Los Angeles, the Angels played their home games at Wrigley Field. Built in the 1920s, once an emblem of a go-go city on the make, the tiny park was breathing its last breaths. The Coast League Angels, its onetime tenant, were long gone. When the Dodgers arrived they spurned the field in favor of the far larger Coliseum. The previous year Wrigley Field had hosted a television series, *Home Run Derby*, in which Willie Mays, Frank Robinson, Eddie Matthews, and other sluggers competed in home run hitting contests for cash prizes. The program, an early forerunner of the long-ball hitting contests that are part of today's All-Star game festivities, lasted only one season and ended sadly; months after its final show its producer, Mark Scott, died of heart failure.

Wrigley Field in Los Angeles would later meet the same fate as other Coast League parks of its era and be destroyed, but for one season it got to be a major league ballpark. The year 1961 saw Roger Maris of the New York Yankees hit sixty-one home runs to break Babe Ruth's long-standing single-season record; four of those home runs came at Wrigley. Many others hit home runs there as well; in fact, the 248 that were hit that season at Wrigley still stand as the most ever for one season at a major league park. William Wrigley's hitter's paradise remained true to itself to the end. Fittingly, the last major league home run hit there—number 248—was by an Angel, Steve Bilko, who hit twenty on the year and played first base with such skill that it brought back memories of his glory days. A season after his season of redemption, Bilko hung 'em up for good.

★   ★   ★   ★   ★

At about this same time Jay Johnstone was living the carefree life of a suburban southern California teenager: "Crewcuts, Pendleton shirts, white socks, loafers, cars, hangin' out in the sunshine, listening to music, playing sports and looking at girls. What else was there?" He and his friends would go down to the Bob's Big Boy in West Covina, order a cup of coffee and a doughnut for a dime apiece, and shoot the breeze until something better came along. Sometimes they stole a car just for kicks and went joyriding, but mostly they kept their noses clean, cruised around in cars they or their parents owned, and played sports.

The lefty-hitting, righty-throwing Johnstone easily moved up through the youth ranks: Little League, Pony League, American Legion, and Edgewood High, where he starred in football and basketball in addition to baseball. Out of high school he signed a contract with the Los Angeles Angels organization and played minor league baseball in Texas until being forced to make a decision: either enlist in the military or be drafted. "It was one of those 'I've-got-to-do-something' situations that confronted every healthy, eighteen-year-old man in the mid-1960s," said Johnstone.

American combat troops began arriving in large numbers in Vietnam in 1965, the year Johnstone was in the minors. What he decided to do, after the season was over, was enlist. A month before his twentieth birthday he joined the United States Marines Corps Reserve, Platoon 291, and went to Camp Pendleton in Oceanside, California, for his basic training. With the war in Southeast Asia growing, and hundreds of thousands of men no older than Johnstone being sent to fight in the jungles of Vietnam, his outlook and his expectations in life had suddenly changed.

Fellow Marines that Johnstone served with, men he knew, went to Vietnam, but he did not. The call for him never came and he finished his active duty commitment at a Naval base in Los Alamitos, receiving his discharge in the spring of 1966, in time for a new baseball season.

Returning to the life he loved, he went back to his old minor league club in Texas and started slamming the ball. Though he had missed spring training because of his military commitments, being in the Marines had made him fitter than the other players. In less than two weeks he made the step up the organizational hierarchy to a team in Seattle, where his slamming continued. Then in July the Angels told Johnstone to get on a plane because he was coming to the big leagues.

By 1966 the Angels were no longer the Los Angeles Angels, they were the California Angels; and they had left Los Angeles for Anaheim in Orange County, playing in a ballpark affectionately known as "the Big A." The newly opened stadium drew its name from the giant $1 million A-frame structure beyond the left field fence that featured a scoreboard and display screen inside the A. The A stood for both Anaheim and the Angels and, joked sportswriter Ross Newhan, "Agony," a reference to the hard luck and losing seasons that would plague the club for so much of its existence.

After their first season at Wrigley Field, the Angels had moved over to Dodger Stadium, which opened in 1962. Their initial season there started with a bang. Left-hander Bo Belinsky won his first five starts of the season, one of which was a no-hitter, and the cocky, street-smart East Coast hipster—"My only regret in life is that I can't sit in the stands and watch me pitch," he once said—became an immediate sensation, particularly with the ladies. Ann-Margaret, Tina Louise, and other Hollywood beauties were seen around town with him, and he was even briefly engaged to buxom B-movie queen Mamie Van Doren. While Belinsky and fellow night crawler Dean Chance were sampling all that the Sunset Strip nightlife could offer, their second-year expansion team held first place in the American League as late as the Fourth of July. The Angels slipped to third by season's end, but drew more than one million fans.

Things steadily deteriorated from there for the Angels—on the field, in the numbers of people who came to see them, and in their relations with their co-tenants, the Dodgers. Los Angeles, they learned, *was* Dodgertown. The Dodgers had the cool, classy uniforms, the stars on the field and in the seats, Vin Scully on the radio. They had a superheated rivalry going with San Francisco—which boiled over into ugliness in 1965 when Juan Marichal of the Giants hit Dodger catcher John Roseboro over the head with a bat during a game—and they were winning pennants and world championships. The Dodger Stadium showcase was hailed as one of the best places in America to watch a ballgame and, as the name indicated, it was the Dodgers' place, not the Angels'. As a further aggravation to the Angels, the Dodgers charged them rent and expected them to pay half the cost of landscaping, window cleaning, parking lot resurfacing, and other maintenance bills at the stadium. The two teams even squabbled over the toilet paper bill; the Dodgers maintained that the Angels should pay half, while the Angels argued that their share should be prorated because their games had fewer fans who used the restroom less.

Given these circumstances, it was probably to be expected that the Angels went shopping for a new place to play, with Gene Autry insisting only that the team remain in the Los Angeles area. They found the match they were looking for in Anaheim with its upbeat mayor, Rex Coons, who thought a big league club would give his bustling city and Orange County a new national image. Known mainly as the home of Disneyland, Anaheim was at the center of a growing suburban and metropolitan area. Seven million people lived less than an hour away by car, said Coons, and the future would certainly bring more. Autry agreed, and the Angels announced their intention to leave Los Angeles in spring of 1964 for the city where the teenaged Walter Johnson had once pitched. A site for a new stadium was found in a field of alfalfa, corn, and

Angels manager Gene Mauch, left, and Gene Autry, early 1980s. Security Pacific Collection/Los Angeles Public Library

oranges, and the Singin' Cowboy, dressed in alligator boots and a tan Western suit, shoveled the honorary first clump of dirt at the groundbreaking.

The Big A opened on April 9, 1966, with an exhibition between the Angels and the Giants. The visitors won the first of the two-game series in front of 40,735 fans, but the home team took the next one on a Jim Fregosi home run in the tenth inning. The regular-season home opener for the Angels took place about ten days later.

Jay Johnstone made his major league debut with the Angels in July of that season, beginning a twenty-year career in which he played on two world championship clubs, including the 1981 Dodgers. The reputation he developed over the years was as a jokester and a merry prankster, but when he first came to the Angels Johnstone had only been out of the Marines for a few months. War was being fought overseas while race riots were breaking out in the cities and civil unrest was sweeping through university campuses and across the nation. He was lucky to be where he was, and he knew it, because guys he had met in the service—friends of his—were going to Vietnam and some of them were coming home in a box. Having a laugh or two and not taking everything so serious, Johnstone always figured, was maybe not such a bad thing after all.

The Next
Generation

SATURDAY, MARCH 22 — 2:15 P.M.
SUNDAY, MARCH 23 — 2:15 P.M.
— 1947 —

ABLISHED PRICE - $3.33
ERAL TAX - .67   Total $4.00

HIS PORTION OF TICKET NOT GOOD FOR ADMITTANCE
DETACH SEPERATE COUPONS FOR INDIVIDUAL GAMES

Tommy Lasorda was working a living room, and when Tommy Lasorda worked a living room, nobody was better at it in baseball. At least that was the view of many in the Los Angeles Dodgers organization, where the outgoing, talkative Lasorda served as a scout.

In scouting parlance, "working a living room" means that the scout is inside a prospect's house delivering his pitch on why the prospect should sign with the scout's organization. Lasorda loved talking to people, loved schmoozing, but it was not just a sales hustle for him. A former left-handed pitcher who got his first break in the major leagues with the Brooklyn Dodgers (though it was a brief one, and he spent nearly all of his career in the minors), Lasorda honestly believed the Dodgers were the best organization in baseball. Thus, according to this reasoning, the best thing the prospect could do for himself was sign with Lasorda. And lots of them did.

The Dodger brass liked this quality about Lasorda—that yes, he could sell a cup of sand to a man who lived in the desert, but also that he was an organization man, totally loyal. And so in late 1962 Al Campanis, the head of scouting

Tommy Lasorda celebrates after the Dodgers' 1981 world championship.
Security Pacific Collection/Los Angeles Public Library

for the Dodgers in Los Angeles, called Lasorda at his home in Norristown, Pennsylvania. Lasorda's scouting terrain had been the East, but Campanis needed a man in the West to work alongside him, and he wanted Lasorda to be that man. A job transfer of this kind represented a big change for Lasorda, a Norristown native who had basically lived his whole life there, but he decided that if he wanted to get ahead in the organization he needed to be in its head-quarters city, and he and his family moved to Los Angeles.

Like lots of newcomers to the city, Lasorda got lost a lot driving on the freeways, but he managed to find his way around well enough to be invited into the living rooms of top young California baseball prospects. In this case the prospect was a speedy seventeen-year-old high schooler named Rick Monday, and Lasorda was sitting with him and his mother in the Mondays' home in Santa Monica. The three of them had moved out of the living room and into the kitchen, where Lasorda was trying to close the deal. The contract was on the table, and he had given his pen to Monday's mother. All she needed to do was put her signature on the contract (her son was underage and could not legally sign), and Rick Monday would be a member of the Los Angeles Dodgers organization.

In his autobiography Lasorda tells what happened next like it was a vaudeville comedy sketch. After he offered a $10,000 signing bonus, Monday's mother said that sounded fine. But then Lasorda immediately upped the offer to $12,500. Monday's mother said, "That sounds fine too," and almost as soon as the words left her mouth he was boosting the offer again, to $15,000. Monday's mother said that sounded fine as well, and Lasorda went up to $20,000. "I couldn't understand how she kept agreeing to the price," he said, "and the price kept going up."

Lasorda may have kept raising the price because he sensed her indecision and thought perhaps that more money would help her make up her mind. He really wanted to land Monday; he felt certain he was going to become a major leaguer, and possibly a high profile one. To make Monday a Dodger, Lasorda had courted him relentlessly: "I spent so much time at his house that he began to think I was a boarder." This may have been another reason why he so badly wanted to sign him: to make all his time and work pay off.

Lasorda first saw Monday when Lasorda managed him on the Dodger Rookie team. Just making the Rookies was an accomplishment in itself for a teenager. First the Dodgers invited some top local prospects to a tryout, which Lasorda supervised. The best of this bunch were invited to a second tryout. Then the Dodgers skimmed the cream from this group and those were the ones who made the amateur Rookies, who played a forty-game schedule against college teams, minor leaguers, and semipros.

Besides Monday, one of the best of the Dodger Rookies was Willie Crawford, another kid with the major leagues written all over him. Crawford went to Fremont High in Los Angeles—two of his classmates were Bobby Tolan and Bob Watson, both of whom became high-impact major leaguers—and he was one of a group of talented inner city players developed by Chet

Brewer, the former Negro League pitcher who coached youth baseball and also scouted for the major leagues himself. As with Monday, Lasorda was all over Crawford, picking him up after school to drive him to practice or run errands and frequently having dinner with him and his mother Clara at their house. A scout needs to develop trust with the prospect and his parents, and the way he does that is by hanging around a lot, being there, and sometimes making himself useful in unexpected ways. The day before Crawford graduated from high school, his grandfather, a former church deacon, died, and Lasorda attended the memorial service as a show of respect for the family. When he showed up at the church, the minister who was leading the service asked him to say a few words to the congregation. Never at a loss for words, Lasorda spoke eloquently about a man he had met only once before.

The day after the service Lasorda and Al Campanis appeared at the Crawford house ready to present their final offer to Willie. But when they arrived they had to wait outside while the owner of the Kansas City Athletics presented *his* final offer. The Athletics owner had been pursuing Crawford as relentlessly as the Dodgers, calling him every day to persuade him to sign with him. To show how much he valued Crawford he had flown out from the Midwest to make a personal pitch to Willie and his mother in their living room. And this owner knew how to work a living room too. He was Charlie O. Finley.

★   ★   ★   ★   ★

If, in late 1960, Gene Autry had not stepped in with his last-minute bid to buy the expansion Angels, the new American League franchise in Los Angeles might have gone to Finley, who also made an offer for the team. But the baseball owners, who had the last say in the matter, approved Autry's bid, leaving Finley to look elsewhere for a team. This search led him to the Kansas City Athletics, whose owner, Arnold Johnson, had died of a heart attack. After buying a controlling interest in the club from Johnson's widow, then purchasing the remaining shares from the minority owners, Finley was in as an owner in a game he had relished since he was a boy.

Finley, who was bald with a fringe of hair that turned white in his older years, always dressed "with conservative class," said the writer Bill Libby. His business motto, "Sweat Plus Sacrifice Equals Success," reflected a background in which Finley, following his father and grandfather into the Gary, Indiana, steel mills, gradually moved into the insurance business, where he became a top salesman. While recovering from a severe case of tuberculosis that nearly took his life, he conceived of a group medical insurance plan for physicians, then an innovative idea that, once he was back on his feet again, he tried unsuccessfully to sell to numerous insurance companies. Finley finally found an insurance carrier to underwrite his plan and when the American Medical Association and other physician groups endorsed it, he was on his way to earning his first million with offices in Chicago and a farm in La Porte, Indiana, where he lived with his large family.

At times—such as when he was sweet-talking Willie and Clara Crawford in Los Angeles—Finley could be smooth and charming, a salesman of the first rank. Many in baseball who had frequent interactions with him report that these times were few and far between, however. One sportswriter who knew Finley described him as "a man of despicable qualities": cheap, rude, a serial pincher of ladies' bottoms, manipulative, controlling. His ideas on how to improve baseball, his disrespectful attitude toward his players, whom he fought with constantly, and his managers, whom he hired and fired at will, generated controversy and often disdain. But when it came to signing and developing young talent, Finley emerged as one of the top owners in the game. When he saw a sure-thing future major leaguer like Willie Crawford, he donned his salesman's suit and shoes and went after him.

The Athletics, despite Finley's personal appeal, did not land Crawford; the Dodgers did. Every scout always wants to be able to make the last offer to a prospect, so that way he can top all the offers that came before. Finley made the second-to-last offer to the Crawfords, but after he left, Lasorda and Campanis went inside the house and made their offer, and this was the one Willie chose. With his one-hundred-thousand-dollar signing bonus he bought his mother a house. He went on to have a fine fourteen-year career as an outfielder in the majors, almost all of them with Los Angeles, and at the end of his career he even played for the A's and Charlie Finley.

Lasorda may have won the bidding contest for Willie Crawford, but Rick Monday's mother proved to be too tough of a match for him. Despite raising the offer for Monday several times, the Dodger scout had to sit, in silent agony, as his mother put the pen down on the kitchen table and explained that she felt her son was not quite ready for professional baseball.

"I just don't think he's mature enough," she said, adding that she wanted Rick to go to college for a couple of years first. Then he would sign with the Dodgers. "I give you my word," she said.

There was nothing for Lasorda to do except watch as Monday, per his mother's wishes, entered college, specifically Arizona State University. Then in the summer of 1964 Monday went to Alaska with other gifted young prospects who represented a new generation of ballplayers on their way up.

Charlie O. Finley, 1974.
Doug McWilliams Collection

Both Monday, who was born in late 1945, and Crawford, who was born the next year (but did not play in Alaska), were on the front edge of what is known as the baby boom generation. This generation, whose births spanned the end of World War II into the early 1960s, was the largest in American history, and on the strength of sheer numbers alone it has influenced every aspect of American society, including baseball. When Monday joined the Alaska Goldpanners he played with other Californians of his generation who would, when their time came, make people remember their names. One of them was a nineteen-year-old from San Diego with an unusual first name, Graig Nettles, who later became an All-Star third baseman with the New York Yankees and hometown Padres.

Graig's mother named him. She did not like either Craig or Greg separately, but she liked them when they were combined. Her son did not think anything about his name until he reached high school, when his teachers and everybody else seemed to either misspell it or mispronounce it or both.

San Diego High, where Nettles went to school, was in "a very mixed part of town." Whites, blacks, Mexicans, rich kids, poor kids. "It was a melting pot. It prepared you for life," he said. "There were fights, there were gangs." But Nettles stayed away from the gang scene because he played sports, which enabled him to hang around with guys who, if he had not been an athlete, he might otherwise not have known as well. The San Diego High basketball team consisted of fourteen blacks and Nettles, who is white.

Nettles's best sport in high school was basketball, and it was as a basketball player that he earned a scholarship to San Diego State. Both his parents had gone to State; it was, in fact, where they first met. Graig's father, Wayne, was an Oklahoma native who, along with his twin brother, Bill, had left home during the Dust Bowl, heading off in search of what they could not find in Claremore: work. They said goodbye to their mother and hopped a westward-bound freight train, riding it until the land stopped and the ocean began. Both found jobs in San Diego and later enrolled at the university in town, where they played football. Playing sports at San Diego State was a Nettles family tradition.

Nettles made the basketball team at State, but what really started to come on for him there was baseball. His body grew bigger and stronger, and the balls he hit that used to be routine fly balls started sailing over the heads of the outfielders. This was why he went to Alaska—to keep getting stronger, to keep building up his game.

One of his (and Monday's) teammates on the Goldpanners was Tom Seaver, then only nineteen years old. "Will Seaver ever stop looking like a chubbyish California kid?" the writer Roy Blount asked when Seaver was nearing the end of his Hall of Fame pitching career. If Seaver still looked boyish in his late thirties, one can only imagine how he looked in Alaska or before that, growing up in Fresno. When he was a boy his mother, an enthusiastic baseball fan, let Tom stay home from school during the World Series—the games were played in the afternoon then—so they could watch it on television together. His father, a former Walker Cup golfer, was also athletically minded. Even so, Seaver was a late bloomer in sports, and while he made all-city in his senior season at Fresno High, he drew only yawns from the pro scouts. But the summer after graduation he took a job at the fruit-packing company where his father was vice president, and a few months of lifting crates all day—plus a stint after that in the Marine Corps Reserves—hardened up his body and made him not so chubby in the places where it counted.

For a year Seaver played on the Fresno State College (now University) team, where he roused the interest of both scouts and coaches, including Rod Dedeaux, the headman at the University of Southern California. Dedeaux wanted Seaver to come to USC, but recommended that he first go to Alaska to pitch against other top-notch talent. On the Goldpanners, said Nettles, Seaver just "overpowered" people. But even then he had more than just a great fastball; he was a real heady player, with polish and composure beyond his years.

With Seaver dealing from the mound and the likes of Nettles, Monday, and Glendale native Gary Sutherland (a future thirteen-year major leaguer) in the lineup, the Goldpanners ransacked the local competition. But the club had a problem: it could not afford to take both Nettles and Monday to Wichita, Kansas, to compete in a national championship semipro tournament. Because Nettles had a slightly higher batting average, the Goldpanners kept him for the tournament and sent Monday home to California. Monday then returned the next fall to Arizona State, became the 1965 College Player of the Year, and led the Sun Devils to the national championship. In June he became the first player chosen in the first-ever major league amateur draft. The team that picked him was Charlie Finley's Kansas City Athletics.

By 1965, and surely before, Finley's relationship with Kansas City had gone bad. At first regarded favorably because of his pledge to keep the Athletics in town, he quickly came to be viewed as an absentee owner who cared little about the city or its fans (a reputation he would also carve out for himself in Oakland). His view of Kansas City was equally dim. Unhappy over the club's declining attendance, squabbling constantly with his players and managers, lambasted by the press, he hired a search firm to scout for potential cities to take his team.

One of the interested cities was Oakland. It had a new stadium, the Oakland-Alameda County Coliseum, and was looking for a summertime tenant to complement the football Raiders. But the Athletics would be moving into what had exclusively been the baseball territory of the San Francisco Giants, and many major league owners opposed the shift, partly owing to their widespread dislike of Finley. But Angels owner Gene Autry wanted to see another American League club in California to form a rivalry on the order of the National League Giants and Dodgers, and his support for the change helped carry the day for Oakland. When it was announced that Finley was transferring the Athletics out of Kansas City, Missouri Senator Stuart Symington said, "Oakland is the luckiest city since Hiroshima."

The caravan that Finley brought west with him contained many of the features that are popularly associated with the Athletics in Oakland: the uniforms of gaudy green, "Fort Knox gold," and "wedding gown white" (Finley coined these terms because he felt they sounded flashier than mere gold or white); the white shoes worn by players to round out this fashion ensemble; Harvey the mechanized Rabbit, a device that popped up out of the ground behind home plate to distribute balls to the umpire and then disappeared again after its job was done; orange baseballs (Finley felt they would be easier

Charlie O,
the A's mascot.
Doug McWilliams
Collection

Rollie Fingers.
Doug McWilliams Collection

to see than the standard white ones); and a mule mascot named Charlie O. Another Finley innovation, green- and gold-tinted sheep that grazed beyond the outfield fence in Kansas City, did not make it to Oakland, possibly because the Coliseum lacked an adequate pasture.

Fortunately, though, Finley did not just arrive with a mule and a bag full of promotional tricks; he brought his players with him. In April 1968, when the Athletics opened in front of a capacity crowd at the Oakland Coliseum with Governor Ronald Reagan, American League president Joe Cronin, and other dignitaries looking on, a championship team in the making took the field. Campy Campaneris was at shortstop, Sal Bando at third, Dick Green at second. Dave Duncan was catching a pitching staff that included Catfish Hunter, who threw a perfect game at the Coliseum a month after Opening Day, and Blue Moon Odom. And in a city whose professional baseball team once tried to pass off a black player as a Native American, only to quickly dismiss him once the ruse was uncovered—into this city came Reggie Jackson, an outspoken and powerful young slugger of black and Hispanic descent.

Eventually Rollie Fingers—he, Jackson, and Hunter are all in the Hall of Fame—would find his destiny not in starting pitching but in relieving, Modesto defensive ace Joe Rudi would make left field his home, Vida Blue and his fastball would join the staff and dazzle everyone in baseball, catcher Gene Tenace and other key role-players would enter the scene, and one native-Californian manager (John McNamara) would be replaced by a California-bred one (Pasadena's Dick Williams, a former all-state junior college player). And while fighting constantly with their boss about money and everything else, this crazy-quilt collection of personalities—the Swingin' A's they were called, instantly identifiable by their green and gold uniforms, white shoes, long hair, and mustaches (Fingers's handlebar mustache being the most notable)—would evolve into one of the greatest teams of its era, winning three consecutive World Series titles beginning in 1972.

One person who did not share in Oakland's early glory was Rick Monday. After signing with the Athletics out of Arizona State, he played outfield in both Kansas City and Oakland, but the Athletics traded him away just before the beginning of their world championship run. Monday did, however, get a World Series ring in 1981 after joining the Los Angeles Dodgers and being reunited with his longtime admirer, Tommy Lasorda, who had since moved up the ranks from scouting into managing.

1969

SATURDAY, MARCH 22 — 2:15 P.M.
SUNDAY, MARCH 23 — 2:15 P.M.
— 1947 —
ABLISHED PRICE - - $3.33   Total $4.00
ERAL TAX - - - - .67
HIS PORTION OF TICKET NOT GOOD FOR ADMITTANCE
DETACH SEPERATE COUPONS FOR INDIVIDUAL GAMES

Dick Selma was in a jam. One run was already in, runners were on first and third with only one out, and Curt Blefary, who was nobody's patsy, stood at the plate. Selma knew if he did not get Blefary out he might not make it through the first inning of the biggest game of his life.

It was April 8, 1969. The Houston Astros versus the San Diego Padres at San Diego Stadium in the first major league game in San Diego history. The evening air on the coast felt cool and nice, and more than twenty-three thousand people—what would turn out to be the largest home attendance for the Padres for two years—were in the seats. Everything was perfect—everything except for the fact that the Padres' starting pitcher was in a big hole that looked in danger of getting much bigger.

Selma, who had come to San Diego via the New York Mets in the National League expansion draft held the previous year, had pitched poorly over the spring. But Padres manager Preston Gomez had stuck with him and given him the Opening Night nod. Selma, a native of Santa Ana and a graduate of Fresno High, appreciated this because he recognized what a unique honor it was to start the first game in a new franchise's history. Indeed, this was partly what gave him such anxiety as he fingered the ball on the mound staring down at Blefary in the batter's box. He did not want to screw it all up.

On the scoreboard before the game they had posted the new Padres logo in between two dates: 1769 and 1969. This was the two hundredth anniversary of the founding of San Diego's mission, the first of nine missions established by Father Junipero Serra in California, then called Alta (or "upper") California by the Spanish. Serra and the other members of the Sacred Expedition, including its leader Gaspar de Portolá, had arrived in San Diego in late spring and early summer, eventually moving northward from there to explore and settle the region and spread the Catholic faith.

But you did not have to go all the way back to Father Serra to appreciate what was going on that night in San Diego. There were people present who had seen the old Coast League Padres play at Lane Field in the days when Ted Williams was a spindly-legged teenager who loved to wolf down hamburgers and milkshakes and spend his salary on the pinball machines. Others may have seen John Ritchey of the Padres become the first black to play in the Coast League. In 1958 the club moved into fancy new digs at Westgate Park, which, some felt, was the finest minor league park in the country at the time. But the minor leagues were still the minor leagues, and lots of San Diegans felt their city deserved a major league ballclub of its own.

One of them was San Diego sportswriter Jack Murphy, who used the bully pulpit of a newspaper column to lobby for a major league team and, further, to push residents to build a new stadium. Step one—and it was a big step, because it showed widespread popular support for the idea—was the passage of a stadium-financing bond measure by voters. The $27.5 million San Diego Stadium opened in 1967, receiving wide praise for its elegant design features. Years later, in recognition of his leading role in building the park and bringing major league baseball to the city, San Diego Stadium would be renamed Jack Murphy Stadium.

With the stadium under construction or already built, Arnholt Smith, owner of the minor league Padres, arranged for a meeting with Buzzie Bavasi at Los Angeles International Airport. Smith, a banker who had been involved with Hank Greenberg's failed ownership bid for the expansion Los Angeles Angels, was in charge of the financial side of acquiring a major league franchise. But in order to be successful he needed a baseball man with major league connections, and that was why he wanted to see Bavasi, then the general manager of the Los Angeles Dodgers.

Emil Joseph Bavasi, known to all as "Buzzie," was nothing if not a baseball man, widely admired for his role in building pennant-winning and world championship clubs with the Dodgers, first in Brooklyn and then in Los Angeles. Building a major league team from scratch clearly represented a challenge of another sort, and a huge one at that, but Bavasi, who eventually came in as a part owner, agreed to work with Smith in putting a bid together.

Despite the challenges, Bavasi felt there were considerable reasons for optimism, beginning with San Diego Stadium. Add to this a large and growing population, a solid financial package headed by Smith, and year-round sunny weather in which a bad day was when a cloud appeared in the sky. This package proved irresistible to the baseball owners, who chose San Diego to be one of the National League's two new expansion franchises. (The coming of the major league Padres meant the end of the minor league Padres and, with Sacramento having ceased play years before, the end of Pacific Coast League baseball in the state. It would be decades before the Coast League would return to California.) After hearing the good news at the owners' meeting in Chicago, Bavasi flew back to the Coast to begin the job of constructing a big league franchise.

One of his first hires was manager Preston Gomez. Gomez, whose birth name was Pedro, was called Preston apparently in reference to the town in which he was born, Preston, Cuba. Friendly and good-natured, Gomez was a veteran of both the major leagues (ever so briefly; he played only a handful of games) and the Coast League. His coaching staff included Sparky Anderson in his rookie year as a major league coach; Roger Craig, a one-time Dodger pitcher (and future Giants manager); and Whitey Wietelmann, a crusty, well-liked longtime San Diego baseball hand (he also lived in the area) who wore number 19 for the Padres before the arrival of the man who would retire the number, superstar Tony Gwynn.

For months the club had looked ahead to the October expansion draft when Bavasi, Gomez, and the scouting staff would pick the players who would comprise the team. But they were realistic about the general quality of the players that would be available from the other National League clubs. Early on the morning of draft day in Montreal, Bavasi told his staff, "This is the day we get to buy $10 million worth of turkeys."

Their first pick in the draft, the original Padre, was ex–San Francisco Giants outfielder Ollie Brown. The Giants and the other established clubs could only protect a certain number of their players; those left unprotected could then be drafted by San Diego or Montreal, the other new National League expansion team. (The American League also had new expansion teams in Kansas City and Seattle.) Whenever they could, to the extent possible, the Padres chose younger players, figuring they would lose lots of games in the beginning but grow and develop into winners in the future. On the New York Mets, left unprotected and available for selection by the Padres, was a young left-handed pitcher whose future would turn out to be very bright, Tug McGraw.

McGraw's first name was Frank, like his father. But his mother, Mabel, named him Tug because of the aggressive way he latched on to her as a baby when she was breast-feeding him. Tug was always Tug, never Frank. If a teacher or someone asked for Frank McGraw, Tug replied, "That's my father and he's already been to school. I'm Tug."

Born in the East Bay town of Martinez, the birthplace of Joe DiMaggio, McGraw grew up across the strait in Vallejo, a small working-class town that was the home of Mare Island Naval Base until its closure in recent years. After World War II and into the 1950s with the Korean War, McGraw remembers that part of San Francisco Bay as being "like one huge naval base," with ships steaming in and out of port and off-duty sailors around town. But McGraw as a boy was happily focused on sports and little else, playing pickup games with his brothers at Wilson Park and in the Junior Peanut and Peanut Leagues. His baseball coach in the city's Recreation Department league was Dick Bass, who later became a star running back with the Los Angeles Rams.

As an adult McGraw described himself thusly: "Not too short, maybe an inch under six feet, maybe 185 pounds when he's in shape, 200 when he's not. Light-haired, sunny, volatile, as talented as a burglar, as mad as a March hare." But his size only came later; when he was young he was always the little guy, racing to keep up with his older brother Hank, who was bigger, faster, and stronger and the best all-around athlete, by far, at St. Vincent's High School. Tug pushed himself to be as good as Hank, who signed with the New York Mets organization after his senior year.

Hank's signing bonus of fifteen thousand dollars could not have come at a better time for the family. His father, a fireman who had once worked three jobs at the same time to pay the bills, was deep in debt. A trucking business of his had failed. He and Mabel were divorced, but after the marriage broke up the McGraws decided their sons needed the guidance of a parochial school, and that cost money too. Hank gave his bonus money to his father to get him out of debt.

Despite his early prowess Hank McGraw never reached the major leagues, but he turned out to be a stand-up guy for his brothers and his family. Hank agreed to sign with New York only if Roy Partee, the Mets scout, gave Tug a fair look when Tug got older. Partee agreed and Hank signed. Hank also paid Tug's tuition the rest of the way at St. Vincent's and made sure his brother played with the best equipment.

Unlike with Hank, however, Partee and other major league scouts had little to do with Tug after he graduated from St. Vincent's. The scouts only began to get interested during his sophomore year at Vallejo Junior College (now

Solano Community College), when he led his club to the state junior college baseball finals against Mt. St. Antonio Junior College in Los Angeles. But McGraw started the championship game and got knocked out of the box in the third inning, and what interest there was in him dried up and blew away. In frustration Tug called his big brother, who told him to call Partee. Hank may not have said it, but he and Partee had an agreement and it was time to see if the Mets scout was going to honor it.

Partee did. He arranged a tryout for Tug in Salinas with Hank and some other young Met prospects. Tug showed off his stuff, earning a second tryout in Stockton in which he again did well. This persuaded Partee to sign him for a bonus of seven thousand dollars, and suddenly Tug was off to Florida to play for the Mets in their rookie league.

A year or so later when Tug reported to Mets training camp—the one for the big leaguers, not the rookies—he joined another Californian on the way up, shortstop Buddy Harrelson of Hayward. The pair made an impression on their new teammates. Talking first about McGraw, Ron Swoboda, who was a rookie for the Mets that year, said, "He was California all the way, man, full of all these different expressions about things....He and Buddy Harrelson had an extremely different perspective on things. I thought, 'Whoa, man, they've been in the sun too much.'" In two years another Californian by the name of Tom Seaver would arrive on the Mets, and he and Harrelson would become close friends and key contributors (along with McGraw) to New York's '69 world championship team.

McGraw himself bears some similarities to another sun-kissed California guy of this generation, Bill Lee. Like McGraw, Lee—who was born in Burbank, played Little League in the San Fernando Valley with future Giants third baseman Dirty Al Gallagher (the kids called him "Dirty Al" even then), came to live in Marin County after his father's job transfer, graduated from Terra Linda High, and then pitched for a national championship team at USC with fellow Californians Jim Barr, another future Giant, and future Padre Brent Strom—was known for his offbeat comments and behavior, a screwball or "flake" in baseball jargon. Coincidentally or not—it is near axiomatic in baseball that the biggest screwballs are left-handers, and usually left-handed pitchers—both Lee and McGraw were left-handed pitchers. But unlike Lee, who became a fan favorite with the Boston Red Sox and Montreal Expos as a starter, McGraw struggled in this capacity. His brother Hank felt he was being overcoached by the Mets, who had just about given up on both McGraws. In fact, the Mets did release Hank and left Tug unprotected for the 1969 expansion draft, leaving San Diego with the chance to grab him up.

Bill Lee, Montreal Expos, 1983.
Ken Lee copyright 88.

The Padres did not choose McGraw, however, and it is easy to see why they did not. (For reasons known only to them, and perhaps not even them, the Mets decided to pull McGraw back after three rounds and put him on their protected list.) At the time he had moved unimpressively back and forth between the minors and majors and had a developing reputation for eccentricity. The Padres could not have known that by the next spring, McGraw would give up on starting and, first with the Mets and then the Phillies, develop into one of the best relief pitchers of his era. His rallying cry of "You Gotta Believe!" for the 1973 pennant-winning Mets—beaten in the Series by the Oakland Athletics—has become part of the game's lexicon. (His son, Tim McGraw, is a star country-and-western singer.)

Chris Cannizzaro, San Diego Padres, 1969.
San Diego Hall of Champions

Though they did not select McGraw in the draft, the Padres did choose two Californians from the Mets—a catcher from Oakland, Chris Cannizzaro (the first All-Star in Padre history, selected the next year), and Fresno right-hander Dick Selma. The two formed the Opening Night battery for the Padres, and Cannizzaro surely tried to settle Selma down in that rocky first inning. Throughout the inning Selma had had trouble with his slider and could not get it over the plate for a strike, forcing him to rely on his fastball. The Astro hitters, picking up on this weakness early, had jumped all over him. But Selma, looking in on Curt Blefary, had no other choice; all he had to offer was a fastball. He knew it, and Blefary knew it too. The predictable happened. Selma delivered, Blefary swung, and the ball rocketed on a line toward right field.

But then the unpredictable happened; call it providence. Padres second baseman Roberto Pena leaped high and snagged the ball in the air, turning a sure Blefary hit into an out and breathing new life into the suddenly reinvigorated Selma. The next Astro hitter, Bob Watson, went down on a routine fly ball to the outfield, the Padres were out of the inning, and the hometown fans were roaring.

Recovering his slider to go along with his fastball, Selma pitched all nine innings and did not allow another run, finishing with twelve strikeouts and scattering five hits. Third baseman Ed Spiezio achieved a whole handful of Padre firsts in a single at-bat—first home run, first run batted in, first run—to tie the score in the fifth, 1 to 1. In the next inning first-round draftee Ollie Brown doubled home fielding star Roberto Pena for what proved to be the winning run, and after one perfect evening of baseball the undefeated San Diego Padres were tied for first place in the Western Division of the National League.

Decades later, dying of cancer and close to the end of his fifty-seven years, Dick Selma would look back on his Opening Night victory over the Astros as the highpoint of his baseball career and one of the highpoints of his life. He had always wanted to pitch for a major league team in his home state and San Diego gave him the chance. Baseball being what it is, though, disappointment soon followed triumph for Selma who, after only a month with the Padres, was traded to Chicago, where he participated in a vivid Eastern Divisional race that season between the Cubs and Tom Seaver's Mets.

The 1969 major league season actually started the day before the Padres' home opener, when forty-five thousand fans turned out to see the managerial debut of Ted Williams for the hometown Senators at RFK Stadium in Washington, D.C. In the stands that day was the newly elected president of the United States, Richard Nixon, a former congressman and gubernatorial candidate from California. Nixon had won election pledging to end the Vietnam War, which still raged overseas as political turmoil divided the nation at home. Nor was baseball immune from this turmoil. Many people, particularly the young, saw it as irrelevant to their lives—constricted by tradition, too slow and boring, their father's game perhaps but not theirs. During an era of widespread experimentation and a questioning of conventional authority and customs, Bill Lee and Dock Ellis, who claimed to pitch a no-hitter while high on LSD, were among the prominent major leaguers using marijuana and other drugs. These and other players (as well as owners such as Charlie Finley) openly challenged the baseball establishment in a variety of ways.

At the start of the 1960s, another newly elected president, John Kennedy, committed America to the goal of landing a man on the moon by the end of the decade. Two years later an assassin's bullet felled him. More assassinations— of civil rights leader Martin Luther King Jr. and Kennedy's brother Robert, shot dead in a Los Angeles hotel after winning the California primary in his campaign for president—would follow. But amidst these tragedies the country stayed true to Kennedy's goal. When astronaut Neil Armstrong stepped on the moon on July 20, 1969, what was described as the largest global audience in human history watched him on television. In an Angels game in Anaheim, when a message flashed on the Big A scoreboard that a man had just walked on the moon, the nearly eighteen thousand people in the stadium rose to their feet and applauded.

Baseball continued, as always. In a season that would earn him the Most Valuable Player award in the National League, San Francisco Giant star Willie McCovey hit two home runs in the All-Star game in July. The next month McCovey's nemesis on the Dodgers, pitcher Don Drysdale, retired from the game due to an injured right shoulder. His great running mate, Sandy Koufax, had quit a few years earlier, unable to endure any longer the constant pain in his throwing arm. And in September the best player of his generation, Willie Mays, hit his six hundredth career home run. He would hit sixty more before time caught up with him too, and he retired from the game.

Mays with the Giants, and Koufax and Drysdale with the Dodgers, had all come to California as major leaguers in 1958 (McCovey started on the Giants the next year), and their generation was steadily giving way to the next. Members of the California contingent of this new generation—in addition to

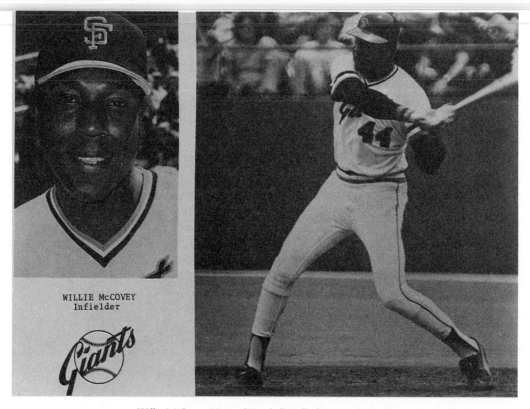

Willie McCovey. National Baseball Hall of Fame Library, Cooperstown, N.Y.

the ones already mentioned, they include Dusty Baker, Bud Black, Bob Boone, Larry Bowa, Bill Buckner, Jeff Burroughs, Enos Cabell, Gary Carter, Jack Clark, Darrell Evans, Dwight Evans, Bob and Ken Forsch, Dave Henderson, George Hendrick, Keith Hernandez, Mike Krukow, Fred Lynn, Jerry Manuel, Buck Martinez, Eddie Murray, Willie McGee, Jesse Orosco, Lance Parrish, Dave Righetti, Ozzie Smith, Reggie Smith, Allan Trammell, Tim Wallach, Don Wilson, Robin Yount, and so many more; too many to list and each with a story of his own—would pass through the major leagues in the next years, enriching the game as it enriched them.

One of the most talented of this new generation, Bobby Bonds of the San Francisco Giants, achieved a benchmark in late 1969, becoming only the fourth player in baseball history to hit thirty or more home runs and steal thirty or more bases in a single season. The reason why this feat is so highly prized is because in order to do it, a player must possess both speed and power, which Bonds certainly did. Born in Riverside and raised in an athletic family—his brother Robert played running back in the NFL and his sister Rose competed as a hurdler in the Olympics—Bonds achieved the magical 30-30 mark in only his second season with the Giants. Whereas aging Giant stars Mays and McCovey represented the glorious past, Bonds seemed to embody a present rich with promise.

A visitor to the San Francisco locker room in those days could also see a glimpse of baseball's future. He was only five years old then, a cute little guy maybe dressed up in a Giants uniform and always carrying around a glove and ball. When not in the clubhouse with his father he could be found out on the field, possibly playing toss and catch games with Mays, his godfather. Though he was a Riverside native too, his family would come to live in the Bay Area. He was Bobby's son, Barry Bonds, and his time was coming.

★   ★   ★   ★   ★

In October, after the end of the 1969 season, the man who would influence this new generation of players coming up—and all the ones who came after them— was sitting in St. Louis with a phone in his hands, too stunned to talk.

"Curt," said the voice on the other end of the line. "You've been traded to Philadelphia. Good luck."

"Thanks," he managed to say. "Thanks a lot."

After graduating from Oakland Tech in the 1950s, Curt Flood entered the Cincinnati Reds farm system, but he blossomed into one of the best outfielders in the game while with the St. Louis Cardinals, for whom he had played twelve seasons. But now his association with the Cardinals was at an end, he learned over the phone. He had just been traded to Philadelphia.

Under baseball's reserve clause, a system that originated in the 1800s, once a player signed with a certain team, that team controlled the rights to his services for the length of his career until it chose to sell or trade or release him. When, as in Flood's case, the Cardinals traded him to the Phillies, he had to go to Philadelphia if he wanted to keep playing major league baseball. The reserve clause made him, in effect—and this term was frequently used in baseball—the "property" of the Phillies, which now held the rights to his services.

But shortly after receiving that phone call, or perhaps in that very moment, Flood decided that he was not going to play for Philadelphia, that he would not accept the trade, and that even if it cost him what was left of his baseball career he was going to challenge, in court, the age-old restrictions of the reserve clause. Though his lawsuit would ultimately be rejected by the United States Supreme Court, it set in motion events that would radically change the way major league baseball conducted its business. Salary arbitration would be instituted, with players becoming "free agents" able to shop their services around to other teams. This, in turn, led to the escalation of salaries and the multimillion dollar contracts of today, although Flood himself never profited from these changes. Except for a brief return to the major leagues two years later, his career did indeed end with his decision to fight the reserve clause.

But Flood could not know any of this on the day he received that phone call in 1969. All he knew was that he no longer wanted to be regarded as someone else's property.

After consulting with an attorney and thinking about it some more, only to become more resolved in his mind, Flood boarded a plane to go see Marvin Miller and discuss with him what to do next. Miller, the executive director of the Major League Baseball Players Association and a seasoned and tough labor negotiator, would become Flood's chief ally in his battle with organized baseball. Miller's office was in New York City.

And so, once again, an American ballplayer of African descent, born in the southern region of the country and raised to manhood in California, would walk into an office in New York City and cause a revolution in the game.

Curt Flood, right, and his attorney, 1970. © Bettmann/CORBIS

Epilogue

Curt Flood's decision to challenge the reserve clause begins a new chapter in baseball (and California baseball) history, but alas, not a new chapter in this book. The intent of *The Golden Game* is to tell the story of California baseball from its origins in the Gold Rush era to the arrival of the major leagues. The San Diego Padres in 1969 became the fifth and (so far) final major league team to come to the state, and so marks the end of this story.

But many of the people referred to in the closing chapters received only a passing mention. The purpose of this epilogue is to briefly update these personalities, beginning with Flood himself:

Flood lived in the Bay Area while playing for the Cardinals in the 1960s but his refusal to accept a trade to the Phillies basically ended his playing career. After retiring as a player he volunteered in Little League baseball and briefly worked as a broadcaster for the Oakland Athletics. His death in 1997, at the age of fifty-nine, drew many former major leaguers to the memorial service held for him at the First African Methodist Episcopal Church in Los Angeles. But few of the game's current stars showed up to pay their respects, which rankled one of the mourners. "He was a great man," ex–Giants shortstop Tito Fuentes said. "I'm sorry that so many of the young players who made millions, who benefited from his fight, are not here. They should be here."

Flood's lawsuit against organized baseball, although unsuccessful, set in motion a series of events that radically changed the business relationship between owners and players. Andy Messersmith, a former all-American pitcher at Cal Berkeley, was an early beneficiary of these changes. Then an All-Star with the Los Angeles Dodgers, Messersmith and Orioles lefthander Dave McNally were declared free agents by an arbitrator appointed to resolve their contract disputes. While McNally retired, Messersmith signed a lucrative deal to jump to the Atlanta Braves, and the era of multimillion-dollar player contracts had begun.

Some have blamed the parsimonious, arbitrary ways of Athletics owner Charlie Finley for poisoning player-management relations during this era. Certainly the coming of free agency led to the demise of the A's championship teams of the early 1970s, as all of their stars—Catfish Hunter, Reggie Jackson, Joe Rudi, Rollie Fingers, Vida Blue, Sal Bando, Campy Campaneris—departed Oakland for bigger paydays elsewhere. In 1980 Finley sold the club to the chairman of Levi Strauss, Walter Haas Jr., and his family.

Under the ownership of the Haas family, which has since sold the team, Oakland developed another championship club in the late 1980s. This power-house team featured a number of California-born and -bred stars: outfielder Rickey Henderson, raised in Oakland, Oakland Tech; pitcher Dave Stewart, Oakland native, St. Elizabeth's High; reliever Dennis Eckersley, Oakland native, Washington High in Fremont; third baseman Carney Lansford, San Jose native,

Wilcox High; and slugger Mark McGwire, Pomona native, Damien High in Claremont, USC. In 1988 the A's won the American League pennant and met the National League champion Dodgers in the World Series. In Game 1 an ailing Kirk Gibson hit a dramatic ninth-inning home run off Eckersley to win it for the Dodgers and propel them to an upset in the Series over the heavily favored A's. The next year Oakland returned to the title match, this time against San Francisco. After the A's won the first two games in Oakland, the Series shifted to San Francisco. A few minutes before game-time the disastrous Loma Prieta Earthquake struck the Bay Area, causing the Series to be postponed. When it resumed ten days later the Athletics swept the next two games and claimed the title.

Despite their success on the field during the Finley years, the Athletics received only paltry fan support in Oakland. This was also true of the expansion San Diego Padres, who, unlike the A's, were miserable on the field as well. In 1973, a mere four years after the Padres arrived in town, owner Arnholt Smith was on the brink of shipping the club to Washington, D.C. All its gear was reportedly loaded into moving vans and ready to head east when a financial angel by the name of Ray Kroc appeared. Kroc, the owner of the McDonald's hamburger restaurant chain and a man who had been a boyhood fan of the Chicago Cubs, stopped the vans from rolling and kept the Padres in San Diego.

In a famous incident on Opening Day of the following year, the crusty, outspoken Kroc endeared himself further to San Diego fans by publicly berating his team and apologizing for its lousy play. This same season, Ted Giannoulas, now known as the Famous Chicken, made his debut as a mascot for the Padres, his antics often giving the locals a reason to come out to see their losing team. A decade passed before the Padres turned from losers into winners. Led by manager Dick Williams (Pasadena Junior College, formerly of the Oakland Athletics), third baseman Graig Nettles (San Diego native, San Diego High), Tony Gwynn (Los Angeles native, Long Beach Poly High, and now head baseball coach at his alma mater, San Diego State), ex–Los Angeles Dodger Steve Garvey, and others, the Padres won their first National League championship in 1984. But their success came too late for Kroc to see it; he died earlier that year.

A similar fate befell the widely admired Gene Autry, who, in his nearly four decades as owner of the Angels, never won an American League pennant. "For sure, baseball has been the most exciting and frustrating experience of my life," he said once. "In the movies, I never lost a fight. In baseball, I hardly ever won one." The Disney Corporation bought the Angels after the Singing Cowboy passed on in 1998 at the age of ninety-one. Autry, who always kept score of every game he watched from his private box at the Big A, was laid to rest with an Angel schedule and an American League pass in his suit pocket.

Autry's memory was frequently evoked in Anaheim during the 2002 World Series between the Angels and San Francisco Giants. The Angels, led by such stars as outfielder Tim Salmon (Long Beach native) and third baseman Troy Glaus

(Newport Beach native, Carlsbad High, UCLA), beat the Giants in seven games to give their former owner what he never received in life: a world championship.

The '02 Giants also had a sizable California contingent, including second baseman Jeff Kent (Bellflower native, Cal Berkeley), first baseman J. T. Snow and closer Robb Nenn (former teammates at Los Alamitos High in Orange County), and Bobby's son Barry Bonds (Riverside native, Serra High in San Mateo), who has grown to become surely one of the ten best players in all of baseball history. But the Series, while ending decades of frustration for the Angels, only evoked painful memories for longtime Giants fans who remembered how close the team came to beating the Yankees in the 1962 World Series. The Giants lost that Series in seven games after Willie McCovey lined out with runners on in the bottom of the ninth inning.

Years after his retirement, McCovey, who also starred for the Padres, remains one of the most popular Giants. When Barry Bonds or anybody else hits a home run beyond the right field stands in SBC Park, the ball carries into a finger of San Francisco Bay known as McCovey Cove. (The Lefty O'Doul Bridge, named after another prominent San Francisco baseball man, carries fans across the cove into the park.) Two other popular ex-Giants remain involved with the club: Orlando Cepeda, who fulfilled Whitey Lockman's prediction and reached the Hall of Fame, operates a barbecue stand at the park; and pitcher Vida Blue is a community relations representative. Original San Francisco Giant Jimmy Davenport briefly returned to manage the Giants, while another original, Felipe Alou, replaced Dusty Baker as manager after the 2002 season. Bill Rigney, the original manager of both the Giants and Angels, who also later served as special assistant to the Oakland Athletics, died in 2001 after a long, full life lived true to his maxim: "There's no such thing as enough baseball."

Willie Mays, the greatest center fielder of the past fifty years and probably the next fifty too, was greeted coolly by local fans when the Giants arrived in San Francisco. Though a native of Alabama who played in the Negro Leagues before joining the New York Giants, Mays was, in the eyes of many San Franciscans, a New Yorker. Mays also had "the temerity"—in the words of his biographer, Charles Einstein—to play center field, the same position as homegrown legend Joe DiMaggio. The unsurpassed excellence of Mays's play would, in the end, win over even the most provincial San Franciscans, and a monumental statue of him stands at Willie Mays Plaza at the entrance to SBC Park.

By the 1970s Horace Stoneham, the man who brought the Giants to San Francisco, was struggling to pay his team's bills, partly because of the newly arrived competition from the Athletics in Oakland, but also because of the cold, windy, fan-repellant climes of Candlestick Park. The Giants might have been sold to a Canadian beer manufacturer were it not for the intervention of Mayor George Moscone, who helped persuade San Francisco financier Bob Lurie and another investor to buy the club. But like his predecessor, Lurie labored under the weight of Candlestick and himself almost unloaded the Giants to an out-of-state buyer, only to have an investment group led by Peter Magowan step in to keep them in San Francisco. Under the guidance of

Magowan, who grew up in New York City and followed the Giants when they played there, the club signed Barry Bonds and did what many people thought was impossible: build a new baseball park in downtown San Francisco to replace Candlestick.

Los Angeles Dodgers owner Walter O'Malley, the man most responsible for bringing major league baseball to the West Coast, died in 1979. Under his ownership the club won three world championships in Los Angeles (it has since won two more), while setting attendance records and becoming the first team to draw three million fans in a season. After his death his son Peter ran the team for almost twenty more years until he sold it to the Fox Corporation. For many observers the sale of the Dodgers signified the end of family ownership in major league baseball and heralded the increasing influence of corporations on the game.

Vin Scully, "the most memorable personality in Los Angeles baseball history" (so said a poll of voters), still broadcasts Dodger games as he has for the past half-century. A recent best-selling biography of Sandy Koufax, who retired in the mid-1960s, attests to his continuing popular appeal. The other half of "the greatest one-two pitching punch in the history of the game," Don Drysdale, became a well-liked and respected broadcaster after his retirement from the game in 1969. Drysdale, who died in 1993, was buried in the same Forest Hills cemetery in Glendale where Casey Stengel was laid to rest.

Drysdale was a southern California native, as was former Compton High star Duke Snider. But unlike Drysdale, Snider's best baseball days were in Brooklyn, and a couple of seasons ago the aging Duke of Flatbush paid a sentimental visit to his old stomping grounds to throw out the first pitch for a minor league game there. Don Newcombe, another Brooklyn Dodger great who came west with the team, successfully battled problems with alcoholism to counsel ballplayers such as Maury Wills, the Dodger base-stealing star of the 1960s who later managed in the majors.

Along with Wills, Drysdale, and Koufax, two other Dodger stars of the 1960s were two-time National League batting champ Tommy Davis and speedster Willie Davis, who, to borrow Satchel Paige's line about Cool Papa Bell, was "so fast he could turn out the light and jump in bed before the room got dark." Future Hall of Famer Tony Gwynn grew up in Los Angeles watching the Dodgers of this era, and he has talked about being inspired by the way Willie Davis ran the bases and flagged down fly balls in the outfield.

Ron Fairly came out of USC to make his major league breakthrough with the Dodgers in 1958; he has since become a popular broadcaster in the old Pacific Coast League city of Seattle. Another Dodger of this era, catcher John Roseboro, will be forever paired in baseball history with a Giant, pitcher Juan Marichal, who hit Roseboro over the head with a bat in a bloody argument during a 1965 game at Candlestick. Though the blow caused a two-inch cut to Roseboro's head, he managed to return to the lineup a few days later; Marichal was suspended, fined, and suffered lasting damage to his reputation. The incident, indicative of the bitter rivalry between the two teams in those days, was thought to be a major reason why Hall of Fame voters rejected Marichal in his first two years of eligibility. But Roseboro spoke out on Marichal's behalf, saying he should be forgiven and the incident should not be held against him. When the former Giant finally won election to Cooperstown, he thanked the former Dodger in his induction speech.

Spanish-language broadcaster Jaime Jarrin, who joined Rene Cardenas in the Dodger broadcast booth in 1959, became a celebrity in his own right, particularly after the arrival, in Los Angeles in 1981, of the left-handed Mexican-born pitching phenomenon Fernando Valenzuela. Jarrin acted as Valenzuela's translator with the English-speaking media, and his broadcasts of Fernando's games at Dodger Stadium—dubbed "Fernandomania" because of the intense excitement surrounding them, particularly among the Latino community—drew vast radio audiences in Mexico and Latin America. The next decade another pitching phenom, Hideo Nomo of Japan, made his debut with the Dodgers. Also immensely popular in Los Angeles—"Nomomania," they called it—the right-hander represented the beginning of an ongoing trend: the influx of Japanese and Asian baseball talent into the American major leagues. But Nomo was only the *second* Japanese-born pitcher to reach the majors; the first was Masanori Murakami, who pitched two seasons for the San Francisco Giants in the mid-sixties. The Giants signed Murakami on the advice of their scout and special assistant Cappy Harada, the former Army Lieutenant who helped organize the 1949 tour of Japan by Lefty O'Doul and the San Francisco Seals that helped erase some of the bitterness felt by Japan and the United States after World War II.

★   ★   ★   ★   ★

This book essentially ends with the arrival of the "next generation" into the major leagues. Many of these California baby boomers had high-impact major league playing careers before they moved into other areas of the game.

As a player Dusty Baker starred for the Los Angeles Dodgers; with the Giants and Cubs, he has since become one of the most respected managers in the game. Bobby Bonds, who, like Baker, grew up in Riverside, died of cancer in 2003. He was memorialized as a gifted outfielder who combined both power and speed. Jerry Manuel has become a well-regarded big league manager. Larry Bowa was a superb, hard-nosed shortstop with the Phillies and later became their manager. Buck Martinez followed a seventeen-year career as an infielder by becoming manager of the Toronto Blue Jays. All four of these men graduated from Sacramento high schools: Baker, Del Campo; Manuel, Cordova; Bowa, McClatchy; and Martinez, Elk Grove. Another pair of Sacramentans, Bob and Ken Forsch, are the only brothers in major league history to each pitch a no-hitter. Bob, a standout for many seasons with the Cardinals, threw two, and Ken did it once for the Astros.

The highlight of Dave Righetti's pitching career was his 1983 Fourth of July no-hitter for the New York Yankees against the Boston Red Sox in Yankee

Stadium. "Rags" also pitched for the Giants and Athletics before becoming pitching coach for the Giants. His counterpart in the '02 World Series was Bud Black, who pitched fifteen years in the bigs for a variety of clubs. Black is a native of San Mateo, and Righetti was born and raised in San Jose.

Long Beach native Mike Krukow won twenty games for the Giants in 1986; he has since become a broadcaster with a knack for colorful language. In Krukow-speak, a short outfield fly that drops in for a base hit is a "dead bird" or a "grenade," a lucky break is a "Happy Birthday play," a home run ball hit into the upper seats is an "upper tank dong," and a player or manager who glares at an umpire is said to give him "the stank eye." Some San Francisco fans may have given former Giants slugger Jack Clark the stank eye when he appeared in San Francisco in 2001 as the hitting coach for the Dodgers. Clark grew up in the southern part of the state, not the north; a teenager with a wild streak, he raced hot rods around the streets of Azusa.

Gary Carter and Eddie Murray were inducted into the Hall of Fame in 2003. Both are products of the talent-rich southern California playgrounds. Carter, born in Culver City, became an all-American in football at Sunny Hills High in Fullerton. A knee injury at the start of his senior season made him shift his focus to baseball, and the Montreal Expos and New York Mets, where Carter had his best years as a catcher, are glad he did. Murray's best years as an RBI man and home run hitter came with the Baltimore Orioles, but before he reached the majors he played under the watchful eye of ex–Negro Leaguer Chet Brewer and at Locke High in Los Angeles. Three other future major leaguers played at Locke with Eddie: his younger brother Rich, a first baseman with the Giants for a short stint; Darrell Jackson, a pitcher with the Twins; and Ozzie Smith.

Smith, who beat Murray into the Hall of Fame by a year, evolved into the best fielding shortstop of his time, but it did not come easy. Most scouts, bug-eyed over the power-hitting potential of his teammate, passed him over at Locke because he was too small. So Smith walked on to the freshman baseball team at Cal Poly San Luis Obispo in central California. Feeling alone and dejected, "a black player on a nearly all-white team in a nearly all-white town," he thought about quitting. But his mother would not hear of it. Marvella Smith had raised six children by herself and she wanted her son to stick it out, which he did. He kept working on his game in San Luis Obispo, including his famous pre-game somersaults, and eventually went on to attain the status of "Wizard" on the Padres and Cardinals.

Robin Yount was a highly sought-after all-around athlete from Taft High in Woodland Hills. He played twenty seasons, at shortstop and center field, all with the Brewers, and in Milwaukee he is as popular as beer. Tim Wallach led Cal State Fullerton to the 1979 College World Series championship. The Huntington Park native starred on the Expos with Gary Carter. Slugging catcher Lance Parrish of the Detroit Tigers attended Walnut High in southern California. Darrell Evans, who finished his major league career with 414 home runs, captained two state junior college championships, in baseball and basketball, for Pasadena Junior

College. Another Evans, name of Dwight (no relation), was born in Santa Monica. He covered right field for the Red Sox at Fenway Park perhaps as well as anybody had since another Californian, Jackie Jensen. Fred Lynn, the pride of El Monte High and USC, teamed up with Dwight Evans and another ex-Trojan, Bill Lee, against Joe Morgan's and Sparky Anderson's Cincinnati Reds in the 1975 World Series, one of the best ever.

Keith Hernandez was born in San Francisco and grew up on the Peninsula. Himself a wizard with a first baseman's glove, he once shared a Most Valuable Player Award with Willie Stargell. Hernandez starred with Gary Carter and Crenshaw High's Darryl Strawberry on the New York Mets. A not-to-be-forgotten member of those Mets was ageless reliever Jesse Orosco, a Santa Barbara native who, at age forty-six, was still pitching major league baseball. (Power-hitting Hall of Famer Eddie Matthews also grew up in Santa Barbara, although he hails from an earlier generation than Jesse.)

The Mets of Orosco, Strawberry, Carter, and Hernandez won the 1986 World Series after Vallejo native and former Napa High star Bill Buckner committed one of the most famous fielding errors in Series history. Playing first base for the Red Sox, he let a ground ball roll under his glove in the bottom of the tenth inning of the sixth game. The Mets scored the winning run on the play and took the Series in seven. As painful as that may have been for Buckner and the Red Sox, the California Angels had experienced similar disappointment earlier in the American League Championship Series. The hard-luck Angels were *this close* to winning their first pennant when Merced's Dave Henderson came up for Boston and hit a dramatic home run with two out in the ninth inning of Game 5. The Red Sox won that game and the next two to eliminate Anaheim, and the Angels had to wait until 2002 for redemption. The Red Sox are still waiting.

Along with Eddie Murray, Enos Cabell of the Houston Astros, George Hendrick of the Oakland Athletics and St. Louis Cardinals, Don Wilson of the Houston Astros, and Reggie Smith of the Los Angeles Dodgers and Boston Red Sox all played youth baseball in Los Angeles for Chet Brewer. Wilson pitched two no-hitters in nine years with the Astros. The switch-hitting Smith, an all-California prep athlete in baseball and football, starred on pennant- and Series-winning teams in Los Angeles. Now a batting instructor in Encino, he taught actors Barry Pepper and Thomas Jane how to hit and handle themselves like big leaguers in the Billy Crystal baseball movie, *61*. (While on the subject of movies, one of the best modern baseball films, *Bull Durham*, was written and directed by Ron Shelton, a native of Whittier who grew up in Santa Barbara. Kevin Costner, the star of *Bull Durham* and another fine baseball movie, *Field of Dreams*, attended Cal State Fullerton and gives financial support to its athletic teams. Yet another popular baseball movie, *A League of Their Own*, featured its star, Oakland's Tom Hanks, uttering one of the game's immortal lines: "There's no crying in baseball.")

Fleet outfielder Willie McGee went from Harry Ells High School in Richmond and Diablo Valley College in Pleasant Hill to star with the St. Louis

Cardinals. After McGee retired, the Cardinals hosted a day in his honor at Busch Stadium. McGee arrived in St. Louis in 1982, the same year Ozzie Smith went to the Cardinals from San Diego. Although not as spectacular a shortstop as Smith, many San Diego–area residents believe that one of their local products, Alan Trammell (Garden Grove native, Kearny High in San Diego), deserves consideration for the Hall of Fame. The Most Valuable Player of the 1984 World Series spent twenty seasons with the Detroit Tigers and went on to manage his former team. George Brett, who spent his entire twenty-one-year career with the Kansas City Royals, was one of the best third basemen of the 1970s and 1980s. A member of the Hall of Fame, he graduated from El Segundo High in Southern California.

The Boones of San Diego County are the most accomplished three-generation family in baseball history. First came Ray Boone, an American League All-Star infielder who, as a boy, shagged flies for a young Ted Williams. Ray's son Bob, a graduate of Crawford High and an all-American at Stanford, was an All-Star catcher for the Phillies and Angels and has since become a big league manager. Bob has two sons, Bret and Aaron Boone, who are both major league All-Star infielders. Bret attended El Dorado High in Placentia with Phil Nevin, who became a big league infielder with the Padres.

Jeff Burroughs of Long Beach was the first player chosen in the 1969 amateur draft. A right-handed slugger with a showcase swing, he became an All-Star in Texas and won an American League Most Valuable Player award. After retiring after sixteen seasons Burroughs did what so many other fathers do: he coached his son's Little League team. The Long Beach Little League All-Stars, starring his son Sean, won back-to-back Little League World Series championships, the first and only repeat champions in Little League history. Sean went on to star for Wilson High in Long Beach (the alma mater of his dad and Hall of Fame pitcher Bob Lemon), contributed to Team USA's gold medal–winning 2000 Olympic baseball team, and is currently an infielder with the San Diego Padres.

Like all businesses, the baseball industry goes up and down. Players come and go, teams move from city to city, ballparks are built and razed. The game has survived depression, wars, racial injustice, scandals, and crises of every description. It has been around for one hundred fifty years. As long as children and families keep playing it, there is every reason to believe it will be around for the next one hundred fifty, too.

Acknowledgments

Many people contributed to this book and made it possible. Michael Duty, the former executive director of the California Historical Society, saw the merits of my idea and gave the green light to the project. Current California Historical Society executive director Stephen Becker kept the project alive after Michael left and helped create the California Historical Society Press, the publisher of this book. Malcolm Margolin, the publisher of Heyday Books, helped steer this book to completion and showed generosity and patience throughout.

Special thanks goes to the entire Heyday staff. Jeannine Gendar, Lisa K. Manwill, Rebecca LeGates, and Kim Hogeland have displayed similar generosity and patience. Their extraordinary work in researching photographs and in other areas has contributed immensely to this book. Before she left Heyday, Karen Lichtenberg made editorial comments that proved beneficial as well.

The staff at the California Historical Society, notably its research library, was helpful to me as I poured through boxes and boxes of photographs, programs, and other material from the Dick Dobbins Collection. The Dobbins Collection is a treasure of Pacific Coast League history, and were it not for the Dobbins family's original gift to the California Historical Society, this book would have never come about. I never met the late Dick Dobbins but I know his best friend, Doug McWilliams, who was kind enough to share with me his vast Oakland baseball collection at his home and his equally vast knowledge of the game.

A number of people took the time to read portions or all of this book and made suggestions that greatly improved it. They were: Dick Beverage, Pamela Hood, Jennifer Kaiser, Lillian Kaiser, Doug McWilliams, Kerry Yo Nakagawa, Henry Reichman, Scott Thomason, Jules Tygiel, and Paul Zingg. What merit this book has is in large part due to their contributions. I made every effort to be accurate; all mistakes are of my own doing.

Dick Beverage, Doug McWilliams, Kerry Yo Nakagawa, Henry Reichman, Jules Tygiel, and Paul Zingg were all members of an advisory board for a proposed California Historical Society exhibit on California baseball, for which I served as guest curator. This book grew out of work done for that exhibit. Other members of the advisory board were: Larry Baer, Nancy Donati, Rob Elias, Bud Geracie, Hank Greenwald, Doug Harvey, Bruce Jenkins, Tom Larwin, David Lander, David Nemec, Scott Ostler, Phil Pote, Ted Robinson, Sam Regalado, Branch Rickey III, Charlie Silvera, Eric Solomon, Andy Strasberg, Bill Swank, and Tim Wiles. Although the exhibit as originally conceived never took place, their contributions to the project and this book are greatly appreciated.

Over the course of three years of research I talked and e-mailed with hundreds of people around the state and nation about California baseball. Many of these individuals graciously shared their memories and knowledge of the game with me. Mel Atwell gave me a personal tour of Pasadena, showed me his collection of House of David baseball material, and his wife, Millie, made a nice lunch for both of us. Baseball collectors Steve Niemand and Kerry Rose bought me dinner in Malibu and talked about the early Los Angeles Dodgers. Bob Reis spread his vintage Los Angeles Angels and Hollywood Stars uniforms around a room of his house and shared his considerable expertise on southern California baseball. I will forever be grateful to historian Don King at the Hall of Champions for giving me directions to Ted Williams's former boyhood home on Utah Street in San Diego. I drove over to North Park and watched a Little League team practice in the place where Ted learned his game.

At Sports Robe in Los Angeles, Alan Ruegsegger (with his son Roric) gave me a tour of his facility and a primer on baseball collecting and history. I spent a fascinating afternoon with Jim Griffith looking at nineteenth-century and early twentieth-century baseball gear at his Marin home. Besides lending his name to our advisory panel, Charlie Silvera talked to me about growing up in San Francisco and his ballplaying memories of his boyhood chums Jerry Coleman and Bobby Brown. Hank Koerper shared with me a research paper of his on Chief Meyers as well as photographs and baseball cards from the Chief's days as a New York Giant. Bill Lange Jr. gave me insights about his late father. Gil Bogen in Florida contributed immensely to my understanding of Frank Chance. Baseball historian John Spalding deserves special mention; everywhere I went in my research of nineteenth-century California baseball history, he had almost always been there before me. Private baseball collectors who also provided assistance to me include: Allen Byer, Bob Choisser, David Eskenazi, Bill Forst, Autumn Keltner, Jessica Harris, Norma Heal, Edgar Hurt Jr., Mark Macrae, Dennis Spillane, Jim Spitser, Charley Thompson, and Kathy Turner. I met some of these individuals and others at Coast League reunion meetings hosted by Dick Beverage in Carson and Bill Swank in San Diego.

Los Angeles journalist David Davis was extremely kind and helpful, giving me phone numbers and leads on people I needed to contact as well as providing articles of his own that proved useful in my research. He and Carolyn Cole of the Los Angeles Public Library provided dozens of photos of southern California ballplayers, some of which found their way into this volume and all of which were helpful in increasing my understanding of the various individuals involved.

In addition to the California Historical Society and the Los Angeles Public Library, I conducted research at several other institutions and museums. Each of the archivists I dealt with were generous with their time, notably Erin Chase of the Huntington Library, Don King and Todd Tobias of the San Diego Hall of Champions, Maria Ortiz of the Fresno Historical Society, Victoria Steele and Simon Elliot of UCLA, Dace Taub of the USC Regional History Collection,

Jim Henley at the Sacramento Archives, Tod Ruhstaller and Susan Benedetti at the Haggin Museum, and Linda Wobbe of St. Mary's College.

Many other people answered questions of mine or provided research and other assistance: Tito Avila, Amaury Pi-Gonzalez, Cesar Love, Scott Ball, Jim Kantor, Jason Pommier, Tom Dalrymple, Bill Weiss, Pamela Hood, Lillian Kaiser, Bill Swank, Kay Roper, Joe Evans, and Scott Thomason. Chuck Nan, Gary Namanny, Kin Robles, Paul Hirsch, and Jay Walker of the Society of American Baseball Research contributed research assistance to another aspect of this project. Bob and Shoba Newlon kindly let me stay at their hilltop Malibu pad on my research trips to Los Angeles. Sadly, Don Crawford, a California Historical Society trustee who was an active supporter and great believer in this project from the very beginning, died before he could see this book in print. Thanks, Don.

I apologize if I have inadvertently forgotten to mention someone who helped me during this project. In the movie *Red River*, a character in it says, "There are three times in a man's life when he deserves to be happy: when he gets married, when his children are born, and when he finishes some big project he probably never should have attempted in the first place." This book surely falls into this last category, and I never could have finished it without my wife, Jennifer. She reads everything I write and, perhaps equally important, she put up with listening to me talk about California baseball practically every day for more than two years. You're better than baseball and chocolate ice cream, my love, and that's saying something.

Kevin Nelson
Benicia, California
October 2003

Bibliography

"1930 National League Highlights." In Thorn et al., *Total Baseball*.

2000 San Diego Padres Media Guide. San Diego Padres Baseball Club.

2001 California Golden Bear Baseball Media Guide. Cal Berkeley Sports Information Department.

2001 USC Baseball Media Guide. USC Sports Information Department.

"'A' was for Ashtray." *Contra Costa Times*. Oct. 21, 2002.

Adelman, Bob, and Susan Hall. *Out of Left Field: Willie Stargell and the Pittsburgh Pirates*. New York: Two Continents Publishing Group, 1976.

Allen, Maury. *Damn Yankee: The Billy Martin Story*. New York: Times Books, 1980.

Almond, Elliott. "Baseball Breaks Another Barrier." *San Jose Mercury News*, May 13, 2003.

Ambrose, Stephen E. *Nothing Like It in the World: The Men Who Built the Transcontinental Railroad*. New York: Simon and Schuster, 2000.

Anderson, Kelli. "Back to the Boardwalk." *Via*, May/June 2003.

Anderson, Sparky, and Dan Ewald. *Sparky!* New York: Prentice-Hall, 1990.

Asinof, Eliot. *Eight Men Out: The Black Sox and the 1919 World Series*. Evanston, Ill.: Holtzman Press, 1963.

Associated Press. "Morgan Eulogizes Stargell." *San Francisco Chronicle*. April 15, 2001.

Autry, Gene, and Mickey Herskowitz. *Back in the Saddle Again*. Garden City, N.Y.: Doubleday, 1978.

Bamberger, Michael. "Dom DiMaggio." *Sports Illustrated*, July 2, 2001.

Bartlett, Arthur. *Baseball and Mr. Spalding: The History and Romance of Baseball*. New York: Farrar, Straus, and Young, 1951.

Berlage, Gai Ingham. "Women, Baseball, and the American Dream." In Elias, *Baseball and the American Dream*.

Beverage, Richard E. *The Angels: Los Angeles in the Pacific Coast League, 1919–1957*. Placentia, Calif.: Deacon Press, 1981.

Bitker, Steve. *The Original San Francisco Giants*. Foreword by Peter Magowan. Champaign, Ill.: Sports Publishing, Inc., 1998.

Bjarkman, Peter C. "Six-Pointed Diamonds." *Elysian Fields Quarterly*, Fall 1992.

———. "The Cuban Comet." *Elysian Fields Quarterly*, Winter 2002.

Blount, Roy, Jr. "How DiMaggio Made It Look Easy." In Okrent and Lewine, *The Ultimate Baseball Book*.

"Blue Chip Bonds." 2001 San Francisco Giants Yearbook. San Francisco Giants Baseball Club.

Brock, Darryl. *If I Never Get Back*. New York: Ballantine, 1989.

Brock, Darryl, and Robert Elias. "To Elevate the Game: Women and Early Baseball." In Elias, *Baseball and the American Dream.*

Brokaw, Tom. *The Greatest Generation.* New York: Random House, 1998.

Broman, Mickey. *California Ghost Town Trails.* Baldwin Park, Calif.: Gem Guides Books, 1992.

Bryant, Howard. *Shut Out.* New York: Routledge, 2002.

Bush, David, and Dwight Chapin. "It Musta Been Rigged." *San Francisco Chronicle,* Feb. 21, 2001.

Calabro, Marian. *The Perilous Journey of the Donner Party.* New York: Clarion Books, 1999.

California Historical Society. "The California Gold Rush." History through the Collections Series. San Francisco: California Historical Society, 2002.

Cartwright, Anne. "Cartwright's Trip West." *The National Pastime: A Review of Baseball History,* 2002.

Center, Bill. "Memory of a Lifetime." *San Diego Union-Tribune,* Aug. 12, 2001.

———. "A Baseball Original, Padres' 'Mr. Indispensable' Dead at 83." In "Echoes from Lane Field," June 2002. Originally published in the *San Diego Union-Tribune.*

Chanin, Abe S. "Golden Memories." NCAA College World Series Program, Host Communications, 1996.

Chapin, Dwight. "Yankees Great Crosetti Dies at Age 91." SFGate.com, Feb. 13, 2002.

"Chris Cannizzaro." 1971 San Diego Padres Program. San Diego Padres Baseball Club.

"Coaches, The." 1969 Inaugural Yearbook, San Diego Padres. San Diego Padres Baseball Club.

Cobb, Sally Wright, and Mark Willems. *The Brown Derby Restaurant.* New York: Rizzoli, 1996.

Cobb, Ty, and Al Stump. *My Life in Baseball.* New York: Doubleday, 1961.

"Commercial Aviation." The History of Aviation. www.history.sandiego.edu. March 21, 2003.

Conner, Floyd. *This Date in Sports History.* New York: Warner Books, 1989.

Cramer, Richard Ben. *Joe DiMaggio: The Hero's Life.* New York: Simon and Schuster, 2000.

Creamer, Robert. *Stengel: His Life and Times.* New York: Simon and Schuster, 1984.

Crisser, Harrington E., Jr. "Baseball and the Armed Services." In Thorn et al., *Total Baseball.*

"Curtis Charles Flood." 1999 Induction Program. Baseball Reliquary, Pasadena, Calif.

Davis, David. "Straight, No Chaser," *LA Weekly,* Aug. 11–17, 1995.

———. "Remembering Mr. Brewer," *LA Weekly,* June 6–12, 1997.

———. "A Field in the Desert That Felt Like Home." *Sports Illustrated,* circa 1999.

Deane, Bill. *Top Ten Baseball Shortstops.* Berkeley Heights, N.J.: Enslow, 1999.

Dickey, Glenn. *Champions.* Chicago, Ill.: Triumph, 2002.

DiMaggio, Dom, with Bill Gilbert. *Real Grass, Real Heroes.* New York: Zebra Books, 1990.

Dobbins, Dick. *The Grand Minor League.* Emeryville, Calif.: Woodford Press, 1999.

Dobbins, Dick, Drew Bruno, and Nancy O'Brien. "A Century of A's Baseball." Oakland Athletics Official Yearbook, 2000.

Dobbins, Dick, and Jon Twichell. *Nuggets on the Diamond*. San Francisco: Woodford Press, 1994.

Donovan, Richard. "The Fabulous Satchel Paige." In Einstein, *The Baseball Reader*. Originally published in *Collier's*, 1953.

Dunne, John Gregory. "Keeping Score." *New Yorker,* Oct. 30, 2000.

Edelman, Rob. *Great Baseball Films*. New York: Citadel Press, 1994.

Einstein, Charles. *Willie's Time*. New York: J. B. Lippincott, 1979.

Einstein, Charles, ed. *The Second Fireside Book of Baseball*. New York: Simon and Schuster, 1958.

———. *The Baseball Reader*. New York: Lippincott and Crowell, 1980.

Elias, Robert, ed. *Baseball and the American Dream*. Armonk, N.Y.: M. E. Sharpe, 2001.

Eskenazi, Gerald. *Bill Veeck: A Baseball Legend*. New York: McGraw-Hill, 1988.

Faraudo, Jeff. "Babe, Gehrig Took Bay Area by Storm." *Oakland Tribune,* Sept. 24, 2002.

Felber, Bill. *125 Years of Professional Baseball*. Chicago: Triumph, 1994.

Felker, Clay. *Casey Stengel's Secret*. New York: Walker and Company, 1961.

Figuracion, Inigo. "Qualcomm/Jack Murphy/San Diego Stadium: What's In a Name?" About San Diego. www.sandiego.about.com/library/blsbsd.htm. June 10, 2003.

Fimrite, Ron. *Way to Go! Heroes and Legends of Bay Area Sports.* Mill Valley, Calif.: Tarquin, 1978.

———. "This Portrait of an American Icon Is No Pretty Picture." *Sports Illustrated,* 2000.

Fine, David. "The Emergence of Los Angeles as Literary Territory." *California History,* Spring 2000.

Fleming, G. H. *The Unforgettable Season*. New York: Holt, Rinehart, and Winston, 1981.

Flood, Curt, and Richard Carter. *The Way It Is*. New York: Trident Press, 1970.

Ford, Richard, and Glenn Stout, eds. *The Best American Sports Writing 1999*. Boston: Houghton Mifflin, 1999.

Franks, Joel. "California Baseball's Mixed Multitudes." In Elias, *Baseball and the American Dream*.

Friedman, Myles E. "Spring Training." In Thorn et al., *Total Baseball*.

Gabriel, Daniel. "Getting a Grip on the Hard One." *Elysian Fields Quarterly,* Winter 2002.

Gardner, Martin, ed. *The Annotated Casey at the Bat*. New York: Dover, 1995.

Gergen, Joe. "Duke of Flatbush Returns Home." *Los Angeles Times,* July 25, 2002. Originally published in *Newsday.*

Gershman, Michael, David Pietrusza, and Matthew Silverman. *Baseball: The Biographical Encyclopedia*. New York: Total Sports, 2000.

Golenbock, Peter. *Bums: An Oral History of the Brooklyn Dodgers*. New York: Putnam, 1984.

———. *Amazin'*. New York: St. Martin's Press, 2002.

Greenwalt, Emmett A. *The Point Loma Community in California, 1897–1942*. Berkeley: University of California Press, 1955.

Guhan, Carol. "History of Santa Catalina Island." Ultimate Insider's Guide to Santa Catalina. www.eCatalina.com, 2002.

Gutman, Dan. *Baseball Babylon*. New York: Penguin, 1992.

Halberstam, David. *Summer of '49*. New York: Avon Books, 1989.

Harris, Beth. "Autry Leaves Legacy of Love with Angels." Associated Press, *Contra Costa Times,* Oct. 19, 2002.

Hart, James D. *A Companion to California*. Berkeley: University of California Press, 1987.

Hawkins, Joel, and Terry Bertolino. *The House of David Baseball Team*. Chicago: Arcadia, 2000.

Henderson, Rickey, with John Shea. *Off Base: Confessions of a Thief.* New York: HarperCollins, 1992.

Hendsch, David A. "Fresno Shows the Japanese How to Do It: Baseball in the Making." In *Northern California Baseball History*. Cleveland, Ohio: Society of American Baseball Research, 1998.

Henstell, John. "A Sky-Minded City." In Meyer, "Los Angeles, 1781–1981," *California History*.

Herbold, John. "Wrigley Field in Los Angeles: One Special Diamond." *Collegiate Baseball*, April 6, 2001.

Highfill, Bob. "A Legend As an Athlete and Person." *Stockton Record,* Feb. 13, 2002.

"Highlights of Ted Williams' Life." *San Diego Union Tribune*. www.signonsandiego.com. July 7, 2002.

Hill, Kimi Kodani. *Topaz Moon: Chiura Obata's Art of the Internment*. Berkeley: Heyday Books, 2000.

Holiday, J. S. *The World Rushed In*. New York: Simon and Schuster, 1981.

Holtzman, Jerome. *No Cheering in the Press Box*. New York: Henry Holt, 1995.

Honig, Donald. *The October Heroes*. New York: Simon and Schuster, 1979.

Hopper, Hedda. *From Under My Hat*. New York: Doubleday, 1952.

Huff, Ryan. "The Wizard of Poly." *San Luis Obispo Tribune,* Jan. 9, 2002.

Hutchinson, W. H. "The Genie of Yang-Na." In Meyer, "Los Angeles, 1781–1981," *California History*.

Inada, Lawson Fusao, ed. *Only What We Could Carry: The Japanese American Internment Experience*. Berkeley: Heyday Books, 2000.

"Jack Roosevelt Robinson." 2000 UCLA Media Guide. UCLA Sports Information Department.

James, Bill. *The Politics of Glory*. New York: Macmillan, 1994.

Jenkins, Chris. "Splendid Splinter Cut Wide Swath from Coast to Coast." *San Diego Union-Tribune,* July 10, 1992.

Johnstone, Jay, and Rick Talley. *Over the Edge*. New York: Bantam, 1987.

Kahn, Roger. *The Boys of Summer*. New York: Harper and Row, 1972.

Kempner, Aviva. "The Life and Times of Hank Greenberg." Documentary film. 1999.

Kiersh, Edward. *Where Have You Gone, Vince DiMaggio?* New York: Bantam, 1983.

Kirkley, Evelyn A. "Images of Women in Point Loma Theosophy." *Journal of San Diego History,* Winter 1997.

Klages, Ellen. "The Girls of Summer." Exploratorium. www.exploratorium.edu. April 16, 2003.

Klein, Gary. "College World Series Spotlight: Rod Dedeaux." NCAA College World Series Program, 1996.

Koerper, Henry. "The Catcher Was a Cahuilla: A Remembrance of John Tortes Meyers." Manuscript, 1998.

Kohout, Martin Donnell. *Hal Chase: The Defiant Life and Turbulent Times of Baseball's Biggest Crook.* Jefferson, N.C.: McFarland and Company, 2001.

Kunz, Bill. "Cal's 1947 NCAA Champion Baseball Team." Cal Baseball Alumni Day Program, 1987.

Kurzman, Dan. *Disaster! The Great San Francisco Earthquake and Fire of 1906.* New York: HarperCollins, 2001.

Larwin, Tom. Pacific Coast League Historical Society presentation, Hall of Champions, San Diego, Feb. 23, 2002.

Lasorda, Tommy, and David Fisher. *The Artful Dodger.* New York: Arbor House, 1985.

Lavoie, Steven. "St. Mary's Has Sent Players to Majors for 100 Years." In *Northern California Baseball History.* Cleveland, Ohio: Society of American Baseball Research, 1998.

———. "When Baseball Discovered Asians." *Oakland Tribune,* n.d.

Lee, Bill, and Dick Lally. *The Wrong Stuff.* New York: Viking Penguin, 1984.

Leutzinger, Richard. *Lefty O'Doul: The Story of the Hall of Fame's Missing Star.* Carmel, Calif.: Carmel Bay, 1997.

Libby, Bill, and Vida Blue. *Vida: His Own Story.* Englewood Cliffs, N.J.: Prentice-Hall, 1972.

Linn, Ed. *Hitter: The Life and Turmoils of Ted Williams.* New York: Harcourt Brace, 1993.

Lockwood, Wayne. "Old Playground Memories Linger for Ted and Pals." *San Diego Union-Tribune,* July 9, 1992.

Love, Cesar. "Mike Garcia: Cleveland Indians Pitcher of the 1950s." *El Tecolote,* July 2001.

Margolin, Malcolm. "Baseball and Bird Songs: Remembering John Andreas." *News from Native California,* Winter 2002/03.

Martin, Billy, with Phil Pepe. *BillyBall.* New York: Doubleday, 1987.

McDevitt, Matthew. "The First Century of St. Mary's College: 1863–1963." St. Mary's College, Moraga, Calif., 1964.

McGraw, Tug, and Joseph Durso. *Screwball.* Boston: Houghton Mifflin, 1974.

Meany, Tom. *The Magnificent Yankees.* New York: Grosset and Dunlap, 1956.

Meyer, Larry L., ed. "Los Angeles, 1781–1981." *California History,* California Historical Society, 1981.

Miller, Max. *I Cover the Waterfront.* New York: E. P. Dutton, 1932.

Moore, Jim, and Natalie Vermilyea. *Ernest Thayer's "Casey at the Bat."* Jefferson, N.C.: McFarland and Company, 1994.

Morgan, Joe, and David Falkner. *Joe Morgan: A Life in Baseball.* New York: W. W. Norton, 1993.

Murphy, Brian. "Ex-Seals Star Fain Dies." *San Francisco Chronicle,* Oct. 20, 2001.

Nachman, Gerald. *Raised on Radio.* New York: Pantheon Books, 1998.

Nakagawa, Kerry Yo. *Through a Diamond: 100 Years of Japanese American Baseball.* San Francisco: Rudi Publishing, 2001.

Nasaw, David. *The Chief: The Life of William Randolph Hearst.* Boston: Houghton Mifflin, 2000.

Nelson, Kevin. "Pioneer in Print." *Women's Sports,* 1981.

———. *Baseball's Greatest Quotes.* New York: Fireside, 1982.

———. *The Greatest Stories Ever Told about Baseball.* New York: Perigee, 1986.

Nemec, David. *The Great American Baseball Team Book.* New York: Penguin, 1992.

———. *The Great Encyclopedia of Minor League Baseball.* New York: Donald I. Fine, 1997.

Nettles, Graig, and Peter Golenbock. *Balls.* New York: Pocket, 1985.

Newhan, Ross. *The Anaheim Angels: A Complete History.* New York: Hyperion, 2000.

Okanes, Jonathan. "Stargell's Death Felt in East Bay." *Contra Costa Times,* April 10, 2001.

Okrent, Daniel. "Scout's Honor." *Sports Illustrated,* Sept. 18, 2000.

Okrent, Daniel, and Harris Lewine. *The Ultimate Baseball Book.* Boston: Houghton Mifflin, 1981.

Ostler, Scott. "Rig's Lessons of Life." *San Francisco Chronicle,* Feb. 23, 2001.

———. "Angels Put Sad History Behind Them." *San Francisco Chronicle,* Oct. 28, 2002.

Pearlman, Jeff. "My, How He's Grown." *Sports Illustrated,* March 18, 2002.

Peterson, Harold. *The Man Who Invented Baseball.* New York: Charles Scribner's Sons, 1973.

Peterson, Robert W. *Only the Ball Was White.* Old Tappan, N.J.: Prentice-Hall, 1970.

Pinelli, John J. "From San Francisco Sandlots to the Big Leagues: Babe Pinelli." In Elias, *Baseball and the American Dream.*

Pitt, Leonard. "The Modernization of a Cowtown." In Meyer, "Los Angeles, 1781–1981," *California History.*

Quay, Jim (Executive Director, California Council for the Humanities), Letter to the Editor, *New Yorker,* April 8, 2002.

Rains, Rob. *Mark McGwire.* New York: St. Martin's Press, 1998.

Rampersad, Arnold. *Jackie Robinson.* New York: Ballantine, 1997.

Rawls, James J., and Richard Orsi, eds. *A Golden State: Mining and Economic Development in Gold Rush California.* Introduction "A Golden State: An Introduction" by James J. Rawls. 1998–1999. California Historical Society and University of California Press, Winter 1988/99.

Ray, Bob. "Joe E. Brown Stars as Sheiks and Reds Split." *Echoes from Lane Field,* Vol. 7, Issue 3, Sept. 2001. Originally published in the *Los Angeles Times,* Sept. 23, 1935.

Reagan, Ronald. *An American Life.* New York: Simon and Schuster, 1990.

Regalado, Samuel O. "Dodgers Beisbol Is on the Air." *California History,* California Historical Society, Fall 1995.

————. *Viva Baseball! Latin Major Leaguers and Their Special Hunger.* Chicago: University of Illinois, 1999.

Reynolds, David West. *Apollo: The Journey to the Moon.* San Diego: Tehabi Books, 2000.

Ritter, Lawrence. *The Glory of Their Times.* New York: Macmillan, 1966.

————. *Lost Ballparks.* New York: Penguin, 1992.

Robinson, Frank, with Al Silverman. *My Life Is Baseball.* New York: Doubleday, 1968.

Robinson, Jackie, with Alfred Duckett. *I Never Had It Made.* New York: Ecco, 1995.

Rogers, Paul. "A Conversation with Bobby Brown." *Elysian Fields Quarterly,* Summer 1999.

Rushin, Steve. "The Most Artful Dodger." *Sports Illustrated,* Aug. 19, 2002.

Rust, Art, Jr. *Recollections of a Baseball Junkie.* New York: Sports Channel, 1985.

Ruth, George Herman. *Babe Ruth's Own Book of Baseball.* New York: Putnam, 1928.

Salan, Tony. "Walter 'Pete' Deas on Billy Hebert." *Mudville Times,* Spring 2000.

Salvaressa, Sandra. "Fond Memories of Grandpa Sam." *Contra Costa Times,* June 1, 2002.

"San Diego Padres." Baseball Library. www.baseballlibrary.com. June 10, 2003.

Schraff, Anne E. *The Great Depression and New Deal.* New York: Franklin Watts, 1990.

Schroeder, W. R. Bill. "The Story of the California League." California League baseball program, 1994.

Silverman, Brian, ed. *Going, Going, Gone.* New York: HarperCollins, 2000.

Smith, Ken. *Baseball's Hall of Fame.* New York: A. S. Barnes, 1947.

Society of American Baseball Research, San Diego Chapter. "Most Influential Figures in San Diego Baseball History." Research paper, 2000.

"Sons of Sacramento." *Contra Costa Times,* Feb. 25, 2001.

Spada, James. *Ronald Reagan: His Life in Pictures.* New York: St. Martin's Press, 2000.

Spalding, Albert Goodwill. *America's National Game.* 1911. Reprint, with a foreword by Benjamin G. Rader, Lincoln, Nebr.: University of Nebraska Press, 1992.

Spalding, John E. *Always on Sunday: The California Baseball League, 1886–1915.* Manhattan, Kans.: Ag Press, 1992.

————. *Sacramento Solons and Senators: Baseball in California's Capital, 1886 to 1976.* Manhattan, Kans.: Ag Press, 1995.

————. *Pacific Coast League Stars, Volume II, 1903 to 1957.* Manhattan, Kans.: Ag Press, 1997.

————. *A Century of Sports in Santa Clara County.* Manhattan, Kans.: Ag Press, 2000.

Steinbeck, John. *Bombs Away: The Story of a Bomber Team.* New York: Viking Press, 1942.

Stump, Al. "Ty Cobb's Wild 10-Month Fight to Live." In Einstein, *The Baseball Reader.*

Sullivan, Neil J. *The Dodgers Move West.* New York: Oxford, 1987.

Sultzberger, C. L. *American Heritage Picture History of World War II.* David McCullough, ed. New York: Simon and Schuster, 1966.

Swank, Bill. *Echoes from Lane Field: A History of the San Diego Padres, 1936–1957.* Paducah, Ky.: Turner Publishing, 1997.

———."Black Balled." *U.S. Athletics*, 2000.

Tennis, Nelson. "Cooperstown a Locke for Murray." CalHiSports.com. May 2, 2003.

Thayer, Ernest Lawrence. *Casey at the Bat: A Centennial Edition.* Afterword by Donald Hall. Boston: David R. Godine, 1988.

Thomas, Bob. "Flashy Hollywood Funerals History, but Graves Popular." Associated Press, *San Francisco Chronicle,* June 1, 2001.

Thomas, Henry W. *Walter Johnson: Baseball's Big Train.* Lincoln, Nebr.: University of Nebraska Press, 1995.

Thorn, John. "Our Game" and "The True Father of Baseball." In Thorn et al., *Total Baseball.*

Thorn, John, Peter Palmer, Michael Gershman, and David Pietrusza. *Total Baseball.* 6th ed. New York: Total Sports, 1999.

Tucker, Bud. "Suddenly the Padres Are Real." San Diego Padres Inaugural Yearbook, 1969.

Tully, Jeff. "Magical Baseball Tour." *Burbank Leader,* May 19–20, 2001.

Tygiel, Jules. *Baseball's Great Experiment: Jackie Robinson and His Legacy.* New York: Oxford, 1997.

———.*Past Time,* New York: Oxford University Press, 2000.

Updike, John. "Hub Fans Bid Kid Adieu." In Einstein, *The Baseball Reader.* Originally published in *New Yorker,* 1960.

Veeck, Bill, and Ed Linn. *Veeck as in Wreck.* Chicago, Ill.: University of Chicago Press, 1962.

Verge, Arthur C. "George Freeth, King of the Surfers and California's Forgotten Hero." *California History,* California Historical Society, Summer/Fall 2001.

Weaver, John. "The Laboratory of Marvels." In Meyer, "Los Angeles, 1781–1981," *California History.*

Weiss, Bill. "The California League in Professional Baseball." In *Northern California Baseball History.* Cleveland, Ohio: Society of American Baseball Research, 1998.

Wiles, Tim. "1888: When It All Began." *Mudville Times,* 2000.

Will, George. *Men at Work: The Craft of Baseball.* New York: Macmillan, 1990.

Williams, Ted, with John Underwood. *My Turn at Bat: The Story of My Life.* New York: Simon and Schuster, 1969.

Willman, Tom. "The Baseball Journey of Jimmie Reese." In *Northern California Baseball History.* Cleveland, Ohio: Society of American Baseball Research, 1998.

Zingg, Paul J. *Harry Hooper: An American Baseball Life.* Chicago: University of Illinois, 1993.

Zingg, Paul J., and Mark Medeiros. *Runs, Hits, and An Era: The Pacific Coast League, 1903–1958.* Chicago: University of Illinois Press, 1994.

Museum and Personal Collections

Bill Lange Scrapbooks

Bob Reis Collection, Los Angeles

Dick Dobbins Collection, California Historical Society, San Francisco

Doug McWilliams Collection, Oakland, Calif.

Fresno Historical Society

Haggin Museum, Stockton, Calif.

Huntington Library Collection, San Marino, Calif.

Los Angeles Public Library Collection

Martinez Museum, Martinez, Calif.

Mel Atwell Collection, Walnut, Calif.

Sacramento Archives and Museum Collection Center

San Diego Hall of Champions

USC Regional History Collection, University of Southern California, Los Angeles

USC Special Collections, University of Southern California, Los Angeles

Web Sites

American Legion Baseball (www.baseball.legion.org)

Baseball Library (www.baseballlibrary.com)

California League (www.californialeague.com)

Hallowed Ground, Baseball's Historical Places (www.hallowedground.org), July 2002

Hickok Sports (www.hickoksports.com)

Little League Baseball (www.littleleague.org)

Major League Baseball (www.mlb.com)

Minor League Baseball (www.milb.com)

Pitch Black Baseball, Negro Leagues (www.pitchblackbaseball.com)

Source Notes

Introduction

More major league ballplayers: Charles C. Alexander, Baseball Library, www.baseballlibrary.com/**Rickey chose Robinson:** Tygiel, *Baseball's Great Experiment,* p. 64/**His father was an Army veteran:** Linn, *Hitter,* p. 29/**Of Hispanic descent:** Williams and Underwood, *My Turn at Bat,* p. 2/**Disapproved of his sons:** DiMaggio and Gilbert, *Real Grass, Real Heroes,* p. 14/**Heart of organized baseball activity:** Dobbins and Twichell, *Nuggets on the Diamond,* p. 25/**Feature [sports] regularly:** Nasaw, *The Chief,* p. 76/**Friend from Harvard:** Gardner, *The Annotated Casey at the Bat,* p. 2/**Most popular American poems:** Hall, Afterword to *Casey at the Bat* by Thayer, p. 23/**Some have claimed that Stockton:** Moore and Vermilyea, *Ernest Thayer's "Casey at the Bat,"* p. 234–35/ **Repeatedly denied:** Ibid., p. 315/**More than half a century in Glendale:** Creamer, *Stengel,* p. 170/**In Oakland where Stengel met Billy:** Allen, *Damn Yankee,* p. 36/**Like father and son:** Ibid., p. 45/**Wherever Martin managed:** Martin and Pepe, *BillyBall,* p. 43/**Railroad in 1869 changed all this:** Ambrose, *Nothing Like It in the World,* p. 369/**The sport's first professionals:** Brock and Elias, "To Elevate the Game: Women and Early Baseball," p. 231/**First Issei baseball club:** Nakagawa, *Through a Diamond,* p. 32/**Part of state's baseball mix:** Ibid., p. 30/**"Baseball Crazy Day":** Ibid., p. 35/**Mother was a Cahuilla:** Koerper, "The Catcher Was a Cahuilla," p. 3/**More than thirty Hall of Famers:** Tennis, "Cooperstown a Locke For Murray" /**His teen years in the oil fields:** H. W. Thomas, *Walter Johnson,* p. 7–8/**Play the ponies:** Fleming, *The Unforgettable Season,* p. 13/**An orange ranch:** Gil Bogen (Chance biographer) to author, early 2002/**An Iowa sportscaster:** Reagan, *An American Life,* p. 77/**Have always outnumbered:** Quay, Letter to the Editor/

Chapter 1

Born on Lombardy Street: Cartwright, "Cartwright's Trip West," p. 14/**A volunteer firefighter:** H. Peterson, *The Man Who Invented Baseball,* p. 1/**A bat and ball game:** Paul J. Zingg (baseball historian) to author, Feb. 9, 2002/**What the Knickerbockers did:** Thorn, "The True Father of Baseball," p. 110/**"The father" of modern baseball:** Smith, *Baseball's Hall of Fame,* p. 85/**People poured into California:** Holiday, *The World Rushed In,* p. 37/**Migration unlike any before:** Ibid., p. 452/**The headline-grabbing announcement:** California Historical Society, "The California Gold Rush," p. 3/**The New York *Herald* wrote:** Holiday, *The World Rushed In,* p. 48/**Wooden wagons actually became part of the game:** Jim Griffith (baseball collector) to author, early 2002/**Cartwright had brought with him:** H. Peterson, *The Man Who Invented Baseball,* p. 110/**Apparently tossed the ball:** Cartwright, "Cartwright's Trip West," p. 14/**After crossing the Sierra Nevada:** H. Peterson, *The Man Who Invented Baseball,* p. 164/**Seemed to be in motion:** Holiday, *The World Rushed In,* p. 300/**The headquarters city:** Ibid., p. 301/**Wagon train had collapsed:** Cartwright, "Cartwright's Trip West," p. 15/**A harrowing story:** H. Peterson, *The Man Who Invented Baseball,* pp. 166–67/**After less than a week:** Ibid., p. 172/**Baseball's Johnny Appleseed:** Ibid., p. 109/**One New York Knickerbocker:** Ibid., p. 168/**Carried an intriguing item:** Zingg, *Harry Hooper,* p. 44

Chapter 2

Sacramento can lay claim: Dobbins and Twichell, *Nuggets on the Diamond*, p. 15/**Caused feathers to be ruffled:** Ibid., p. 15 /**One of the founders:** Dobbins and Twichell, *Nuggets on the Diamond*, p. 33/**The first organized baseball game:** J. E. Spalding, *Always on Sunday*, p. 9/**A nasty squabble:** Dobbins and Twichell, *Nuggets on the Diamond*, p. 17/**The core likely contained:** A. G. Spalding, *America's National Game*, p. 510/ **Fielding gloves were also unheard of:** Jim Griffith (baseball collector) to author, early 2002/**The first state baseball tournament:** Dobbins and Twichell, *Nuggets on the Diamond*, p. 17/**May have traveled via stagecoach:** Hart, *A Companion to California*, pp. 75–76/**In periods of forced idleness:** Paul J. Zingg (baseball historian) to author, early 2003/**A boost in activity:** Brock and Elias, "To Elevate the Game, " p. 227/**The first Pacific Base Ball Convention:** Zingg and Medeiros, *Runs, Hits, and An Era*, p. 2/**The Shepard brothers:** 1866 Photograph, Dick Dobbins Collection/**The second Pacific Base Ball convention:** J. E. Spalding, *Always on Sunday*, p. 9/**Ballplayers during this era:** Dobbins and Twichell, *Nuggets on the Diamond*, p. 19/**The park opened on Thanksgiving:** J. E. Spalding, *Always on Sunday*, p. 10/**National pride and self-interest:** Ambrose, *Nothing Like It in the World*, p. 194/**"The grandest and noblest":** Ibid., p. 82/**Thousands of Chinese immigrants:** Ibid., p. 152/**The hammer hit the spike:** Ibid., p. 364/**The effect of the railroad:** Ibid., p. 369/**A game practiced by amateurs:** Nemec, *The Great Encyclopedia of Minor League Baseball*, p. ix/**Pounded amateur teams:** Brock and Elias, "To Elevate the Game," p. 231

Chapter 3

The most glamorous baseball team: Brock and Elias, "To Elevate the Game," p. 231/**With the financial backing of the city of Cincinnati:** Gershman, Pietrusza, and Silverman, *Baseball*, p. 1257/**A welcoming committee greeted them:** J. E. Spalding, *Always on Sunday*, p. 10/**The talk of the city:** Ibid., p. 10/**The morning *Chronicle*:** Ibid., p. 10/**Bright baseball ideas:** Gershman, Pietrusza, and Silverman, *Baseball*, p. 1256/ **"May they never meet":** J. E. Spalding, *Always on Sunday*, p. 10/**The initial reaction:** Zingg and Medeiros, *Runs, Hits, and An Era*, p.3/**The mother's milk:** Asinof, *Eight Men Out*, p. 10/**Supposedly fired pistols:** Dobbins and Twichell, *Nuggets on the Diamond*, p. 18/**A small but noteworthy event:** Photograph caption, San Diego Hall of Champions Collection/**People cleared off:** Salvaressa, "Fond Memories of Grandpa Sam"/**First organized baseball league:** Dobbins and Twichell, *Nuggets on the Diamond*, p. 25/**A rival to the Pacific:** J. E. Spalding, *Always on Sunday*, pp. 11–12/**Skilled enough to beat:** Zingg and Medeiros, *Runs, Hits, and An Era*, pp. 46–47/**Mentor and advisor:** Nemec, *The Great Encyclopedia of Minor League Baseball*, p. 152/**A native of San Jose:** J. E. Spalding, *A Century of Sports in Santa Clara County*, p. 7/**Father was English:** J. E. Spalding, *Always on Sunday*, p. 15/**Played for St. Mary's:** Zingg, *Harry Hooper*, p. 47

Chapter 4

One fine day in the fall of 1886: Moore and Vermilyea, *Ernest Thayer's "Casey at the Bat,"* p. 178/**Received a telegram:** Gardner, *The Annotated Casey at the Bat*, p. 2/**Son of a well-to-do:** Ibid., p. 2/**"Phinney" to his friends:** Moore and Vermilyea, *Ernest Thayer's "Casey at the Bat,"* p. 95/**Who had come west:** Nasaw, *The Chief*, p. 3/**Remove George's name:** Ibid., p. 63/**Made financial donations:** Ibid., p. 33/**Lots of drunken parties:** Ibid., p. 35/**Crisply parted hair:** Photograph, *Ernest Thayer's "Casey at the Bat,"* by Moore and Vermilyea, front page/**Thayer stayed at first:** Moore and Vermilyea, *Ernest Thayer's "Casey at the Bat,"*

p. 186/**Took a liking to him:** Ibid., p. 194/**"Journalists very much like cattle":** Ibid., p. 197/**Inaugurated a new park:** J. E. Spalding, *Always on Sunday,* p. 27/**Boost the paper's circulation:** Nasaw, *The Chief,* p. 76/**Splashed more crime stories:** Ibid., p. 76/**Friction below the surface:** Thayer Letter, *Ernest Thayer's "Casey at the Bat,"* by Moore and Vermilyea, p. 199/**"No longer a boy":** Ibid., p. 199/**"On a Frisco paper":** Ibid., p. 200/**Snowflake Park:** description attached to 1887 baseball, Sacramento Archives and Museum Collection Center/**Tailor and clothing shop:** Business card, Doug McWilliams Collection, Oakland/**A new competitive league:** J. E. Spalding, *Always on Sunday,* pp. 27–28/**Baseball on Sunday:** Ibid., p. 23/**"Hippodroming":** Nemec, *The Great Encyclopedia of Minor League Baseball,* pp. 5–6/**His charge was to clean house:** J. E. Spalding, *Always on Sunday,* p. 14/**The deciding tilt:** Advertising broadsheet, Steve Niemand Collection, Los Angeles/**Lorrigan[…]took the hill:** J. E. Spalding, *Always on Sunday,* p. 31/**Reading W. S. Gilbert:** Gardner, *The Annotated Casey at the Bat,* p. 177/**"The Shocking Tale":** Ibid., p. 204/**A sea ballad:** Ibid., p. 205/**One authority on Thayer says:** Ibid., p. 2/**Writing unsigned editorials:** Moore and Vermilyea, *Ernest Thayer's "Casey at the Bat,"* p. 233/**Bottom of page four:** Gardner, *The Annotated Casey at the Bat,* p. 208/**A happy accident:** Wiles, "1888: When It All Began," p. 9/**Commanding figure:** Hopper, *From Under My Hat,* p. 10/**The "first major expansion":** Jules Tygiel (baseball historian) to author, early 2002/**A rave review:** Gardner, *The Annotated Casey at the Bat,* p. 8/ **"If the matter were of any importance":** A. G. Spalding, *America's National Game,* p. 452/**A hard-drinking San Francisco–born:** Ibid., p. 453/**Almost any nineteenth-century California town:** Tod Ruhstaller (Director, Haggin Museum) to author, early 2001/**A scrappy club:** Moore and Vermilyea, *Ernest Thayer's "Casey at the Bat,"* pp. 234–35/**"There is no story":** Ibid., p. 315/**The shy bachelor:** Ibid., p. 305/**"More pleasure than annoyance":** Gardner, *The Annotated Casey at the Bat,* p. 9/ **Harvard graduating class:** Ibid., p. 10/**"Too weak":** Ibid., p. 16/

Chapter 5

Planned to cross the Pacific: A. G. Spalding, *America's National Game,* p. 252/**In the opener:** J. E. Spalding, *Always on Sunday,* p. 38/**"We have players":** Ibid., p. 38/**Darkness shut down the game:** Photograph caption, Haggin Museum/**The Southern Pacific was battling:** Pitt, "The Modernization of a Cowtown," p. 45/**These settlers were different:** Ibid., p. 42/**Being buried in hype:** Fine, "The Emergence of Los Angeles as a Literary Territory," p. 5/**Two Pullman cars:** A. G. Spalding, *America's National Game,* p. 253/ **"It was absolutely essential":** Ibid., p. 252/**From a Union soldier:** Ibid., p. 510/**His pitching helped turn:** Smith, *Baseball's Hall of Fame,* p. 145/**The *Chicago Tribune* reported:** Rader, Introduction to *America's National Game,* p. xii/**Spalding had retired:** Ibid., p. xii/**The greatest star of his time:** Gardner, *The Annotated Casey at the Bat,* p. 185/**An ugly piece of business:** R. W. Peterson, *Only the Ball Was White,* p. 29/ **Epithets of this type:** A. G. Spalding, *America's National Game,* p. 30/**Other lesser-known individuals:** Ibid., p. 253/**Also part of the tour:** Ibid., p. 30/ **A song and dance man:** Bartlett, *Baseball and Mr. Spalding,* p. 179/**Sixth Street Base Ball Park:** Map, Bob Reis Collection/**Diners chose from:** Bartlett, *Baseball and Mr. Spalding,* p. 182/**Likely met Spalding:** Jules Tygiel (baseball historian) to author, early 2003/**The king tossed him:** Ibid., p. 186/

Chapter 6

Shameless baseball promoter: J. E. Spalding, *Always on Sunday,* p. 58/**Championship banner:** Ibid., p. 45/**Nickname was the Colonels:** Ibid., p. 45/**Two rubber-armed pitchers:** Weiss, "The California League in Professional Baseball," p. 8/**Greenhood and Moran no longer sponsored:** J. E. Spalding, *Always on Sunday,* p. 39/**First California baseball cards:** Doug McWilliams (Oakland baseball historian) to author, early 2002/**Oil was discovered:** Hutchinson, "The Genie of Yang-Na," p. 46/**The owner of the new franchise:** J. E. Spalding, *Always on Sunday,* p. 58/**A two-team race:** Ibid., p. 58/ **Star-quality looks:** 1890s Photograph, Bill Lange Scrapbooks/**Ran away from home:** Bill Lange Jr. to author, spring 2002/**The Seattle club folded:** Dobbins and Twichell, *Nuggets on the Diamond,* p. 31/**Teams ignored the rule:** J. E. Spalding, *Always on Sunday,* p. 58/**What was known as the National Agreement:** Zingg, *Harry Hooper,* p. 54/**Van Haltren signed:** J. E. Spalding, *Always on Sunday,* p. 58/**Chicago offered train fare:** Bill Lange Jr. to author, spring 2002/**Began in its usual fashion:** J. E. Spalding, *Always on Sunday,* p. 60/**Moved the pitching distance:** Ibid., p. 60/**Colonel Tom's club:** Ibid., p. 60-61/**The first night game:** Weiss, "The California League in Professional Baseball," p. 9/**"Burlesque baseball":** Ibid., p. 9/**First organized baseball team:** 1890s Photograph, Fresno Historical Society/**He attended Washington:** Gil Bogen (Chance biographer) to author, early 2002/**Slugging star of the Fresno Republican Tigers:** 1897 Poster, Fresno Historical Society/**Who spotted him first:** Gil Bogen (Chance biographer) to author, early 2002/**One of baseball's elite:** Gershman, Pietrusza, and Silverman, *Baseball,* p. 637–38/**Why Lange walked away:** Bill Lange Jr. to author, spring 2002/**After retiring from active play:** Ibid./**Less lucky in love:** Ibid.

Chapter 7

San Francisco–born pitcher: Nemec, *The Great Encyclopedia of Minor League Baseball,* p. 761/**He walked off the field:** J. E. Spalding, *Always on Sunday,* p.16/**In the winter of 1887:** Moore and Vermilyea, *Ernest Thayer's "Casey at the Bat,"* p. 223/**Convicted of manslaughter:** Zingg and Medeiros, *Runs, Hits, and An Era,* p.12/**Sweeney received word:** J. E. Spalding, *Always on Sunday,* p. 71/**It resumed operations:** Ibid., p. 68/**Sacramento's Gilt Edge:** Dobbins and Twichell, *Nuggets on the Diamond,* p. 34/**Bringing professional baseball:** K. Anderson, "Back to the Boardwalk," p. 64/**Sold his best player:** J. E. Spalding, *Always on Sunday,* p. 76/**A genuine major league ace:** Dobbins and Twichell, *Nuggets on the Diamond,* p. 35/**Its status had grown:** Weaver, "The Laboratory of Marvels," p. 55/**Home games at Chutes Park:** Bob Reis (baseball collector) to author, summer 2001/**He had seen all there was to see:** J. E. Spalding, *Always on Sunday,* p. 71/**His baseball past:** Dobbins and Twichell, *Nuggets on the Diamond,* p. 33/**League rules at the time:** Ibid., p. 32/**The biggest celebration of all:** Photograph and article, Dick Dobbins Collection/**One car broke down:** Dobbins and Twichell, *Nuggets on the Diamond,* p. 35/**The National Association governed:** Zingg, *Harry Hooper,* p. 54/**A young Japanese immigrant:** Hill, *Topaz Moon,* p. 2/**Studied English:** Ibid., p. 3/**Other passion in life:** Nakagawa, *Through a Diamond,* p. 32/**Artistic flair:** Ibid., p. 32/**Another Issei team:** Ibid., p. 32/**Competed hard against white players:** Ibid., p. 32/

Chapter 8

His father, Raphael: Pinelli, "From San Francisco Sandlots to the Big Leagues," p. 135/**Near where they lived:** Ibid., p. 136/**Always dogging his brother:** Ibid., p. 136/**On the morning:**

Ibid., p. 135/**When the shaking started:** Kurzman, *Disaster!*, p. 187/**Came the fires:** Ibid., p. 62/**"Curtains of flame":** Ibid., p. 84/**Blotted out the daylight:** Ibid., pp. 69–70/**Those who survived:** Ibid., p. 180/**The boats not being used:** Ibid., p. 183/**Recreation Park:** Zingg and Medeiros, *Runs, Hits, and An Era,* p. 25/**Smaller pieces of baseball history:** Dobbins and Twichell, *Nuggets on the Diamond,* p. 19/**Finally sizzled out:** Kurzman, *Disaster!*, p. 226/**Caused the suspension:** Nemec, *The Great American Baseball Team Book,* p. 148/**Morley said he planned:** H. W. Thomas, *Walter Johnson,* p.18/**Growing up on the streets:** Dobbins and Twichell, *Nuggets on the Diamond,* p. 42/**Lodged an official protest:** J. E. Spalding, *Always on Sunday,* p.84/**Used it to save the league:** Zingg and Medeiros, *Runs, Hits, and An Era,* p. 26/**"The final blow":** Dobbins and Twichell, *Nuggets on the Diamond,* p. 42/**Play resumed:** Ibid., p. 42/**Reconstruction in San Francisco:** Kurzman, *Disaster!*, p. 252/**The Paolinellis were recovering:** Pinelli, "From San Francisco Sandlots to the Big Leagues," p.135/**Lived for six months:** Hill, *Topaz Moon,* p. 3/**KNC founder Frank Tsuyuki:** Nakagawa, *Through a Diamond,* p. 58/**The league's new president:** Dobbins and Twichell, *Nuggets on the Diamond,* p. 42/**While the dimensions:** Dobbins and Twichell, *Nuggets on the Diamond,* p. 43/**In late March:** Ibid., p. 45/**The big day finally occurred:** Ibid., p. 45/

Chapter 9

Left New York City: Fleming, *The Unforgettable Season,* p. 13/**Loved to gamble:** Ibid., p. 2/**Ways to relax:** Ibid., p. 10/**Holed up in Glendora:** Ibid., p. 15/**With his wife Edythe:** Gil Bogen (Chance biographer) to author, late 2001/**Sold oranges for one dollar:** Ibid./**Suffered chronic headaches:** Ibid./**His doctors in Los Angeles:** Fleming, *The Unforgettable Season,* p. 15/**The dawn of southern California's beach culture:** Verge, "George Freeth," p. 86/ **While at practice:** Ritter, *The Glory of Their Times,* p. 84/**Bickered back and forth:** Ibid., p. 84/**"Headstrong, quick-tempered":** Ibid., p. 83/**Given their blessing:** Ibid., p. 85/**"The Big Swede":** H. W. Thomas, *Walter Johnson,* p. xiii/**As Johnson wrote:** Ibid., p. 364/**The impetus to leave:** Ibid., p. 6/**Compared to the hardships:** Ibid., p. 7/**Hired some men as "weeders":** Ibid., p. 8/**Home games in Anaheim:** Ibid., p. 8/**Boys from the orange groves:** Ibid., p. 10/**Walter started pitching more:** Ibid., p. 10/**Walter threw so hard:** Ibid., p. 12/**"He ain't got a thing":** Ibid., p. 12/**Sioux Indian:** Ibid., p. 13/**On his recommendation:** Ibid., p. 16/**A commanding athlete:** Ibid., p. 24/**He joined the San Diego Pickwicks:** Ibid., p. 51/**Posed for a team picture:** Photograph, Hall of Champions Collection/**The Chief's given name:** Koerper, "The Catcher Was a Cahuilla," p. 3/**Similar confusion:** Ibid., p. 2/**A Civil War veteran:** Ibid., p. 3/**Before her marriage:** Ibid., p. 3/**Learned to play ball:** Ibid., p. 4/**A team in Los Angeles:** Photograph, Dick Dobbins Collection/**"In those days":** Ritter, *The Glory of Their Times,* p. 175/**The Sherman Institute[...]sponsored:** Franks, "California Baseball's Mixed Multitudes," p. 113/**"For the first time":** Ibid., p. 113/**Entered Dartmouth College:** Ritter, *The Glory of Their Times,* p. 163/**Gavy was short for:** James, *The Politics of Glory,* p. 328/**Outdueling Sleepy Bill Burns:** H. W. Thomas, *Walter Johnson,* p. 52/**Developed a severe ear infection:** Ibid., p. 53/**Spinning tall tales:** Koerper, "The Catcher Was a Cahuilla," p. 9/**Had crafted a special shoe:** Fleming, *The Unforgettable Season,* p. 34/**Summoned his old infield mates:** Gil Bogen (Chance biographer) to author, late 2001/**Being young and playing center field:** Ritter, *The Glory of Their Times,* p. 108/

Chapter 10

Hooper was a rambler: Zingg, *Harry Hooper*, pp. 17–18/**"Garden of the World":** Ibid., p. 20/**Emigrant class ticket:** Ibid., p. 23/**Mary Keller worked:** Ibid., p. 25/**The Hoopers moved:** Ibid., p. 28/**His only sister:** Ibid., p. 51/**Fourth of July picnic:** Ibid., pp. 32–33/**"What a boyhood":** Ibid., p. 28/**A teacher at school:** Ibid., p. 38/**Originally founded:** Ibid., p. 42/**Bay Area all-star team:** Ibid., p. 47/**Another early standout:** J. E. Spalding, *Always on Sunday*, p. 21, 70/**St. Mary's owed some of its success:** Zingg, *Harry Hooper*, pp. 17–18/**A man of immense learning:** McDevitt, "The First Century of St. Mary's College," p. 209/**"The venerable mentor":** Ibid., p. 210/**It was not uncommon:** Zingg, *Harry Hooper*, pp. 39–40/**Thrived in the classroom:** Ibid., p. 52/**One of the best college baseball teams:** Lavoie, "St. Mary's Has Sent Players to Majors for 100 Years," pp. 14–15/**Whose lush farmlands:** Kohout, *Hal Chase*, p. 10/**Provided lumber for:** Ibid., p. 10/**A neighbor remembered:** Ibid., p. 11/**Los Gatos High:** Ibid., p. 12/**The coach when Chase arrived:** Ibid., p. 13/**One game against Cal:** Ibid., p. 15/**He declined offers:** Ibid., p. 19/**A reporter from the *Los Angeles Times*:** Ibid., p. 21/**The umpire of the game:** Ibid., p. 21/**A gold watch:** J. E. Spalding, *Always on Sunday*, p. 97/**"Just wasn't all there":** Kohout, *Hal Chase*, p. 47/**Largely because of his desire:** Ritter, *The Glory of Their Times*, p. 131/**Topped his railroad pay:** Ibid., p. 131/**Graham tipped off:** Ibid., pp. 132-33/**A stylish, rifle-armed graduate:** Ruth, *Babe Ruth's Own Book of Baseball*, p. 114/

Chapter 11

"A ramshackle two-by-four ballpark": Holtzman, *No Cheering in the Press Box*, p. 164/**Known as the Booze Cage:** Ibid., p. 164/**Found some land they liked:** Dobbins and Twichell, *Nuggets on the Diamond*, p. 57/**"The only possible drawback":** Ibid., pp. 57–58/**Behind home plate:** Ibid., p. 58/**The fog was so thick**/Ibid., p. 203/**Forcing him and Ish to sell:** Ibid., p. 60/**Port and trade center:** Hart, *A Companion to California*, p. 377/**Two "swing hitters":** Ruth, *Babe Ruth's Own Book of Baseball*, p. 153/**One Saturday at work:** J. E. Spalding, *Pacific Coast League Stars*, p. 25/**A scout from the Northwest:** Ibid., p. 25/**How he chose his new last name:** Zingg and Medeiros, *Runs, Hits, and An Era*, p. 35/**"The World Champion of Home Runs":** Dobbins and Twichell, *Nuggets on the Diamond*, p. 51/**"First great American opportunity":** Halberstam, *Summer of '49*, p. 248/**One of the longest home runs:** J. E. Spalding, *Pacific Coast League Stars*, p. 26/**Bodie's five-year-old son wandered:** Holtzman, *No Cheering in the Press Box*, p. 171/**Created an opening for other people:** Nakagawa, *Through a Diamond*, p. 32/**"Many diverse immigrant groups":** Ibid., p. 30/**Built ballfields of their own:** Ibid., p. 30/**Sunday afternoons were set aside:** Ibid., p. 35/**Dressed formally in suits and ties:** Ibid., p. 30/**Earn respect:** Ibid., p.40/

Chapter 12

Decided to replace: Dobbins and Twichell, *Nuggets on the Diamond*, p. 210/**Clean, simple lines:** Ibid., p. 57/**Hired a new pitcher:** Ibid., p. 210/**An early California minor leaguer:** Zingg and Medeiros, *Runs, Hits, and An Era*, p. 119/**A contest between black employees:** Ibid., p. 119/**The *Los Angeles Times* noted:** Franks, "California Baseball's Mixed Multitudes," p. 109/ **"This is the first time":** Ibid., p. 109/**Two parks with this name:** Maps, Bob Reis Collection/**Nearby was the White Sox Café:** Advertisement, Bob Reis Collection/**First all-black baseball team:** Photograph, Fresno Historical Society/**Pioneer Rube Foster:** R. W.

Peterson, *Only the Ball Was White*, pp. 103–11/**Biographical details:** Dobbins and Twichell, *Nuggets on the Diamond*, p. 210/**A photographer from Zeenuts:** Ibid., p. 210/**Showed up a few years later:** Ibid., p. 210/

Chapter 13

Two fellows had tried to bribe: Kohout, *Hal Chase*, p. 235/**Who denied everything:** Ibid., p. 235/**Two thousand dollars to players:** Ibid., p. 235/**Authorizing sweeps:** Dobbins and Twichell, *Nuggets on the Diamond*, p. 65/**One of the people banned:** Kohout, *Hal Chase*, p. 235/**A string of questionable incidents:** Gutman, *Baseball Babylon*, pp. 182–83/**An inquiry into his behavior:** J. E. Spalding, *Pacific Coast League Stars*, p. 10/**A new home in Los Angeles:** Kohout, *Hal Chase*, p. 234/**"If reports are true":** Ibid., p. 235/**Threatened to sue:** Ibid., p. 236/**The crowd cheered:** Ibid., p. 236/**The magic of telegraph wires:** 1921 Photograph, Dick Dobbins Collection/**Arrested Arnold "Chick":** Kohout, *Hal Chase*, p. 247/**His son denied involvement:** Ibid., p. 247/**A former San Franciscan:** Asinof, *Eight Men Out*, pp. 26–27/**He met Bobby Keefe:** Kohout, *Hal Chase*, p. 15/**Arrested Chick Gandil:** Ibid., p. 246/**Ran away from home:** J. E. Spalding, *Pacific Coast League Stars*, p. 11/**"A big, rough-hewn man":** Ibid., p. 11/**Agreeing to a contract:** Ibid., p. 11/**The dicks found:** Asinof, *Eight Men Out*, p. 131/**Punched an umpire:** Ibid., p. 208/**"A hard guy":** Ibid., p. 209/**Open a restaurant:** Ibid., p. 137/**Could not be extradited:** Kohout, *Hal Chase*, p. 246/**Offered to go to Chicago:** Ibid., p. 248/**Almost from its inception:** Asinof, *Eight Men Out*, p. 28/**Ended up in California:** Ibid., p. 284/**Drifted from place to place:** Kohout, *Hal Chase*, p. 249/**Suffering from health problems:** Ibid., p. 270/**1940s-era poll:** Ibid., p. 271/**To his deathbed:** Ibid, p. 274/

Chapter 14

About as scrawny: Ritter, *The Glory of Their Times*, p. 265/**Close to a cemetary:** Ibid., p. 263/**Coach, surrogate father:** Ibid., p. 263/**"Spike was a big man":** DiMaggio and Gilbert, *Real Grass, Real Heroes*, p. 17/**Quickly released him:** J. E. Spalding, *Pacific Coast League Stars*, p. 59/**Worked in the shipyards:** Ritter, *The Glory of Their Times*, p. 263/**"Our regular third-baseman":** Ibid., p. 264/**Did not know a thing:** Ibid., p. 265/**Average ticked higher:** J. E. Spalding, *Pacific Coast League Stars*, p. 59/**The boy shouted:** Ritter, *The Glory of Their Times*, pp. 266–67/**Outfielder from Sacramento:** J. E. Spalding, *Pacific Coast League Stars*, p. 67/**Open, bright-faced:** 1921 Photograph, Dick Dobbins Collection/**Jimmy's world fell:** J. E. Spalding, *A Century of Sports in Santa Clara County*, p. 28/**Another version of events:** Dobbins and Twichell, *Nuggets on the Diamond*, p. 66/**People expressed shock:** J. E. Spalding, *Pacific Coast League Stars*, p. 68/**Played outlaw baseball:** Kohout, *Hal Chase*, p. 256/**Spotted and signed:** Ritter, *The Glory of Their Times*, p. 279/**An ole country boy:** Ibid., p. 280/**Take the ferry:** Ibid., p. 280/**Shagged balls in the outfield:** Ibid., pp. 281–82/**"I all but lived":** Deane, *Top Ten Baseball Shortstops*, p. 23/**One of four high schools:** Tennis, "Cooperstown a Locke For Murray"/**A high-strung shortstop:** Ruth, *Babe Ruth's Own Book of Baseball*, p. 20/**Moon shots at Jackson Playground:** Dobbins and Twichell, *Nuggets on the Diamond*, p. 140/**Sickly as a child:** Chapin, "Yankees Great Crosetti Dies at Age 91," p. 2/**A reserved and quiet life:** Highfill, "A Legend as an Athlete and Person"/**Working his way up:** Pinelli, "From San Francisco Sandlots to the Big Leagues," p. 136/**Help groom Frankie:** Dobbins and Twichell, *Nuggets on the Diamond*, p. 83/**"Ping Bodie Day":** 1928 Photograph caption, Dick Dobbins Collection/

Chapter 15

The first European ship captain: Guhan, "History of Santa Catalina Island," p. 1/**A succession of businessmen:** Ibid., p. 2/**Added to his baseball holdings:** Beverage, *The Angels*, p. 17/**Camera-shy son:** Gershman, Pietrusza, and Silverman, *Baseball*, pp. 1258–59/**Switched their spring training:** Friedman, "Spring Training," p. 571/**New home for the Angels:** Ritter, *Lost Ballparks*, pp. 197–98/**Hosted its last Coast League game:** Bob Reis (baseball collector) to author, early 2002/**Fence for the power alleys:** Beverage, *The Angels*, pp. 32–33/**"A completely motorized":** Pitt, "The Modernization of a Cowtown," p. 63/**The earliest photographs:** Photograph, *Lost Ballparks* by Ritter, p. 196/**"It wasn't a feminist matter":** Cramer, *Joe DiMaggio*, p. 59/**Adopted this policy:** Beverage, *The Angels*, p. 49/**"Built on heroic lines":** Zingg and Medeiros, *Runs, Hits, and An Era*, p. 62/**A day in his honor:** 1927 Photograph, Dick Dobbins Collection/**A native of New York City:** Willman, "The Baseball Journey of Jimmie Reese," p. 57/**Caught a break:** Ibid., p. 57/**Tried out for the Seals:** Ibid., p. 58/**The spinning and leaping:** Ibid., p. 58/**A skill with a fungo bat:** Dobbins, *The Grand Minor League*, p. 210/**While vacationing in California:** Asinof, *Eight Men Out*, p. 137/**Traveled up to Weed:** Leutzinger, *Lefty O'Doul*, p. 74/**A photographer snapped him:** 1924 Photograph, Haggin Museum/**Played the lead:** Edelman, *Great Baseball Films*, p. 34/**Two other baseball movies:** Ibid., pp. 34–35/**Rolph personally greeted:** Faraudo, "Babe, Gehrig Took Bay Area by Storm"/**"Eminent home run specialists":** Ibid./**Its stop at Oaks Park:** Ibid./**Moving on to Fresno:** Nakagawa, *Through a Diamond*, p. 69/**Babe gave a quarter:** Ibid., p. 69/**A somewhat different look:** Ibid., p. 69/**Sneaked off to games:** Ibid., p. 85/**Found work:** Franks, "California Baseball's Mixed Multitudes," p. 108/ **Supervised the building:** Davis, "A Field in the Desert That Felt like Home"/**Took on all comers:** Nakagawa, *Through a Diamond*, p. 66/**They played hard:** Ibid., p. 72/**Attended a banquet:** Ibid., p. 70/**Another Hollywood credit:** Edelman, *Great Baseball Films*, p. 33/

Chapter 16

Growing up on the family ranch: J. E. Spalding, *Sacramento Solons and Senators*, p. 85/**Will played outfield:** Ibid., p. 85/**Cy paid him one thousand dollars:** Kohout, *Hal Chase*, p. 61/**One of the words:** Ibid., p. 61/**Threatened to move:** Ibid., p. 64/**Offered him a job:** Ibid., p. 273/**Ultimately left baseball:** J. E. Spalding, *Always on Sunday*, p. 92/**The behind-the-scenes man:** J. E. Spalding, *Sacramento Solons and Senators*, p. 66/**He approached his hometown:** Ibid., p. 40/**Biggest item on Lew's punch list:** Ibid., p. 46/**Restrooms for women:** Ibid., p. 46/**More wins than any other left-hander:** Zingg and Medeiros, *Runs, Hits, and An Era*, p. 79/**Worked as a bank clerk:** J. E. Spalding, *Sacramento Solons and Senators*, p. 74/**Up for sale:** Ibid., p. 69/**After Black Thursday:** Schraff, *The Great Depression and the New Deal*, p. 18/**Lost their jobs:** Ibid., pp. 20–21/**Des Moines hosted Wichita:** "1930 National League Highlights," p. 2110/**Landis came to see it:** J. E. Spalding, *Sacramento Solons and Senators*, p. 71/**Thinking about installing:** Ibid., p. 71/**Total illumination:** Ibid., p. 71/**"The ball was visible":** Ibid., p. 71/**More than ten thousand people:** Ibid., p. 71/**Adding to the evening's excitement:** Ibid., p. 71/**A fruitless mining scheme:** Ibid., p. 85/**So popular in Los Angeles:** Beverage, *The Angels*, pp. 59–60/**New baseball palace:** Ritter, *Lost Ballparks*, p. 170/**Public address system:** Dobbins and Twichell, *Nuggets on the Diamond*, p. 115/

Chapter 17

Led an all-black squad: J. E. Spalding, *Sacramento Solons and Senators*, p. 48/**Frequently took to the road:** R. W. Peterson, *Only the Ball Was White*, p. 124/**A big occasion:** Tygiel, *Past Time*, p. 117/**Barnstorming pilots usually performed:** Lillian Kaiser (semanticist) to author, early 2002/**A fastball that buckled the knees:** Donovan, "The Fabulous Satchel Paige," p. 77/**A traveling all-star team:** Ibid., p. 85/**The *Los Angeles Times* bragged:** Weaver, "The Laboratory of Marvels," p. 60/**His gateway into professional baseball:** J. E. Spalding, *Always on Sunday*, pp. 68–69/**A second career:** Ritter, Introduction to *The Unforgettable Season* by Fleming, p. viii/**Moved to California:** Edelman, *Great Baseball Films*, p. 203/**Technical assistance:** Ibid., p. 28/**Actors interviewing for jobs:** Ibid., p. 142/**Their boss sometimes stopped shooting:** Ibid., p. 142/**A new screen version:** Ibid., p. 160/***Fireman, Save My Child*:** Ibid., p. 163/**Through a ballpark fence:** Ray, "Joe E. Brown Stars as Sheiks and Reds Split"/**Made cameo appearances:** Ibid./**Glove with hole in its palm:** 1941 Photograph, Dick Dobbins Collection/**Record for longevity:** Beverage, *The Angels*, p. 137/**Would call him up:** Ibid., p. 81/**Last as president:** Richard E. Beverage (baseball historian) to author, Oct. 2002/**Sunk a drill:** Zingg and Medeiros, *Runs, Hits, and An Era*, p. 95/**Also constructed Gilmore Stadium:** Ibid., p. 95/**Following every pitch:** Veeck and Linn, *Veeck as in Wreck*, p. 182/**"The greatest pitchers' battle":** Ibid., p. 182/**Back to California:** Donovan, "The Fabulous Satchel Paige," p. 85/**"The games against big leaguers":** Ibid., p. 85/**In their matchup:** Ibid., p. 85/

Chapter 18

His father, Eugene: Leutzinger, *Lefty O'Doul*, p. 27/**Joined these rumbles:** Dobbins and Twichell, *Nuggets on the Diamond*, p. 138/**"The essential fundamentals":** Ibid., p. 139/**Work in his father's trade:** Leutzinger, *Lefty O'Doul*, p. 28/**Led the Native Sons:** Ibid., p. 28/**Received a one-thousand-dollar cash prize:** Ibid., p. 43/**"The gift of greeting life":** Cramer, *Joe DiMaggio*, p. 70/**Bought his first green suit:** Leutzinger, *Lefty O'Doul*, p. 127/**Invited to tour Japan:** Ritter, *The Glory of Their Times*, p. 248/**Persuade Babe Ruth:** Leutzinger, *Lefty O'Doul*, p. 58/**"I like people":** Ibid., p. 62/**Invaded Manchuria:** Sultzberger, *The American Heritage Picture History of World War II*, p. 44/**At a hardware store:** J. E. Spalding, *Sacramento Solons and Senators*, p. 75/**Kept a scrapbook:** Nakagawa, *Through a Diamond*, p. 63/**Played ukulele and sang songs:** Ibid., p. 63/**Listed his age as:** Ibid., p. 64/**"A few more like Nushida":** Ibid., p. 64/**Hong's real name:** Lavoie, "When Baseball Discovered Asians"/**Youngsters out of trouble:** Franks, "California Baseball's Mixed Multitudes," p. 107/**The Wa Sungs:** Ibid., p. 108/**One of Oakland's largest crowds:** J. E. Spalding, *Sacramento Solons and Senators*, p. 75/**Set off firecrackers:** Ibid., p. 75/**"Fallen in love with":** Leutzinger, *Lefty O'Doul*, p. 58/**With Babe Ruth:** Ibid., p. 58/**Sprung Japanese professional baseball:** Ritter, *The Glory of Their Times*, p. 248/**"You'll Meet Everybody":** Advertisement, Dick Dobbins Collection/**Could not leave until:** Cramer, *Joe DiMaggio*, p. 71/**One year leading a Nisei team:** Nakagawa, *Through a Diamond*, p. 64/**A barnstorming team:** Ibid., pp. 21–22/

Chapter 19

Lived on a tiny island: Historical Records, Martinez Museum, pp. 36–37/**Wrote them letters:** Cramer, *Joe DiMaggio*, p. 16/**Pregnant with their first child:** Ibid., p. 16/**Known as Portugese Flats:** Ibid., p. 17/**In their cabin Giuseppe:** Photograph, Historical Records,

Martinez Museum/**Enlisted in the Rough Riders:** Linn, *Hitter*, p. 29/**Hispanic girl:** Williams and Underwood, *My Turn at Bat*, p. 2/**A hard decision for her:** Linn, *Hitter*, p. 29/**Moved to San Diego:** Ibid., p. 29/**Sunshine Maternity Hospital:** "Highlights of Ted Williams' Life," *San Diego Union Tribune*, www.signonsandiego.com/**Raised chickens, hogs:** Rampersad, *Jackie Robinson*, p. 14/**Owned by a white man:** Ibid., p. 14/**Daughter of slaves:** Ibid., p. 11/**In honor of former president:** Ibid., p. 11/**This was a lie:** J. Robinson and Duckett, *I Never Had It Made*, p. 3/**In retaliation he threw:** Ibid., p. 4/**Stayed in the home of a relative:** Rampersad, *Jackie Robinson*, p. 16/**Well-dressed, nice-talking:** Ibid., p. 16/**Discouraged blacks from leaving:** Ibid., p. 16/**Three dollars, which was all she had left:** Ibid., p. 18/**Stopped and questioned her:** Ibid., p. 16/**No. 58 train:** Ibid., p. 17/**"The first Italian superstar":** Halberstam, *Summer of '49*, p. 248/**Hardly the chic:** Fimrite, "This Portrait of an American Icon Is No Pretty Picture"/**Too small to go onto the open waters:** Cramer, *Joe DiMaggio*, p. 19/**Home was on Taylor Street:** DiMaggio and Gilbert, *Real Grass, Real Heroes*, p. 14/**Grazed its horses:** Cramer, *Joe DiMaggio*, p. 8/**Sneaking out of junior high:** DiMaggio and Gilbert, *Real Grass, Real Heroes*, p. 13/**Long, sweet face:** Photograph, USC Special Collections/**Become an opera singer:** Bamberger, "Dom DiMaggio," p. 109/**A man who did not work:** Cramer, *Joe DiMaggio*, p. 16/**Forging Giuseppe's signature:** Ibid., p. 22/**Years would pass before:** Ibid., p. 22/ **"He'd swing at balls":** Earl Keller, quoted in *Echoes from Lane Field* by Swank, p. 31/**Getting Joe started:** Dobbins and Twichell, *Nuggets on the Diamond*, p. 150/ **"There may never":** Fimrite, "This Portrait of an American Icon is No Pretty Picture"/**Called him "Coscilunghi":** Cramer, *Joe DiMaggio*, p. 4/**She told stories:** Ibid., p. 23/**She stuck up for Joe:** DiMaggio and Gilbert, *Real Grass, Real Heroes*, p. 14/**Wild throws from shortstop:** Holtzman, *No Cheering in the Press Box*, p. 172/**"Hell of an arm!":** Ibid., p. 172/**Fielded his position with skill:** Dobbins and Twichell, *Nuggets on the Diamond*, p. 150/**With Joost at second:** Cramer, *Joe DiMaggio*, p. 41/**Yelled dirty names:** Ibid., p. 41/**DiMaggio went over to him:** Ibid., p. 41/**Continued to play on semipro:** Ibid., p. 105/**"Italians, bad at war":** Halberstam, *Summer of '49*, p. 46/ **"A magnet of ethnic pride":** Dunne, "Keeping Score," p. 98/**Finally Oakland's Ed Walsh Jr.:** Dobbins and Twichell, *Nuggets on the Diamond*, p. 151/**More than Giuseppe made:** Cramer, *Joe DiMaggio*, p. 44/**Rose before the sun:** Ibid., p. 47/**His son's name:** 1935 San Francisco Seals Program, Dick Dobbins Collection/**Dom DiMaggio's name first appeared:** Cramer, *Joe DiMaggio*, p. 47/**Hit for a high average:** DiMaggio and Gilbert, *Real Grass, Real Heroes*, p. 14/**Moved Dom from shortstop:** Ibid., p. 18/**Hauling and lifting mattresses:** Ibid., p. 18/ **"Down I went":** Cramer, *Joe DiMaggio*, p. 62/***Examiner* assigned a reporter:** Ibid., p. 62/**Play with torn ligaments:** Dobbins and Twichell, *Nuggets on the Diamond*, p. 153/**Essick was a scout:** Cramer, *Joe DiMaggio*, p. 66/**A medical evaluation:** Ibid., p. 66/**Considerably lower than the $100,000:** Dobbins and Twichell, *Nuggets on the Diamond*, p. 153/**Taught him about hitting:** Ibid., p. 153/**Two other San Francisco Italians:** 1936 Photograph, Dick Dobbins Collection/**His new Ford:** Cramer, *Joe DiMaggio*, p. 78/**"If I had had my mother's name":** Williams and Underwood, *My Turn at Bat*, p. 2/**A highly visible personality:** Linn, *Hitter*, p. 33/**Soft round face:** Ibid., p. 29/**Tirelessly raised money:** Ibid., p. 30/**Walked the streets:** Ibid., p. 31/**Modest one-story home:** Observed by author, San Diego, early 2001/**Could not afford to buy:** Linn, *Hitter*, p. 33/**Not afford to buy:** Ibid., p. 30/**"The more his wife":** Halberstam, *Summer of '49*, p. 169/**Sat on the front porch:** Ibid., p. 169/**Danny got into trouble:** Linn, *Hitter*, p. 32/**Showing up on his doorstep:** Ibid., p. 35/**Out the classroom door: Ibid., p. 34/**Made breakfast for himself:** Williams and Underwood, *My Turn at Bat,* p. 19/**Noon he ran home:** Ibid., pp. 19–20/**Hit balls with him:** Ibid., p. 22/**Thanked both Luscomb and Caldwell:** Ibid., p. 249/**"What's your name, kid?":** Ibid., p. 37/**Pounded down malted shakes:** Ibid., p. 38/**Started showing up at his house:** Lockwood, "Old Playground Memories Linger for Ted and Pals"/**He loved to fish:** Ibid./**Jackrabbits and quail:** Jenkins, "Splendid Splinter Cut Wide Swath from Coast to Coast"/**Using a Model 12:** Williams and Underwood, *My Turn at Bat,* p. 25/**Being a new school:** Linn, *Hitter,* p. 39/**Batted close to .600:** Ibid., p. 39/**Felt awkward around girls:** Williams and Underwood, *My Turn at Bat,* p. 32/**Did not drink or party:** Ibid., p. 32/**Played hitting contests:** Lockwood, "Old Playground Memories Linger for Ted and Pals"/**Paid younger kids to shag:** Linn, *Hitter,* p. 36/**One of the kids:** Ibid., p. 70/**Questioned later by his mother:** Ibid., p. 36/**Paid him three dollars:** Ibid., p. 41/**Three future Hall of Famers:** Rampersad, *Jackie Robinson,* p. 37/**"A little hamburger town":** Swank, *Echoes from Lane Field,* p. 30/ **"A tough, gruff":** Williams and Underwood, *My Turn at Bat,* p. 40/**After striking it rich:** Swank, *Echoes from Lane Field,* p. 6/**After a poll of fans:** Tom Larwin, Pacific Coast League Historical Society presentation, Hall of Champions, San Diego, Feb. 23, 2002/**With the assistance of:** Ibid./**Opening Day parade:** Ibid./**The hometowners whipped:** Ibid./**Money was being discussed:** Williams and Underwood, *My Turn at Bat,* p. 30/**Doing the shopping:** Linn, *Hitter,* p. 43/**Keep her son in San Diego:** Ibid., p. 47/**One hundred fifty dollars:** Williams and Underwood, *My Turn at Bat,* p. 38/ **"Like a fairyland to me":** Linn, *Hitter,* p. 53/**Baffled him at first:** Ibid., p. 53/**Docked a portion:** Williams and Underwood, *My Turn at Bat,* p. 40/**His mother asked Lane:** Linn, *Hitter,* p. 53/**The pair then dropped out:** Swank, *Echoes from Lane Field,* p.18/**Single-seat Chevy:** Ibid., p.19/**Investing in the phone company:** Halberstam, *Summer of '49,* p. 113/**From a baseball family:** Ibid., p. 113/**First thing father and son did:** Ibid., p. 113/**Such a baby face:** Ibid., p. 114/**Put the Red Sox onto Williams:** Ibid., p. 170/**Shook hands on the deal:** Linn, *Hitter,* p. 65/**On street corners she talked:** Ibid., p. 73/**Only a half-dozen times:** Williams and Underwood, *My Turn at Bat,* p. 206/**Roamed the stands:** Linn, *Hitter,* p. 73/**May was not happy:** Ibid., pp. 46–47/**Hard Rock denied:** Ibid., pp. 67–68/**Ted did not stand:** Halberstam, *Summer of '49,* p. 169/**Torrential rains hit:** Williams and Underwood, *My Turn at Bat,* p. 40/**Hired a pair of ham:** Ibid., p. 40/**Rickey chose Robinson:** Tygiel, *Baseball's Great Experiment,* p. 64/**"The most beautiful sight":** Rampersad, *Jackie Robinson,* p. 18/**Found an apartment:** Ibid., p. 18/**A white family** Ibid., p. 18/**Next twenty years:** Ibid., p. 18/**For its gardens:** Ibid., p. 20/**Across a length of land:** Observed by author, Brookside Park, Pasadena, Calif., with Mel Atwell, Mar. 2003/**Bought a home:** Rampersad, *Jackie Robinson,* p. 19/**White neighbors did not want them:** Ibid., p. 24/**Burning a cross:** Ibid., p. 24/**Prayed every night:** Ibid., p. 25/**"Didn't allow us":** J. Robinson and Duckett, *I Never Had It Made,* p. 6/**After feeding her family:** Ibid., p. 24/**First experience with open racial:** Ibid., p. 5/**A gang of boys:** Ibid., p. 6/**A sheriff caught Jack:** Ibid., p. 6/**Unholstered his gun:** Ibid., p. 6/**For whites only:** Rampersad, *Jackie Robinson,* p. 35/**Stood outside the fence:** Ibid., p. 35/**Restrictions on blacks:** Ibid., p. 35/**"Full-fledged juvenile delinquent":** J. Robinson and Duckett, *I Never Had It Made,* pp. 6–7/**Did not talk down:** Ibid., p. 7/**One direction: sports:** Ibid., p. 9/**"Special little boy":** Rampersad, *Jackie Robinson,* p. 17/**In the big showdown:** Ibid., p. 38/**The Owl League:** Ibid., p. 44/**"It's grand larceny":** Ibid., p. 44/**Brookside Plunge hosted:** Ibid., p. 31/**Listened to the race:** Ibid., p. 31/**National junior college records:** Plaque observed by author, Pasadena Community

College Athletic Hall of Fame, Pasadena, Calif./**Sweeping the streets:** Rampersad, *Jackie Robinson*, p. 31/**Wore his USA Olympic:** Ibid., p. 31/**"You would hear":** Ibid., p. 49/**One night a patrolman:** Ibid., p. 50/**Open to young people:** J. Robinson and Duckett, *I Never Had It Made*, p. 7/**"Those of us":** Ibid., p. 7/**Kawai sometimes roomed:** Nakagawa, *Through a Diamond*, p. 74/**Early May 1938:** Rampersad, *Jackie Robinson*, p. 54/**Starred for the Pasadena Sox:** Ibid., p. 55/**"If that kid was white":** Ibid., p. 55/**Attracted as many as five thousand:** Ibid., p. 56/**Dazzling huge crowds:** Ibid., p. 57/**Watching from the stands:** Ibid., p. 57/**Ward Snider knew:** Kahn, *The Boys of Summer*, p. 382/**Throw a football:** Ibid., p. 382/**Pete Rozelle, the future commissioner:** Ibid., p. 382/**"The first of the California surfer types":** Golenbock, *Bums*, p. 343/**"Whites as well as blacks":** Rampersad, *Jackie Robinson*, p. 27/**Two white policemen:** Ibid., p. 60/**Went for treatment:** Ibid., p. 60/**"Felt like an intruder":** Ibid., p. 61/**Known for his fairness:** Ibid., p. 62/**Earned four varsity letters:** "Jack Roosevelt Robinson," 2000 UCLA Media Guide, p. 87/**In his debut game:** Rampersad, *Jackie Robinson*, p. 73/**Winning long jump:** Ibid., p. 75/**Lifting weights:** Ibid., p. 55/**Wearing white shirts:** Ibid., p. 78/**A well-put-together freshman:** Ibid., p. 76/**"I thought to myself":** Ibid., p. 78/**Each was intrigued by the other:** J. Robinson and Duckett, *I Never Had It Made*, p. 10/**Decided to quit college:** Ibid., p. 11/**Campus newspaper reported:** Rampersad, *Jackie Robinson*, p. 82/**Summer camp director:** Ibid., p. 84/**Traveled to Hawaii:** Ibid., p. 86/**Playing poker:** Ibid., p. 87/**Moved in and out of the sea lanes:** Ibid., p. 87/**Two monumental busts:** Observed by author, Pasadena, Calif., Mar. 2003/

Chapter 20

A daring plan: Autry and Herskowitz, *Back in the Saddle Again*, p. 149/**Checked into train schedules:** Ibid., p. 149/**Took place December 8:** Ibid., p. 149/**Did not bother to read:** Ibid., p. 150/**Reviving the idea:** Sullivan, *The Dodgers Move West*, p. 90/**The Atwells:** Author interview with Mel Atwell, Mar. 2003/**Highest-paid performer:** House of David letter, Feb. 9, 1936, Mel Atwell Collection/**Gave the go-ahead:** Zingg and Medeiros, *Runs, Hits, and An Era*, p.101/**Lifted this ban:** Ibid., p. 101/**Gliding around center field:** Cramer, *Joe DiMaggio*, p. 208/**Two other San Francisco major leaguers:** Crisser, "Baseball and the Armed Services," p. 2516/**A graduate of Roosevelt High:** Murphy, "Ex-Seals Star Fain Dies"/**A tryout in San Pablo:** Salan, "Walter 'Pete' Deas on Billy Hebert," p. 16/**"I never saw a ballplayer":** Ibid., p. 16/**With its palm up:** DiMaggio and Gilbert, *Real Grass, Real Heroes*, p. 41/**Made sure not to touch:** Salan, "Walter 'Pete' Deas on Billy Hebert," p. 16/**Sometimes featured whites:** Nakagawa, *Through a Diamond*, p. 20/**Were playing in Los Angeles:** Franks, "California Baseball's Mixed Multitudes," p. 108/**Rounded up all persons:** Inada, *Only What We Could Carry*, p. 413/**9066 broadly applied:** Nakagawa, *Through a Diamond*, p. 76/**Italian Americans also argued:** Ibid., p. 76/**Fled the state:** Lavoie, "When Baseball Discovered Asians"/**An artist and a professor:** Hill, *Topaz Moon*, p. 9/**It is wrong:** Ibid., p. 16/**Refused to accept:** Ibid., p. 16/**Needed special permission:** Ibid., p. 16/**The Minetas:** Brokaw, *The Greatest Generation*, p. 218/**Slept in horse stalls:** Davis, "A Field in the Desert That Felt like Home"/**Left California for the Gila River:** Nakagawa, *Through a Diamond*, p. 83/**In search of rock:** Ibid., p. 79/**Brought over a hose:** Ibid., p. 79/**At Tule Lake:** Ibid., p. 79/**On Opening Day:** Ibid., p. 87/**The grandest of the internment camp fields:** Ibid., p. 83/**Next they laid pipe:** Ibid., p. 83/**Holman's sent boxes:** Ibid., p. 86/**Gila River camp closed:**

Inada, *Only What We Could Carry,* pp. 416–17/**Gyo Obata never went:** Hill, *Topaz Moon,* p. 109/**Ford formally revoked:** Inada, *Only What We Could Carry,* pp. 410–11/**"Cannot restore lost years":** Ibid., p. 412/

Chapter 21

A similar shortage of men: Nelson, "Pioneer in Print," p. 16/ **"Too bad you're a girl":** Ibid., p. 16/**Sure she knew sports:** Ibid., p. 17/**Headed straight for the public library:** Ibid., p. 17/**Had to keep score:** Ibid., p. 17/**Trivia expert on the *Call-Bulletin*:** Ibid., p. 17/**Name was shortened:** Ibid., p. 17/**Walt Daley returned:** Ibid., p. 17/**Fifty thousand combat planes:** Henstel, "A Sky-Minded City," p. 59/**"Hostile to blacks":** Rampersad, *Jackie Robinson,* p. 87/**Rowland announced that:** Dobbins and Twichell, *Nuggets on the Diamond,* p. 212/**Former engineering student:** Ibid., p. 212/**Pitched against the likes of:** R. W. Peterson, *Only the Ball Was White,* p. 125/**"I know how good you are":** Dobbins and Twichell, *Nuggets on the Diamond,* p. 212/**Took his case to:** Ibid., p. 212/**Refused to let them:** Ibid., p. 212/**Letters of protest:** R. W. Peterson, *Only the Ball Was White,* p. 180/**Gifted inner-city players:** Davis, "Remembering Mr. Brewer," p. 24/**Driving a truck for Lockheed:** Rampersad, *Jackie Robinson,* p. 88/**Worth fifty thousand dollars:** Ibid., p. 89/**Received his orders:** Ibid., p. 89/**Turned him down:** Ibid., p. 91/**Revised its stance:** Ibid., p. 93/**The second lieutenant:** Ibid., p. 94/**Studying nursing:** Ibid., p. 95/**Boarded an Army bus:** Ibid., p. 102/**Test of his faith:** Ibid., p. 105/**"Vent their bigotry":** Ibid., p. 109/**Trying out, with two other blacks:** R. W. Peterson, *Only the Ball Was White,* p. 185/**Constant travel around the country:** J. Robinson and Duckett, *I Never Had It Made,* p. 23/**Did not drink or smoke:** Rampersad, *Jackie Robinson,* p. 118/**Considered quitting the game:** J. Robinson and Duckett, *I Never Had It Made,* p. 25/**Sukeforth approached Robinson:** Ibid., p. 30/**Had been surveying:** Ibid., p. 32/**"Mr. Rickey, here is":** Okrent, "Scout's Honor," p. 28/**Closing the door behind them:** Jules Tygiel (baseball historian) to author, early 2003/**At the Independent Church:** Rampersad, *Jackie Robinson,* p. 133/**Bartlett, who had introduced:** Ibid., p. 133/**North to San Jose:** Ibid., p. 134/**Requested that Rachel come:** Ibid., p. 134/

Chapter 22

Moved to Oakland: Fimrite, *Way to Go!,* p. 38/**Worked long hours:** Ibid., p. 38/**"The rent came due":** Ibid., p. 38/**"Blond and broad shouldered":** Ibid., p. 34/**Pushing the idea:** Chanin, "Golden Memories," p. 18/**All-Star game in Boston:** Ibid., p. 18/**Playoff did not seem so crazy:** Ibid., p. 18/**Veterans who filled the rosters:** Kunz, "Cal's 1947 NCAA Champion Baseball Team," p. 3/**Struggling with his control:** Ibid., p. 3/**Unusual coaching arrangement:** 2001 USC Baseball Media Guide, p. 49/**Calling everyone he met "Tiger":** Anderson and Ewald, *Sparky!,* p. 60/**"The greatest farm club":** Jim Murray, *Los Angeles Times,* 1976 (2001 USC Baseball Media Guide), p. 10/**Moved to Los Angeles:** Anderson and Ewald, *Sparky!,* p. 9/**The house in Los Angeles:** Ibid., p. 57/**A little privacy:** Ibid., p. 57/**Tape his ears:** Ibid., p. 57/**"A little kid":** Ibid., p. 3/**Lived only a few blocks:** Ibid., p. 59/**"Where's the boss?":** Ibid., p. 59/**"Taught me more":** Ibid., p. 59/**Go outside with his brother:** Ibid., p. 58/**House painter by trade:** Ibid., p. 54/**"Lead-pipe tough":** Ibid., p. 54/**Crenshaw Post American Legion:** Ibid., p. 58/**Arranged a summer job:** Ibid., p. 61/**Worked at the Virtue Brothers:** Ibid., p. 62/**One year in Texas:** Ibid., p. 41/**Batboy at USC for six years:** Ibid., p. 59/**Went on to face Yale:** Chanin, "Golden Memories," p. 18/**Pushed across a run:**

Ibid., p. 19/**Leaving college early to play:** Fimrite, *Way to Go!*, p. 39/**A fear of flying:** Dobbins, *The Grand Minor League*, p. 185/**East-West Shrine:** Doug McWilliams (Oakland baseball historian) to author, Oct. 2003/**Once again led by:** 1948 Photograph, USC Regional History Collection/

Chapter 23

Until the fall of 1940: Schroeder, "The Story of the California League," p. 59/**This latest version:** Ibid., p. 59/**Owls could not afford:** Weiss, "The California League in Professional Baseball," p. 10/**Could not last the season:** Ibid., p. 10/**Rare baseball photograph:** 1880s Photograph, Huntington Library Collection/**A "Mexican marvel":** Franks, "California Baseball's Mixed Multitudes," p. 109/**Such names as:** Ibid., p. 109/**"Spanish-Irish":** Baseball Register, *The Sporting News*, 1940, Mel Atwell Collection/**A tough competitor:** Holtzman, *No Cheering in the Press Box*, p. 171/**Andreas was the patriarch:** Margolin, "Baseball and Bird Songs," p. 2/**Boys' summer league:** Ibid., p. 2/**Boarded a train:** Love, "Mike Garcia," p. 18/**Radio communications:** Ibid., p. 18/**Another meeting:** Schroeder, "The Story of the California League," p. 62/**This time the cities:** Ibid., p. 62/**Many Latino barbershops:** Love, "Mike Garcia," p. 18/**One out of four major leaguers:** Weiss, "The California League in Professional Baseball," p. 10/**Moved to the Bay Area:** Klages, "The Girls of Summer," Exploratorium, www.exploratorium.edu/**Played in the home parks:** Dobbins and Twichell, *Nuggets on the Diamond*, p. 213/**Often hit leadoff:** Dobbins, *The Grand Minor League*, p. 214/**"Green-eyed ballplayer":** Ibid., p. 214/**With blacks and whites:** Ibid., p. 214/**"Johnny Baseball":** Swank, "Black Balled," p. 11/**Traveled to Spartanburg:** Ibid., p. 10/**Told to leave the field:** Ibid., p. 10/**"In those days":** Ibid., p. 10/**Five battle stars:** Ibid., p. 11/**The scouts passed over:** Swank, *Echoes from Lane Field*, p. 87/**A Brooklyn native:** Ibid., p. 34/**Actually pinch-hit:** Don King (Curator, Hall of Champions) to author, late 2001/**"The Coast League was lily white":** Swank, *Echoes from Lane Field*, p. 36/**"He was thrust":** Dobbins, *The Grand Minor League*, p. 214/**Roomed by himself:** Ibid., p. 214/**No Padre pitcher:** Ibid., p. 214/**Came into the plate:** Ibid., p. 214/**Noticed a change:** Swank, "Black Balled," p. 11/**Shipped to Vancouver:** Ibid., p. 12/**"Endured his pioneering ordeal":** Tygiel, *Baseball's Great Experiment*, p. 258/**First taste of Alaskan king crab:** Swank, *Echoes from Lane Field*, p. 101/**First baseball uniform:** Regalado, *Viva Baseball!*, pp. 43–44/**Stayed with a family:** Swank, *Echoes from Lane Field*, p. 100/**"Opened the door":** Ibid., p. 100/**Substituted its regular balls:** Don King (Curator, Hall of Champions) to author, late 2001/**He liked for his teammate:** Swank, *Echoes from Lane Field*, p. 103/**"I say to Luke":** Ibid., p. 100/**"Handicapped to start with":** Ibid., p. 29/**Slapped the ball:** Zingg and Medeiros, *Runs, Hits, and An Era*, p. 125/**Volunteered to room:** Tygiel, *Baseball's Great Experiment*, p. 255/

Chapter 24

Left his hometown: Allen, *Damn Yankee*, p. 19/**Girl he left behind:** Ibid., p. 19/**Once a stop for Pony Express:** Ibid., p. 20/**Crammed with ten children:** Ibid., p. 19/**Outhouse in back tumbled:** Ibid., p. 20/**Floated it on the bay:** Ibid., p. 20/**Coins onto the living room:** Ibid., p. 20/**Handsome, dark-eyed:** Ibid., p. 21/**Liked to play at more than music:** Ibid., p. 21/**Smashed the windows:** Ibid., p. 21/**Circumcised downstairs:** Ibid., p. 18/**Married Jack Downey:** Ibid., p. 22/**She bit their hand:** Nelson, *The Greatest Stories Ever Told About Baseball*, p. 72/**Did not own a refrigerator:** Martin and Pepe, *BillyBall*, p. 54/**"I ate stale bread":**

Allen, *Damn Yankee*, p. 25/**West Berkeley neighborhood:** Ibid., p. 25/**"When nothing talks":** Nelson, *The Greatest Stories Ever Told About Baseball*, p. 73/**A laundry owned by the Galan family:** Martin and Pepe, *BillyBall*, p. 55/**Pictures of Augie taped:** Ibid., p. 55/**Games at James Kenney Park:** Ibid., p. 56/**Only had two meager lights:** Allen, *Damn Yankee*, p. 25/**Too small to be considered:** Ibid., p. 27/**Played for the Oakland Junior Oaks:** Martin and Pepe, *BillyBall*, p. 56/**Down on a broken arm:** Ibid., p. 57/**When Martin showed up to sign:** Ibid., p. 57/**A suit to bury him:** Ibid., p. 57/**Held a big party:** Allen, *Damn Yankee*, p. 30/**Introducing Stengel to a girlfriend:** Creamer, *Stengel*, p. 158/**"Tall, slim":** Ibid., p. 158/**Had moved the family:** Ibid., p. 158/**An extra in several silent films:** Ibid., p. 158/**Keen mind:** Ibid., p. 158/**Asking for her hand:** Ibid., p. 158/**Edna proudly displayed:** Felker, *Casey Stengel's Secret*, p. 58/**Built a house:** Creamer, *Stengel*, p. 170/**Scouting the young Ted Williams:** Linn, *Hitter*, p. 66/**Operated a chain of movie theaters:** Dobbins, *The Grand Minor League*, p. 113/**"Bag Night" promotions:** Ibid., p. 113/**Poured a few hundred thousand:** Dobbins and Twichell, *Nuggets on the Diamond*, p. 179/**Pledge to bring a flag:** Ibid., p. 180/**"Everywhere I go":** Creamer, *Stengel*, p. 207/**Hosted a barbecue:** Dobbins, *The Grand Minor League*, p. 147/**With his bare right hand:** Ibid., p. 192/**First look at Martin:** Allen, *Damn Yankee*, p. 36/**"If he done it in Africa":** Nelson, *The Greatest Stories Ever Told About Baseball*, p. 77/**Martin showed up:** Allen, *Damn Yankee*, p. 38/**Hitting grounder after grounder:** Ibid., p. 36/**Tuning into the mental side:** Ibid., p. 39/**"Fresh kid":** Creamer, *Stengel*, p. 209/**"Growled at [Martin]":** Ibid., p. 209/**A telling photograph:** 1948 Photograph, Doug McWilliams Collection/**Strategy of "platooning":** Allen, *Damn Yankee*, p. 43/**A fan of Stengel's:** Creamer, *Stengel*, p. 208/**Riding in an open convertible:** 1948 Photograph, Dick Dobbins Collection/**Expected to follow him:** Allen, *Damn Yankee*, p. 45/**A nobody compared to Jensen:** Ibid., p. 49/**On Stengel's recommendation:** Ibid., p. 49/**His "big-nosed player":** Creamer, *Stengel*, p. 209/**See whose schnozz was bigger:** Ibid., p. 209/**Gotten a nose job:** Allen, *Damn Yankee*, p. 49/**F-10 Corsair:** Doug McWilliams (Oakland baseball historian) to author, Oct. 2003/**Off-season salesman's job:** Ibid., p. 33/**Stream of inspirational letters:** Meany, *The Magnificent Yankees*, p. 183/**Return to active duty:** Ibid., p. 189/**Drove a United States Mail truck:** Ibid., p. 134/**Two other San Francisco schoolboys:** Charlie Silvera to author, early 2002/**Enrolled at Stanford:** Rogers, "A Conversation with Bobby Brown," p. 60/**During the war he transferred:** Ibid., p. 61/**Often reporting late:** Ibid., p. 63/**Reported to San Francisco County:** Ibid., p. 73/**Grew up on Guerrero Street:** Charlie Silvera to author, early 2002/**"Our major leagues":** Ibid./**Later became a major league coach:** Ibid./**Moved into umpiring:** J. E. Spalding, *Pacific Coast League Stars*, p. 70/**Overcome a once-volatile temper:** Ibid., p. 68/**Second most famous image:** 1956 Associated Press Photograph, Doug McWilliams Collection/**Blamed his longtime mentor:** Martin and Pepe, *BillyBall*, p. 50/**Stopped talking:** Ibid., p. 50/**Stengel received a parade:** 1960 Photograph, USC Special Collections/**"Don't Cry Casey":** 1960 Photograph, USC Special Collections/**Key to the city:** 1960 Photograph, USC Special Collections/**As a son:** Allen, *Damn Yankee*, p. 45/**"I loved the old man":** Ibid., p. 42/**"Much of what I am":** Martin and Pepe, *BillyBall*, p. 43/**In every manager's office:** Ibid., p. 43/ **"I feel greatly honored":** Creamer, *Stengel*, p. 316/**Series of strokes:** Ibid., p. 330/**Visiting her every day:** Ibid., p. 330/**Mass of minor dings:** Martin and Pepe, *BillyBall*, p. 52/**License was suspended:** Ibid., p. 52/**When the Glendale police:** Ibid., p. 52/**Appeared at Dodger Stadium:** Creamer, *Stengel*, p. 331/**Checked into Glendale Memorial:** Ibid., p. 332/**"One last time":** Ibid., p.

332/**Postpone Casey's funeral:** Ibid., p. 332/**Services were held:** Ibid., p. 332/**Slept in his old bed:** Martin and Pepe, *BillyBall*, p. 52/**Made trips to Stengel's grave:** Ibid., p. 52/

Chapter 25

Opened up the sports page: Cramer, *Joe DiMaggio*, p. 321/**Posing with her:** Ibid., p. 320/**After the picture appeared:** Ibid., p. 321/**First date:** Ibid., p. 321/**"I found myself staring":** Ibid., p. 321/**Not crude or rough:** Ibid., p. 321/**Her appendix removed:** Ibid., p. 326/**"Fed on sexual candy":** Nelson, *The Greatest Stories Ever Told About Baseball*, p. 61/**One of the places they went:** Cramer, *Joe DiMaggio*, p. 336/**A half-block down:** S.W. Cobb and Willems, *The Brown Derby Restaurant*, p. 9/**Four Derbies:** Ibid., p. 15/**Low-slung leather booths:** Ibid., p. 20/**A Montanan by birth:** Ibid., p. 9/**Handmade leather shoes:** Ibid., p. 10/**Private label rum:** Ibid., pp. 96-97/**"While my mother":** Ibid., p. 10/**Sunk some money into the Stars:** Ibid., p. 10/**Later sold his shares:** Autry and Herskowitz, *Back in the Saddle Again*, p. 152/**All-wood ballpark:** 1939 Photograph, Dick Dobbins Collection/**Caught the ceremonial first-pitch:** Photograph, *Runs, Hits, and An Era* by Zingg, p. 96/**Football, baseball and track:** Spada, *Ronald Reagan*, p. 12/**Worked as a lifeguard:** Ibid., p. 12/**Following graduation:** Ibid., p. 16/**This experience enabled:** Ibid., p. 16/**Gave Reagan an idea:** Reagan, *An American Life*, p. 77/**Came to California for the first time:** Ibid., p. 77/**A bad storm hit the area:** Ibid., p. 78/**Met an old friend:** Ibid, p. 78/**Grimm ragged on him:** Ibid., p. 80/**Offered him a seven-year:** Ibid., p. 81/**Commanded a $1 million:** Spada, *Ronald Reagan*, p. 19/**Could be seen around town:** Tully, "Magical Baseball Tour"/**Also notable in that its cast:** Edelman, *Great Baseball Films*, p. 212/**Graduate of Fremont High:** Beverage, *The Angels*, p. 208/**Marks the screen debut:** Hallowed Ground: Baseball's Historical Places, www.hallowedground.org, July 2002/**Posing for a gag shot:** 1947 Hollywood Stars Program, Dick Dobbins Collection/**"Shave Their Legs":** Zingg and Medeiros, *Runs, Hits, and An Era*, p. 134/**Angel-Star brawl:** 1953 Photographs, Dick Dobbins Collection/**A band of revelers:** Photograph, Los Angeles Public Library Collection/**From the Bamboo Room:** 1953 Photograph, Los Angeles Public Library Collection/**Had become a superstar:** Cramer, *Joe DiMaggio*, p. 343/**His dislike of show business people:** Ibid., p. 345/**"Wouldn't be an easy":** Ibid., p. 351/**Drove south down the coast:** Ibid., p. 353/**Japanese felt resentment:** Nakagawa, *Through a Diamond*, p. 101/**One of his aides:** Ibid., p. 101/**More than half a million:** Leutzinger, *Lefty O'Doul*, p. 65/**Pitched the final game:** Ibid., p. 65/**A diplomatic triumph:** Nakagawa, *Through a Diamond*, p. 102/**An invitation to visit:** Leutzinger, *Lefty O'Doul*, p. 65/**Crowded the Tokyo airport:** Cramer, *Joe DiMaggio*, p. 356/**Realized what a huge, huge star:** Ibid., p. 358/**Packed up his things:** Ibid., p. 369/**His face a mask of contained grief:** 1962 Photograph, Los Angeles Public Library Collection/**Arranged her funeral:** B. Thomas, "Flashy Hollywood Funerals History, but Graves Popular"/

Chapter 26

A Texas woman: F. Robinson and Silverman, *My Life Is Baseball*, p. 21/**Split up when little Frank:** Ibid., p. 21/**Letters to Texas:** Ibid., p. 23/**Opportunity for work:** Flood and Carter, *The Way It Is*, p. 19/**Your own bed:** Ibid., p. 20/**Father drank too much:** Adelman and Hall, *Out of Left Field*, p. 20/**And better, atmosphere:** Ibid., p. 20/**Decided to follow the lead:** Morgan and Falkner, *Joe Morgan*, p. 32/**One of the first black families:** Ibid., p. 33/**The Myrtle Street block:** F. Robinson and Silverman, *My Life Is Baseball*, p. 24/**At Tompkins**

Street: Ibid., p. 26/**Fourteen players from those:** Ibid., p. 32/**Felt distanced:** Ibid., p. 32/**"He'd invite me over":** Ibid., p. 33/**"A stocky guy":** Ibid., p. 31/**Not quite good enough:** Author interview (for article in *Rossmoor News*) with George Powles, Feb. 9, 1987/**Found out about Robinson:** F. Robinson and Silverman, *My Life Is Baseball*, p. 31/**"Even as a kid":** Author interview of George Powles, Feb. 9, 1987/**Second on his team:** F. Robinson and Silverman, *My Life Is Baseball*, p. 40/**"We had nothing":** Flood and Carter, *The Way It Is*, p. 19/**Recycled the same Christmas tree:** Ibid., p. 21/**"Conventionally squalid":** Ibid., p. 19/**All the whites Flood saw:** Ibid., p. 25/**When Curt was ten:** Ibid., p. 23/**"If I now see whites":** Ibid., p. 26/**If he had received better instruction:** Adelman and Hall, *Out of Left Field*, p. 24/**Down to the lumberyard:** Ibid., p. 19/**"Exposed to everything":** Ibid., p. 21/**Slept on fold-up cots:** Ibid., p. 22/**Threatened him with shotgun:** Ibid. p. 21/**So discouraged:** Ibid., p. 22/**One of his first lessons:** Morgan and Falkner, *Joe Morgan*, p. 33/**Joe and his father:** Ibid., p. 36/**Most notorious brawls:** Dobbins and Twichell, *Nuggets on the Diamond*, p. 208/**May's bonus:** Morgan and Falkner, *Joe Morgan*, p. 43/**Lavagetto saw a smart kid:** Ibid., p. 46/**Joe's father invited him:** Ibid., p. 47/**Played with Flood and Robinson at McClymonds:** F. Robinson and Silverman, *My Life Is Baseball*, p. 30/**Raised in nearby Richmond:** Bryant, *Shut Out*, p. 8/**His brother Cornell:** Ibid., p. 9/**After his horrific:** Adelman and Hall, *Out of Left Field*, p. 22/**Baseball and football fields are named after him:** Okanes, "Stargell's Death Felt in East Bay"/**Morgan said he chose:** Associated Press, "Morgan Eulogizes Stargell"/

Chapter 27

Dodgers flew cross-country: Sullivan, *The Dodgers Move West*, p. 87/**A helicopter ride:** Ibid., p. 87/**The search focused:** Ibid., p. 84/**His opposition to the referendum:** Ibid., p. 86/**Tried unsuccessfully to interest:** Ibid., p. 87/**Old potter's field:** Hart, *A Companion to California*, p. 91/**Sheriff's Department provided:** Rampersad, *Jackie Robinson*, p. 301/**First freeway:** Hart, *A Companion to California*, p. 216/**O'Malley and Supervisor Hahn shook hands:** Ibid., p. 87/**Son of a New York city commissioner:** Ibid., p. 29/**Hung out his attorney's shingle:** Ibid., p. 29/**Struggle for control:** Ibid., p. 29/**"First to say out loud":** Ibid., p. 29/**Business suit and tie:** 1959 Photograph, USC Special Collections/**A photograph during this era:** 1957 Photograph, Los Angeles Public Library Collection/**Issued a study:** Sullivan, *The Dodgers Move West*, p. 88/**Left untouched was:** Ibid., p. 88/**Changed the power equation:** Beverage, *The Angels*, p. 231/**Flew with a delegation:** Sullivan, *The Dodgers Move West*, p. 96/**"Promised O'Malley the moon":** Ibid., p. 96/**"You had to be crazy":** DiMaggio and Gilbert, *Real Grass, Real Heroes*, p. 51/**On the verge of proposing:** Autry and Herskowitz, *Back in the Saddle Again*, p. 149/**Air transportation:** "Commercial Aviation," The History of Aviation, www.history.sandiego.edu/**Formation of Mutual Radio Network:** Zingg and Medeiros, *Runs, Hits, and An Era*, p.129/**Major league search committee:** Bitker, *The Original San Francisco Giants*, p. 3/**$5 million bond measure:** Ibid., p. 3/**Christopher called Poulson:** Ibid., p. 4/**Asked Christopher to support:** Ibid., p. 4/**"Intended to move":** Sullivan, *The Dodgers Move West*, p. 117/**Wanted a new park:** Ibid., p. 115/**First choice was Minneapolis:** Ibid., p. 117/**Face-to-face with Stoneham:** Bitker, *The Original San Francisco Giants*, p. 5/**Talk exclusively over the phone:** Ibid., p. 5/**City would build new stadium:** Ibid., p. 5/**Received a memorandum:** Ibid., p. 6/**Directors voted their approval:** Ibid., p. 6/**Less polarizing figure:** Sullivan, *The Dodgers Move West*, p. 115/**Craft a

winning agreement: Ibid., p. 99/**Owners had unanimously:** Ibid., p. 100/**A tumultuous session:** Ibid., p. 103/**Extended their deadline:** Ibid., p. 104/**Announced they were finished:** Ibid., p. 135/**"More important to Los Angeles":** Ibid., p.4/**The best thing:** Thorn, "Our Game," p. 9/**"Call itself the national":** Ibid., p. 9/**Nicaraguan-born journalist:** Regalado, "Dodgers Beisbol Is on the Air," p. 282/**Immigrated to the city:** Ibid., p. 282/**"Imagine a Spanish man":** Ibid., p. 282/**Went to see William Beaton:** Ibid., p. 284/**Jumped to 1.4 million:** Regalado, *Viva Baseball!,* p. 175/**"Why not do it in Spanish?":** Regalado, "Dodgers Beisbol Is on the Air," p. 282/**Hundreds of Spanish announcers:** Ibid., p. 285/**Former New York prep schooler:** Gershman, Pietrusza, and Silverman, *Baseball,* p. 1014/**El Chelito:** Regalado, "Dodgers Beisbol Is on the Air," p. 282/**Meet the club's number-one:** Ibid., p. 285/**Sunny and mild:** Bitker, *The Original San Francisco Giants,* p. 14/**Began lining up:** Ibid., p. 12/**Mannequins in the Macys:** Ibid., p. 14/**Greeted the Giants:** Ibid., p. 12/**A welcoming parade:** Ibid., p. 15/**Awarded the key to city:** Ibid., p. 15/**Coach told him to go home:** Ostler, "Rig's Lessons of Life"/**Grew up in Red Bluff:** Bitker, *The Original San Francisco Giants,* p. 178/**Never set foot in the city:** Ibid., p. 80/**"A year away from what?":** Ibid., p. 115/**Spoke only limited English:** Ibid., p. 99/**Would repeatedly fine:** Ibid., p. 72/**Many played hurt:** Ibid., p. 101/**Playing stickball:** Ibid., p. 111/**Ceremonial first pitch:** Ibid., p. 15/**Lived in North Beach:** Ibid., p. 15/**Wore their game uniforms:** 1958 Photograph, USC Special Collections/**Some female May Co.:** 1958 Photograph, USC Special Collections/**From Chicana women:** 1958 Photograph, USC Special Collections/**Settled on the cavernous:** Sullivan, *The Dodgers Move West,* p. 141/**Adjustments had to be made:** Ibid., p. 143/**Ran an avocado ranch:** 1955 Photograph and caption, USC Special Collections/**A re-creation of their wedding cake:** 1959 Photograph and caption, USC Special Collections/**Due to financial constraints:** Regalado, "Dodgers Beisbol Is on the Air," p. 285/**Virtually simultaneous:** Ibid., p. 285/**First Spanish-language broadcasts:** Regalado, *Viva Baseball!,* p. 176/**Opponents had gathered:** Sullivan, *The Dodgers Move West,* p. 138/**Sentiment had turned:** Ibid., p. 144/**"Yea on Baseball":** Ibid., p. 154/**His immediate popularity:** Ibid., p. 145/**Lose their homes:** Ibid., p. 147/**Urged a yes vote:** Ibid., p. 159/**Telethon in the evening:** Ibid., p. 160/**Ruled unanimously:** Ibid., p. 172/**Who refused to go:** Ibid., p. 179/**Owned as many as nine homes:** Ibid., pp. 179–80/**Entire Coliseum went dark:** 1959 Photograph and Caption, USC Special Collections/**Fairer to hitters:** Sullivan, *The Dodgers Move West,* p. 177/**Joined Rene Cardenas:** Regalado, "Dodgers Beisbol Is on the Air," p. 286/**Series attendance record:** Thorn et al., *Total Baseball,* p. 376/**Dismissed the final appeals:** Sullivan, *The Dodgers Move West,* p. 188/

Chapter 28

Star in *Somewhere in Georgia*: Edelman, *Great Baseball Films,* p. 31/**"A production aimed":** Ibid., p. 31/**Managed Willie Kamm:** J. E. Spalding, *Pacific Coast League Stars,* p. 59/**"The Einstein of average":** Updike, "Hub Fans Bid Kid Adieu," p. 322/**"Up from the South":** Smith, *Baseball's Hall of Fame,* p. 102/**"Egotistical, brash":** Gershman, Pietrusza, and Silverman, *Baseball,* p. 213/**One of the dignitaries:** Zingg and Medeiros, *Runs, Hits, and An Era,* p.68/**Invited Cobb to sit beside him:** Cramer, *Joe DiMaggio,* p. 41/**Brought in Cobb as an advisor:** Ibid., p. 73/**Against a team managed by Cobb:** Nakagawa, *Through a Diamond,* p. 24/**Appeared on the field:** Dobbins and Twichell, *Nuggets on the Diamond,* p. 120/**Fathers told their sons:** David L. Nelson (baseball enthusiast) to author, early 2003/**"Wild eyes":**

Stump, "Ty Cobb's Wild 10-Month Fight to Live," p. 299/**Asked him to invest:** Leutzinger, *Lefty O'Doul*, p. 70/**Socialized at the Domino Club:** Stump, "Ty Cobb's Wild 10-Month Fight to Live," p. 285/**"I'll hate to leave":** 1957 Associated Press Photograph and Caption, USC Special Collections/**Stands in the driveway:** Ibid./**"Held a ball game":** Stump, "Ty Cobb's Wild 10-Month Fight to Live," p. 293/**There he was again:** Bitker, *The Original San Francisco Giants*, p. 15/**Balloou, who liked to wind down:** Cramer, *Joe DiMaggio*, p. 58/**McKercher, who was a batboy:** Bitker, *The Original San Francisco Giants*, p. 262/**Two working businesses:** Ibid., p. 262/**Creation of a new $15 million stadium:** Ibid., p. 17/**Old park should be saved:** Ibid., p. 17/**The weather would be better there:** Ibid., p. 17/**Citizens' lawsuit:** Ibid., p. 13/**Approved the final plans:** Ibid., p. 18/**Overly optimistic:** Ibid., p. 13/**Met the wrecking ball:** Ritter, *Lost Ballparks*, p. 175/**Cobb showed up there:** Stump, "Ty Cobb's Wild 10-Month Fight to Live," p. 295/**Sneaked out of Stanford:** Ibid., p. 295/**A wreck of a human being:** Ibid., p. 283/**"Kept coming to games":** Ibid., p. 297/**"Hit for ridiculous averages":** Ibid., p. 297/**Stayed at a motel:** Ibid., p. 284/**Speedboat had sunk:** Ibid., p. 291/**Packed $1 million:** Ibid., p. 297/**Next they traveled:** Ibid., p. 298/**Slept with his pants:** Ibid., p. 298/**No lights, no heat:** Ibid., p. 293/**"Die a little at a time":** Ibid., p. 298/

Chapter 29

"Built like a packing crate": Gershman, Pietrusza, and Silverman, *Baseball*, p. 89/**With a broad face:** 1957 Photographs, Dick Dobbins Collection/**A temporary sauna:** Zingg and Medeiros, *Runs, Hits, and An Era*, p.144/**One of the best minor league clubs:** Beverage, *The Angels*, p. 226/**Such a popular figure:** Ibid., p. 215/**Hired only two days before:** Newhan, *The Anaheim Angels*, p. 24/**"Boyhood passion":** Autry and Herskowitz, *Back in the Saddle Again*, p. 151/**With the likes of Dizzy Dean:** Ibid., p. 151/**Could not see walking away:** Ibid., p. 151/**Arrived in town:** Ibid., p. 37/**"Formless, too sprawling":** Ibid., p. 37/**Ninety movies and six hundred:** Newhan, *The Anaheim Angels*, p. 12/**When the Dodgers decided to shift:** Ibid., p. 146/**They assured Autry:** Ibid., p. 147/**"A born boat-rocker":** Ibid., p. 147/**Member of Beverly Hills:** Kempner, "The Life and Times of Hank Greenberg"/**"I didn't play tennis":** Ibid./**And his group:** Newhan, *The Anaheim Angels*, p. 17/**Considered to be a lock:** Veeck and Linn, *Veeck as in Wreck*, p. 355/ **Picked out a site:** Ibid., p. 360/**Greenberg group balked:** Ibid., p. 362/**Old friend of Autry's:** Autry and Herskowitz, *Back in the Saddle Again*, p. 148/**Guarantee arrived in time:** Ibid., p. 149/**The other bidder:** Ibid., p. 149/**Strapping former Stanford:** Newhan, *The Anaheim Angels*, p. 17/**"What amounted to grazing rights":** Autry and Herskowitz, *Back in the Saddle Again*, p. 150/**Open tryout:** Newhan, *The Anaheim Angels*, p. 36/**Aspiring infielder named Charlie Pride:** Ibid., p. 36/**Held spring training:** Ibid., p. 31/**"Biggest thrill":** Autry and Herskowitz, *Back in the Saddle Again*, p. 153/**Hosted a television series:** Herbold, "Wrigley Field in Los Angeles," p. 9/**Died of heart failure:** Silverman, *Going, Going, Gone*, p. 131/**Last major league home run:** Ritter, *Lost Ballparks*, p. 202/**"What else was there?":** Johnstone and Talley, *Over the Edge*, p. 27/**Bob's Big Boy:** Ibid., p. 28/**Edgewood High, where he starred:** Ibid., p. 27/**'I've-got-to-do-something-':** Ibid., p. 30/**Joined the United States Marine Corps:** Ibid., p. 30/**Finished his active duty:** Ibid., p. 35/**Get on a plane:** Ibid., p. 36/**"My only regret":** Nelson, *Baseball's Greatest Quotes*, p. 106/**Fellow night crawler:** Autry and Herskowitz, *Back in the Saddle Again*, p. 154/**Pay half the cost:** Newhan, *The Anaheim Angels*, p. 80/**Squabbled over the toilet paper bill:** Ostler, "Angels

Put Sad History Behind Them"/**Its upbeat mayor:** Newhan, *The Anaheim Angels*, p. 83/**At the center of a growing:** Ibid., p. 84/**Field of alfalfa, corn, and oranges:** Ibid., p. 86/**Dressed in alligator boots:** Ibid., p. 87/**An exhibition between:** Ibid., p. 102/**Guys he had met in the service:** Johnstone and Talley, *Over the Edge*, p. 35/

Chapter 30

Nobody better at it: Lasorda and Fisher, *The Artful Dodger,* p. 101/**Believed the Dodgers were the best:** Ibid., p. 101/**Called Lasorda at his home:** Ibid., p. 111/**Got lost a lot:** Ibid., p. 111/**Contract was on the table:** Ibid., p. 117/**A vaudeville comedy sketch:** Ibid., p. 117/**"I spent so much time":** Ibid., p. 117/**First saw Monday:** Ibid., p. 117/**Best of the Dodger Rookies:** Ibid., p. 114/**All over Crawford:** Ibid., p. 114/**Attended the memorial service:** Ibid., p. 116/**Pursuing Crawford as relentlessly:** Ibid., p. 115/**Might have gone to Finley:** Autry and Herskowitz, *Back in the Saddle Again*, p. 149/**"Conservative class":** Libby and Blue, *Vida*, p. 38/**"Sweat Plus Sacrifice":** Ibid., p. 38/**Following his father and grandfather:** Ibid., p. 37/**Severe case of tuberculosis:** Ibid., p. 37/**Insurance plan for physicians:** Dickey, *Champions*, p. 10/**Smooth and charming:** Ibid., p. 9/**"Despicable qualities":** Ibid., p. 8/**Cheap, rude, a serial pincher:** Ibid., p. 8/**Make the last offer:** Lasorda and Fisher, *The Artful Dodger,* p. 115/**Bought his mother:** Ibid., p. 116/**"Don't think he's mature enough":** Ibid., p. 117/**Monday joined the Alaska Goldpanners:** Nettles and Golenbock, *Balls,* p. 21/**Graig's mother named:** Ibid., p. 19/**"A very mixed":** Ibid., p. 20/**Fourteen black athletes and Nettles:** Ibid., p. 20/**Scholarship to San Diego State:** Ibid., p. 21/**An Oklahoma native:** Ibid., p. 19/**One of his (and Monday's):** Ibid., p. 21/**"Chubbyish California kid":** Roy Blount, "How DiMaggio Made It Look Easy," p. 207/**Let Tom stay home:** Honig, *The October Heroes*, p. 104/**A former Walker Cup golfer:** Golenbock, *Amazin'*, p. 186/**Drew only yawns:** Ibid., p. 186/**Job at the fruit-packing:** Ibid., p. 186/**"Overpowered" people:** Nettles and Golenbock, *Balls,* p. 21/**Club had a problem:** Ibid., p. 22/ **Relationship with Kansas City:** Dobbins, Bruno, and O'Brien, "A Century of A's Baseball," p. 12/**Looking for a summertime tenant:** Dickey, *Champions*, p. 7/**"Luckiest city":** Nelson, *Baseball's Greatest Quotes*, p. 110/**Coined these terms:** Doug McWilliams (Oakland baseball historian) to author, early 2002/**Green- and gold-tinted sheep:** Dobbins, Bruno, and O'Brien, "A Century of A's Baseball," p. 12/**Joe Cronin, and other dignitaries:** Ibid., p. 14/**All-state junior college player:** Plaque observed by author, Pasadena Community College Athletic Hall of Fame, Pasadena, Calif./

Chapter 31

Selma was in a jam: Center, "Memory of a Lifetime"/**Pitched poorly over the spring:** Ibid./**Did not want to screw it up:** Ibid./**Sacred Expedition:** Hart, *A Companion to California*, p. 466/**Lobby for a major league team:** "San Diego Padres," Baseball Library, www.baseballlibrary.com/**Receiving wide praise:** Figuracion, "Qualcomm/Jack Murphy/San Diego Stadium," About San Diego, www.sandiego.about.com/**Arranged for a meeting:** Tucker, "Suddenly the Padres are Real," p. 11/**Needed a baseball man:** Ibid., p. 11/**Reasons for optimism:** Ibid., p. 11/**His coaching staff:** "The Coaches," 1969 Inaugural Yearbook, San Diego Padres, p. 9/**Who wore number 19:** Center, "A Baseball Original," p. 2/**"Worth of turkeys":** Tucker, "Suddenly the Padres Are Real," p. 11/**Chose younger players:** Ibid., p. 12/**Mother, Mabel, named him:** Golenbock, *Amazin'*, p. 203/**"One huge naval base":**

McGraw and Durso, *Screwball*, p. 58/**At Wilson Park:** Ibid., p. 17/**Recreation Department league:** Ibid., p. 60/**"Not too short":** Ibid., p. 10/**Hank, who was bigger:** Ibid., p. 63/**Hank's signing bonus:** Ibid., p. 68/**Gave his bonus money:** Ibid., p. 63/**Agreed to sign with New York:** Ibid., p. 78/**Knocked out of the box:** Ibid., p. 80/**Showed off his stuff:** Ibid., p. 80/**Joined another Californian:** Golenbock, *Amazin'*, p. 160/**"California all the way":** Ibid., p. 202/**Played Little League:** Lee and Lally, *The Wrong Stuff*, p. 6/**Live in Marin:** Ibid., p. 3/**Pitched for a national championship:** Ibid., p. 17/**Left Tug unprotected:** Golenbock, *Amazin'*, p. 205/**Pull McGraw back after three rounds:** Ibid., p. 205/**A catcher from Oakland:** "Chris Cannizzaro," 1971 San Diego Padres Program, p. 19/**Trouble with his slider:** Center, "Memory of a Lifetime"/**Pena leaped high:** Ibid./**A whole handful of Padre firsts:** 2000 San Diego Padres Media Guide, p. 70/**High points of his life:** Center, "Memory of a Lifetime"/**Largest global audience:** Reynolds, *Apollo*, p. 137/**A message flashed:** "'A' was for Ashtray," *Contra Costa Times*/**Raised in an athletic family:** "Blue Chip Bonds," 2001 San Francisco Giants Yearbook, p. 60/**"You've been traded":** Flood and Carter, *The Way It Is*, p. 185/**After receiving that phone call:** Ibid., p. 186/**Consulting with an attorney:** Ibid., p. 190/**Boarded a plane to go see:** Ibid., p. 190/

Epilogue

"A great man": "Curtis Charles Flood," 1999 Induction Program, Baseball Reliquary, Pasadena, Calif./**A former All-American pitcher:** 2001 California Golden Bear Baseball Media Guide, p. 44/**Loaded into moving vans:** Don King (Curator, Hall of Champions) to author, late 2001/**"Never lost a fight":** Harris, "Autry Leaves Legacy of Love with Angels"/**Laid to rest with:** Newhan, *The Anaheim Angels*, p. 12/**"No such thing as enough baseball":** Ostler, "Rig's Lessons of Life"/**Greeted coolly by local fans:** Einstein, *Willie's Time*, p. 111/**"The temerity":** Ibid., p. 111/**Who grew up in New York City:** Magowan, Foreword to *The Original San Francisco Giants* by Steve Bitker, p. vii/**"The most memorable personality":** Gershman, Pietrusza, and Silverman, *Baseball*, p. 1014/**Paid a sentimental visit:** Gergen, "Duke of Flatbush Returns Home," p. D7/**Successfully battled problems with alcoholism:** Davis, "Straight, No Chaser," p. 20/**Roseboro spoke out on Marichal's behalf:** Gershman, Pietrusza, and Silverman, *Baseball*, p. 710/**Acted as Valenzuela's translator:** Regalado, "Dodgers Beisbol Is on the Air," p. 288/**Signed Murakami on the advice of:** Nakagawa, *Through a Diamond*, p. 119/**Graduated from Sacramento high schools:** "Sons of Sacramento," *Contra Costa Times*/**Walked on to the freshman baseball team:** Huff, "The Wizard of Poly"/**"A black player":** Ibid./**Wanted her son to stick:** Ibid./**Coached his son's Little League:** Pearlman, "My, How He's Grown"/

Note: Statistical information from Thorn et al., *Total Baseball*.

Index

Kevin Nelson worked on *The Golden Game* for nearly three years. He traveled the state on a baseball odyssey, going to games, visiting ballfields and playgrounds, trooping around historic baseball sites, walking the old neighborhoods where Joe DiMaggio and Ted Williams and Jackie Robinson grew up and played ball as kids, attending the conventions of retired ballplayers, and speaking to hundreds of people—all to help him tell the more than 150-year history of California baseball.

Nelson has written fifteen books and numerous articles about sports. He is married with three children and lives in the Bay Area.

Hank Greenwald is best known as the voice of the San Francisco Giants (1979–86 and 1989–96). In his more than thirty years as a radio and television broadcaster, he has called games for the New York Yankees and several professional basketball teams, and in 2004 he will return to baseball as a part-time announcer for the Oakland Athletics. He is the author of the memoir *This Copyrighted Broadcast*.